# COMMUNICATION IN EASTERN EUROPE

## *The Role of History, Culture, and Media in Contemporary Conflicts*

# Contents

# *Preface*

ONCE UPON A TIME . . . All good fairy tales seem to start that way. Unfortunately for our contemporary world, the beginning of recent sociocultural and economic/political difficulties also can be traced back to a time when (mostly Northern or Western) political leaders forced their concepts of state building on the people of their times, simply because they had the power to do so. Lebanon, Yugoslavia, and even the Soviet Union under Stalin's influence, became frightening examples of outside forces used to develop institutions that ignored, and even tried to destroy, the cultural foundations and value systems that human beings found necessary for their long-term interactions. All of that was done in order to strengthen politically ordered and economically founded concepts of states developed by their leaders.

Few, if any, scholars are suggesting at this point that the basic model of the state, as it emerged after the Thirty Years War, may be flawed. However, most are beginning to become aware of the power that culture and cultural associations, which developed over centuries, exert over human beings *even* today. The hope still seems to be, however, that somehow these factors can (or should) be overcome, if not locally or within a country, then perhaps by building a brave new world. In that world, or as McCluhan misnamed it for his own emotion-charged purposes, "the global village," electronic communication and technology are assumed to finally have the power to eliminate cultural diversity as they were not able to do within the state or internationally.

It appears high time to look in some detail at what is now happening in Eastern Europe. In the pages that follow, the reader will find a clear attempt to learn something from the events in Eastern European countries that does not *start* with simplistic, or old assumptions based on convenient Western communication models. If chaos theory could fundamentally change how physicists looked at order in the universe, then it may just be of value for communication scholars to attempt to *understand* the diversity of chaos or order in the *human* universe, rather than attempting to force existing models on it for their own explanatory purposes.

This volume is not merely based on the study of select groups of university students or on laboratory settings created in the minds of social scientists. This is an attempt to understand some of the "real world," including the historical backgrounds and the theoretical assumptions brought to our studies of intercultural conflicts. Scholars writing in this volume, using personal and professional insights developed during first-hand contacts with existing situations, illustrate some of the realities by using the complexity of changes in Eastern European states during this final decade of the 20th century. From education to business, from the role of women to the role of mass media, from the impact of political systems to the impact of history, communication between those who are culturally diverse, though they may have been arbitrarily forced to live under the same "political roof," is the theme of their studies.

My own reason for developing this volume of original essays is my belief that diversity rather than assumed similarity or even sameness, based on the use of inadequate terminology, is necessary if we are to learn from contemporary human experiences. I believe that diversity and the significant roles of cultural values as well as of history need to become key concepts in the model with which we *start* when it comes to the study of various aspects of intercultural communication. It is, therefore, vital that scholars who represent various points of view and backgrounds contribute to that process. After all, our understanding of what is happening in the world is centrally anchored in or related to effective and successful "intercultural" communication between scholars who have different academic and personal backgrounds.

*Fred L. Casmir*

# COMMUNICATION IN EASTERN EUROPE

## *The Role of History, Culture, and Media in Contemporary Conflicts*

# I

# FOUNDATIONAL ISSUES

Fred L. Casmir

A serious problem that faces all those interested in the study and understanding of intercultural, cross-cultural, or international communication is the fact that very often little or no attention has been paid to historical factors that underlie current events. Preoccupation with the *now* and the *future* has caused many Americans to pay little attention to the past. When that kind of historical orientation to the past of one's own country becomes almost routinely translated into a lack of concern with the history of other countries and other cultures, the possibilities for misunderstandings or misinterpretations are greatly increased.

Considering the recent 50th anniversary of D-Day, especially the invasion of Normandy, the implications of lacking historical perspectives become apparent. The anniversary probably could have been virtually ignored had it not been for the fact that mass media in the United States turned it into a major news event. Another generation now *knows* or *understands* what happened 50 years ago, because its members *saw it on television*. The information gained, the emotions experienced are now truly the result of a week-long media blitz in June of 1994 (not 1944). The role that the media played during that week of *historical remembrances* illustrates the impact of contemporary mass media most dramatically. When Walter Cronkite, former newscaster, walked to the speaker's podium, shadowed by an African-American general in uniform, to serve as master of ceremonies for a major commemorative D-Day event, it became even more evident who plays a major role in creating our historic images.

At the beginning of this volume, chapter one was designed to focus on the importance of historic foundations in the study of contemporary events. It demonstrates this book's emphasis on the values, the concerns, and the images that, at the very least, help to shape *cultures*, societies, and human beings.

Stephen challenges us to examine the common belief that our perception of the Cold War caused us to see it as an ideological dispute that resulted in an apparent historical discontinuity. That assumption of discontinuity, in turn, changed our view of the importance of broad-based historical processes. Unfortunately, such an uncritical and often uninformed point of view was also held by many social scientists, including communication scholars, who attempted to interpret for others the important political, social, and cultural changes in our world. As the influence of positivism has diminished, concern with *social* history, and its role in the study of interpersonal and intercultural communication has increased. Throughout this volume, note the interest of the authors in connecting the historic past to contemporary insights and challenges, as a *fundamental* requirement for meaningful intercultural-communication studies.

In that process, the established, changing, and emerging roles of the so-called mass media have to be studied. I use the term *so-called* advisedly, because one current debate among those interested in human communication deals with the question of whether or not the term *mass* best identifies contemporary media and electronically or print-mediated messages. We are thus confronted by the conflict of our conviction that mass media do have an influence, which is coupled with our uncertainty as to what, exactly, that impact is, how it can be identified and measured, and what role individuals play in the process. Consideration of such issues is especially important when one deals with the role of media in inter- or cross-cultural communication. After all, even in the former dictatorially controlled states of Eastern Europe, state-owned media were *not* able to permanently eliminate racial, ethnic, religious, or cultural differences and conflicts. In some cases, the mass media actually played a role in the eventual collapse or destruction of the Communist dictatorships that controlled them.

There has been an easily identifiable displacement in Eastern Europe, and there has been increasing evidence that state control, including that of mass media in former Communist states, had not established any permanent basis that could prevent the social aggressiveness we are witnessing almost every day. Ethnic, racial, cultural, historical divisions thus were not overcome by a new ideology. Nevertheless, it is vital for us to understand what results when certain issues or concepts are taken off the agenda or added to it by so-called mass media. There are many things to be learned from the role mass media played in the slide to disintegration and even in the destruction of the Communist system. Nor should we automatically assume that there is nothing like a collective learning process resulting from historical experience, which may well counteract the attempts of modern states to enforce their political- or economically based concepts of unity. Even while Communist state governments were in supposed total control of media in Eastern Europe there were those who used contemporary technology and convictions, as well as religious or ethnic concerns as the bases for mediated messages that ran counter to their governments' ideals.

This book is not intended to present *extensive* historical, cultural, or media data. In effect it deals with communication; that is, it is concerned with gaining better insights and understanding of that *intersection* of culture, history, media, and human beings that is the subject matter of communication—and certainly of intercultural communication—studies. We are thus concerned with what developing or emerging symbolic processes we can identify between human beings from different cultural backgrounds, as they build the future together or refuse to do so.

How then are contemporary cultures produced, and how are traditional cultures continued? Ultimately, for the purposes of this volume, which is concerned with the role of culture, history, and media in human symbolic activities, the question becomes how our world is held together, and how our rather subjective understanding of reality translates into foundations for the future.

# 1

## *Interpersonal Communication, History, and Intercultural Coherence*

Timothy Stephen
*Rensselaer Polytechnic Institute*

Notwithstanding the views of experts who examine world history from a unique vantage (e.g., Fukuyama, 1992), for the ordinary individual in the 1950s, 1960s, and 1970s, the postwar division of the world into two hostile camps seemed to constitute a fundamental discontinuity in the flow of international relations, a recalibration of the world system from one in which national and ethnic factions were embroiled routinely in local conflicts to a new global stability. Everyone knew that the standoff between the Warsaw Pact and the NATO Alliance was without historical precedent and though its apocalyptic potential terrorized the world, the separation of the globe into two ideologically opposed camps also stabilized world relations by suppressing long-standing local conflicts between national and ethnic groups.

At least on the surface, the Cold War was understood to be an ideological dispute between capitalism and Communism and therefore seemed to be about something more substantial and foundational than the smaller issues (e.g., border and trade disputes, local religious or ethnic wars, etc.) that have typically fueled the myriad conflicts filling the pages of world history. Because the Cold War seemed to represent a break with the past, it encouraged the view that world affairs had set off on a new track after World War II. Most important, this apparent discontinuity in the history of international relations encouraged the view that broad-based historical processes were less important in the modern world than they may have been in former times. This was one sense in which history was discounted in the 20th century.

History was also discounted by social scientists, who, during the post-war period, adopted wholesale a positivist model for research that granted almost exclusive priority to information obtained through experimental methods. Within this model of inquiry, historical influences were easily overlooked because they have no opportunity to display their effects in a laboratory or field study. Typically, communication research relied on cross-sectional designs, focusing almost exclusively on the location of immediate rather than ultimate causes. It was therefore virtually impossible to take account of the effects of broad-span historical processes. Indeed, as Shils (1981) noted, in the main, the research technologies of 20th-century social scientists are practical only on living persons, fostering another source of bias against historical information. Social scientists have therefore given short shrift to the influences of history and tradition in their studies. Paradoxically, though social scientists are usually also university professors, an occupation that must rank among the most tradition-bound, their scientific efforts frequently fail to account for the influence of tradition in the behavior of the individuals they study. With most social scientists dismissing or ignoring historical factors in their analyses of social life, and with the world seeming to have evolved to a new globalism marking the end of historically fueled local conflicts, the post-war era had severed its ties with the past. History lost relevance in the analysis of human affairs.

The end of the Cold War has dramatically reawakened awareness of historical processes in world conflict and this has happened at approximately the same time as the fall from preeminence of the positivist position in social science. With these changes has come a new appreciation of historical influences both at the level of international and intercultural relations and at the level of social interaction. In the wake of the collapse of the Soviet Union, ageless conflicts have resurfaced. What is striking about the post-Cold War "new world order" is how distressingly much it resembles the world as it existed before World War II. In the face of renewed conflict in the Balkans, the resurfacing of fascist elements in Germany, and the renewal of radical fundamentalism in some Islamic societies, history's relevance to the analysis of modern international relations is suddenly all too obvious.

Similarly, with the decline of positivism and the broader acceptance of diverse methodologies within the social sciences has come a new interest in exploring the ways that historical analysis can inform studies of interpersonal communication (e.g., Stephen & Harrison, 1993). Social history has now emerged as a discipline in its own right, a branch of social science that actively forges links between historical processes of everyday life and everyday life today. Scholars have expanded the domain of historical studies from one dominated by biographies of famous men and women and accounts of major political/military upheavals to a more general study of the evolution of society on both the macro- and microlevels. The history of human relations has taken center stage in the new appreciation of the importance of the long view in understanding the nature of contemporary social action.

This chapter discusses the relevance of historical analysis to an appreciation of the way in which modernity is manifest in cross-cultural communication. Proceeding from an analysis of the relationship between modernity and social life, a framework is presented for understanding differences in interpersonal relations within societies displaying different configurations of factors related to modernity. Particular attention is directed to two such factors: the degree to which a society is pluralistic (i.e., the degree to which members of a society hold disparate beliefs and the extent of role complexity and role variation) and the degree to which a society is egalitarian (especially the extent of difference in social power for men and women). This framework is considered within the context of Central and Eastern European societies.

It is argued that communication exhibits different unintended consequences in societies configured differently with respect to these key factors because they establish conditions under which the self is experienced differently. In a modern pluralistic society, in which the maintenance of self-identity is chronically problematic (e.g., Taylor, 1989), interpersonal communication must do extra duty as a vehicle for maintaining self and for constructing symbolic bridges between existentially isolated individuals. In traditional societies, however, the self is not as plastic and, in consequence, interpersonal communication does not carry the hidden burden of negotiating self-identity; rather, communication simply conveys information between individuals whose lived experience is grounded in traditional, consensual definitions of self and other. Modernity tends to promote formal egalitarianism, whereas traditional societies tend to be structured hierarchically, especially with respect to gender roles. Interpersonal communication between social equals is more likely to provide a basis for the joint construction of reality, a condition that creates bonds between members of modern societies but is not as relevant a source of bonding in traditional, nonpluralistic societies.

Differences in the degree of modernity within two cultures increases the potential for cross-cultural misunderstanding and conflict because members of the two cultures use mutually incomprehensible methods to place themselves within their social milieu. In Riesman, Glazer, and Denney's (1961) terminology, the representative of modernity is "gyroscopically controlled"—guided by his or her own individual standards—whereas the behavior of the representative of traditional society is "radar controlled"—guided externally by the force of tradition.

## TRADITIONAL AND MODERN SOCIETIES

In sociological and anthropological writing traditional societies are often identified with reference to several classic distinctions: (a) Life in traditional societies is guided by religious or mystical conceptions of the world rather than secular/scientific conceptions; (b) traditional society is hierarchical rather than egalitarian; (c) traditional societies are predominantly agrarian and oriented to a subsistence economy rather than industrialized and driven by a market economy; (d) life in traditional societies is centered in the local community rather than in a diffuse mass culture; (e) the population of a traditional society is stationary rather than mobile; and (f) traditional society is characterized by consensually held beliefs rather than a pluralistic mosaic of socially constructed realities.

In traditional society life may be guided more by religion and mystical traditions. According to Tuan (1982), Western culture evolved from a largely undifferentiated social and material gestalt to one that is profoundly segmented. In traditional societies the natural and the social orders are indistinct and religion and mysticism permeate everyday life. People tend to look backward to traditional sources (e.g., opinions of elders, religious texts, customs, rituals) for guidance rather than to science or other sources of secular expertise. Because they are principally agrarian, traditional societies connect more closely to nature and structure day-to-day life in accordance with natural rhythms. The artificial structuring of time characteristic of industrial societies is unnecessary because the local community is the center of all social activity and commerce. A nonmobile, community-centered people has no need to coordinate definitions of time with other external groups, though such coordination is essential in industrial society. As historian Michael O'Malley (1990) noted, prior to the revolution and the onset of industrialization in the United States, American communities kept time according to purely local standards, a practice more in harmony with the rhythms of nature but utterly impractical for travel and commerce.

Shils (1981) argued that tradition is evident to a degree in all societies, traditional or modern. For example, science—the paragon of modernity—is a highly conservative institution guided by the clinical rationality of the laboratory but also by elements of traditional and ritualistic practice. But the predominance of mystical or religious formulas for living over formulas based in the rational analysis of empirical data separates traditional from modern societies. It is also true that, regardless of the ultimate basis for action, action in a modern society is warranted in reference to rational criteria; in traditional society action is more often warranted in reference to sacred definitions of propriety (e.g., "divine Providence," "the will of Allah"). The modern scientist may select a research focus on grounds that are traditional (e.g., he or she wants to study a topic in the mainstream of a discipline's interest) or even pious (e.g., he or she chooses a topic to honor a disciplinary demigod), but will nevertheless justify the choice in terms of dispassionate rationality. This is not to say that the rationality of modern societies is insubstantial; rationality is a key factor in modernity that penetrates to core definitions of self. Rather, it is to acknowledge that no society is completely rational or free of tradition (Shils, 1981). The difference between traditional societies and modern societies is one of degree.

Modern societies are characterized as well by a formal egalitarianism. This is not to say that they are not stratified or that they are classless. On the contrary, as argued by historians studying the evolution of social etiquette (e.g., Elias, 1978; Kasson, 1991), one characteristic of modernity has been the gradual unfolding of forms of behavior that serve to enunciate class distinctions. According to Elias codes of courtly behavior established originally distinctions between powerful social elites and the masses; however, the behavior of those at the upper ranges of society tends to be emulated and appropriated eventually by the larger population. Thus there is a tendency for behavior to be refined continually at the top as this serves to keep members of the elite distinct. Refined behavior constitutes a visible badge of class (cf. Fussell, 1983), but the sign loses distinction if everyone wears it. Thus, in order for refined behavior to continue to serve its purpose as a mechanism for distinguishing social class it must evolve continuously. This is one sense in which in modern society social norms for communication are dynamic though society is hierarchical overall. It is in their legal/political organization that modern societies tend toward increasing egalitarianism. As Fukuyama (1992) argued, liberal democracy has become the predominant structure of modern nations in the 20th century. With the broad acceptance of liberal democracy has come the belief in universal rights and the gradual eradication of barriers to enfranchisement. The progress of this process is perhaps most evident in the area of the liberation of women and racial minorities, an area in which clear differences are visible across societies, even those that are otherwise at the forefront of modernity.

Industrialization has inescapable concomitants. A society cannot move from a predominantly agricultural economy to a market-driven manufacturing and service economy without incurring certain impacts in its institutions and structures. The family provides a clear example of one such institution that has been affected profoundly by modernity. To begin with, family life is restructured as members are drawn from their labors at home to work in centralized organizations and factories. In the United States, this process began during the early 19th century as men left home to work in newly created industrial centers. It was during this period that women were recast as domestic experts, a new role that they had not previously enacted (e.g., Mintz & Kellog, 1988).[1] By the late 20th century, however, women too were drawn from home into the industrial labor pool. In America and Europe, the shift to industrial society brought a need for a highly trained workforce and in consequence education was extended and the period of childhood prolonged (cf. Demos, 1986; Mitterauer & Sieder, 1982). An industrial economy requires a mobile workforce concentrated in urban environments and social mobility and urbanization have profound impacts on the family and on social relations generally. In addition, an industrial economy feeds on infrastructure improvements, particularly in transportation and mass communication. These processes result in an urbanized mass society.

Berger, Berger, and Kellner (1974) described the link between bureaucratized, high-speed mass society and the consciousness of those who live within its domain. They believed that modern individuals, thrust into a secular, rational, bureaucratized, and market-driven world, suffer from a deepening condition of "homelessness"—the individual's understanding of self and world are no longer supported by external societal structures. The fact that there are few non-self-referential sources of meaning in modern society leads to a sort of permanent identity crisis. The urban mass culture is of course antagonistic of community bonds, a state of affairs that some contend has reached critical proportion in the United States (e.g., Bellah, Madsen, Sullivan, Swidler, & Tipton, 1985). Kasson (1991) argued that in America, urbanization shifted the population from villages and towns, in which everyone knew everyone else, to environments in which all are strangers to each other. Similarly, Giddens (1991) remarked that the concept of "stranger" actually lost meaning as a result of urbanization and population expansion because these processes created strangers out of everyone. Pluralization was so extensive that no matter where one lived, it was no longer possible to take one's neighbor's beliefs and values for granted.

Anthony Giddens (1990, 1991) added to these basic distinctions between traditional and modern societies the following abstract characteristics of modernity: time-space distanciation, disembedding, and reflexivity. Time-space distanciation results from the universality of time measurement. As already noted, in traditional cultures time is defined locally rather than universally. In consequence virtually all social interchange must take place in a face-to-face context because there is no other basis for coordinating action. Because time and place are defined with reference to local coordinates they are closely interdependent concepts.

[1]See Pietrow-Ennker (1992) for a description of the manner in which this process operated in Poland in the 19th century.

The fact that they are defined universally and are independent of each other in modern societies means that social systems can be disembedded—lifted out of local contexts, their transactions conducted across vast expanses of time and space. This is a prerequisite for the development of complex social systems such as international corporations. Complex social organization also depends on the universal willingness of individuals to rely on the invisible hands of experts (e.g., air traffic controllers) to safely and rationally structure and control the technologies of modern life that make time-space distanciation possible. Thus trust takes on special significance in modernity.

Giddens (1990, 1991) is perhaps best known for his description of modernity as a reflexive system. Within this framework, regardless of what an individual may be able to say about his or her intentions, action is rooted ultimately in a kind of preconscious awareness of the possibilities, the requirements, and the constraints of particular situations (Giddens referred to this as "practical consciousness"). Purposive action results simultaneously in both intentional and unintentional outcomes. These outcomes may serve to perpetuate or to alter the structural prerequisites for action occurring in similar situations at future points in time. Action is situated within the constraints of larger social structures and reconstitutes such constructions, giving rise to what Giddens called the "duality" of structure: Actors draw upon structure to constitute their social practices and, in so doing, structure is itself reconstituted in the knowledgeable production of social practice. The individual therefore exists in a mutual causal relationship with social structure, though he or she may have little or no conscious awareness of this process.

The reflexivity of modern societies enmeshes the individual in a dynamic that poses problems for self-definition. If self is dependent on social structure for definition, what does it mean that social structure (indeed all knowledge) is continually in flux? Moreover, what does it mean that the individual's own actions, ostensibly in response to changes in societal conditions, actually contribute to further change in those conditions? The reflexivity of modern societies places the individual in a house of mirrors from which there may seem to be no escape. Without a transcendent personal philosophy, existence under these conditions can quickly lose meaning. It is in this sense that Charles Taylor (1989) argued that modern existence is animated by fear of a "terrifying emptiness" should one fail to construct a satisfying personal account of self and world. For better or worse, the modern individual must rely upon his or her own devices in this endeavor. Traditional and religious definitions of self have lost ground to secular rationality, which means that the individual, dimly aware that definitions of self founded on external role categories (e.g., I am a professor) are without fixed reference, must construct a self from the ground up.

In a traditional culture, this is not the case. Personal identity originates in consensually held categories derived from tradition. Richard Sennett (1976) cited examples of consensually held codes of dress and behavior that were used to demarcate individual identity: "... [D]ress in 1750 was not a matter of what you feel; it was an elaborate, arbitrary marking of where you stood in society" (p. 147). According to Sennett, in Europe, the body was regarded as a sort of mannequin and speech was impersonal and signlike, blotting out all personal expression in public. In fact, though perhaps rarely enforced, "sumptuary" laws existed for a time in preindustrial England assigning to each social station a set of clothes that could be worn by no other.

Colonial New England provides a similar example of such a consensual and rigidly structured society. Puritan society was patriarchal with male prerogative derived from "... a continuous chain of hierarchical and delegated authority descending from God" (Mintz & Kellogg, 1988, p. 8). In colonial New England, the law regarded a wife as a husband's property and laws existed that provided for the death of children who cursed or struck their fathers (Mintz & Kellogg, 1988). Women were regarded as intellectually inferior to men. In a well-known example, the wife of the governor of Connecticut was thought to have gone insane from too much reading (Morgan, 1966). In such a society the self derives from social position and from consensually defined roles. How distant this is from modern societies in which role definitions—the way one understands the duties, powers, and character of individuals within occupational categories (e.g., priest, professor, mother, father, president)—are continually undergoing change and are therefore unreliable anchors for identity. Thus in traditional societies, the self does not rely upon an active process of social construction and maintenance; it is more or less presented to the individual from external sources.

Industrialization and its concomitant processes—urbanization, secularity, social mobility, bureaucratization, pluralism, and so on—have gradually differentiated the modern world, transforming it from a relatively simple and coherent structure into a fragmented mosaic. The ever more complex differentiation of occupational specialties and the bureaucratic compartmentalization of everyday life necessitate that the individual must daily interpolate experiences situated within the frameworks of many specialized communities of knowledge. According to Holzner (1968), "the general trend of social change throughout world history bears out, beyond any possible doubt, that the existence of specialized modes of knowledge which depart significantly from the knowledge of the common man occurred increasingly with increased social differentiation ..." (p. 125).

The family provides a concrete example of this process. Once the common environment of husband and wife who participated in the shared tasks of farm operation and parenting, the modern family has gradually spun off its functions to bureaucratized agencies operated by specialists. It is now increasingly common for child care to be provided in professional agencies, education to be handled by the state, and health care to be given over to an elaborate professional bureaucracy. Even aspects of relationship maintenance have been spun off to experts in the mental health and human relations industry. On top of this, husband and wife frequently work in disparate external occupations, the basis of their shared existence continually threatened by the increasingly difficult task of reintegrating their day-to-day lives.

Each venue of social activity presents its own rules for communicating and its own method of prioritizing knowledge—in Holzner's (1968) term its own "epistemology." The individual who must navigate these structures—even if only dimly aware of the problem—must become adept at interpolating between the versions of reality supported within each epistemic community. Although it is now common to speak of the evolution of a "corporate culture" in reference to the phenomenon of work groups that evolve their own visions of reality and patterns of discourse, there are more or less discrete visions of reality and patterns for discourse to be found within each segment of the modern world, each one placing the actor in a slightly different set of interactional demands and a different framework of sensibility. An individual must adopt one framework while at work, another when in contact with the health care system, another with government agencies, another at church, another when interacting with his or her spouse, and so on. All these are separate "cultures" of a sort. One understands that different procedures are followed in determining scientific "facts," legal "facts," religious "facts," the intimate "facts" that bind members of a marriage or friendship, and so forth. As Berger et al. (1974) noted, the modern individual's continual exposure to a multiplicity of epistemic communities relativizes every one of them.

In illustration of the contrast between the manner in which individuals in traditional and modern societies process reality, Rose Coser (1991) related a Dutch newspaper story from rural Pakistan in which 12 members of the same family were asphyxiated in sequence. The first family member descended into a well to fix a broken pump. When he failed to emerge, the next family member went in after him. This was repeated until all 12 family members went down the shaft and were asphyxiated, presumably because the pump was emitting toxic gas. Coser contrasted this with another newspaper story from the same year in which an 8-year-old boy from Illinois "... responded to his four-year-old brother's fall into a 40-foot well by throwing two life preservers into the well, calling the telephone operator for help, and then running for assistance" (p. 76). Clearly, these responses reflect vastly different modes of understanding the world. In the case of the rural Pakistani family, the response is organized around a simple principle of family relatedness. As Coser noted, the role sets of these individuals are restricted within the confines of the primary social group. The child from Illinois, however, at only 8 years of age already sees the world in terms of a set of elaborated compartments of expertise and organizes his response accordingly.

Thus the world as experienced by the modern actor is comprised of a plurality of epistemic communities. In order to move fluidly among them, the individual must adopt a relativistic perspective. This is one sense in which the modern world is said to be highly pluralistic. It is the result of the progressive fragmentation of society that occurs with industrialization and its concomitant processes.

According to historian John Kasson (1991), the fragmentation of society has been mirrored by a fragmentation of self.[2] In navigating the complex external world, the modern individual by necessity differentiates between the private or personal self and the public self. The public self, a kind of *Gesellschaft* personae—to use Coser's (1991) terminology—is tailored specifically to withstand the travails of presentation in multiple epistemic contexts. It is carefully manufactured in ways that protect the individual to a degree from the anguish of existence in a profoundly relativistic social milieu. According to Kasson (1991), emotional control, a critical component of this process, is a concomitant outcome of modernity:

> Before the seventeenth and eighteenth centuries, extremes of jubilant laughter, passionate weeping, and violent rage were indulged with a freedom that in later centuries would not be permitted even to children. . . . there appeared in the eighteenth century a decisive shift in notions of appropriate behavior, including a new stress upon emotional control that was profoundly extended in the course of the nineteenth century with the development of an urban-industrial capitalist society. The feeling rules of the eighteenth-century gentleman, like other popularized elements of etiquette, proved to have (in Max Weber's phrase) an "elective affinity" with the demands of nineteenth-century urban life. (p. 166)

With the development of this gap between the personal and the public, individuals in modern societies have struggled with the problem of bringing the private self into the light of public examination. Popular opinion holds that the private self is the "true self" whereas the public self is regarded as an unreliable front. From the introduction of phrenology in the 19th century, through hypnotism and psychoanalysis, electroencephalography, and the development of a virtual industry devoted to person-

---

[2]Berger et al. (1974) believed that the process of pluralization extends to the private sphere as well, endowing the modern individual with a variety of private identities.

ality testing, science (and pseudoscience) has attempted to find ways to bring the private self under public scrutiny and control. Of course, the private self is a construction as well. Pluralism brings definition to the private self and makes its construction and maintenance problematic and this alters fundamentally the nature of everyday communication.

In traditional societies communication occurs within the context of consensual knowledge. Participants in interaction relate within a framework of role definitions that are taken for granted. There is no need to convince others about the significance of information and no guesswork about how to approach one's interactional partners. Within this context it is possible to speak of communication as a process of information exchange rather than as a process in which reality is negotiated. In the modern world, by contrast, except in special and often limited circumstances, one can rarely assume that an interactional partner will assign the same significance to information. Further, one must probe to establish the correct modality in which to address one's partner lest dialogue devolve into conflict over self-definition before content issues have a chance to be addressed. "Who am I?" must be resolved satisfactorily and anew in every interpersonal encounter because in modern societies the negotiation of identity is a persistent and thorny problem.

Only with the resolution of the issue of mutual recognition of identity can the interactants move on to the next task, which is the negotiation of other forms of shared meaning. In interpersonal encounters individuals become bonded through the process of coming to terms with each other's perspectives on the world. As the sum of a history of ordinary conversations through which they coordinate their perceptions of themselves and the world around them, individuals in sustained interaction gradually generate a framework of shared meaning. Over time, each interactant comes to supply uniquely for the other a source of confirmation and support for the particular outlook on reality that is the shared product of their interactions through time. The more radical the shared framework (i.e., the more difficult it would be to locate others who would easily understand or support it), the greater the power of this type of interpersonal bond, a bond that I have elsewhere referred to as "symbolic interdependence" (Stephen, 1986, in press). Vivid examples of this type of bond are evident among individuals who have shared profoundly adverse and unusual circumstances such as battlefield combat, but the process also operates in more routine circumstances (e.g., marriages and friendships) though it may be less well understood for what it is.

Interaction in modern societies is further complicated when it occurs between individuals who are not coequal. One consequence of pluralistic society is that much of the important work of creating and maintaining a stable personal account of reality is transferred to intimate relationships such as friendships and marriages (Stephen, in press). Only in such relationships, in which members have prolonged cross-contextual information about each other, is it possible to obtain meaningful validation for core aspects of self-identity. Thus intimate relationships carry a profound burden in modern egalitarian societies that they do not carry in traditional societies: They become the principal venue for the construction of a coherent account of self and the larger world. They constitute a "home" in the otherwise "homeless" modern world described by Berger et al. (1974).

The degree to which this process can be effective is mediated by the relative social status of the relationship partners. In a relationship of unequal partners—for example, in a patriarchal marriage—it is doubtful that the partner of lesser status will as meaningfully influence the shared reality of the interactants as would be the case if the partners were on equal footing. In a traditional society, in which role prescriptions are often patriarchal, rigid, and consensual, identity is derived from cultural resources rather than creatively generated by relationship members. To the extent that one relationship member is of lower social status than the other, it is likely that the low-status member's views will be subordinated. In such a case, interpersonal communication will function more to convey information than to construct a shared reality. Thus, under such circumstances interpersonal communication is less likely to serve as a bonding force. In a modern pluralistic and egalitarian society, where all knowledge and role definitions are up for grabs, communication may become a principal bonding force and interpersonal relationships that are unable to accomplish a shared construction of reality may not survive.

To summarize, I have argued that two characteristics that differentiate modern and traditional societies have important consequences for interpersonal communication. The first dimension is pluralism. In traditional societies beliefs are consensual and communication functions mainly to convey information and to coordinate action. Modern societies are highly pluralistic. Beliefs are up for grabs and communication is used to create shared constructions of reality—local pockets of consensus—that provide stability and bridge existentially isolated individuals. Interpersonal communication thus acquires a bonding power that it does not possess in traditional societies.

The second dimension is egalitarianism. If a society is predominantly hierarchical rather than egalitarian—as may more often be the case in traditional societies—interpersonal interaction occurs predominantly between individuals of unequal social power. This circumstance makes it more difficult for communication to operate to create shared constructions of reality. Egalitarianism tends to be characteristic of modern societies.

## THE CASE OF EASTERN EUROPE

What does this theoretical framework suggest about the nature of communication in Central and Eastern Europe? Unfortunately, this is a difficult question to answer in the general case. Central and Eastern Europe as a geopolitical region has undergone momentous change during the 19th and 20th centuries. Nations have formed and been transformed through partition, revolution, the ravages of two world wars, and the Cold War. Soviet domination of the region after World War II stabilized national boundaries but had varying impacts on economic development. In only the last 4 years Germany has been reunified,[3] the breakup of the former Soviet Union resulted in the restoration of the autonomy of the Baltic States and other former Soviet republics, Czechoslovakia split into the Czech and Slovak Republics, and civil war in Yugoslavia resulted in a new Balkan map. There is little about the history of Central and Eastern Europe that all the peoples of the region have experienced in common. Even during the relatively stable Cold War years, the political and economic climate varied significantly from one country to the next.

The region is a complex ethnic patchwork, which Palmer (1970) divided into four main groups: the Western Slavs (Poles, Slovaks, Czechs, and Ruthenes), the Southern Slavs (Serbs, Croats, Slovenes, Bulgarians, and Macedonians), the Hungarians (Magyars and Szeklers), and the Latins (Romanians). However, there are also Greeks, Turks, Albanians, Germans, Russians, and Italians mixed in. Indeed, part of an explanation for the degree to which national frontiers have been in flux can be found in the desire to sort the area into stable geopolitical units that honor ethnic and religious boundaries. The fact that this tendency has been expressed internally as well as by dominant nations outside the region (e.g., in the Congress of Vienna in 1815, the Congress of Berlin in 1878, the Versailles Settlement in 1919, and again following World War II) speaks to the persistent power of ethnicity as a source of external identity for individuals in Central and Eastern Europe.[4] As Palmer noted, the geography of the area is also complex: ". . . there are few other areas in the world where the interplay of geography and history . . . has made it possible . . . to meet such sudden changes in social characteristics between settlements separated by a few miles" (p. 1).

---

[3]Reunified at least politically (see chap. 2 in this volume).

[4]There are of course other important explanations for the frequent and dramatic changes since 1800 in the map of Eastern and Central Europe, not the least of which is that the region served as a buffer between the Ottoman, Austro-Hungarian, German, and Russian empires.

Hence, there are few generalizations that are likely to hold up across this complex region. The foregoing analysis, however, points to the relevance of indices of modernity in examining communication across cultural or national boundaries. Without suggesting that modernity as it is known in Western Europe and North America constitutes either an historical necessity or a desirable or ultimate target of development, it is nevertheless possible to distinguish between societies on the basis of the degree to which certain characteristics of modernity are or are not present. As suggested earlier, the two global dimensions of particular relevance are the degree to which the life worlds of citizens are pluralized and the degree to which the society in which they live is structured along egalitarian lines. How can one assess these dimensions?

## Pluralism

Pluralism is reflected indirectly in a range of national characteristics. These include the diversity of media sources (TV and radio stations, newspapers, magazines, etc.), the literacy level, the extent of annual gross national product that derives from agriculture as opposed to the manufacturing and service sectors of the society, the quality of the transportation infrastructure, and especially the degree of urbanization. These data cannot tell the whole story and, in addition, one must keep in mind that nationally aggregated statistics may not reflect accurately local conditions. However these data can serve as rough indicators of the cultural context of a nation as a whole. A thorough analysis of these dimensions is beyond the scope of this chapter but a brief examination of some relevant data is suggestive.

Urbanization has come recently to many Eastern European nations. For example, Turmock (1989) reported that only 23% of Romanians lived in urban areas in 1950. (As a point of comparison, 60% of the U.S. population lived in urban areas at that time—Monkkonen, 1985—a figure that increased to 70% by 1980.) By 1980 Romania was still at less than 50% urban. Bulgaria was less than 30% urban in 1950 but had reached 62% urban by 1980 (Turmock, 1989). Czechoslovakia was also approximately 60% urban in 1980 but change was much less dramatic there because it was already over 50% urban in 1950. On the other hand, Albania was less than 20% urban in 1950 and remained less than 40% urban in 1980. On the whole, the region did not rank among the world's most urbanized areas in 1980 but there is considerable variation among nations and the overall trend has been substantial increases in urbanization in the second half of the 20th century. To the extent that modernity is reflected in urbanization, it is not as advanced in the region though it is clearly on the rise.

Literacy levels are generally high in Central and Eastern European countries ranging from a low of 72% in Albania and 93% in Bulgaria to 96% or better in Hungary, Czechoslovakia, Poland, Romania, and Austria (Central Intelligence Agency, 1992). Media exposure, as reflected in the combined number of television and radio stations, is quite low in contrast to other modern states. This number ranges between 10 and 100 stations per country across the region. In contrast, the United Kingdom has over 900 stations, Italy has over 225, Switzerland has more than 250, and Spain has over 290 (Central Intelligence Agency, 1992). Radio and television stations are certainly more pervasive in Western European nations, even when the figures are adjusted for population size. The same pattern holds for daily newspapers (UNESCO, 1978). The average number of newspapers published per nation in the Central and Eastern European nations of Albania, Austria, Bulgaria, Czechoslovakia, Hungary, Poland, Romania, and Yugoslavia in 1977 was 11. The average number for Western European nations (exclusive of the German Federal Republic) was closer to 80. Adjusting these numbers for population, the rate was one newspaper for every 640,000 population in the eight Eastern European nations as compared to one newspaper for every 240,000 population for the Western European sample. Western European nations with smaller populations (e.g., Switzerland—population 6 million with 95 newspapers) tended to produce more newspapers than Central or Eastern European nations with larger populations (e.g., Romania—population 21 million with 20 newspapers).

The Central and Eastern European region is more heavily agricultural than Western Europe as reflected in the percentage of the labor force involved in agriculture. The average for Central and Eastern Europe is 19% but this ranges from an extraordinary high of 60% in Albania to less than 6% across the former Yugoslavian republics of Serbia, Croatia, and Bosnia-Hercegovina. Poland, Romania, and Bulgaria all invest more than 20% of their labor force in agriculture and Hungary invests 18%. Consistent with its higher pattern of urbanization, the former Czechoslovakia invests only 12%. Representative figures for Western European countries are 14% for Spain, 10% for Italy, 7% for France, and 2% for Great Britain (Central Intelligence Agency, 1992).

As a final indirect indicator of pluralism, it should be mentioned that the average density of roads and railways as represented in data for 8 Central and Eastern European nations (Albania, Austria, Bulgaria, Czechoslovakia, Hungary, Poland, Romania, and Yugoslavia) is approximately half that for a comparison sample of 12 Western European nations (Belgium, Denmark, France, Italy, Luxembourg, Netherlands, Norway, Portugal, Spain, Sweden, Switzerland, and the United Kingdom). In Central and Eastern Europe there are an average of .06 kilometers of railroad track per square kilometer of land whereas in the Western European sample there are .13 kilometers per square kilometer (*The Economist*, 1981). For roads the figures are .71 kilometers per square kilometer for Central and Eastern Europe and 1.6 kilometers per square kilometer in the Western European sample. Roadways and railways are channels of communication that increase the mixture of people, goods, and ideas. The infrastructure supporting these activities is nearly twice as dense in Western Europe.

Egalitarianism is reflected indirectly in data on the relative status of men and women across the countries of Central and Eastern Europe as compiled by the United Nations (1991). There are clear indications to support a conclusion that gender role equality is considerably more advanced in Central and Eastern Europe than it is in Western Europe.[5] For example, on the average, women in 1987 occupied 23% of legislative seats in Albania, Austria, Bulgaria, Czechoslovakia, Hungary, Poland, Romania, and Yugoslavia. The comparison figure for a sample of Western European countries (Belgium, Denmark, France, Italy, Luxembourg, Netherlands, Norway, Portugal, Spain, Sweden, Switzerland, and the United Kingdom) is 17% though it should be noted that the Scandinavian countries (Denmark, Norway, and Sweden), with an average of 31%, were responsible for raising the Western European average 7 points above its otherwise paltry 10% level. A comparison of data for the Federal Republic of Germany (15%) and the former German Democratic Republic (32%) is consistent with this trend, which suggests that greater gender role equality may have been evident under Communism than under capitalism.

The number of women per 100 men enrolled in tertiary-level education supports a similar conclusion. The average for Central and Eastern Europe (Albania, Austria, Bulgaria, Czechoslovakia, Hungary, Poland, Romania, and Yugoslavia) is 98.7 (United Nations, 1991). For the Western European sample (Belgium, Denmark, France, Italy, Luxembourg, Netherlands, Norway, Portugal, Spain, Sweden, Switzerland, and the United Kingdom), the average is 86. The difference is reflected in comparison data for the Federal Republic of Germany (72 women per 100 men) and the former German Democratic Republic (114 women per 100 men). Similarly, the number of hours per week spent on wage-earning economic activity showed consistent differences for the two regions. In a Central and Eastern European sample consisting of Bulgaria, Czechoslovakia, Hungary, Poland, and Yugoslavia the average was 27.7 hours for women and 44.9 hours for men, meaning that men engaged in this type of activity 1.6 hours for every hour that women put in. In a sample of Western European

---

[5]However, there are also alarming indications now beginning to come to light that with the fall of Communism, gender role egalitarianism is being replaced by historic patterns of male domination (e.g., Newman, 1993).

nations consisting of Belgium, France, Federal Republic of Germany, Netherlands, Norway, and the United Kingdom, the average was 15.2 hours for women and 38.31 hours for men for a much larger ratio of 2.5 hours of work for men for each hour for women. Clearly, women are better represented in economic activity in former Communist countries than in their capitalist counterparts. It will be instructive to see if women retain their status in Eastern Europe in the wake of the recent repudiation of Communism.

Finally, gender role egalitarianism is also reflected indirectly in national fertility statistics. The higher the fertility, the more likely it will be that women will not participate in public/economic life. With regard to the United States, Degler (1980) argued that the profound drop in fertility from 7.04 births per White woman in 1800 to 3.56 in 1900 was a necessary prerequisite to progress in gender role equality (the current U.S. fertility rate is 1.8 births per woman across the whole population—United Nations, 1991). Fertility in some areas of the world remains high. For example, in many African and Asian countries fertility levels are still higher than 5. Assuming decreasing rates of child mortality and assuming that women almost universally provide primary care of children, fertility at this level makes it difficult for a woman to participate in the public/economic sector. Fertility in Central and Eastern Europe is slightly higher than in Western Europe. The average for the sample consisting of Albania, Austria, Bulgaria, Czechoslovakia, Hungary, Poland, Romania, and Yugoslavia is 2.07 ranging from a high of 3.0 in Albania to a low of 1.5 in Austria. For the Western European sample (Belgium, Denmark, France, Italy, Luxembourg, Netherlands, Norway, Portugal, Spain, Sweden, Switzerland, and the United Kingdom) the average rate is 1.65.

## DISCUSSION

I have elsewhere presented an analysis of transitions in the context of interpersonal communication in the United States with reference to the broad cultural dimensions of pluralism and egalitarianism (Stephen, 1994).[6] That historically based model suggests that American culture evolved from a period during which egalitarianism and pluralism were low—characteristics of a traditional culture—to a modern configuration characterized by high egalitarianism and high pluralism. This shift was of monumental consequence for the role of interpersonal communication

[6]That analysis focused explicitly on the marital context and the dimension of egalitarianism was compounded with that of the separation of spheres of experience for men and women.

in everyday social relationships. It transformed communication from a vehicle for coordinating action and sharing information to a medium for the social construction of self and world. Communication ceased functioning as a mere conveyor of information and gradually began to function as a process that anchors identity and forges bonds between self and other. A modern individual from the late 20th century would find interpersonal relationships in colonial America bewilderingly rigid in their unquestioned and unquestionable meaning, their fixed social positions, and their presumption of ties between character (self) and role. On the other hand, an individual from 17th-century America thrust into the late 20th century would find meaning insubstantial, complex, and impossibly abstract and life blasphemous, irreverent, and superficial.

Although there are certainly circumstances today in which members of modern cultures interact with members of traditional cultures, encounters between individuals from societies so distant from each other have little to do with intercultural communication involving Central and Eastern Europe. The region is advanced industrially and possibly more egalitarian than many Western countries with unbroken traditions of capitalist market economies.[7] However, the structural evidence suggests that Central and Eastern European societies may not be as compartmentalized and fragmented as is the case in the West, at least not at the moment. Although there seems every reason to anticipate that the nations of Central and Eastern Europe that were economically held back throughout the Cold War will eventually catch up with their neighbors to the West, the data suggest that for the time being there will remain an odd moment of historical disjunction during which communication between individuals from Central and Eastern Europe and more modern societies may be burdened by a degree of mutual incoherence as individuals from these two contexts may understand the process of interpersonal interactions in different ways. If so, this is one sense in which historical processes may be impacting on social behavior in contemporary life.

Of course there are many other historical threads that must also be followed in coming to terms with the unique context of communication in Central and Eastern Europe, as the region is far too variable and complex to be described reliably in general terms. In the foregoing discussion, for example, Austria has been included in the data on Central and Eastern Europe and, though it belongs to the region geographically, it is clearly separate from other Central and Eastern European countries in that its fate was determined principally by the Western powers rather than the Soviet Union at the end of World War II. Austria is part of Central Europe and its history is deeply intertwined with the other nations

[7]However, for a different perspective on this see Goode (1993).

of the region, but Austria's recent economic history has isolated her from her neighbors.

Insofar as political action often supplies the vital force for structuring social life, political history is clearly important in understanding the way in which society shapes communication practices. No great effort need be expended in locating recent examples from the Cold War era of radical political policies that impacted fundamentally the nature of interpersonal relations in Central and Eastern European countries. Communication not only constitutes social structure, it is also constituted by and takes place within existing social/political structures. Nevertheless, political events have received a disproportionate amount of attention by historians. To understand how a culture establishes and sustains meaning through communication, it is also vital to come to grips with microhistorical trends, with the gradual, evolutionary patterns of change in the everyday life circumstances of the individual members of a society. Hence, it seems clear that research on intercultural communication would proceed most profitably if it operated at the level of specific national subgroups and only then if it is appropriately informed by a full appreciation of the historical background, the unfolding economic and political context, the religion, traditions, and other life circumstances of the people involved.

A considerable body of scholarship suggests that it may also be instructive in assessing the social context of communication to appreciate the structure of family relations within the cultures under study. For example, a body of linguistic theory reported by Borkenau (1981) suggests that the group of Indo-European languages represented throughout Europe evolved quite differently with respect to the point at which they provided a detached subject in speech—an "I-form," as in "I, Hlegestr, sailed the ship" rather than "Hlegestr sailed the ship" (in which the author refers to himself in the third person). This showed up first in Nordic lands and suggests the possibility of a distinctly different heritage of perception for individuals in linguistic cultures that adopted this particular distinction of speech and thought early on. In one account (which Borkenau disputes) this was a product of the early Nordic adoption of a particularistic family form instead of the common patriarchal family structure. As Todorova (1993) suggested, some areas of Eastern Europe may have continued to employ the patriarchal pattern as the basic structure of the family longer than in many Western European countries, possibly helping to sustain traditionalism.

The foregoing discussion of Central and Eastern European social structure and communication is admittedly speculative. It should be clear that coming to terms with the theoretical ideas outlined previously will require an examination in depth of the particular subcultures whose intercultural interaction is of interest. Methodologically speaking, what is advocated is a sort of "historical ethnography"—a study in depth of a culture that also extends backward through time. Such a study must consider the interrelationships between macrolevel characteristics including relevant patterns of historical evolution and macrostructures of the surrounding society and microlevel detail of the specific symbolic environment of specific people. Each interaction involves specific people and occurs within a particular social structure and against a particular historical backdrop. This is especially clear in Central and Eastern Europe.

## REFERENCES

Bellah, R. H., Madsen, R., Sullivan, W. M., Swidler, A., & Tipton, S. M. (1985). *Habits of the heart: Individualism and commitment in American life*. New York: Harper & Row.

Berger, P., Berger, B., & Kellner, H. (1974). *The homeless mind: Modernization and consciousness*. New York: Vintage.

Borkenau, F. (1981). The rise of the I-form of speech. In R. Lowenthal (Ed.), *End and beginning: On the generations of cultures and the origins of the West*. New York: Columbia University Press.

Central Intelligence Agency. (1992). CIA world fact book: 1992 [Electronic data source]. Langley, VA: Author.

Coser, R. L. (1991). *In defense of modernity: Role complexity and individual autonomy*. Stanford, CA: Stanford University Press.

Degler, C. N. (1980). *At odds: Women and the family in America from the revolution to the present*. New York: Oxford University Press.

Demos, J. (1986). *Past, present, and personal: The family and the life course in American history*. New York: Oxford University Press.

*The Economist*. (1981). *The world in figures*. London: The Economist Newspaper Limited.

Elias, N. (1978). *The history of manners*. New York: Pantheon.

Fukuyama, F. (1992). *The end of history and the last man*. New York: Avon.

Fussell, P. (1983). *Class*. New York: Ballantine.

Giddens, A. (1990). *The consequences of modernity*. Stanford, CA: Stanford University Press.

Giddens, A. (1991). *Modernity and self-identity: Self and society in the late modern age*. Stanford, CA: Stanford University Press.

Goode, W. J. (1993). *World changes in divorce patterns*. New Haven, CT: Yale University Press.

Holzner, B. (1968). *Reality construction in society*. Cambridge, MA: Schenkman.

Kasson, J. F. (1991). *Rudeness & civility: Manners in nineteenth-century urban America*. New York: The Noonday Press.

Mintz, S., & Kellogg, S. (1988). *Domestic revolutions: A social history of American family life*. New York: The Free Press.

Mitterauer, M., & Sieder, R. (1982). *The European family*. Oxford, England: Basil Blackwell.

Monkkonen, E. H. (1985). *America becomes urban: The development of U.S. cities & towns 1780–1980*. Berkeley: University of California Press.

Morgan, E. S. (1966). *The Puritan family: Religion and domestic relations in seventeenth-century New England* (rev. ed.). New York: Harper & Row.

Newman, B. (1993, November 19). Women in Poland find little liberation in shift to democracy. *The Wall Street Journal*, p. 9.

O'Malley, M. (1990). *Keeping watch: A history of American time*. New York: Penguin.

Palmer, A. (1970). *The lands between: A history of East-Central Europe since the Congress of Vienna*. New York: Macmillan.

Pietrow-Ennker, B. (1992). Women in Polish society. A historical introduction. In R. Jaworski & B. Pietrow-Ennker (Eds.), *Women in Polish society* (pp. 1–29). Boulder, CO: East European Monographs (No. CCCXLIV).

Riesman, D., Glazer, N., & Denney, R. (1961). *The lonely crowd: A study of the changing American character*. New Haven, CT: Yale University Press.

Sennett, R. (1976). *The fall of public man: On the social psychology of capitalism*. New York: Vintage.

Shils, E. (1981). *Tradition*. Chicago: University of Chicago Press.

Stephen, T. (1986). Communication and interdependence in geographically separated relationships. *Human Communication Research, 13*, 191–210.

Stephen, T. (1994). Communication in the shifting context of intimacy: Marriage, meaning, and modernity. *Communication Theory, 4*, 191–218.

Stephen, T., & Harrison, T. (1993). Interpersonal communication, theory, and history. *Communication Theory, 3*, 163–172.

Taylor, C. (1989). *Sources of the self: The making of the modern identity*. Cambridge, MA: Harvard University Press.

Todorova, M. N. (1993). *Balkan family structure and the European pattern*. Washington, DC: The American University Press.

Tuan, Y.-F. (1982). *Segmented worlds and self: Group life and individual consciousness*. Minneapolis: University of Minnesota Press.

Turmock, D. (1989). *The human geography of Eastern Europe*. New York: Routledge.

UNESCO. (1978). *Statistical yearbook: 1977*. Paris: Author.

United Nations. (1991). *The world's women: The trends and statistics 1970–1990*. New York: Author.

# II

# GERMANY AND UNIFICATION

Fred L. Casmir

Probably, no event in recent history demonstrates the dangers of inadequate understanding and analysis of cross- or interculturally significant events than the unification of Germany during the last two decades of the 20th century.

Emotions ran high when the wall separating East and West Germany was finally knocked down, with the feared *Volkspolizei* looking on without preventing its destruction. As a matter of fact, the wall had become such a symbol, often unrelated to political, cultural, and economic *realities*, that the public, which had only mass media images on which to build its opinions, could be readily forgiven for concluding that many more positive results were involved than the mere collapse of a wall.

After 40 and more years of East–West confrontations citizens of our world, and especially Americans, were weary. In addition, they were overwhelmed by the mediated images of Germany and Germans becoming *one*. It seemed obvious that the final, permanent collapse of Communism was being witnessed, something that the experts had been unable to predict. What was perhaps less acceptable was the fact that these same kinds of experts were unable or unwilling to interpret the events portrayed by our mass media in such a way as to truly make sense of them, while not contributing to the euphoria binge.

Looking at the case of East and West German unification, or reunification, through the eyes of someone who was born and educated in Germany, but who has long been acculturated into the American society, provides us with an opportunity to better understand the intercultural challenges a country faces, even if the outside world identifies it all too readily as *one nation*. Much of our confusion results when we make the mistake of equating a state, a political entity, with a nation, a people, or a culture. It is no wonder that so many people expected unity where only political, and often coerced, unification had been achieved within the borders of a modern state. Casmir traces historic developments over many hundreds of years, which need to be understood if one is to meaningfully analyze events in a country that has all too glibly been identified by the term *Germany*.

Only if one develops foundations for adequately evaluating contemporary events on the basis of cultural and historical differences as well as similarities, all of them rooted in almost 2,000 years of history, can one hope to understand what difficulties the Federal Republic and the former People's Republic of Germany faced when they decided to become one state. At the same time, the deeply rooted cultural images of a nation, one *Volk*, a dream never quite realized by Germans, are such powerful motivators that even a modern state cannot ignore them. Although the example of Germany, because it was so unexpected by many, is especially startling to all who hoped for simple answers to the challenges of the *"new world order,"* later chapters in this volume demonstrate that the German experience is not unique in Eastern Europe.

How far-reaching the impact of cultural differences, and how great the roles of mass media in dealing with them have already been, is repeatedly demonstrated by Boyle. Like Casmir, her insights are based on extensive personal and professional contacts and on long-term interests in developments in that part of Europe. Particularly challenging is her insistence that the mass media have taken over the role of traditional social and cultural organizations that once helped to weave the social fabric. That role becomes significant in dealing both with the Nazi past of Germany, East and West, and contemporary problems related to *outsiders*, refugees and others, who have entered Germany in large numbers. Not only has the *new Germany* had to deal with enormous problems caused by political and economic unification, some social and cultural problems have been virtually ignored until they became so overwhelming that they had to be recognized. The study of contemporary Germany produces a much clearer understanding of the fact that no state can reorganize itself without taking into consideration the intercultural problems that exist within its own borders, and those global challenges that are increasingly the result of what may well be the largest dislocation and relocation of human beings in the history of the world.

It is also important for us to recognize that the challenges faced by the modern state require consideration of more than the traditional cultural, ethnic, racial, and religious divisions or categories, which we have commonly used when dealing with inter- and cross-cultural communication. Rosenberg makes very clear in her chapter that gender issues are just as problematic, and that they have been just as consistently and thoughtlessly ignored as is true of other cultural differences and similarities. Only recently have some of us become aware of the fact that many East German women have experienced a *loss* of what they saw as social and political rights, which were made readily available to them in the former Communist People's Republic of Germany. Not only does such a fact fly in the face of preconceived ideas about which of the two former German states was more *democratic,* it incapacitates us if we do not adequately consider its implications as far as future interactions between women and women, and women and men in East and West Germany are concerned. Once more, the complexities of inter- or cross-cultural communication in a country that many of us saw as simply being reunited, because it had always been one *Volk,* are thus demonstrated.

# 2

# *"Wir sind ein Volk": Illusions and Reality of German Unification*

Fred L. Casmir
*Pepperdine University*

## FOUNDATIONAL CONCEPTS

No subject has been of more consistent concern to scholars of human communication than the complexities of interpersonal relations within and between cultures. Because of the centrality of that issue, and because of the pervasive probems existing in human interactions, it is easy to understand that both scholars and practitioners have attempted to develop relatively simple explanatory systems. That has certainly been the case in what we call intercultural or cross-cultural communication.

### Hall's Pioneer Work

The writings of Edward T. Hall are indicative both of our concerns and the progressions of our thinking. In his earliest work, Hall presented us with a framework for the study of intercultural communication as well as a new term, *proxemics*. In both cases the systematic approach he provided was highly linear, simplistic, and strongly influenced by his predilection to define human interactions in relation to the use of space, on the basis of cultural groups, and as fit subjects for the application of quantitative methods (E. T. Hall, 1969, 1973). As his insights increased, and his work became more indicative of the complexities he discovered, other books followed. However, Hall continued to use one of his early categories almost unchanged. References to "nations" or "cultures" continued, when in effect he was referring to states. He wrote, for instance, "American time is what I have termed 'monochronic' . . . when Americans interact with people of foreign cultures, the different time systems cause great difficulty" (E. T. Hall, 1976, p. 17). Claiming more inclusivity for his system he eschewed other approaches, though he considered them valid, because he felt ". . . it is more important to look at the way things are actually put together than at theories" (E. T. Hall, 1976, p. 16). That is especially important because Hall (1976) felt that if one touched culture in one place that everything else was affected, that, in effect, not even one aspect of human life is untouched or unaffected by culture.

E. T. Hall's (1976) concept or identification of a culture (or of a nation) became even more central to the total scheme of his system. In an attempt to understand and describe what he had observed, Hall provided us with short-cut explanations like the following: "In bicultural cases, I have seen people shift from a Spanish to a German way of interacting without knowing that the shift occurred. Also, I have seen others start with a Greek pattern and slip automatically into a German-Swiss pattern as the situation demanded" (p. 43). In this way, Hall continued a system of categorizations that made it easy to ignore individual differences, and that even overlooked significant regional and cultural differences within the borders of a political state, such as Germany, for the sake of simplicity. My own concern with the confusion in our terminology that results when we make no distinctions between nations, cultural groups, or subcultures and states that are politically and economically determined entities, has been dealt with elsewhere (Casmir, 1991, 1992).

### Hofstede's Cultural Communication Model

However, the work of E. T. Hall is not the only model that has been embraced, often uncritically, by those wishing to gain insights into intercultural relations and communication. Geert Hofstede (1980) provided us with another systematic attempt to explain why cultural factors play a significant role in such interactions and how they can serve to predict certain types of relations. Even more than was true in E. T. Hall's work, culture, for the sake of making it accessible to certain mathematical manipulations, was thus defined as follows: "The word 'culture' is usually reserved for societies (in the modern world we speak of 'nations') or for ethnic or regional groups, but it can be applied equally to other human collectivities or categories: an organization, a profession, or a family" (Hofstede, 1980, p. 27).

Hofstede's (1980) conceptualization is clearly indicated and further elaborated when he stated, "The degree of cultural integration varies between one society and another, and may be specially low for the newer nations . . ." (p. 26). By this time the confusion between such terms as society, culture, nation, state, and even family had become almost institutionalized, making the following statement seem logical: "This book is about differences in national culture among 40 modern nations" (p. 26). Actually, Hofstede was, of course, referring to modern states, and simply brushed off significant regional and subcultural differences in such modern states by referring to the work of anthropologists who studied nonliterate cultures on the basis of small samples.

Hofstede's (1980) attempt to provide us with a statistically manipulable sample concept comes full circle when he wrote, "From such in-depth sample studies, anthropologists draw conclusions on the culture as a whole, including 'modal personality' or 'national character'" (p. 37). It would almost appear that culture now has been defined as an artifact of the method rather than something separately identifiable. Hofstede based his entire effort in studying employees of the HERMES corporation as "representatives" of cultures in the hope that the quality of matching narrow samples can "only be proved ex post facto" (p. 38). He did not adequately consider the possibility that his findings, once again, could be the result of the method applied and not of factors inherent in cultures, individuals, or the situation.

The attempt to simplify our task is even more startling when one considers Hofstede's (1980) claim that "In order to learn about differences among societies we need not necessarily study what is modal in each society; we can also learn from a comparison of marginal phenomena" (p. 39). The pervasiveness of such confusions that influence our work as intercultural communication scholars becomes once more evident when, based on his assumptions, Hofstede simply stated (ignoring the size, makeup, or cultural representativeness of his chosen sample) that "The main purpose of this book is a comparison by country" (pp. 72–73).

There can be little doubt that the severity of conflicts that face us in our contemporary world call, or perhaps put more accurately, scream for solutions. There can also be little doubt that we need to develop both conceptual frameworks and methods that allow us to address these challenges. However, my concern is that it will be difficult to adequately target problems if our bases for their identification are flawed.

### Shuter's Emphasis on Culture

Shuter (1990) had good reason to laud E. T. Hall's and other anthropologists' passionate concern for culture. He had equally meaningful reasons to remind communication scholars that they frequently lacked that passionate concern in their work, even if they laid claim to contributions in what we call inter*cultural* communication: ". . . [M]uch of the published research in intercultural communication, particularly in the national and regional speech communication journals, is conducted to refine existing communication theories: culture serves principally as a research laboratory for testing the validity of communication paradigms" (Shuter, 1990, p. 238). Even more challenging is his statement that "Intercultural studies in national and regional speech-communication journals are neither of an etic or emic nature: they are products of a nomothetic model developed in psychology that drives communication research . . ." (p. 239). Shuter's essay should influence us to consider the significant cultural problems many societies (or states) face, including those in Eastern and Western Europe, as far as *intra*cultural communication issues are concerned.

Because I agree with Shuter's (1990) assertion that we need research in particular countries to "generate cultural data that not only creates understanding of a society, but also serves as a springboard for developing intracultural communication theory" (p. 242), I am including a variety of insights in the following case study of East German–West German cultural conflicts.

One issue, however, needs some elaboration here. Shuter (1990) preferred the term *co-cultures* when dealing with such conflicts. I continue to use the term *subcultures*, simply because, as my case study clearly indicates, cultural relationships are often, if not always, related to power relationships. My underlying assumption behind the issues discussed in this chapter is the fact that we do not merely face "cultural conflicts," but also relational conflicts when human beings attempt to dominate others who are identifiable as "culturally different," and often as culturally less developed, less valuable, or less desirable.

## Defining Culture

For the purposes of this chapter, culture is dealt with as a human sense-making, explanatory tool whose institutionalized uses serve various control purposes. First, there is control over human beings both inside and outside a group of individuals who have associated themselves with others. Second, culture serves the purpose of interpreting the environment in which human beings exist, encouraging the common use of various familiar artifacts, symbols, and institutions. Either by means of adaptation, conquest, or a combination of both, human beings thus bring some regularity or control to their environment and existence. Just as important, through the use of a common language, they are able to share and pass on those concepts on which they have agreed, resulting in a feeling of safety and assurance over extended periods of time. Art, science, religion, economics, and politics are only some of the cultural institutions used in various societal settings that serve those purposes.

Among all of these factors, the most important to the scholar of cultural and intercultural communication is the fact that none of the processes involved in instituting, maintaining, transmitting, or even destroying cultures is possible without communication.

## 2,000 YEARS OF GERMAN UNIFICATION ATTEMPTS

Although it would be patently absurd to try and review any state's or nation's history in a few summary pages, the central theme of this book demands more than the description of contemporary events. Pointing to a number of cultural and historical explanations directly related to the subject at hand should aid us in better understanding the cultural conflicts in the recently unified Germany.

As Pflanze (1963) explained,

> In western civilization the idea of a nation has been reached from two different directions. Among the Atlantic peoples the molding force was that of the state. Here the awareness of nationality developed from a common political allegiance and experience. But in central and eastern Europe the awareness of nationality preceded and even helped in the creation of the nation-state. Here national consciousness grew from the chrysalis of individual cultures. (pp. 32–33)

Germany has been one of the countries in which such cultural factors as language, folkways, and ethnic origin have played a significant role. However, the commonly used umbrella terms *German* or *Germany* have obscured important subcultural differences that even today can be observed in such factors as customs, institutions, and regional or even local dialects. The latter would make it almost impossible for all Germans to communicate with each other, were it not for the agreed-upon cultural artifact of the common written language called High German.

### Charlemagne's First Empire

The term *empire* can, of course, be used in many ways. I am employing it here in much the same way as Owen and Ehrenhaus (1993) did who considered it to be organic, explaining its concern with feeding, or "... with nourishment for perpetuation and growth. Empire has voracious appetites; it thrives by feeding on those less well positioned in the world. ... Its perpetuation requires domination over those both within its boundaries and without" (p. 170).

One of the inheritors of Roman power and civilization were the Germanic people, especially the Lombards and Franks, the latter a collection of tribes that had united (Wells, 1898). This Frank confederation of several tribes inhabited the Rhine districts, never leaving their old lands in spite of the pressures created during the invasion of the Huns, although conquering new areas. Even then, two distinct groups, the Salians near the mouth of the Rhine, and the Ripurians on the right bank of the Rhine, emerged. Whereas other tribes became more Romanized, including those in what later would become France, the Franks of the Rhineland "remained for the most part German in speech and culture" (Davies, 1948, p. 10). As war became an almost permanent state of affairs, temporary tribal war-chieftains were replaced by more permanent kings. In these historic beginnings can we recognize the beginnings of German or Germanic unification efforts.

The old tribal customs and religions disappeared, opening the way for a significant impact of Christianity and the Papal empire, as it replaced the old Roman state. Clovis was the first Frankish king to develop the dream of an empire uniting all German tribes (Wells, 1898). Not intent on fusing Romans and Germans but rather relying on a common Christian faith, Clovis found that faith to be an important unifying factor. Under Charlemagne's eventual influence the imperial idea became that of a Christian empire, with a new David, a kind of continuation of a Biblical royalty (Sullivan, 1954). Thus began a long history that would lead to the "great modern states of western Europe, including Germany" (Wells, 1898, p. 31). Although the notion of empire came to the Germans from Rome, it was not an inherently Germanic concept, and the Roman empire's foundations, requiring complete integration of its members, never really became part of any of the German empires (Sullivan, 1954).

Clovis distributed the kingdom among his sons, as was the Germanic custom, based on a concept of family unity. It was Charles, eventually to be known as The Great (or Charlemagne), who later became the most powerful inheritor of that dream of an empire. A powerful Germanic mythology developed during the days of Charlemagne, including the person of the emperor himself. It also included a belief that the nation had descended from Troy, and that indeed it was a chosen nation, particularly dear to God. The belief that its king, emperor, or ruler was beloved and elected by God would reappear in various forms in centuries to come (Sullivan, 1954).

The unifying role of the Christian faith became even clearer with Charles' eventual canonization through the combined efforts of Emperor Frederick I and King Henry II of England, with the agreement of both the antipope Paschal and the rightful pope Alexander III. After all, following St. Boniface's efforts to bring about an alliance between the Papacy and the Frankish empire, it had been Charles who became the protector of the Papacy, and whose coronation in Rome during the year 800 became an important symbol of that relationship (Sullivan, 1954).

The concept of unity was upheld by Charles' son and heir Louis, but the underlying forces of disunity were too strong to maintain the first Germanic empire beyond his rule, "... for in spite of the underlying race unity of the German people, there were between the various tribes which had come to make up the empire vast differences which seemed to offer well nigh irresistible obstacles to real union" (Wells, 1898, p. 374). The key concept in that statement is "tribes which had come to make up the empire," indicating a confederative rather than an integrated association.

Unification through the efforts of a strong leader making use of some overriding common religious or ideological concept became a pattern to be repeated twice more in German history, but lasting union was much more difficult to achieve. Davies (1948) reminded us that, although modern pan-Germans have striven to create the idea of Germans as a separate race, anthropologists tell us that the differences between so-called Germans, Celts, Slavs, and so forth are not so much racial as they are descriptive of language and culture. Davies concluded that "... the most potent influences in the formation of 'national' character are facts of geography and climatic surroundings, modified by special cultures and political conditions that have arisen in large measure out of this environment" (p. 12). Probably Rome's influence on Gaul and what was later to become France, based on its genius for organization, had a great deal to do with that country's later unity. But the Germans never allowed Rome's political impact—they expelled Rome and returned to disunity. Charlemagne's empire never was based on organic unity, but he had suggested to Germans for the first time an ideal of unity under one ruler (Davies, 1948).

### The Second German Empire

The real beginning of a German "nation" may be traced back to the Treaty of Verdun in 843 when the empire of Charlemagne was divided by his three grandsons (Davies, 1948). Significantly, centuries of disagreements and wars between Germany and France can be traced back to those days. Territorial claims and counterclaims, insistence that Charles was either "German" or "French," and the political implications of those claims, poisoned relationships between the two countries for many centuries—but eventually it was those conflicts and that rivalry that became one of the major factors in bringing about the second German empire.

For centuries, in spite of attempts to keep the so-called Holy Roman Empire or the Holy Roman Empire of Germanic Nation in existence, disunity, strife, war, and bloody struggles for succession were the rule. Attempts, for instance, to build some sort of unified German empire under Hapsburg rule, thus including the strong central influence of Austria, came to naught. Austria built its own empire, and whatever had remained of the German empire came to an end in 1806 when Napoleon forced Francis II to abandon the by now empty title of emperor of the Holy Roman Empire (Davies, 1948).

Against this historic backdrop it is reasonable to make the claim that "Bismarck [the chancellor of Prussia] did not set out at the beginning of his official career to build up a new Germany . . ." (Davies, 1948, p. 95). During the intervening centuries since Charlemagne's empire, the very idea of a unified German people had become more mythology or a romantic dream than a clear model. At the same time, national awakening in Germany was part of a greater, Europe-wide movement following the French Revolution. National unity was a logical consequence of that general mood (Ritter, 1968).

The Congress of Vienna in 1815 had played a significant role in German history, as an attempt was made to redivide and reorganize the world along strictly statist lines. It was against that backdrop that in Germany the choice between a Greater German Republic (*Grossdeutsche Republik*) or a Lesser German Empire (*Kleindeutsches Reich*) with Prussian leadership was debated. The latter concept became strongly linked to the romantic doctrine of *Volkstum* (national heritage, in the German sense) as well as old imperial ideals (Schnabel, 1968). However, the German Confederation that emerged from diplomatic efforts in Vienna was not really a sovereign body, but rather something like a miniature United Nations including 38 states, which Bismarck could never quite entice to give up their rights and privileges for the sake of a unified empire or the romantic concept of one *Volk* (Pflanze, 1963).

An early and important advocate of the idealized national concept was the founder of the German "Turner" associations, the so-called "*Turnvater*" Jahn. Concepts like the national spirit (*Volksgeist*), national heritage (*Volkstum*), and the rejection of Austria as a leader because of its "mixture" of peoples, were central to his literary conception of Germany's future. These concepts did not necessarily originate with Jahn. German poets, philosophers, and writers like Herder had extensively used the term *Volksgeist* before, and Schiller had drawn the conclusion that the German spirit was not only different from but also superior to others, causing him to write, "Every people had its day in history, but the day of the German is the harvest of all time" (see Pflanze, 1963, p. 33).

Jahn's Greater Germany would have included all German-speaking peoples including Swiss, Dutch, and Austrians under the motto: "*So weit die deutsche Zunge klingt*" ("Wherever there is heard the German tongue") (Schnabel, 1968). The roots of Hitler's later romantic version of a Greater Germany become clearly visible in these earlier conceptualizations, many of them resulting from a widespread feeling of national disunity and powerlessness, especially under Napoleonic occupation.

A number of other events prepared the way for the attempt to unify German-speaking people as well, including the less than successful revolution of 1848. Two concepts, part of a political slogan of the day, were central to events during that period: "Unity, Freedom, and Power" (*"Einheit, Freiheit, und Macht"*). The first and the last of these terms indicated the desired bases for German statehood as well as the contemporary vision of Germany's future role in Europe (Namier, 1968). However, the lack of unity proved to be the most serious challenge to achieving the perceived need for power. The Frankfurt Parliament of 1848 developed the vision of a Pan-Germany with a Great Prussia or Great Austria at its core. Bismarck, for a variety of reasons, would later reject that greater vision for a so-called Lesser Germany with Prussia at its center, whereas Hitler would embrace it. At the same time, the Frankfurt Parliament insisted on the general human right of self-determination for all people, although laying the foundations for later problems with German unification as it finally accepted more realistic, *"kleindeutsche,"* limits for the German state. These were based on political and statist considerations rather than the earlier emotional romanticized cultural or language-oriented idealism (Pflanze, 1963, 1968).

When a European power vacuum was left after the collapse of the French Empire following the Franco-Prussian war, Bismarck decided that the time had come to use the existing coalition of states for building a German empire. Out of an earlier Northern German Federation, a loose Custom Union, and a combined effort by many of the small states in the German Federation to defeat France under Prussian leadership, therefore, emerged Bismarck's empire, once more federative rather than national or organically unified (Haffner, 1989).

There was little or none of the fanaticism, romanticism, or idealism of other attempts at German national unification about the so-called Iron Chancellor's efforts. Although he would link his plan back to Germany's past by insisting that his was a "Christian state" and that the basic purpose of political institutions was the "realization of Christian doctrine," he subordinated the church to the state. The tax-supported state-church lost more and more of its spiritual impact on Germany, making it eventually easy for Hitler to control and use it during his reign (Pflanze, 1963). Bismarck used other emotional and romantic concepts for his own state-building purposes as well. His insistence on the term *Kaiser* (emperor) was an attempt to exploit both German nationalism and historic idealism for the purposes of unity and centralization (Pflanze, 1963).

Finally, as Charles had been crowned in Rome, the king of Prussia, after much quarreling, the granting of special exceptions and privileges to kingdoms like Bavaria, and last-minute avoidance of using either the title "Emperor of Germany" (on which the new emperor insisted) or the title "German Emperor" (which several other rulers in the new empire wanted), was crowned outside German territory once more, this time in Versailles (Davies, 1948). It seemed that German unity, including the fact that the idea of a "greater" Germany incorporating Austria and other German-speaking states was abandoned, was defined more in relationship to inside and outside political forces than internal cultural, racial, or even language factors.

Bismarck's most important and yet historically ironic legacy was his eventually unsuccessful effort to produce lasting national unity. His Lesser Germany, without Austria, became the historic backdrop for a Greater Germany, led by an Austrian, Adolf Hitler. Where Bismarck tried to avoid expansionism, Hitler's efforts were diametrically opposed to that policy—and they were greeted with great enthusiasm by the German people when he came to power (Haffner, 1989).

## The Third Reich

Adolf Hitler, native of Austria, did not take the title of Kaiser. He linked his empire to the mystical past, to the superior Germanic "race" (the Aryan superman), and to the longings of a German people once more defeated in war, once more divided into feuding parties and states, once more powerless.

One of Hitler's favorite slogans changed the realistic demands embraced by those who attended the earlier Frankfurt Parliament from unity, freedom, and power to the emotion-laden assertions "*Ein Volk, Ein Reich, Ein Führer*." Unity was assumed to exist in the fact that Germans were one race, of one blood, "one people" (or nation). The existence of "one (unified) state" (or empire) was simply asserted as the basis of power. Added was the personality cult of a "leader," in the tradition of the old Germanic tribal chief, "chosen" by his people, and protected by whatever god there was (Davies, 1948; Shirer, 1960).

Hitler destroyed internal opposition or even imagined rivals in bloody purges, eliminated the political parties that opposed him, and set up one of the most effective police states in the history of the world. At the same time the Führer used the concept of *Volk, Volksgeist*, and historical myth to create feelings of unity and national purpose not achieved in Germany before him. That successful combination would not be forgotten by the later East German Communist state.

Some have pointed to the fact that Hitler's movement was theoretically imprecise, and that much of what he presented to the people was highly emotional, rambling, and, again, imprecise and anti-intellectual (Koch, 1985). The point that is often missed by such critics is that all these factors made it possible for Germans to "read into" his messages whatever they wanted—imprecision allowed Hitler to become all things to all people. In many ways Hitler made modern advertising concepts the basis for his messages.

The Fuehrer's seeming belief in what he called "*gesundes Volksempfinden*" (the inherently healthy feeling of the people—once more including the term *Volk*) is one such example. His second concept, the classless national community (note the use of the term community as opposed to state), the so-called *Volksgemeinschaft*, was so appealing that even those who later tried to assassinate him felt they could not do without it as they planned a political entity to replace Hitler's Reich. Koch (1985) insisted that even the economic miracles in West Germany and East Germany (certainly compared to other Eastern European Communist countries) following World War II could not have been achieved without the ideal of a classless society, born in the trenches of World War I, and encouraged by Hitler for his own purposes of German unification. Even the concept of "racial purity" had its adherents among the conspirators who decided to kill Hitler, specifically a representative of the traditional, elitist military leadership, Colonel von Stauffenberg, who placed the bomb in the Führer's headquarters (Koch, 1985).

Hitler's personal dynamism and appeal reached beyond the German people, however. Even foreign diplomats and visitors were deeply impressed by it (Koch, 1985; Shirer, 1960). For years I owned a picture of Hitler addressing German and foreign athletes in his Berlin Chancellory during the 1936 Olympic Games. Few could understand him, but every head was turned toward him; all faces showed complete absorption. Hitler became a prophet who partook of the divine, at least in the eyes of his admirers; he was a charismatic miracle worker whose movement took on religious dimensions.

Little wonder then that the Führer would end some of his speeches with an "Amen" (Angebert, 1974). The head of the German Labor Front, Dr. Ley, was quite precise in his own identification of the faith dimension of Hitler's movement: "Our faith, which alone can save us, is National Socialism, and this religious faith does not tolerate any other faith alongside itself" (Angebert, 1974, p. 201). National Socialism was a state religion based on blood and race, a *Weltanschauung* with a highly visible messiah and high priest to boot. The dream, the religion, the empire collapsed, not after 1,000 years as Hitler had prophesied, but after some 12 years.

The longing for German unity has not disappeared, but whether it will become the basis for real unity at the end of the 20th century is still questionable, as the next segment of this chapter indicates. Much of what has been summarized in the preceding pages is proof that history is not merely the consequence of impersonal forces or currents—people make history. Nor is formal logic the answer to the kind of logic that has developed out of the needs of people, over time (Koch, 1985). Culture is more than science, or economics, or politics—all these factors are the result of larger sociocultural developments. Contemporary German history indicates that that particular lesson of history has not yet been learned.

## ONE MORE TIME

The world can be forgiven for expecting too much from the destruction of the Berlin Wall and the collapse of Communism both in Russia and East Germany. Decades of conflict and uncertainty, after all, had led to a weariness on all sides, which caused most of us to conclude that a new age was dawning in which all the old problems would disappear or in which they could be readily resolved. No wonder then that German unification was seen only in the light of contemporary political and economic realities, without any consideration being given to cultural and historical factors that would have a significant impact. In some ways, empire building, with all of its inherent problems, once more became the model for unification. Economic penetration, cultural domination, and the shaping of consciousness became the major tools in the renewed attempt to unify Germany (see Owen & Ehrenhaus, 1993).

The terms German and Germany almost automatically conjured up images of one country that had been only temporarily divided because of outside political forces. It may be well to remember throughout this discussion a factor that was considered in an editorial (signed "m.s.") in the *Frankfurter Allgemeine Zeitung*: ". . . the old question about 'the typically German' is here again. However, explanations of collective characteristics are as questionable as they are stimulating, as unscientific as they are irresistible" ("Die Einen und Die," 1990). In the same newspaper an editorial signed "G. Ho" ("Des Deutschlands," 1990) had earlier suggested to simply forget about cultural and other divisive features when speaking of "Germany," and to make the term stand only for a geographic area. The following pages indicate why that solution is highly simplistic.

### Setting the Stage

The first sections of this chapter have indicated how much Germany has struggled, over many centuries, to become a unified political state. The roles mystical concepts, and especially the concept of *Volk*, have played in those attempts have been repeatedly stressed.

Prior to and following the unification of East and West Germany, the term *Volk* was used in order to further a variety of political agendas.

(Note: The lowercase *east* and *west* Germany are used throughout the remainder of this chapter to indicate the situation following German unification. Use of the uppercase *West* and *East* Germany refers to the period prior to German unification.)

The Communist regime of East Germany had used the concept of *Volk* to indicate its own identity vis-à-vis West Germany as well as to soften the harsh realities of its regime. The terms *Volkspolizei* (People's Police) and *Volksarmee* (People's Army), to cite only two examples, were attempts to achieve that purpose.

When the final confrontations between the people and government of East Germany spilled into the streets and market squares of such large cities as Leipzig, a central rallying cry, challenging the claims of the government that it was representative of the *Volk*, became: "*WIR sind das Volk!*" (WE are the people). German journalists present at and reporting on these events provided interesting insights in their letters to me (R. Fricke, personal communication, July 10, 1992; M. Gensicke, personal communication, June 26, 1992; C. Wernicke, July 2, 1992). All those I consulted seemed to agree that this slogan became part of the Monday demonstrations in Leipzig or, more generally, the fall demonstrations of 1989 in Saxony. The slogan related powerfully to the self-concept of demonstrators during the historic mass meetings of October 8 and 9, 1989, that took place during Gorbachev's visit to Berlin, when some 70,000–80,000 people took to the streets in spite of tanks and *Volksarmee* units arrayed against them in Berlin, Jena, Leipzig, Dresden, and Plauen (C. Wernicke, personal communication, July 2, 1992). In Berlin, in front of the Palace of the Republik, the crowds shouted: "*Gorbi, Gorbi,*" and "*Wir sind das Volk.*"

However, a significant change occurred when that reidentification of who represented the people changed to the slogan: "*Wir sind EIN VOLK!*" (We are ONE NATION/PEOPLE). Even the morgues and research centers of such prominent German newspapers as *Die Zeit*, *Wochenpost*, *Neues Deutschland*, and *Frankfurter Allgemeine Zeitung* were little help in determining who used this changed appeal to German unity first, or when it was first used. C. Wernicke (personal communication, July 2, 1992) indicated that "at the very latest" it was used at the beginning of December 1989 during demonstrations in Saxony, especially in Leipzig. He pointed to the fact that it became a massive influence after the Christian conservative "Alliance for Germany" began using it on millions of signs and bumper stickers. R. Frick (personal communication, July 10, 1992) wrote of a "rumor" that the *Bundesrepublik* (West Germany), or the Christian Democratic Union (CDU) of West Germany, introduced and promoted the use of the slogan. M. Gensicke (personal communication, June 26, 1992) also mentioned the possibility that Chancellor Kohl promoted this change in a significant way, when he used the slogan during his speech in Dresden following unification.

What then went wrong? Why was the initial elation replaced by anger, mutual mistrust, and a feeling of resentment? The following three interlinked factors are possible explanations:

1. A common currency and a realignment of borders were assumed to be the primary tasks facing those desiring German reunification.

2. Opting for the traditional statist/political model did not make it possible to consider possible significant cultural differences that developed during 45 years of separation and that resulted in very different value systems. Political slogans asserting the existence of one nation thus were used to cover up important differences.

3. Embracing the idea that the West German model of success and so-called progress could not only be more or less easily transferred to East Germany, but that it would also be seen as desirable by East Germans, led to a situation remarkably similar to that found in the U.S. South following the Civil War during Reconstruction. The major difference is that the South was "swallowed" by the North following a military defeat, whereas East Germany took on the status of a subculture following a political arrangement.

Several years after the initial euphoria about the collapse of the hated wall had abated, U.S. journalists began to reassess the situation. For example, Nenneman (1992) wrote, "Two strong images emerge from the 'New Germany': That of two brothers separated at birth who, upon being reunited, find they don't even recognize each other, and that of a bird set loose that hasn't learned to fly" (p. 41).

Indicative of the underlying power struggle now going on in a supposedly unified Germany is a contemporary joke frequently heard in East Germany. A well-meaning, jovial West German (Wessie) meets an East German (Ossie) acquaintance and attempts to establish a feeling of solidarity by putting his arm around his shoulder, smiling at him, and reassuring him: "*Wir sind ein Volk!*" (We are one nation, one people). Whereupon the Ossie smiles back and says: "Yes! And so are we!" Remove the smiles and close physical proximity, and one has much of the current confrontation explained in a nutshell.[1] At the same time, in post offices and other public places, brochures were made available with the government's message "Get the wall [that used to separate East and

---

[1]The author's first language is German, and he is responsible for all translations from German as well as the interpretations of texts.

West Germany] out of your head," in order to bring about national unity. As we see later, there are those in contemporary Germany who long for a return of that wall.

## Intra-German Culture Shock

The rude awakening after Germany was declared to be one state has been indicated in many ways. Meier (1992) provided both the basic question and a common answer, "To grow together, to lead together, to weld together?—Whether or not in the unified Germany that is really growing together which belongs together, is met by more and more serious doubts every day" (p. 19). Why such doubts? Because there are many factors that have divided Germans from Germans during the past 40 years. As Meier explained it, the West Germans were mostly observers, touched, but more concerned with not disrupting their own lives. One fifth of the people in the new Germany, namely those living in the east, were excited, confused, seeing totally new possibilities and a new playing field when unification became a possibility, but in many cases they needed assistance and help, even basic explanations.

***Confusion on All Sides.*** Of course, it was not only the East Germans who were not sure of how to act and in need of help because the old order and structures had collapsed, taking with them familiar landmarks and surroundings. Langenstein, during a reaction session following a formal presentation as part of the Mainzer Tage dealing with the integration role of television (quoted in P. C. Hall, 1992), explained plaintively that when he sits down with a French or Italian friend for breakfast, he knows how to act—but "When I travel into the DDR [Note the use of the old designation for East Germany] I have difficulties. I am without a clue; I do not know how one lives there, what the normal everyday life looks like" (p. 61). Putting conflicts in the terms of "gallows' humor," Fuelberth (1991) wrote of "Ossimisten" and "Wessimisten" (east and west German pessimists, respectively). The latter tend to assume that it can't get any worse, and the former, pointing to both the past and the future, are sure that it will.

Thus we cannot assume that negative feelings or confusion are only one-sided—they represent truly intercultural problems. An East German spoke about it this way, "My half of the world has been lost. That simply is not of interest. Like a fastgrowing weed, another life-culture, which is in many ways tempting and convincing, is covering up my familiar environment. I have to exert myself to remember past feelings, they are disappearing just like the objects . . . I must learn about the other half of the world, in a crash course" (Sylvester, 1992, p. 3). The fact that many cultural differences have come to separate East and West Germany may not be readily apparent to the casual observer, but they are central factors standing in the way of easy reunification. As Zglinicki (1992) related:

> I have gotten rid of the habit of shaking hands with someone when I greet them. At least if the other is a West German ... Every time I sat in the Comic-Opera after November '89, I had a clear feeling that I was the only human being from the east in the hall ... I remain cautious for fear of being easily hurt by side-remarks. In the local bar: "But you haven't been—I mean to say, you haven't ALWAYS been from the East? ... You know, by the way, how I recognize the people from here [the East]? By the color of their skin! They are so pale because they did not get enough fruit and vegetables." (p. 3)

Those of us who have faced culture shock recognize and appreciate the seriousness of such confusions, and the inability to communicate effectively and the fear of reacting inappropriately.

***Learning New Rules of the Game.*** Sylvester (1992) identified what is one of today's central intercultural problems in communication efforts between Germans: "It is difficult to learn the rules of the game, because no one explains them" (p. 3). Of course, a West German may see the roots of such problems quite differently, because supposedly it is easy to just sit together with West Germans and get to know them. "With West Germans that is uncomplicated. Not with East Germans. They just don't ask any questions" (Bartz, 1992, p. 3). His East German respondent, however, pointed out the danger of asking questions when West Germans may judge silence as an indication that an individual has something to hide, whereas those who speak up too readily are thought of as being shameless, unwilling to wait for a "decent" length of time before entering the east–west dialogue (Maihorn, 1992, p. 3). What has developed, in effect, is an "... interwoven pattern of mutual assertions of hidden motives, descriptions and criticisms of the other, a continuous development and rejection of images and definitions ..." (Bischoff, 1992, p. 3). A dominant and a subculture exist in today's Germany, both of which still find it difficult to understand each other.

***The Third Road?*** Lang (1990) indicated a hope that many Germans held, that of a "third road" between socialism and capitalism that could bring east and west together. In reality, however, she found that anything even "smelling of being socialistic" is rejected and replaced by hasty steps toward a free market orientation. Others have written of that third choice, that new road created and built by Germans together—in a new Germany. Meier (1992) insisted that four fifths of a nation cannot expect to continue as they have lived, and expect the other one fifth to simply fit in: "In reality in such a unification there must, much rather, emerge something that is a third choice. I don't mean by that a new Constitution (that is another, perhaps not quite so important question), but rather: a nation" (p. 26).

Fischbeck (1992), although welcoming the new freedom and the release from the old political system, was saddened by the fact that, "Our hope was gigantic, namely that the historically unique chance provided by peaceful instability could lead to the emergence of a 'Gemeinwesen' [communal society] in which democracy would saturate all areas of life, including the economic system" (p. 65). That such a development is not easy is Ruge's (1990) argument. He claimed that the rejection of East Germans by those in the west results when all those who "went along" with the Communist regime are classified as either dumb or without scruples, and neither group is seen as being able to make a meaningful contribution to the future of a united Germany. No wonder that in a cartoon, one East German informs another, "Well then, I want to become jobless as soon as possible, so that I get it all behind me more quickly" (Glotz, 1992, p. 26).

***Learning to Communicate Interculturally.*** There are some deep insights in many of the statements cited here concerning the communicative and other cultural aspects that are needed to truly forge a new nation. Hennis, in another discussion during the Mainzer Tage (in P. C. Hall, 1992), pointed out that anything in a given group that serves the purpose of holding it together must be considered in that process: "Integration is only a word for the comprehension of the unique process of life, [a word] for the continuous process of reaching agreement with one another, [a word for] survival" (p. 67). The economic and political survival of what is now considered to be a unified Germany will depend on an integrative process in which all Germans can participate meaningfully.

***Ein Volk.*** The word *Volk* takes on special meaning in this connection. Its almost mystic or mythological aspects are difficult for anyone to appreciate who has not read or heard it used the way Germans do. Lang (1990) mused about the change in meaning from the expression the people (nation) to one people (nation) after unification mentioned earlier in this chapter, which most likely was not the initial impulse of those rebelling against Communist rule.

The role of the people, of the nation is something that others have certainly dealt with, including in German literature. In his drama "Danton's Death," Buechner (1958), for instance, had one of his "citizens" state, "We are the people [*Wir sind das Volk*], and we will that there be no law; thus that will is the law, thus in the name of law there is no law, thus it's been beaten to death!" (p. 16). That tortured reasoning about the will of the people, and the nature of a nation is just one more indication of the difficulties Germany has faced since 1989—and before. In effect, East Germans found themselves drawing the conclusion, once they saw what things were really like in the west after unification, that they no longer counted ("*Schatten des Westens*," 1990). The author speculated, after citing Johannes Piskorz, a medical doctor and psychotherapist, whether East Germany had merely been the dark shadow of what life could have been like in the West following World War II. That West Germany may have succeeded by mere historical chance, not merit, was something that had to be denied, and the "dark shadow" of the East had to be ignored. During the constitutional conference of September 16, 1990, in Weimar, Dr. Wolfgang Ullmann (1990) asked whether or not Germans indeed are one nation, and he stressed that the question had to be answered. But, whenever Germans tried to speak of one nation (*Volk*), he claimed, ". . . we struggle not only for words, but for a [common] language."

## The Complexity of Intercultural Challenges

One issue that has been stressed in the preceding sections is the fact that today's Germany faces intercultural challenges in a large number of areas. The following instances are only representative not comprehensive.

***Women, Children.*** Two examples can stand here for many. One aspect of unification is that women in east Germany now make up nearly two thirds of the unemployed. Formerly, not only was abortion on demand available, but a plethora of state-supported day-care centers, kindergartens, and youth clubs assisted women in taking care of their children while they worked right alongside men. The result, according to Editha Beier, commissioner of women in the east German state of Saxony-Anhalt, is that increasing numbers of east German women are having themselves sterilized to be able to hold on to their jobs. Companies, though the charge is difficult to prove, appear to encourage such sterilization (Fisher, 1992b).

For children, the changing environment also means that there are no more youth clubs or supervised activities readily available, nor is there adequate job training or the assurance of adequate numbers of jobs. Besides the strain this is putting on the society's general fabric, the strain on families is great as well. Some cope by continuing the rituals embraced during Communist rule, which replaced such Christian concepts as First Communion or Confirmation. Thus the old East German rite of passage, the *Jugendweihe*, remains a viable alternative (Fisher, 1992a).

Others have difficulty even maintaining family ties. The example of 13-year-old Christian who brags about the fact that he can get his parents, especially his father, furious by putting on parts of his old Communist Youth organization's uniform, and singing one of the old marching songs, is one case among many (Weidt, 1992). Such young people seem to feel almost a longing for the "good old days." Intercultural communication problems take on additional meaning when we read, "In the [East] German families, an honest confrontation between parents and their children seems hardly ever to take place" (Weidt, 1992, p. 31). This is an important factor in east Germany where family relations and interactions had been an important part of the value system, holding society together even during Communist rule.

*The Workforce.* Workers in East Germany had a great deal of job security, though their incomes were often far behind those of West Germans in similar situations. Since unification many factories have been closed, many jobs lost. Whitney (1992) pointed to the significant problems underlying recent strikes: "This strike has been not so much about money, as about the dark side of unification" (p. 1). West German workers are bitter about increases in their taxes caused by unification; east German workers are bitter not only about job losses, but that their incomes continue to lag significantly behind those of west German workers. The argument comes down to a basic point: equal pay for equal productivity.

But the existing complexities of the situation include such factors as former East German factories and equipment that are not up to date, or the fact that public transportation in east Germany continues to be heavily subsidized by the state to make changes from the Communist system less severe. If one adds to that the genuine problem that many East German workers were spoiled by a Communist system that assured them job security even if they did not produce adequately, it becomes clear that the entire work ethic or culture is in a crisis state (Guertler, 1992). One east German labor leader indicated his dilemma when he wanted to assure west German workers striking independently of those in east Germany that their east German colleagues would not increase production to make up for the western production decline—as a sign of labor solidarity. By the same token he knew that he was denying his east German colleagues a chance to increase their income. Such problems resulted because two separate and unequal labor union systems were allowed to emerge and function for some time, supposedly to ease integration. It is no wonder that the title of the article cited here, "It Is Easy to Talk About Solidarity" ("Ueber Solidaritaet," 1991), implies that dealing with the underlying problems is much more difficult than talking about them.

*Business.* Things are no better in business and industry, where bitter feelings also exist. As Fisher (1992d) wrote, "Unfortunately, the Western arrogance is also here, in the form of Western managers who mistrust

Eastern talents and instead insist on importing their top staff from the West. Some Easterners are fighting a rear-guard action, hoping to retain some of the openness and informality that had developed in their long years of isolation . . ." (p. 8). In effect, it is often left to non-Germans to provide some encouragement and direction. Representatives of one group of U.S. consultants are quoted as feeling that, "More than anything else, we found ourselves having to say to them [east Germans], 'Protect your traditions; don't be so hard on yourself; don't believe all the bad things the West Germans say about you' " (Fisher, 1992c, p. 13).

One representative example of widespread discrimination, which Halentz (1992) cited, is that of a highly qualified industrial scientist who worked for a major electrical company in East Germany, and who was offered a job by a western company at 60% of the income his west German colleagues make—with the assumption that his talent would benefit the west German firm. Similar discrepancies in pay are the bane of virtually every area of employment in east Germany.

Then there are the absurd situations that develop when the new east Germany simply cannot afford to dump the talents left over from the Communist regime, even if these individuals were ranking party members. One example is that of Siegfried Wagner who headed one of the Communist state-owned farmer's cooperatives—after the state nationalized the agrarian sector. First local farmers wanted to lynch him after unification. When they found later on that none could take his place as head of the new, democratic farmer's cooperative, they elected him to that new position (Rechenbach, 1992). As indicated earlier, when the old landmarks are taken away confusion rules. At least that is true until valid new ones can be found, or the old are appropriated once more and redefined through the use of a new language, which is adopted from the new, dominant culture for survival reasons. The relationship of the east German subculture to the west German dominant culture is defined by such processes that may return later to haunt all those involved.

Speaking of a new language, many east Germans find it even difficult to understand and trust pronouncements of such institutions as their new internal revenue service (Schwenkenbecher, 1992), or they find that experienced east German architects are not considered to be the equals of their western colleagues, in part because they do not find it easy to speak the new market-oriented language that comes so easy to west Germans (Schoenball, 1992).

***The University.*** While teaching in east Germany, I saw, repeatedly, the lists of faculty members who requested rehabilitation following unification, because of their dismissal from Schiller University in Jena during the Communist era.[2] This is just one indication of a past that has to be dealt with by east Germans, as painful as the process often is. But an even more serious question remains: How does one restore the good name or career of an academician, who was fired simply because he or she did not support the Communist political system, when east German universities' budgets are being cut? ("Rehabilitierungsverfahren," 1992).

The other side of this coin is the ongoing replacement of faculty members who are now being rejected because of their earlier relationship to the Communist regime. That problem is directly connected to the availability of qualified teachers and the unwillingness of west Germans to teach in the east, in spite of the high salaries offered them. This is at least the third major restructuring of east German universities—following the impact of National Socialism and Communism—in 60 years. One possible result of that fact is a withdrawal into "pure" science because the sciences were supposedly less influenced by politics than were the humanities and philosophy (Glotz, 1992; Simon, 1990). Entire curricula have been changed dramatically to align eastern universities with those in the west, and to provide students with a preparation for the west German political and economic culture (Reich, 1992). Universities that were once leading institutions in German cultural development thus are often reduced to following contemporary western trends. The question still remains whether west German faculty replacements with no cultural roots or experience in east Germany, the flight of east German students to west German universities (or the reverse), or simple submission by students to new requirements can improve the situation in the near future (Zeller, 1991; "Zu wenig Feuer," 1992).

To these problems one can add the fact that the current situation has created competition for limited resources among existing and planned east German universities (Stadler, 1992). The challenge to the university and east German culture in general is made even greater by the fact that, for a lifetime and more, East Germany was cut off from the rest of the world, or at least severely hampered in its efforts to "keep up." As Vollrath (1992) saw it after contacts with Americans at Harvard, the challenge is to remember that the world consists of more than Germany, in spite of the need to deal with past history and the contemporary German situation. Again, in many such instances the experience, the language, the intercultural expertise are simply lacking.

---

[2]The author returned in August of 1992 from teaching assignments in Europe, including a guest professorship and substitution for the holder of the chair in Rhetoric and Speech Science, at Schiller University, Jena, East Germany, from March through July of 1992.

***There Is More.*** I could continue with similar examples from different, specific areas. Wiegand (1990), for instance, wondered what contributions the arts in east Germany can make to a unified Germany, or if it is a foregone conclusion that western pop culture, music, and youth culture become dominant? Can east German concerns about ideological influences become an insightful gift to west German artists? It is important at this point, however, not to let the huge number of available details obscure the central theme of this chapter, as I conclude my observations.

## SOME CONCLUSIONS

There are some important lessons to be learned from the east German experience. Decreeing unity has never worked for Germans or Germany, at least not beyond the lifetime of a strong ruler. Thousands of years of history have not made it any easier for Germans to submit individual and cultural differences to the demands of a state or empire. By the same token, Germans also lack highly developed skills for intercultural communication. In the second half of the 20th century the need to recognize cultural differences between various segments of Germany, and the need to build a future *together,* provide at least some hope that more than political unification or economic *Gleichschaltung* will be seen as desirable.

Our world demands recognition of the benefits of diversity and the cooperative, respectful effort required in the building of third roads or third cultures. As Bergmann (1991) pointed out, that takes effort and a similar dedication on all sides. Unity or unification does not require homogenization, unless the leaders of a state are so insecure that it seems the only road to stability.

In all of this, the mass media have played major roles in the past. Without them the unification process would not have been possible as it developed, yet Germans were not adequately prepared by the media for the vast changes facing them. Now the question is whether the media can do a better job to help in an ongoing process of integration (Nowottny, in P. C. Hall, 1992). The 24th Mainzer Days dealing with a critical evaluation of television, and specifically its role in the German integration process (for a detailed report, see P. C. Hall, 1992), were mentioned previously. They are one positive step in that direction. How difficult that task can be has been demonstrated throughout this chapter. That fact needs to be addressed not only by intercultural communication scholars but also by media practitioners, as Simon-Zuelch (1992) understood when she cited one example: "Family, to be sure, is in both East and West the word for the same life form [institution]. What hides behind that word, however, are the differences in [peoples'] historic experiences" (p. 161).

It behooves us to understand these differences better if we are to deal with each other as human beings, not merely as parts of a political or economic entity, and that cannot be done only through use of the mass media. As this chapter has shown through the extensive citation of media sources, the debate about German unification, and its implications to the present and future, has been fed and kept alive by both print and electronic media. Thus the media can play a significant role in helping us to stay aware of concerns as we attempt to *define* and *apply* new, common concepts, rules, and cultural value systems that a future Germany needs to become united in spite of, or maybe with the help of, cultural diversity.

What is being considered here is first of all the development of an "ethic" of intercultural communication, an ethic useful for the *mutual* discovery of ways to live, act, and create together, not merely a technique. In a recent essay, Farrell (1992) discussed the role of rhetoric's eliptical tradition, which has consistently led to a necessarily imperfect body politic. He suggested that in that setting "... 'truths' are not found but invented, ... reason must be creative if it is to have any voice at all" (p. 156). Invention and creation suggest communication.

Once the progress of *creating* the future can be seen as just that, not merely the *rediscovery* of relevant features from the past that can be reused in the present, *intercultural* communication becomes a meaningful tool toward the end of creating third ways, third cultures, finding third roads, in a never-ending process of renewal that uses all of the available resources while inventing necessary and acceptable truths or values, and creating common reasons.

For many it is difficult, against the backdrop of their limited knowledge of what Germany is, has been, and can be, to appreciate the significant intercultural problems faced by the citizens of that country after unification. Walls have been torn down, universities have been liberated, a common currency is making possible a common market-oriented society, but, as we have seen, "What should have brought joy, suddenly produces second thoughts. Fears develop and create separation, distance" (Wirsing, 1990a, p. 38). The title of the editorial from which this quote was taken is significant: "David Against Goliath—Who Must Succumb?" Four months later, and only a short time after unification, the same prestigious west German publication used a headline, "We Now Speak of Victors and (the) Defeated," under which Wirsing (1990b) summarized the feelings of many of her east German compatriots: "What concerns him, is the disappearance of cultural uniqueness which developed in the DDR [East Germany] under the cover of all imaginable pretenses" (p. 35).

Is anything worth saving of the old East German culture? That may be difficult to decide, but it is certain if that decision is made only by west German "carpetbaggers," the result may be similar to the hundred years of confrontation between South and North experienced in the United States. For us, as intercultural communication scholars, however, this case study should serve as a warning not to speak too readily of a state as if it were a culturally united nation, or to indicate that we can deal only with "modal" cultures as we study interpersonal relations related to intercultural conflicts that take place even within what we call too readily *ein Volk*.

## REFERENCES

Angebert, J. M. (1974). *The occult and the third reich* (L. A. M. Sumberg, Trans.). New York: Macmillan.

Bartz, D. (1992, May 7). Keine Fragen. Oder? *Wochenpost, 20*, 3.

Bergmann, C. (1991, December 10). Mauer im Kopf? *Frankfurter Allgemeine Zeitung, 286*, B 20.

Bischoff, M. (1992, June 22). Kinderglueck in einem Meer aus Luegen. *Frankfurter Allgemeine Zeitung, 142*, 30.

Buechner, G. (1958). Danton's Tod. In *Werke und Briefe*. Wiesbaden, Germany: Insel Verlag.

Casmir, F. L. (1991). *Communication in development*. Norwood, NJ: Ablex.

Casmir, F. L. (1992). Third-culture building: A paradigm shift for international and intercultural communication. In S. Deetz (Ed.), *Communication yearbook* (Vol. 16, pp. 407–436). Beverly Hills, CA: Sage.

Davies, J. S. (1948). *From Charlemagne to Hitler*. London: Cassell.

Des Deutschlands? (1990, July 4). *Frankfurter Allgemeine Zeitung, 152*, 27.

Die einen und die anderen Deutschen. (1990, July 28). *Frankfurter Allgemeine Zeitung, 173*, 28.

Farrell, T. B. (1992). On the disappearance of the rhetorical aura. *Western Journal of Communication, 57*(2), 147–158.

Fischbeck, H-J. (1992, January 21). Opposition ohne Hoffnung? *Der Weltbuehne, 87*(4), 65.

Fisher, M. (1992a, May 25). East Germans' once-red rite of passage endures. *International Herald Tribune*, p. 1.

Fisher, M. (1992b, May 29). Berlin wall down, gloom and sterilization up. *International Herald Tribune*, p. 2.

Fisher, M. (1992c, June 3). From Lenin to Apple chips. *International Herald Tribune*, p. 13.

Fisher, M. (1992d, June 5). Visiting Dresden: Signs of life, no room at the inn. *International Herald Tribune*, p. 8.

Fuelberth, G. (1991, May 21). Missglueckte Modernisierung. *Der Weltbuehne, 86*(22), 652.

Glotz, P. (1992, June 17). Die intellektuelle Vereinigung. *Wochenpost, 26*, 26.

Guertler, D. (1992, April 9). Lohn, Preis, Produktivitaet. *Wochenpost, 16*, 22.

Haffner, S. (1989). *The ailing empire*. New York: Fromm International Publishing Corporation.

Halentz, R. (1992, June 17). High-tech in der Wueste? *Wochenpost*, 26.

Hall, E. T. (1969). *The hidden dimension*. New York: Anchor.

Hall, E. T. (1973). *The silent language*. New York: Anchor.

Hall, E. T. (1976). *Beyond culture*. New York: Doubleday.

Hall, P. C. (Ed.). (1992). *Fernseh kritik: Ein Bild der Deutschen Wirklichkeit*. Mainz, Germany: v. Hase & Koehler Verlag.

Hofstede, G. (1980). *Culture's consequences: International differences in work-related values*. Beverly Hills, CA: Sage.

Koch, H. W. (Ed.). (1985). *Aspects of the third reich*. New York: St. Martin's Press.

Lang, S. (1990, December). Briefe aus Berlin. *Liber, 6,* 14.

Maihorn, K. (1992, May 7). Keine Fragen. Oder? *Wochenpost, 20,* 3.

Meier, C. (1992). Arbeit an der mentalen Infrastruktur. In P. C. Hall (Ed.), *Fernseh Kritik: Ein Bild der Deutschen Wirklichkeit* (pp. 19–29). Mainz, Germany: v. Hase & Koehler Verlag.

Namier, L. (1968). Frankfurt, 1848: Start of Germany's bid for world power. In O. Pflanze (Ed.), *The unification of Germany, 1848–1871* (pp. 85–87). New York: Holt, Rinehart & Winston.

Nenneman, R. A. (1992, June). Europe's center of gravity. *World Monitor,* pp. 40–45.

Owen, A. S., & Ehrenhaus, P. (1993). Animating a critical rhetoric: On the feeding habits of American empire. *Western Journal of Communication, 57*(2), 169–190.

Pflanze, O. (1963). *Bismarck: And the development of Germany.* Princeton, NJ: Princeton University Press.

Pflanze, O. (Ed.). (1968). *The unification of Germany, 1848–1871.* New York: Holt, Rinehart & Winston.

Rechenbach, B. (1992, April 9). Ich bin ein Hiesieger. *Wochenpost, 16,* 24.

Rehabilitierungsverfahren. (1992). *Alma Mater Jenensis, 3*(12), 2.

Reich, J. (1992, April 9). Der Steinbruch lockt. *Wochenpost, 16,* 29–30.

Ritter, G. (1968). National state more realistic than federalism. In O. Pflanze (Ed.), *The unification of Germany, 1848–1871* (pp. 99–105). New York: Holt, Rinehart & Winston.

Schatten des Westens. (1990, May 21). *Frankfurter Allgemeine Zeitung, 117,* 33.

Schnabel, F. (1968). Federalism preferable to a national state. In O. Pflanze (Ed.), *The unification of Germany, 1848–1871* (pp. 88–98). New York: Holt, Rinehart & Winston.

Schoenball, R. (1992, April 29). Neuer Schinkel gesucht. *Wochenpost, 19,* 24.

Schwenkenbecher, C. (1992, April 29). Ruhe vor dem Sturm? *Wochenpost, 19,* 35.

Shirer, W. S. (1960). *The rise and fall of the third reich.* New York: Simon & Schuster.

Shuter, R. (1990). The centrality of culture. *The Southern Communication Journal, LV*(3), 237–249.

Simon, D. (1990, August 11). Kader auf Lebenszeit. *Frankfurter Allgemeine Zeitung, 185,* 21.

Simon-Zuelch, S. (1992). Unerwartete Buendnisse, ruhiges Innehalten. In P. C. Hall (Ed.), *Fernseh Kritik: Ein Bild der Deutschen Wirklichkeit* (pp. 159–161). Mainz, Germany: v. Hase & Koehler Verlag.

Stadler, S. (1992). Radikaler Rueckschnitt. *UNI F.A.Z., 38,* 8.

Sullivan, R. S. (Ed.). (1954). *The coronation of Charlemagne: What did it signify?* Boston: Heath.

Sylvester, R. (1992, April 29). Meistens gingen die Meisten hin. *Wochenpost, 19,* 3.

Ueber Solidaritaet laesst sich leicht reden [A conversation with members of industrial-companies' boards]. (1991, April 29). *Wochenpost, 19,* 20.

Ullman, W. (1990, October 2). *Sind wir ein Volk?* [Transcript of a speech]. *Thueringer Land Zeitung, 16.*

Vollrath, S. (1992, April 9). Zimmer mit Aussicht. *Wochenpost, 16,* 28.

Weidt, B. (1992, April 23). Heute sollen wir alles duerfen. *Wochenpost, 18,* 31.

Wells, C. H. (1898). *The age of Charlemagne.* New York: The Christian Literature Co.

Whitney, C. R. (1992, May 8). Labor strife shows nation is still far from united. *International Herald Tribune,* p. 1.

Wiegand, W. (1990, October 2/3). Im Schmelztiegel. *Frankfurter Allgemeine Zeitung, 229–230,* 33.

Wirsing, S. (1990a, May 17). David gegen Goliath—Wer muss unterliegen. *Frankfurter Allgemeine Zeitung, 114,* 38.

Wirsing, S. (1990b, September 28). Von Siegern und Besiegten ist nun die Rede. *Frankfurter Allgemeine Zeitung, 226,* 35.

Zeller, B. (1991, December 18). Deutschland einig Wessiland. *Studentisches Kruetzel, XXI,* 3.

Zglinicki, C. von (1992, April 9). Kleine Stiche. *Wochenpost, 16,* 3.

Zu wenig Feuer unterm Hintern [A conversation with German students, led by A. Baum, R. Halentz, L-B. Keil]. (1992, April 23). *Wochenpost, 18,* 27.

# 3

# *The Crisis of Citizenship: The East German Media, Nazis, and Outsiderness*

Maryellen Boyle
*University of California, Santa Cruz*

Reunified Germany is culturally in flames. The west Germans wish the Wall would go back up, the east Germans reconsider their Communist era experiences with some nostalgia. The youth (in the east and west) are turning in alarming numbers to Nazi rhetoric and violence. The American press tells us that the cultural chaos is in great measure the result of increasing unemployment. Once Germans get jobs again, according to this logic, the Germans will stop hating each other and stop threatening foreigners. This standard interpretation assumes that Germany can be rid of its Nazi past only under the conditions of full employment. I challenge that interpretation, arguing that party politics and not the German propensity to hatred structure works to inhibit east German integration into the west and to establish foreigners as the scapegoat for the dislocations generated by unification. Ethnic hatred is not the "natural" outcome of social dislocation.

In post-Communist eastern Europe the mass media play a more important role than they do in the west, for the weave of established social interactions in which conversation can occur has become frayed, or no longer exists. And, many in the newly liberated east say, the new dog-eat-dog competitive environment has destroyed the old solidarities. Totalitarian theorists like Hannah Arendt argue that the inhabitants of Communist societies lived in the grip of the state. The Communist Party, she argued, set about dismantling secondary associations characteristic of liberal or traditional societies. This absence of buffers between the individual and the state made the individual totally dependent on the state and vulnerable to state propaganda. We now know that people in Communist eastern Europe had a vast web of information and emotional relationships at the workplace and within state-structured associations, like unions or the youth league (Konrad, 1984). One of the ironies of the freedom from Communism has been the disintegration of these very bonds. The youth leagues are gone, the old unions are gone, and the jobs are frequently gone. In no eastern European country is this more the case than in the former East Germany, for west German political architects have attempted to destroy all remnants of the Communist past. In this new alienating existence east Germans must learn to be west Germans, to fit into the unified Germany. The primary agent of this integration into freedom is the east mass media.

This chapter analyzes how and why east German mass media, particularly public broadcasting, approach the issue of strangers and foreigners, of insiders and outsiders, of those who belong and *Auslaender* (outsiders, foreigners) in the Federal Republic of Germany. Public discussion in the east of the *Auslaender*, neo-Nazi and citizenship crisis is structured by two conditions—the fundamental *Auslaender* status of the east Germans and the political party domination of the most important zone and agent for public conversation—public broadcasting. Reconciliation with the "other"—learning to live in a world beyond the mental framing of a kith-and-kin nation, can only begin in the east when the now taboo subject of the east *Auslaender* condition becomes a legitimate theme for public conversation, when east Germans can discuss in public the situation of their own citizenship.[1]

I focus our attention on the eastern public broadcasting corporations—the East German Broadcasting Corporation (ORB) and the Middle German Broadcasting Corporation (MDR)—for as regional members of the ARD public broadcasting network, their task is to concern themselves with the problems of the public—their local *Publikum*. Perusing the regional TV guide and watching/listening to the programming will tell us what is produced, but it won't tell us why. Why is a very important question when studying media products. The why here has less to do with producer interests and broadcasting finances, and more to do with formal politics, for as all familiar with Germany know, public broadcasting is to a considerable degree the ideological domain of the ruling political parties (Boyle, 1992, 1993, 1994, 1995; Goetz, 1992). Ruling power in eastern Germany belongs, with the exception of the state parliament in Brandenburg, to the Christian Democratic Union (CDU). This translates into CDU media production power. The question of the "other" belongs

---

[1]See Ash, 1993.

to the domain of public discussion, and this is the territory of the parties. As a result, we must explore the intersection of this *Parteipolitik* and the media institutions to understand media coverage and practices.

## THE PROBLEM OF "SKINS IN GOVERNMENT"

Public broadcasting in eastern Germany has a specific social role: to nurture democratic will formation and to assist east German integration into the Federal Republic of Germany. In 1989 Willy Brandt told his east German siblings: "What belongs together will grow together." These words were on the lips of public commentators in the East and West, and became part of the Social Democratic Party campaign platform in the first post-Communist elections, held March 18, 1990.[2] That east and west Germans belonged together seemed natural to most Germans, and this integration of the people from the two states was expected to come about naturally. That has not turned out to be the case. People in the east and west, we are told in Germany, have begun to hate each other. This is a common theme in television sitcoms, like the controversial "Motzki" mocking east German ways, or in studies of the east German society, as in Bitterman's (1993) *Der rassende Mob. Die Ossis zwischen Selbstmitleid und Barbarei* (The racist mob. The easterners between self-pity and barbarity), or Peter Schneider's (1991) *The German Comedy: Scenes of Life After the Wall*. This hatred has its roots in formal politics and not merely in a clash of values or customary ways of living, we are told by the intellectual luminary Günter Grass.

Günter Grass is one of (west) Germany's cultural treasures. Literary figures hold a special position in German society: they are recognized by society as the voice of the German conscience. Günter Grass has a particular importance in this discussion of east and west problems, for he was born in the eastern German city of Danzig, in the state of Silesia. As part of the postwar dismantling of the German Reich, that eastern portion of Germany is now Poland, and Danzig is now the famous Polish city Gdansk, the birthplace of Solidarity. After the war most of the Germans were driven out of that region. From their new homes in western Germany they (and now their offspring) have organized themselves into a League of Exiles and have demanded a return to the 1937 German borders.

---

[2]In 1989–1990 three phrases were on the lips of all public commentators (from East and West Germany): Mikhail Gorbachev's off-the-cuff remark to journalists during his visit to the GDR in October 1989—"History punishes those who come too late"; West German Chancellor Helmut Kohl's campaign promise—"No one will be worse off after unification"; and Willy Brandt's "What belongs together will grow together." These phrases were taken up, in doctored form, in advertising campaigns and in the east graffiti.

Unlike his exile compatriots, Grass has argued for decades that the division of Germany is the logical and appropriate result of German militarism and barbarism. In fact, Grass opposed German reunification in 1989 and 1990 (Grass, 1990). *The New York Times* (Fein, 1992) printed a disturbing Günter Grass interview in which he made what many far away from Germany would find a startling accusation: "We have skins in the Government. . . . They are nicely dressed with beautiful hair, educated. They speak well. But they think the same way as the young kids who shave their heads and carry swastikas and demonstrate. They encourage these ideas and these brutal actions." Grass was not speaking about the far right party, the Republicans, which has its counterparts in most countries of Europe. Grass referred to those in government, not the fringe. At the time of this interview the German federal parliament was locked in a stormy debate about deleting from the constitution the generous guaranteeing of the right to political asylum. Since the collapse of the iron curtain, several hundred thousand individuals have sought safe haven in the Federal Republic of Germany, more than in the rest of Europe combined. Proponents for the constitutional change (primarily members of the Christian Democratic Union) argued "the boat is full," that the asylum seekers were merely taking advantage of German generosity. Those opposed to limiting the right to asylum argued that this constitutional protection was Germany's compensation to the world for creating the greatest European refugee crisis of the 20th century. They argued that "cramped nationalisms of one kind or another" and *Volk* sentiments did not belong in the new Europe. The catalyst for this round of the reoccurring debate was the shocking reemergence of neo-Nazi violence directed at foreigners: over 2,400 racially motivated attacks in 1992 and the same rate in 1993. In 1992 and 1993 this neo-Nazi violence has accounted for more than 30 deaths; the police reported 76 firebombings in the first 9 months of 1993. Between 1926 and 1931 there were 80 desecrations of Jewish cemeteries—the same number as in the year of 1992. Those proposing the constitutional changes claimed that the shocking reemergence of xenophobia was the result, in part, of Germans feeling culturally "overwhelmed" by the flood of foreigners. Günter Grass had a different perspective on this rise in violence and the general social crisis which has engulfed Germany, *The New York Times* noted:

> "Many people from the East hoped to join the West with their own face, their own experiences," he [Grass] said. "But the West was coming like colonial masters, treating them like children. It was shock for many. They were astonished. There is no longer a wall or an iron curtain, but Germany is divided socially and economically. There are Germans first and second class . . ."

> He [Grass] said he believed that the violence against immigrants was not so much an expression of true hate against outsiders as much as it was the weakest members of German society fighting their own lowly status.
>
> "The hate between Germans is the root of this violence," he said. "But they know that they cannot take on the other Germans, the stronger Germans, with their jobs and their money and their cars, so they go for the weakest. In many ways it is an expression of their own self-hate, which was bound to happen with reunification.... And so the weakest of East and West Germany got thrown to the bottom, and they are fighting to be above somebody or really anybody. And who is beneath them? The foreigners." (Fein, 1992, p. B1)

Günter Grass, long critical of the CDU government's laissez faire attitude toward the far right, has embarked on a campaign to expose these "skins in government" (Grass, 1990). In an address to his fellow Social Democrats in November 1992, Grass placed the blame on the politicians.

> The government policies of the last three years, which are to blame for this most recent relapse into German barbarity, have not been altered in the slightest, because none of their proponents see anything wrong with them. ... It is not only, and not primarily, the skinheads who are shattering the democratic consensus of our society with their telegenic theatrics; rather it was certain politicians whose verbal pyrotechnics ignited the subject of immigration and made the desperation of refugees and asylum-seekers a permanent campaign issue. Meanwhile the individual right to asylum—a jewel in our Constitution—is being put on the auction block to satisfy the instincts of the *Volk*, which the Nazis insisted on characterizing as "sound." (Grass, 1993, pp. 179–180)

Günter Grass is not the only figure in Germany to make this accusation. The more fundamental question attempting to define the relationship between the ruling government and the far right is commonplace in all the German *print* media. *The New York Times* (Kinzer, 1993) reported on a case receiving considerable attention in the German press:

> When the police quickly released four of the five skinheads accused of beating an American athlete last weekend, they were acting under criminal justice policies that are coming under increasing attack here. Many politicians and criminologists complain that the German legal system is "blind in the right eye," meaning that the police, prosecutors and judges tend to be lenient when dealing with rightists or neo-Nazis. (Kinzer, p. 9)

Grass's linkage of reunification and "German barbarity" might be discussed in the halls of the Social Democratic Party in Bonn, but these views are generally not expressed in discussions on east German television and radio.

In post-Communist Europe, citizenship has become once again problematic. The logic for the old borders and passports no longer obtains in many parts of the region. The German state after 1989 became, overnight, highly porous: 17 million east Germans voted themselves in; nearly 1 million ethnic Germans from Poland, Romania, and the former Soviet Union "returned home" between 1988 and 1990, and 2 million more throughout the former Soviet east threaten to exercise their constitutional right to return; some 6.1 million noncitizen residents push for a more protected legal status (including naturalized citizenship); and hundreds of thousands of war refugees seek permanent political asylum status. It is not surprising that the political leaders in Bonn as well as the taxpayers feel under siege.

Since 1949 the Federal Republic of Germany has had an "ethnic German" policy that encouraged and financed Germans who were "coming home."[3] In part this *Volk* German policy was based on the assumption that German "blood" and German culture were one and the same. In this way of thinking, the Germans in the vast regions of the east are the same people as those in the west. But everyday experience with these Germans contradicts the ideological underpinnings of this state policy. The Germans of the east are different, and many don't even speak German. It was official state policy to lure these Germans back into the ethnic *Heimat*. The policy worked, and the Germans have come home. But today the west German taxpayers no longer wish to finance this homecoming. The west Germans would like the old wall between east and west to go back up, as one learns today in the west media. From the perspective of the east Germans, this supposedly natural "growing together" has produced another set of problems.

---

[3]Between 1945 and 1950 official statistics indicate that 8.3 million ethnic Germans returned to West Germany from the Soviet-occupied east, including parts of Poland, the Sudetenland, and the Soviet Occupation zone of Germany. Between 1949 and 1961 at least 2.7 million inhabitants of the German Democratic Republic fled to West Germany. The Berlin Wall, erected in August 1961, ended this westward flow, and conflicts between German refugees and the West Germans abated. As labor developed once more in the 1960s in the midst of the greatest economic boom in German history, the German government recruited southern Europeans to meet this deficit. After the 1973 oil crisis and the collapse of the German economy, the German government canceled its guest worker policy and sought to send all these foreigners home.

Nearly a million more east Germans have moved to west Germany since the fall of the Berlin Wall in 1989, many of whom are descendants of Germans who had migrated eastward centuries ago.

According to German workforce data, some 1.8 million foreigners (non-citizens) are now part of the labor force. In 1990, approximately 52% of the foreigners had lived in Germany for a minimum of 15 years; of the 1.3 million foreigner children living in Germany, 69% were German-born. See also Mehrlaender and Schultze (1992).

## THE INSIDER–OUTSIDER PROBLEM

The victims of the politicians' "telegenic theatrics," "verbal pyrotechnics," and "German barbarity" weren't only hapless asylum seekers in eastern Germany; they were also Turkish guest workers and their (west) German-born offspring. Virulent xenophobia is as much a problem in the west as in the east, although west publicists attributed the eastern xenophobic hate to 40 years of Communist totalitarianism. Cultural observers in the west went back to the drawing boards for a new interpretation when the firebombings in Moelln and Solingen brought world cameras into democratic west Germany (Erb, 1993; Funke, 1993; Kramer, 1993; Leggewie, 1993; Lummer, 1992; Nivuman, 1992; Siegler, Tolmein, & Wiedemann, 1993).

In the five new federal states of eastern Germany the problem of "the other" is intricately intertwined with the fundamental east German crisis of being a *Bundesbuerger*, a citizen of the West German state. The easterners have difficulty with outsiders because they—*Volk* Germans, those who should be insiders—are also outsiders. In that December 1992 interview with *The New York Times*, Günter Grass claimed that "the violence against immigrants was not so much an expression of true hate against outsiders as much as it was the weakest members of German society fighting their own lowly status" (Fein, 1992, p. B1). *Immigrants* was a term nonexistent in official public discourse. According to Chancellor Helmut Kohl (CDU), "Germany is not an immigration country." The 6.1 million "foreigners" in Germany, many of whom were born on German soil and speak German as their first language, are guests or outsiders. The insiders, according to the Constitution, are *Volk* Germans, the blood Germans.

### German Anger

Until the Berlin Wall was breached on November 9, 1989, the *Übersiedler* (the so-called "wall-jumping" East Germans) were welcomed in the Federal Republic. They were immediately granted insider status, which means in the German calculus a German passport *and* access to generous social welfare benefits (including being put at the top of the housing waiting list). These benefits were part of the West German *Übersiedlerpolitik*. This *Übersiedlerpolitik*, the postwar continuation of the once lethal pan-Germanism, created in the east German mind, even when it resided on the east side of the Wall, the expectation that *Volk* status guaranteed preference, or at least equality.

Today this *Übersiedlerpolitik* and the Berlin Wall are gone, having been replaced by another *Politik*, Günter Grass and others say, by *Besatzungspolitik* (occupation politics), and a psychological wall perhaps more impenetrable than its cement-and-guns predecessor. Instead of being at the head of the benefits queue, east Germans claim to be in the second-class queue. Salaries and pensions—the material proof that east Germans are full partners in the economic wonder of the Federal Republic—are only 70% of those in the west. Commodity prices are higher in the east than in the west. East Germans feel they are merely a market for western products rather than being bona fide insiders. Why should the eastern factories and fields lie fallow when the western industry and agriculture blossom, they ask.[4] Why should east Germans give up every one of their traditions? Why can't the west accept some practices from the east?

The discussion in eastern Germany is the same from one kitchen table to the other: forced retirement, early retirement, layoffs, part-time make-work, the dole, unemployment. Unemployment will exceed 35% by 1994, as the make-work jobs disappear and unemployment benefits run out. East Germans need a public dialogue about their condition, about the issue of this new citizenship, about what they miss from the past and what they hate about the present. Yes, they need to talk about the *Stasi* (secret policy) legacy, but also about youth problems then and now, women's options then and now, and so on. They need to find a way to recoup their losses and orient themselves to this new life. In 1990 and 1991 the CDU argued that the east Germans suffered no losses; they gained freedom. The east Germans wonder about the value of this freedom if one is unemployed and powerless, again. The influential liberal west weekly *Die Zeit*, in a September 10, 1993 article, noted that the "east Germans are stuck in a unification shock" (*Einigungsschock*). The *Einigungsschock* will remain, with all its inner-directed and *Auslaender*-directed anger, until public dialogue becomes possible. The 1989 appeal of the citizens' movement New Forum to the East German Communist regime seems once more appropriate:

> The communication in our land between state and society is manifestly disturbed.... The disrupted relationship between state and society paralyzes the creative potential of our society, and hinders the resolution of local and global problems at hand ... And the communication about the state of affairs is cramped and obstructed. In private circles we can each offer our own diagnoses and solutions. These wishes and proposals differ, and we aren't able to rationally weigh one against the other to test their feasibility.... To recognize all the contradictions, to listen to and to judge the opinions and arguments, to sort out the general from specific interests,

[4]That west German industries buy up east German industries in order to close them down and eliminate competition, was exactly what the hunger strikers in the Bischofferode potash dispute claimed in their appeal for support in the summer of 1993 to the European Community in Brussels and to the Pope in Rome. The European Community Court, in an October 1993 ruling supporting the workers' claim, held that this west German ownership and its practices violate the European Community monopoly regulations.

> we need a democratic dialogue about the tasks of a constitutional state, the economy and culture. Together we must bring all this out into the public arena—to think about all this and discuss it with one another. (Michaelis, 1990, p. 1)

The problem in eastern Germany today is that, for the most part, these interwoven issues of outsiderness remain outside official—public broadcasting—discourse. Jürgen Habermas, in *The Structural Transformation of the Public Sphere*, defined the public sphere as a sphere that mediates between society and state, in which the public organizes itself as the bearer of public opinion (Eley, 1992). As essential outsiders, the east Germans are not part of this self-organization of public opinion for they have no access to the technology of the public sphere—the mass media. These east German complaints remain part of the everyday mutterings among neighbors and family members, again often "cramped and obstructed" as was the space for dialogue during the Communist era. Western chief editors (and most of the editors are from the west) tell their eastern staff that they don't want to fill the newspaper pages with east "whining." This has been the state of affairs in the German east since 1991.

## The Foreign "Outsider" in Eastern Germany

During the last year of the Communist regime in the GDR, 120,000 Vietnamese and Africans worked in menial positions under state-to-state contracts. After reunification, when their jobs began to disappear, most of these contract workers accepted the federal government's invitation of a paid one-way trip home. Perhaps some 20,000 remained, with either legal work permits or with applications pending consideration. In 1993, on the steps of the Leipzig train station, the Vietnamese stand and sell the very right-wing west German tabloid *Bild-Zeitung* that condemns their presence in Germany. The east Germans don't know these foreigners and probably have never exchanged a single word with them other than at various official rituals. With the exception of university life, where contacts with exchange students from other socialist nations were plentiful, east Germans and foreigners lived distinctly separate lives. At the same time, East Germans were expected to report any contacts they had with individuals from "nonfriendly" (nonsocialist) countries. East Germans knew very little about the lives of the contract workers, and believed that they received considerable social welfare benefits from the GDR state, all in the name of "socialist solidarity." Most East Germans were unaware of the details of the foreign workers' status (such as their low wages, unsafe working conditions, greater restrictions on personal mobility, the fact that they had no right to marry, nor that they had privacy in their cramped living quarters).

By 1990/1991 new foreigners had arrived in the east—political refugees from behind the former Iron Curtain: Romas (Gypsies), Poles, Russians, Bosnians, and Bulgarians. They were joined by refugees from other political crises: Indians, Pakistanis, Tibetans, and Africans. Each state in the Republic received its quota of refugees who were assigned housing in asylum homes (in the east often former Soviet military barracks, in the west former American military barracks) pending review of their claims of political persecution by state and federal officials.

These asylum petitions work their way slowly from one bureaucratic office to another, frequently taking years to complete. Critics of the government's asylum policies, such as Winfried Deters-Schneider of the Leipzig branch Friedrich-Ebert Political Foundation, complain that the petitions are "stuck for years in the morass of the hyper-bureaucratized and politicized asylum paperwork."[5] Gabriele Hartig, a county-level foreigners counselor in the state of Brandenburg, sees another source of the problem:

> The paperwork moves from one level in the government where the Social Democrats controls the petition machinery to another level where the CDU policy guides decision-making. The CDU wants to find reason to reject the petitions, the SPD has traditionally rejected ethnic-based nationalism and has had a sympathetic view toward 'immigration.' The petitions bounce back and forth.[6]

Another problem is basic understaffing. Reviewing petitions requires considerable expertise and knowledge of the political climate in the relevant country. Staffing levels lag behind review demand. In the meantime, supplicants must remain in asylum homes, they are not allowed to work, and, for that reason, are totally dependent on the state social welfare system for food, housing, and pocket money. The east Germans imagine that these foreigners receive enormous cash welfare benefits. This question of welfare benefits is a highly sensitive issue, for the CDU-controlled federal government voted, in 1993, to reduce the social welfare benefits of all Germans, the first reduction since the founding of the Federal Republic.

There is yet one more set of outsiders in Germany, the *Aussiedler*, or ethnic Germans (or descendants of these ethnic Germans) who for decades or centuries have lived in the "east," in present-day Poland, Romania, and in the former Soviet Union. Their numbers have increased dramatically since the collapse of the Soviet Empire. These Germans seem like total foreigners to the east Germans, for these Germans frequently do not

---

[5]Winfried Deters-Schneider interview.

[6]Gabriele Hartig interview.

speak German and practice folkways which have long since disappeared from Germany, east or west. The east Germans consider these blood relatives "Russians" or "Poles."

When east Berliners first went to west Berlin after the opening of the Wall, they encountered the large Turkish community living primarily in the Kreuzberg district of West Berlin. Eberhard Seidel-Pielen, a student of neo-Nazi youth gangs, noted that, "The east Berliners, unsure of their status in unified Berlin, are shocked to see Turks—*non-Germans*—living better in the Federal Republic than they do. Germans should live better than the foreigners."[7] East and west Germans believe that these foreigners rob Germans of their rightful job opportunities, even though most of them either take jobs Germans won't accept, or they work in ethnic enterprises (Farin & Seidel-Pielen, 1993a, 1993b, 1993c).

Since the firebombings in Solingen and Moelln (in west Germany), Turkish residents have begun to appear on television (in small numbers and in rare occasions) discussing their existence in (west) Germany, and challenging the commonplace German notion that the Turks are taking advantage of German generosity. German media critics complain that any coverage in which the "foreign" voice is present is rare. One reason for this absence, German analysts note, is that the "man on the street," the unaffiliated individual, German or foreigner, rarely appears on television. Germany is known as a corporatist society, and typically journalists interview *representatives* from societal organizations. Turkish radio broadcaster Erkin Örzguc, a 20-year veteran of (West) Berlin Sender Freies Berlin public broadcasting corporation, remarked that Turks were only able to petition the government and obtain any attention in public life after they formed centralized ethnic associations and delegated spokespersons for their community, a typical German practice but novel to the Turks.[8] The nascent public discussion between Turks and Germans is essentially a west German phenomenon, for the Turks live in the west and have their history with the west. In the east, on regional television and radio, one does not hear the voice of the foreigner. They are spoken about, but not spoken to.

### *Parteipolitik* and Government Policies

The CDU *Auslaenderpolitik* has remained consistent since Helmut Kohl was elected chancellor in 1981: The guest workers (Turks, Italians, Greeks) who were needed in the 1960s and early 1970s were no longer needed in the economy after the 1973 oil crisis. These guests, no longer necessary, were expected to go home. Germany is not an immigration

---

[7]Eberhard Seidel-Pielen interview.

[8]Erkin Örzguc interview.

land.[9] Ideally, only ethnic Germans should have the right to German citizenship; the rare right to naturalized citizenship should be limited to adult individuals educated (minimum 8 years) in Germany who are born of German-born parents, and have a strong familiarity with German culture. The CDU has been opposed to dual citizenship rights, which are becoming more and more the norm throughout Europe. For over a decade the CDU was unable to convince its partner in the ruling coalition, the Free Democrats, to accept this *Auslaenderpolitik*, so the federal bureaucracy was paralyzed.

At the end of 1992, with asylum homes in flames (visible to the world on their television screens), and neo-Nazi youth threatening foreigners throughout the country, the federal parliament voted to change the constitution to limit the right of asylum. According to new provisions, in effect since July 1, 1993, the new law turns back asylum seekers who do not come directly from a country that is regarded as a dictatorship or that is at war. Germany will not accept or even consider applicants for political asylum if they enter Germany through a third nation which itself is not considered a nation practicing political persecution. Before July 1993, Romanian, Chinese, or Pakistani refugees entered Germany via Poland or the Czech Republic or Austria. Under the new law, these so-called "third nations" have the responsibility for such individuals. Only those who fly into Germany directly from a nation considered a human-rights violator can petition for political asylum. Germany has worked out agreements with Poland, Slovakia, and the Czech Republic on the basis of which of these neighbors will hold back the tide of immigrants in exchange for monetary compensation. In an arrangement with Romania, the Federal Republic pays the state to take back any of its refugee citizens. Critics of this policy argue that sending Romanians, primarily Roma gypsies, to the east in German trains reminds the modern public of the Nazi trains carrying Romas to their deaths in Treblinka and Auschwitz.

## THE BROADCASTING SYSTEM IN THE FEDERAL REPUBLIC

The German-German Unification Treaty provided for a 1-year transition period after the October 3, 1990 unification. During that time the newly elected state parliaments were to develop new public administrative infrastructure, including state constitutions. One highly debated provision in the Treaty (Article 36) dealt with the electronic media which, according to the German Constitution, fell within the jurisdiction of the federal

[9]For the Social Democratic Party challenge to this CDU immigration policy, see Donhoff, 1992.

states. The Treaty called for the transformation of the Berlin-based, centralized GDR (German Democratic Republic) national broadcasting system into a state-based, federalized public service structure under public control (under the direction of a citizens' governing board of directors).

The Federal Republic of Germany had, since its founding, a 3-channel public broadcasting system financed by fees levied on the owners of television and radio sets. The public system has the obligation to provide "basic services," which means a programming mix of information, education, and entertainment. As a result of Goebbels' use of radio to propagate Nazi ideology, the Allies (particularly the British) insisted that postwar German broadcasting has an obligation to promote democratic ideas and to contribute to the ongoing building of a democratic society. Commercial broadcasting, introduced only in the mid-1980s, offers primarily entertainment and is exempt from formal "democracy-building" obligations. Both commercial and public broadcasting are obligated to adhere to the constitutional provisions protecting children and banning racist, revanchistic public speech.

Broadcasting was the focus of considerable attention in the drafting of the unification treaty, for election campaigns are broadcast *gratis* over the public channels. The political parties and the German public believe that control of the airwaves ensures control of politics (Humphreys, 1990). All but one of the regional directors of German television are dues-paying members of political parties, and public affairs programming in each of the broadcasting regions is geared to the interests of the ruling party in a given regional parliament.

## The New East German Public Institutions and the Unification Shock

After considerable wrangling, two eastern public broadcasting corporations were established by the newly elected state parliaments. In three states (Saxony, Saxony-Anhalt, and Thuringia) the CDU became the ruling party in parliament, each with a *west* German holding the office of governor. These three "CDU parliaments" jointly established one public broadcasting corporation—the Middle German Broadcasting Corporation (*Mitteldeutscher Rundfunk*). The state of Brandenburg's SPD/Free Democrats/Alliance 90 parliamentary coalition established a one-state broadcasting organization—the Brandenburg East German Broadcasting Corporation (*Ostdeutscher Rundfunk Brandenburg*). East Berlin and the small state of Mecklenburg on the North Sea merged with already existing west public broadcasting corporations.

The Brandenburg East German Broadcasting Corporation (ORB) and the Middle German Broadcasting Corporation (MDR), the two eastern organizations, are constituent members of the ARD, the national public broadcasting network that produces collectively a national television channel (the ARD First Program).[10] In addition to this collective national channel, each of the member organizations produces a regional channel (the ARD Third Program) and an array of radio stations. Each regional channel produces a full range of news and public affairs programming addressing international, national, and regional issues.[11] There exists a second national public television organization, ZDF, whose board of directors is made up of representatives from each of the federal states. Unlike the ARD, all the ZDF professional staff are hired by that central organization. Every public broadcasting corporation is governed by a broadcasting council, a public body comprised of representatives from "socially relevant groups in society" appointed by each state parliament. These public boards of directors were established to serve as a buffer between the state and the broadcasting organization itself. From their very beginnings in the 1950s, however, these public boards have been little more than extensions of the political parties in power. When a new political party comes to power, a new board is appointed. The politicization of broadcasting reaches into the senior staffing. The directors of all but one of the public broadcasting corporations are dues-paying members of the ruling political party. Changes in political power in state parliaments also always result in changes in broadcasting directors.

In this study we are interested in the two ARD regional broadcasting corporations in the east, for this is where we can observe the eastern German party politics and east German journalistic treatment of local issues.

## The Middle German Broadcasting Corporation

The large three-state Middle German Broadcasting Corporation (MDR), with its base of 10 million viewers, is informally characterized in the ARD network headquarters in west German city of Munich as the *"Besatzungs-*

---

[10]As an example of the collective work style, the public service North German Broadcasting Corporation (*Norddeutscher Rundfunk*), based in Hamburg, produces the daily news programs "Tagesschau" and "Tagesthemen," which are broadcast on the national channel. The larger the broadcasting organization, its size based on user fees levied on each television-owning household, the greater presence the regional organization has in the national program. Because the Middle German Broadcasting Corporation is the second largest affiliate in the ARD network, it will, when fully funded, contribute substantially to national programming. At the same time, these regional channels produce their own news programming, which covers international, national, and regional issues.

[11]The network system in the United States is organized in a different manner, with the national network providing prime-time programming and the local affiliate responsible for the so-called "off hours." Here national and local programming share one television frequency. In Germany within each region the national broadcaster utilizes one channel, the regional broadcaster utilizes a second channel.

*anstalt*"—the occupation corporation, for 10 of the 11 senior managers and programmers are party-affiliated *west* Germans. (Only the facilities manager is an east German.) Appointing west Germans to the senior production positions within the broadcasting organization served to ensure implementation of the organization's programming objectives established by the state parliaments. The Broadcasting Council and broadcasting executive director Udo Reiter, a member of the ruling Christian Democratic Union party and former director of Bavarian Broadcasting Radio, have the charge to transform the "east" citizens into "west" citizens. This CDU political project has its opponents in the east who believe that unification should have resulted in a new Federal Republic, with contributions from the east and the west. The west and east CDU (and most west Germans) did not understand this newly merged "east–west" society to be the unification mandate. The CDU believed in a shock therapy approach, effecting a dramatic break with the programming past.[12] When the new regional channel began its radio and television programming on January 1, 1992, audience complaints flooded the station management. According to Reinhard Krug, an east German member of the executive director's senior administrative staff, "The audience missed the personalities from the GDR-era programs. We finally bowed to this pressure, and brought back some of the former showmasters."[13] It was all right to bring back some of the former stars, but Saxony member of parliament Herbert Goliasch was adamant that "the MDR was not to be a forum for GDR nostalgia, not to be the zone of east whining."

Banning "whining" means no on-air discussions of social problems if such discussions lead to the support of social programs not endorsed by the CDU. For example, everywhere in the east (and the west) one hears discussion of the "youth crisis." There are many ways to frame this discussion: Question—Why have the eastern youth turned to violence? Answer A—Their family life is empty because the parents, in supporting the Communist regime, have lost their moral standing. Discussion—The evil life of the past, the lack of courage. Answer B—Because young people have no economic future and the government is spending education dollars supporting foreign freeloaders. Discussion—Get rid of the foreign freeloaders. Answer C—The youth have been stripped of the fabric of social life, live in a social vacuum without hope of meaningful employment, and hear Nazi ideas at home from their grandparents, the only

[12]This is per interview with Herbert Goliasch, chairman of the CDU faction in the Saxony state parliament and a member of the MDR Broadcasting Council. During the Communist era Goliasch worked as a journalist for some years in the east CDU press. In 1994, after accusations that he had worked for 20 years as an "informal" spy for the Soviet Union, Goliasch resigned his position as leader of the CDU faction within the Saxony parliament.

[13]Reinhard Krug interview.

family members familiar with a non-Communist Germany. Discussion—What is it that the youth need now, and what about these Nazi grandparents? What is it that young people hear from their grandparents? Why do their elders cheer or quietly support the attacks against asylum seekers? Answer D—The destruction of GDR-era youth organizations and leisure-time activities are no longer free. The youth lack the spending money their siblings in the west possess. Feeling inferior, the youth attack the weaker. Discussion—The crisis of entering a highly commodified culture. The problem of the economy and the bureaucratic barriers to becoming self-reliant. These discussions are tricky, for any of them can lead dangerously back to what might be conceived as positive features of the GDR era. In a way, this is like the famous *Eiertanz* (walking on eggs) problem journalists faced during the Communist era. Discussion of the current crisis leads in everyday discourse so often to a critique of current politics (CDU politics). That is taboo.

What about the depiction of foreigners and foreigner issues in the MDR region? The Romas (the Gypsies) come on to the TV screen as news objects, as thieves, and as burdens on the social welfare system. There is no discussion, for example, of how the bureaucracy could be reformed to facilitate faster processing of asylum applications. There are no televised interviews with these refugees to find out exactly why they left their homes, what their particular political problems were, and what their problems are today. The war in the former Yugoslavia was a nightly news topic, and the general plight of the war victims "over there" received considerable public attention and empathy. But the refugees from that same war, housed in asylum homes in Germany, receive no sympathy. Hoyerswerda, the site of a shocking attack on foreigners in 1991, in which police and the community watched rather than tried to stop the violence, is located in Saxony, within the MDR region. Television images of the violence and Nazi regalia shocked the nation and the world. Although the CDU state government was quite embarrassed by the extraordinary passivity of the state police in the face of neo-Nazi violence, the subject of the role of the mass media and neo-Nazi violence was never the subject of the public Broadcasting Council attention. Each state and city (in the east and the west) has a Commissioner for Foreigner Affairs who is responsible for dealing with foreigner issues. In spite of hefty criticism of media coverage of foreigners in the region and the neo-Nazi violence, the Commissioner of Foreigner Affairs has had no relationship with the regional public broadcasting organization.

Content analyses reveal that the regional press framed the foreigner issue narrowly, depicting foreigners primarily as culprits in crime stories (Friedrich-Ebert Foundation, 1993; Hamann, 1993). Foreigners themselves never come to word in the mass media. During the past 6 months the daily newspaper *Leipziger Volkszeitung* quoted a Roma only once, and that was to report that since the city had decided to give out food stamps rather than cash for food, the Roma family had withdrawn its asylum applications and decided to go home. A photograph of Roma families in a bus accompanied this story. The newspapers and television news focus on Romas' taking advantage of hapless Germans. The Germans are depicted as under siege. Some shopkeepers in the center of Leipzig put a broom in the show window next to the front door to warn the Romas not to enter the shop, or face being swept out. In response to a query as to why this broom condition has not been newsworthy, local journalists indicated to the author that situation of Romas fell outside the standards of newsworthy items. Bosnian refugees receive the same treatment, for, the journalists noted, "Bosnians look just like the Romas." Economics determines what is in the newspaper: The local readers aren't interested in Roma stories so the paper doesn't write about them, an editor explained. Because there is no full discussion of the social welfare benefits extended to asylum applicants assigned to barracks in Leipzig, for example, the local east Germans believe that their welfare benefits rights are reduced to support the dreaded Romas. In fact, the federal government finance minister Theo Waigel makes this very point. This is the "skinhead" rhetoric Günter Grass condemns.

Inasmuch as foreigners are most likely only to come into eye of the media through crime stories, senior editor Uwe Winkler's observations on crime reportage are interesting:

> We in our editorial staff discussed one day the raging xenophobia in the region. We noticed that the police, in their criminal reports which we receive, always listed the race of the foreign criminals, but never listed "German" when a German was a criminal. That was CDU policy throughout the country, we were told by the police here in Thuringia. Newspapers, taking the easy road, often just reprint these police reports. The cumulative effect of this on the reader is to link foreigners with criminality. We decided to eliminate ethnicity from our crime stories. But I think our discussions about this, and our decision to eliminate these references, are unusual in journalistic practices here in Germany. Just look at the crime reports in the newspapers![14]

Newspapers, as the *Leipziger Volkszeitung* chief editor noted, are not social welfare institutions; they are a business, to sell news and entertainment.[15] Public broadcasting is in the social welfare business.

---

[14]Uwe Winkler interview.

[15]Interview with chief editor Hartwig Hochstein.

### The Brandenburg East German Broadcasting Corporation

The state of Brandenburg has had its share of social dislocation and neo-Nazi violence, noted Gabriele Hartig in an interview with this author, a foreigners advisor in Brandenburg.

> People of color do not use public transportation after 7:00 p.m., relying on private vehicles. Too dangerous. Violent youths will attack them. And in the rural communities of Brandenburg, where the collapse of the agricultural economy threatens the entire way of living, the residents support these neo-Nazis. You know, Nazi ideas never really did die out among the old people. They just kept them to themselves, until now.

She explained that the state and municipal governments in Brandenburg have approached the basic *Auslaender* issue differently than the three states in the southern part of eastern Germany. Many of the Brandenburg state public institutions governed by a coalition of Social Democrats, Free Democrats and the grass-roots Alliance 90 reflect the legacy of the pre-unification "citizen politics" or *Buergerbewegung*. The Brandenburg East German Broadcasting Corporation senior producers and management are a mix of east and west Germans (Spielhagen, 1993). According to the members of the Broadcasting Council, the west German director of the Brandenburg corporation was selected not in the political party back rooms but by the full public Broadcasting Council after *it*, not the parliamentary leaders, conducted a search. A second contrast is the background of the east German senior staff. The Director of Television, the Executive Producer of Radio, and the audience research coordinator all were leading figures in the post-Communist media reform movement. They were the senior officials of GDR broadcasting after the overthrow of the Communist regime, and held these positions until the regional corporations were established. By contrast, no senior MDR staff held any position of importance in the post-Communist GDR broadcasting.

Executive Director Hansjurgen Rosenbauer understands the Brandenburg organization as a transitional broadcasting endeavor in two ways. The two states of Brandenburg and Berlin are to merge at a yet to be determined date, and the two broadcasting organizations of these two states will likewise merge. (As east–west relations further deteriorate, this merger seems more and more remote. Berlin is seen as a western state, and Brandenburg as an eastern state.) More significantly for this discussion here, the Brandenburg organization has a mission to assist east Germans in their difficult transition to *Bundesbuerger* thinking (citizen of the Federal Republic). Unlike the MDR Corporation under the leadership of the Christian Democrats, the Brandenburg political and broadcasting leadership do not subscribe to shock therapy transition.[16] Nor do they believe that GDR culture was, in the words of the CDU, nothing more than *Stasi* culture (secret police culture). Pre-Communist East German life is not alien to the Director of Television Michael Albrecht, for he has experienced it himself and lives in an east German social world. According to Director Albrecht, who believes television must bring the good and the bad from the GDR past into public discussion:

> We have to know what happened to us, and how we lived, in order to understand what is happening to us now, and how we should live. No, I don't want old showmasters. We are very different from the MDR. They have brought the showmasters from the past, but only the politics from the west. We don't want imported politics. I think we need to talk about women's issues as they relate to us here, for example. And show great old DEFA films. We have to deal with our histories.[17]

Unlike its counterpart at the MDR Corporation, the Brandenburg Broadcasting Council understands one of its tasks is to work to eradicate xenophobia, both of the violent or nonviolent kind. To this end the Brandenburg Broadcasting Council and the Brandenburg Commissioner for Foreigners have met on several occasions to both discuss the general problems and to develop a systematic approach to dealing with the issues in everyday programming. The youth are the target of concentrated attention. One of Brandenburg's program offerings is the youth radio station "Radio Fritz." During the Communist era every Communist country had a youth organization and a youth league newspaper. In the logic of the Communist order, a youth station is not one that merely features music for a particular age group, as we see in the west. Rather, it provides information, education, and entertainment to the youth. This logic remained in the post-Communist mind of the east German broadcasters. Even before the multicultural issue commanded such attention, the youth program was important. Brandenburg youth programming includes music and interviews with musicians (much like that found on MTV), but also programs focusing on youth issues such as: how to live in the new society, discussions of the apprentice, university and education opportunities, safe sex, travel opportunities, and so forth. It was therefore natural to address multiculturalism issues in the youth programming. This multicultural awareness resulted in changes in music choice, interview subjects, and public service messages.

"Radio Fritz" and the other Brandenburg radio and television programming promote an antiviolence message. The broadcasters organized

---

[16]Per interviews with Brandenburg senior management and six members of the Broadcasting Council.

[17]Director of Television Michael Albrecht interview.

a "Violence without me!" (*Gewalt ohne mich!*) rock concert in Spring 1993 in which east German rock stars appeared and performed. Their message in the music and in the talk—stop the violence, learn to live with others, have a European mentality, be world citizens. The broadcaster supplied the paid technical staff and equipment, recorded the event, and produced a CD "*Gewalt ohne mich!*" which is available at music stores and broadcast over the airwaves. A similar rock concert was organized in west Germany, but by private organizations. The public broadcaster ZDF covered the concert, but did not organize, finance, or produce it.

According to the Brandenburg Broadcasting Council president Lutz Borgmann, "Brandenburg Broadcasting must be a leader in society. This means going into society, not just sitting in our meetings."[18] Leaving the newsroom and entering society was one hallmark of the Leninist press system, and we can now see it at the Brandenburg organization, but without the Leninist Party directing activities (Boyle, 1993b).

Executive Director Rosenbauer finds himself in an usual work situation in the east. An activist broadcasting council is new to this west media professional. Another difference, he notes, is the eastern journalists' reluctance to even film shocking racist events. The eastern journalists argue that this sets a bad example and presents a poor image of Brandenburg for TV viewers. Rosenbauer had to insist on aggressive coverage, arguing that the broadcasting organization has a responsibility to report such events. The executive director and the news staff often argue about issues like this. What is unusual is the fact that unlike the situation at the MDR Corporation, the eastern viewpoint is expressed at Brandenburg at the managerial level, and not just in the staff canteen. As the Brandenburg Executive Director sees it, "we *Ossis* and *Wessis* don't always see eye-to-eye, but we have to learn to do so, in a united Germany and here at the Brandenburg Broadcasting."[19]

## SUMMARY

In east and west Germany alike, talking about Nazis, foreigners, and youth violence is talk about Germany and Germans. This has been an historic problem in West Germany, where the dark shadow of German history continues to prevent open discourse. The shadow now has a broader range, and is tangled up in the project of "belonging together and growing together." Observers of this somewhat acrimonious German growing together have their hopes and fears. The CDU political leaders

---

[18]Lutz Borgmann interview.

[19]Director Hansjurgen Rosenbauer interview.

hope is that they will be successful in absorbing the east Germans into the German system as it existed before reunification. This is the absolute view of the west CDU. The east CDU elected officials are of a mixed mind. They totally reject the political system of the past, but recognize that the east way of thinking is not necessarily crippled in desperate need of cultural therapy. They too want to bring something of the east into the west, but are not sure exactly what this might be, or how it might be carried out. They fear the whole unification experiment will blow up in their faces at the polls (in the east and the west). They fear what they call an east–west "Italianization" of Germany, with power and riches concentrated in the west, and discontent and poverty dominant in the east.[20] Many German social observers fear ever-increasing social strife. Their European neighbors likewise watch with great apprehension the escalating conflicts, well aware that domestic German problems have all too often developed into Europe's problems.

The CDU leadership in the east and west believe they must redouble their efforts to communicate their political objectives to the east voters. Their challenging task is made even more difficult by the fact that although the MDR Corporation is a well-known and large organization, its regional television and radio programming has not found great acceptance by the local population. Monthly audience studies conducted by the network show that more than 75% of the regional viewers turn to the commercial channels. The MDR management argues that their low share of the audience market is the result of television technology: At least 70% of the television viewers opt completely out of the terrestrial broadcasting order that the MDR dominates, choosing cable or personal satellite dishes. The MDR programming was not carried on the more than 4,000 cable networks in the region, nor was it retransmitted via the ASTRA satellite, the major broadcasting communication satellite in Central Europe.[21] To rectify this situation, MDR began transmitting its signals on the ASTRA satellite in July 1993. Although this costs the public broadcaster hundreds of thousands of dollars annually, the only alternative was to lose the majority of its potential market.

Critics of MDR's programming practices argue that local audiences find more of relevance for their lives on the commercial stations, which

---

[20]In the 1994 Italian parliamentary elections, the Northern League received the majority of votes from the electorate in the north by vowing to end the northern tax subsidies of the impoverished south.

[21]Unlike in western Germany, where the Bundespost operates cable services, apartment dwellers in the east have established their own building cable cooperatives, wire their own buildings with low-quality cable, purchase a satellite dish for less than $250, and bring into the building complex six or seven ASTRA satellite-transmitted programs. These gerry-rigged collective cable systems do not have the 32-program choices characteristic of western German cable organized by the Bundespost. See Boyle, 1995.

also produce some public affairs programming. According to these critics, MDR is losing its audience because of its perceived rejection of east German way of thinking. They claim that the audience, in turning off MDR, has tired of the CDU, and will turn it out of office in upcoming elections. The eastern CDU elected officials are having to confront their constituents' anger about the social crisis in the east. As a result, the eastern CDU is more willing today to challenge the views endorsed by the western CDU.

Two of the political parties in the majority coalition in the Brandenburg parliament (the Social Democrats and Alliance 90) are, on the other hand, part of the formal opposition in the federal parliament. The leadership in Brandenburg likewise fear a social explosion in the east, but as we have seen, it has embarked on a different approach to resolving the problems. The Brandenburg public broadcasting organization has founded considerable acceptance from its audience base. In spite of the competition from commercial stations and from Berlin public radio stations and television channels, the Brandenburg public broadcasting corporation regularly captures more than 50% of the viewing market, the highest level for any broadcasting organization, public or commercial. The Brandenburg Broadcasting Council believes that this remarkable viewer acceptance level reveals the fact that eastern Germans don't merely want to be entertained by American sitcoms and western German showmasters. They want serious dialogues with their past and an east German consciousness in the programming.

Mikhail Gorbachev (1987) noted the following about the two German states:

> What has formed historically here is best left to history. This also holds true for the issue of the German nation and of the forms of German statehood. What is important now is the political aspect. There are two German states with different social and political systems. Each of them has values of its own. Both of them have drawn lessons from history, and each of them can contribute to the affairs of Europe and the world. And what there will be in a hundred years is for history to decide. (pp. 185–186)

Since 1987 much has changed in the world. The two German states as they were then no longer exist. But Gorbachev was correct in noting that each of these two societies has drawn different lessons from history, and each has contributions to make. The role of east German public broadcasting could be to bring these "east perspectives" into the light of day. Another mission could be to reach or even capture an audience made up of these new citizens. As we watch east Germany today, we see more of an attempt, in politics and in broadcasting, to capture and subdue than any efforts to encourage dialogue and understanding. The official language of contemporary German politics is one of exclusion. One result of this is the nation's youth turning to alternative ideologies, including Nazism. Germany's most important challenges to the reunification process may well be found in the role mass media will play in the development of both positive intra-German and multicultural processes.

## REFERENCES


Ash, M. (1993, May). *Otherness in Germany: Then and now.* Paper presented at the German Studies Association annual meeting, Washington, DC.

Bitterman, K. (Ed.). (1993). *Der rassende mob. Die ossis zwischen selbstmitleid und barbarei.* Berlin: Tiamat.

Boyle, M. (1992). The revolt of the communist journalist: East Germany. *Media, Culture & Society, 14*(1), 133–139.

Boyle, M. (1993, October). *Is Leninist journalism in the coffin with the Leninist party? Observations on east German broadcasting.* Paper presented at the colloquium on the restructuring of central east European Television. University of Westminster, London.

Boyle, M. (1994). Building a communicative democracy: The birth and death of citizen politics in eastern Germany. *Media, Culture & Society, 16*(2), 183–215.

Boyle, M. (1995a). The public sphere after Communism in Eastern Europe: Television and the new political class. In P. Wasburn (Ed.), *Research in political sociology.* Greenwich, CT: JAI Press.

Boyle, M. (1995b). Eastern Germany after unification: Between east and west. In C. Sparks (Ed.), *After 1989 in East and Central Europe.* London: British Film Institute.

Donhoff, M. (Ed.). (1992). *Weil das land sich aendern muß. Ein manifest.* Reinbeck bei Hamburg: Rowohlt.

Eley, G. (1992). Nations, publics, and political cultures: Placing Habermas in the nineteenth century. In C. Calhoun (Ed.), *Habermas and the public sphere* (pp. 289–339). Cambridge, MA: MIT Press.

Erb, R. (1993, May). *Aktuelle tendenzen des rechtsextremismus in Deutschland 1989 bis 1993.* Paper presented at the German Studies Association annual meeting. Washington, DC.

Farin, K., & Seidel-Pielen, E. (1993a). *Krieg in den staedten. Jugendgangs in Deutschland.* Munich: Beck'sche Reihe.

Farin, K., & Seidel-Pielen, E. (1993b). *Rechtsdruck: Rassismus im neuen Deutschland.* Berlin: Rotbuch Verlag.

Farin, K., & Seidel-Pielen, E. (1993c). *Skinheads.* Munich: Beck'sche Reihe.

Fein, E. (1992, December 29). Günter Grass finds politics inescapable. *The New York Times,* p. B1.

Friedrich-Ebert Foundation (1993). *Entstehung von fremdenfeindlichkeit: Die verantwortung von politik und medien.* Bonn.

Funke, H. (1993). *Brand-Stifter. Deutschland zwischen demokratie und voelkischem nationalsmus.* Gottingen, Germany: Lamuv.

Gorbachev, M. (1987). *Perestroika: New thinking for our country and the world.* New York: Harper & Row.

Goetz, F. (1992). Rundfunk in den neuen bundeslaendern. Vom partei- zum parteienrundfunk. *Kritische Zeitschrift,* pp. 463–472.

Grass, G. (1990). *Two states—One nation?* San Diego: Harcourt Brace.

Grass, G. (1993, Spring). On loss: The condition of Germany. *Dissent,* pp. 178–188.

Hamann, P. (Ed.). (1993). *Das bild des auslaendischen mitbuergers in den massenmedien des freistaates Sachsens*. Leipzig: Forschungstelle Massenmedien und soziale Integration in der Gesellschaft fuer Jugend- und Sozialforschung.

Humphreys, P. (1990). *Media and media policy in West Germany*. New York: Berg.

Kinzer, S. (1993, November 7). Germany's justice system said to favor rightists. *The New York Times*, p. 9.

Konrad, G. (1984). *Antipolitics*. New York: Holt.

Kramer, J. (1993, June 14). Neo-Nazis: A chaos in the head. *The New Yorker*, pp. 51–70.

Leggewie, C. (1993). *Druck von rechts. Wohin treibt die Bundesrepublik?* Munich: Beck'sche Reihe.

Lummer, H. (1992). *Asyl! Ein missbrauchtes recht*. Frankfurt: Verlag Ullstein.

Mehrlaender, U., & Schultze, G. (1992). *Einwanderungskonzept fuer die Bundesrepublik Deutschland: Fakten, argumente, vorschlaege*. Bonn: Friedrich-Ebert-Stiftung.

Michaelis, J. (Ed.). (1990). *Die ersten texte des neuen forum erschienen in der zeit vom 9. september bis 18. dezember 1989*. Berlin: BasisDruck.

Nivuman, B. (Ed.). (1992). *Angst vor den deutschen. Terror gegen auslaender und der zerfall des rechtsstaates*. Reinbeck: Rowohlt.

Schneider, P. (1991). *The German comedy: Scenes of life after the wall*. New York: Noonday Press.

Siegler, B., Tolmein, O., & Wiedemann, C. (1993). *Der pakt: Die rechten und der staat*. Gottingen, Germany: Verlag die Werkstatt.

Spielhagen, E. (1993, May). *Mass media and politics in East Germany: Observations of a revolutionary*. Paper presented at the International Communication Association annual meeting, Washington, DC.

# 4

# *Stepsisters: On the Difficulties of German–German Feminist Cooperation*

Dorothy J. Rosenberg
*Bowdoin College*

> *After the Wall fell, Western feminist curiosity about our Eastern sisters continued to be limited. At first perhaps there was still hope of finding allies, that is co-believers for a Western-defined project. When this proved not to be the case, rejection and retreat, the establishment of property rights and defense of our own achievements quickly followed.*
>
> (Thürmer-Rohr, 1992, p. 15)

> *After a short phase of euphoric sisterliness, differences of opinion and massive disruptions in communications soon appeared. For some time now, the relationship between Eastern and Western sisters has been characterized by the demarking of boundaries, speechlessness and mutual prejudices.*
>
> (Dölling, 1992, p. 3)

These two comments, one written by a Westerner, the other by an Easterner, characterize the relationship between East and West German feminists. East–West feminist cooperation, which seemed about to blossom in 1989, quickly faded. Despite their similar cultural background, East and West German feminists do not share a common history as feminists, common theoretical assumptions, common current socioeconomic conditions, or future prospects. Failure to initially recognize these differences, followed by a more or less mutual withdrawal of cooperation when they could no longer be ignored, doomed early efforts at a joint campaign to preserve at least some of the former GDR's (German Democratic Republic) exemplary women and family social legislation through the unification process.

The East German case is unique among the countries of Eastern Europe, primarily because it involves the imposition of an external (West German) elite along with its political and economic system instead of a politically contested transformation within a single population. Nonetheless, it has broader implications, including serving as an illustration of some of the difficulties characteristic of East–West communications in general.

## EAST MEETS WEST

One striking common aspect of the transformation processes that followed the "revolutions" of 1989 is how quickly all of the women disappeared. Women were an often decisive presence in the human rights opposition and among the leaders of peaceful mass demonstrations against the old regimes, but were virtually nowhere to be seen when political power was assumed by former dissidents (e.g., Poland or Czechoslovakia). Even more problematic, the newly elected parliamentarians seemed to find nothing more vital to cementing the triumph of democracy than the attempt to repeal as much progressive social legislation as possible—liberal abortion laws, along with affirmative action regulations and publicly funded child care have been favorite targets across Eastern Europe. (The only country that did not try to limit abortion or outlaw it outright is Romania, where it was illegal before 1990.) Women's employment outside the home has been proposed as the probable root cause of virtually every social evil and their removal from the labor force is presented as the obvious solution to reform-induced "labor shedding." Female unemployment remains nearly twice that of men in Poland, Slovakia, and the former GDR whereas the situation in Russia and the Commonwealth of Independent States is even more negative. Worse yet, not only did the few women still in government fail to oppose these trends (Suchocka/Poland, Merkel/Germany), until 1993 the majority of women voters supported parties whose programs promise to return them to economic dependency in the private sphere as quickly as possible.

Eastern feminists who had attacked the "real socialist" systems for failing to live up their promises of gender equality are now trying to prevent the programs they previously criticized from being totally abolished, with limited success. The initial shock at seeing droves of their compatriots in what appeared to be a headlong flight from emancipation back into a kind of crude gender subordination has faded as women respond to the realities of unemployment and rapidly declining standards of living. Still, most feminists continue to feel isolated in societies in which feminism was routinely presented as a perverse or self-indulgent Western aberration. Nearly all are fighting overwhelming odds in their efforts to rescue some bits of the reproductive rights, pronatalist measures, and full employment policies that gave women in Eastern Europe, especially women with children, a degree of economic security unimaginable in the West.

Western feminists, critical or ignorant of many details, watched with anger and confusion as programs they had spent years struggling for at home being dismantled across Eastern Europe to the apparent satisfaction of many of the beneficiaries. Communication between Western feminists and their Eastern European counterparts has been limited, often difficult, and characterized by mutual misunderstandings whereas attempts at cooperation have been, with a few encouraging exceptions, disappointing. Nowhere is the relationship more strained than in the recently united Germany.

## The German Anomaly

In 1989 it was widely thought that transition in East Germany would be a simpler and less disruptive process than in the rest of Eastern Europe. Given a clearly articulated, successful economic and political model and supported by huge transfers of human and material resources from the West, a rapid and stable transition appeared to be only a matter of applying the resources to implement the model.

Unfortunately, this prediction was based on deeply flawed economic assumptions (Pickel, 1992). Worse yet, it failed to take any account of either postwar German history or the people who had lived it. The postunification imposition of West German culture—its legal, economic, educational, political, and social systems—as normative, must be seen against the background of German history. Virtually overnight in 1945, everything associated with the Nazis had become officially vile, despite the fact that much of the National Socialists' popular success had been based on their skilled use of widely held values and stereotypes and their implementation of beneficial social programs. Germany was suddenly transformed into a nation of victims and resisters, while a conspiracy of silence protected the vast majority of perpetrators and fellow travelers (Browning, 1992; Müller, 1987).

Once again in 1989, overnight, everything associated with the GDR was to be publicly rejected, removed, replaced, and criticized on pain of social ostracism and/or economic sanction. A West German author noted that, "Surveys all tend to show that the East Germans appreciate their newly acquired freedom to travel, but that most of them do not believe that they have gained any greater freedom of speech. On the contrary, . . . 'now you can no longer say anything at all, otherwise you won't get a job' " (Beer, 1993, p. 7). Masses of victims and self-declared members of the opposition popped up like mushrooms, and a McCarthyite witch hunt for the perpetrators and their henchpersons swung into action. (The significant number of individuals who suffered political persecution, especially in the early postwar period, should not be confused with the majority of those who now declare themselves, ex post facto, the heroic resisters and persecuted victims of the 1980s.) Observers are left with an unsettling sense of déjà vu.

Unable to either invoke a German nationalism tainted by National Socialism or appeal to geography as a defining parameter, the two postwar German states fell back upon culture as the foundation upon which to construct a national identity. Picking and choosing from the midden heap of German history those values, heroes, and works of art that could be woven into a more or less coherent continuum, the two postwar German states developed mutually exclusive versions of a past upon which to base their competing claims to legitimacy as the true heirs of the German cultural and political tradition. Thus, the East built upon the Peasant Revolts, Rosa Luxemburg, and Karl Liebknecht, whereas the West referred themselves to Bismarck and the Second Reich. United in rejecting the immediate past as an ahistorical aberration, both claimed the resistance to fascism, but the East made the Red Orchestra, a Communist international underground network, their symbol of heroism whereas the West celebrated the nationalist military officers' July 20, 1944 plot to assassinate Hitler.

The two Germanys rarely settled on the same figure in constructing what became virtual mirror images, because neither acknowledged that the other's heroes existed. This arrangement remained unproblematic until the late 1960s when the West German student movement discovered large blank spots in its history. Left-wing student groups duly disinterred the German left tradition and read Marx, Engels, Luxemburg, Liebknecht, and Brecht, frequently in East German subsidized editions, before the 1972 *Radikalenerlass* (Law Against Radicals) and the antiterrorist campaign of 1974–1975 drew clear boundaries for political speech as well as action (Braunthal, 1990). Even before, the reception and interpretation of such figures fell into distinctly different configurations in East and West. After his death in 1956, Brecht was also performed in the West, but was interpreted primarily as an aesthetic theorist and resister to fascism. Brecht's support for socialism was either relativized or ignored. The procollectivization prologue to the *Caucasian Chalk Circle*, for example, was simply omitted from most Western performances. His frequently cited comment on the 1953 workers' protest that "Perhaps the leadership should elect another population" consistently omitted his conclusion that the time had come for him to join the Party.

As a result, the differences between East and West German intellectuals (feminist or otherwise) are not just a question of whether they took required or elective courses in Marxism or are familiar with the latest trend in French theory or total quality management, but in their fundamental and oppositional valorization of German social and cultural history. It is also not simply a matter of whether 40 years of life in a "real socialist" system led to a separate "GDR identity" based on shared values or rules of etiquette, but of a differently structured understanding of what constitutes a *German* identity.

All societies include a variety of interpretations of who or what they are, put forward by different groups contesting for dominance or legitimacy and changing over time. The present German case is complicated by both the mutual exclusivity of its two prior dominant versions and by the taboo nature of their predecessor, the undigested National Socialist vision of German national identity. It is further complicated by the circumstance that in each case, the new orthodoxy has been imposed by external forces (political or economic defeat) rather than achieved through internal evolution or consensus. The absence of this vital social process may offer a partial explanation of the current resurgence of that taboo identity among neo-fascist and skinhead groups and the apparent appeal of certain aspects of it in both East and West.

The tension between denial and subliminal identification with taboo memories has also produced repeated attempts by conservative politicians and historians to reclaim, rehabilitate, rewrite, or relativize constituent parts of this past. A recent example is provided by the *Neue Wache* war memorial on *Unter den Linden*, the processional avenue of (the former East) Berlin. Until 1990, the war memorial was a bare room containing an eternal flame and a dedication "To the Victims of War and Fascism" above a crypt holding the remains of an unknown German soldier and an unknown concentration camp victim. The postunification renovation replaced the specific terms *war* and *fascism* with the generic *terror* and *tyranny* and the confessionally neutral flame with an oversized version of a Käte Kollwitz sculpture strongly suggestive of a Christian Pietà. After Jewish organizations refused to participate in the rededication ceremony, a plaque listing the names of concentration camps was affixed to the facade of the building, in effect symbolically displacing even this oblique reference to German agency to an external space clearly separated from the Christian interior from which the memory of fascism had been obliterated.

## PHILOSOPHICAL FOUNDATIONS OF FEMINIST THEORY EAST VERSUS WEST

A further barrier to cooperation between Eastern and Western feminists has been the difference in both the content of their concerns and their underlying assumptions and analytical approaches. As Bassnett (1992) noted, "The cult of individualism is not part of the Eastern European experience" (p. 12). To make a very broad generalization, East and West German feminists proceed from fundamentally different understandings of the relationship between the individual and the state or society, which has led to serious misunderstandings and failures in communication. To summarize very briefly: Eastern European societies officially subscribed to an ideology of egalitarianism and the subordination of individual interests to those of the collective. Although individualism obviously did not disappear, certain aspects of Western individualist value structures either failed to develop or became socially unacceptable (e.g., large income disparities or conspicuous consumption). GDR theorists distinguished between a "Darwinian individualism" based on purely self-interested competition and "humanist individuality," which posited a collective with common interests composed of separate individuals with their own rights and needs. Within this ideological framework various social identities developed or were preserved as a result of tradition, agreement, habit, or simple pragmatic adjustment. Some of these identities (work groups) were encouraged and supported by the state, others (the family) were largely accepted and effectively reinforced, whereas others (dissidents) were persecuted. To oversimplify, individuals tended to see themselves as members of a group—often a family or friendship network defined against the outside society—within which men and women pursued a common interest, occupied the same social category, and were expected to act in solidarity rather than in competition with one another.

Within a structure of formal equality and very nearly equal powerlessness in the public sphere, gender tended to be seen as a secondary and biological rather than social category. Systematic forms of discrimination against women in the public sphere (such as ever fewer women at higher levels of power) were registered, but generally understood to derive from the lack of time to devote to advancement resulting from women's (biologically determined) double burden of work and family. Individual forms such as sexual harassment tended to be regarded as social failings (lack of manners or culture) rather than expressions of power in a system where power resided in the state (and Party members were often disciplined for moral infractions). Within the family, women were perceived as the central figure, generally responsible not only for reproductive labor but also controlling family finances and major decision making. Just as the effects of war and older cultural patterns had removed men physically to the periphery of the family unit, full employment and pronatalist policies reduced or eliminated their economic centrality.

In contrast most Western feminists, proceeding from the assumptions of liberal individualism, tend to see the state as a neutral entity, or even a possible ally that can be pressured to intervene in the interest of fair competition between gendered individuals or on behalf of individual rights. In the East, by contrast, the state had intervened with positive discrimination in favor of women. Rather than seeing men primarily as members of the same social category equally oppressed by the system (although differently advantaged by biology), in the Western framework men tend to appear as the unfairly advantaged competitor or active exploiter, individually and as a group, both in the public sphere and in the family where male economic centrality continues virtually undiminished.

This different self-positioning of Eastern and Western feminists in relation to the state and to men is complicated by their different visions of the relationship between the individual and society. Although a female group identity based on common interests is often postulated, gender solidarity in the West is hopelessly fractured by class, race, and other competing identity and social group interests. In practice, West German feminist reliance upon the liberal individualist model, which regards individuals as free to make choices, but also as individually responsible for the consequences of those choices, has led to a Western feminist activism centered on abortion and equal opportunity individual rights issues, while neglecting full employment, day care, or child welfare payments, all entitlement issues. In contrast, East Germans still tend to hold the view that society as a whole bears a moral and economic responsibility for its members and regarded the aforementioned as basic social services.

As a case in point, a Western feminist arrived at the negative conclusion that GDR policy addressed women primarily as mothers (Gerhard, 1991–1992) and only secondarily as individuals. In fact policy was generated by social needs: most women in the GDR were mothers, a significant number of whom were not married. By guaranteeing women access to both easily affordable child care and paid employment, GDR policy broke the nexus between motherhood and economic dependency, which remains in force in the West. In an article in the same volume, another Western feminist pointed out that since 1945, FRG (Federal Republic of Germany) law and social policy have defined women primarily as wives—legally subordinate to and economically dependent on men—secondarily as mothers, with women as individuals trailing a distant third (Ostner, 1991–1992).

### The Postunification Blues

The postunification period has produced an economic disaster that has led to an unprecedented onslaught across nearly the entire spectrum of social policy measures, with predictably negative results for women. Although interest has focused on the loss of GDR women and family policy measures and the economic impact of "shock therapy" in the East, a less dramatic but equally problematic decline has also been taking place in the West.

A few numbers help to illustrate the magnitude of the problems facing women (and men) in the former GDR, now referred to as the five new states. Although the official unemployment rate in the East continues to hover around 15%, between 1989 and 1992 the number of people in eastern Germany with actual jobs (Berufstätige/Erwerbstätige) fell from 8.54 million to 2.92 million (Winkler, 1990b; Statistisches Jahrbuch, 1993). By June 1994, the rest had been shunted into early retirement, retraining, or temporary job creation programs (ABM), were working involuntary short-time, had migrated to West Germany, were commuting to work in West Germany, or were officially unemployed. Women's share of employment had fallen from 49% to 43% whereas their share of the unemployed had risen to 67%. The female unemployment rate at 21% was a little more than double that of men ("East Germany," 1994). West German total unemployment was 9% in January 1994, with a female rate roughly 50% higher than men ("Skirmishes," 1994, p. 50).

These changes have been exacerbated by the loss of guaranteed full-day day care and after-school care, which have shifted women rapidly toward the West German model in which social expectation and government policy as well as tax, pension, labor, and family law strongly favor single-earner families and stay-at-home mothers (Rosenberg, 1991). Even West German liberals who accept the participation of women in the public sphere advocate the serial rather than simultaneous practice of work and motherhood (called the three-phase model), supporting generous parental leave followed by (often illusory) reentry into the labor market (Berghahn & Fritzsche, 1991; Helwig, 1987).

Almost twice as many women worked outside the home in the former GDR (91%) as in the FRG (55%) (Statistisches Bundesamt, 1990; Winkler, 1990a). In terms of family earnings, East German women contributed an average of 40% of total household income, whereas West German women's contribution was only 18% (Gornig, Schwarze, & Steinhoefel, 1990; Winkler, 1990a). This disparity in economic contribution is also reflected in women's differential bargaining power within the household, men's contribution to housework and child care, and less measurable considerations, such as women's sense of self-worth (Meyer & Schulze, 1992).

Another factor to be considered in comparing women's experience in the East and West German systems are the effects of labor market and child-care policies as expressed in women's childbearing decisions. Although neither German state has achieved simple reproduction (births = deaths) since 1972, the West German rate of 10.5/1,000 is among the lowest in the world. The East German rate, previously 12.9, has fallen by over 50% since unification (Eberstadt, 1994; Statistisches Bundesamt, 1992; Winkler, 1990a). The higher birthrate in the GDR was not a result of women having more children, but can be attributed to a far higher proportion of women having children. Whereas 90% of the women in the GDR had at least one child, the comparable figure for the Federal Republic is only 74%. An even more striking difference between the two systems is the incidence of unmarried motherhood. The mothers of slightly more than one third (35%) of all children born in the GDR were unmarried; the parallel figure for the Federal Republic is 10.2% (Duggan, 1993; Winkler, 1990b).

The sudden shift to the West German family model has increased the burden of reproductive labor within the family on women in the former GDR. Mass unemployment and poor prospects of finding new employment have at the same time increased their need for and financial dependence on an employed partner, weakening their position within the family. The loss of day care and after-school care has meant both more child care within the family and the need to provide extensive after-school homework supervision, if their children are to succeed in the Western model school system (Enders-Dragässer, 1991). The loss of school and factory hot midday meals has meant more shopping and more food preparation within the home. Finally, care of the sick, elderly, and the handicapped, which was largely provided by social institutions in the GDR, has been privatized. Over 80% of elderly relatives are cared for in the home in West Germany, primarily by daughters or daughters-in-law. Federal law stipulates that first-degree relatives (parents, children, siblings) are directly financially responsible for each other in the first instance (*Familienhaftung*), making state welfare payments contingent upon family, rather than individual means testing (Meyer & Schulze, 1992).

Eastern German women have thus been moved from a system in which a wide array of forms of reproductive labor had been socialized into one in which they have remained privatized within the family and located within the home, at a time when West German social support measures are being drastically reduced. The *Standort Deutschland* structural reform package passed on December 21, 1993 limited or reduced welfare benefits, unemployment insurance, and supplementary jobless benefits, subjected supplementary benefits to means testing (excluding women with an employed spouse), reduced child-welfare payments, increased health care copayments, and reduced public pensions (*Bundesgesetzblatt*, 1994; "Vermittlungsausschuß," 1993).

## FEMINIST RESPONSES TO THE DE-PRIVILEGING OF WOMEN

The protests of feminists and women's organizations against the massive removal of women from the labor force and the relocation of reproductive labor in the home have been almost totally ineffective. The failure of feminists, East or West, to pressure the federal government into taking measures to confront blatant gender discrimination in the process of restructuring East German industry and infrastructure, or even prevent its active collusion in the relegation of women to their traditional position of economic and social dependency, has a number of causes. First and probably primary is the fact that feminists and other advocates of women's emancipation or equality between the sexes represent a small minority and enjoy little popular political support in either eastern or western Germany. An inability or unwillingness to communicate across class, gender, ethnic, or ideological boundaries has effectively prevented the development of broader interest or cooperation.

## A Short History of Second-Wave German Feminism

The postwar West German feminist movement grew out of the student movement of 1968 in a break motivated by the failure of attempts to integrate women's issues into the radical left political agenda. The first and only major political mobilization undertaken by the West German women's movement was the (unsuccessful) campaign to legalize abortion in the early 1970s. Frustrated again by this lesson in the limits of democratic consensus in the face of entrenched conservative resistence, the West German feminist movement fractured into "liberal" and "autonomous" factions (Nelles, 1991–1992). The autonomous feminists rejected "mainstream" politics and withdrew from national and state-level politics, abandoning women's issues at the policy level to nonfeminist parties like the Greens or the Social Democrats (SPD). The autonomous women's movement is made up of small, independent, issue-oriented groups at the grass roots, which have confined themselves to local politics and small projects such as safe houses, cafes, bookstores, and study groups, although some informal networks have developed. In another split, feminist intellectuals withdrew from the practice-oriented groups, some electing to remain within the universities, whereas others insisted that feminist theory and education could only be developed outside of male-dominated institutions in independent or parallel structures (Allen, 1994).

The autonomous movement, including many feminist intellectuals, also emphasized feminist separatism, banning men from its organizations, meeting places, and projects (Kulawik, 1991–1992). According to most observers, separatism is a core value of autonomous feminism and the signal of its distinction from mainstream or liberal feminism. The autonomous feminists' preferred strategy of establishing projects run by women for women does not actually make women independent, because virtually all autonomous projects rely on some form of public funding and thus require official approval (Ferree, 1991-1992; Gerhard, 1992). The rejection of cross-gender cooperation is still a central characteristic of the autonomous movement, and it remains a significant limitation of the sphere of autonomous feminist action as well as a source of friction in East–West contacts (Diemer, 1992). Because East German (along with most other Eastern European) women tend to identify themselves first as "people" and only secondarily as "women," they tend to feel themselves discriminated against as East Germans rather than specifically as women, and many regard men as potential allies and partners (Schenk & Schindler, 1993; Streit, 1991–1992). The Western feminist insistence on banning men from their meetings led, on several occasions in 1990 and 1991, to East German women walking out in solidarity with their male colleagues—after being ridiculed by the Western feminists for having brought them along (author's observation).

The mainstream or liberal feminists meanwhile worked their way up through the existing infrastructure of the political parties, trade unions, and administrative bureaucracies with mixed success. One result has been a significant increase in women in the *Bundestag*, currently 21.6% (Riding, 1993), some of them in high-visibility public positions such as Rita Süssmuth (Christian Democratic Union—CDU), President of the *Bundestag*, or Monika Wulf-Matthies, former President of the Public Employees Union (ÖTV). On the other hand, the increased visibility of women in politics has not led to a parallel increase in the presence of women in positions of authority in the private sector: Only 5.9% of middle- or higher level personnel are women. In 1993, the managing boards of Germany's 626 largest companies included 2,286 men and 12 women (Protzman, 1993). Public sector institutions show equal reluctance to promote women. In 1990, women held 2.3% of professorships and 5% of nontenured teaching positions in West German universities (Meyer-Renschhausen, 1990). Finally, despite women's increased presence within political bodies and the adoption of modified feminist agenda items into mainstream political party programs, comparatively little progressive legislation has resulted (Kulawik, 1991–1992). In fact, Turgeon (1989) argued that improvements in West German women's policy and family policy prior to 1989 are more directly attributable to the competitive pressure of East German social policy initiatives than to West German feminist activism. Although both caucuses and informal networks exist, there are no institutional structures supporting cooperation between the various party, union, private-sector- or civil-service-based mainstream feminists, and contacts between mainstream and autonomous feminists have remained sporadic and not infrequently hostile.

The reasons for the retreat of the West German feminist movement from the political arena are complex. Among the factors to be considered is the role played by the wave of internal anti-Communism in response to fear of East German infiltration in the process of the gradual normalization of relations. Although the professional bans resulting from the 1972 Degree Against Radicals led to only a small number of leftists being removed from the civil service or prevented from exercising their professions, the surveillance and political evaluation of over 3 million students had a distinctly chilling effect on political activism (Allen, 1994; Braunthal, 1990). The wave of hysteria provoked in the mid-1970s by the RAF (Red Army Faction), a small terrorist group, several of whose leaders were women previously active in the student and peace movements (e.g., Ulrike Meinhof, Gudrun Ensslin), exacerbated an already tense situation.

By the late 1970s, the political radicalism that had accompanied the student movement had been effectively suppressed and, except for a very small minority of feminists (Nienhaus, Haug), the socialist feminist approaches deriving from such role models as Rosa Luxemburg or Alexandra Kollontai, which remained vital in England, France, or Italy, had faded as a legitimate subject of West German academic or political discourse. Thus, radical feminism quickly separated from feminist radicalism.

The leaders of the German bourgeois women's movement in the early 20th century, Lily Braun or Gertrud Bäumer, for example, were also problematic role models. Many of their programs, such as the separation of spheres or the professionalization of household management, had been adopted by the Nazi women's organizations that followed (and, in Baümer's case, coopted) them. As a result, the West German feminist movement's search for historical continuity has been seriously hampered by the postwar generations' difficulty in dealing with their mothers' lives in Nazi Germany. The mid-1980s rush of feminist research on daily life under fascism almost invariably portrayed the older generation in the role of passive victims or heroic resistors (Bock, 1986; Szepanski, 1983, 1986). A nearly complete taboo on addressing women's active participation in fascist ideology and organizations has only recently been broken ("Frauen," 1993; Gravenhorst & Taschmurat, 1990), whereas efforts by U.S. feminist historians to challenge this model (Grossman, 1991; Koonz, 1987) have been sharply attacked. Although this strategy successfully avoids the problem of women's agency in the fascist period, it offers little in the way of positive political or socially active role models for their daughters. It also fails to provide a consistent historical framework within which to locate West German feminism. The passive victim model tends to fix women exclusively within the domestic sphere, often bordering on (and sometimes actively embracing) feminist essentialism or the ideology of "motherliness" (Grossman, 1991, p. 350), conveniently sidestepping the issue of women's complicity in racism and anti-Semitism, past and present.

Taken together, these factors help to explain the striking popularity of separatism among West German feminists. Assigning primacy to a presumed polar gender opposition allows the postwar generation of West

German autonomous feminists to preserve a seamless and unchanging victim–perpetrator dichotomy between men and women. Denial of the possibility of intergender common interests today allows autonomous feminists to reject working within male-dominated structures. At one stroke, autonomous groups avoid direct political challenge to the system on which they depend for project funding, while simultaneously preserving their political purity by allowing them to escape the messy and unsatisfactory compromises of the political process.

This combination of fragmentation and withdrawal has left West German feminists unable to develop a larger coalition and thus without any vehicle for exercising concerted pressure on the political system. Gender equality receives a nod in the West German constitution, but plays the role of morally correct decoration and is not reflected in actual labor market or social policy (Maier, 1992). Existing equal opportunity law holds violators liable for neither lost earnings nor punitive damages, effectively removing any economic pressure on employers to comply. Victims entitled only to recovery of actual out-of-pocket losses have neither the means nor motivation to sue. Recently proposed legislation, which would finally forbid gender-specific job advertising and sexual harassment (but not age discrimination), mandates no monetary damages, creates no enforcement mechanism, includes no funding to monitor compliance, and applies only to federal employees ("Gesetzesentwurf," 1993; Protzman, 1993). Without effective public pressure groups to force political action, very little change can be expected in legislation, funding, or enforcement.

The "women's affairs officers" (*Frauenbeauftragte*), initiated in the early 1980s in West Germany, provide a case in point. According to Myra Marx Ferree (1991–1992):

> Their charge was usually very global and their actual budget and legal authority minimal . . . they were typically given a staff position directly reporting to the mayor or governor, but had no line of authority or ministry of their own. . . . Whether the *Frauenbeauftragte* had influence or not depended more on the quality of the working relationship she established with this official than on her formal authority. . . . (p. 55)

Much like the creation of a separate Ministry for Women (and Youth) in 1991, the women's affairs offices are largely publicity gestures, confined to symbolic recognition of "women's issues" and assigned tasks such as lobbying for better lighting in parking garages rather than anything of legal substance. Like the federal *Ausländerbeauftragte* (Office for Foreigners), they have remained ceremonial public relations efforts without any law-making or enforcement power.

The most striking example of the inability of West German feminists to successfully confront the political functionalization of women's issues is provided by the abortion debate. Initial attempts to preserve the GDR's progressive abortion law (which enshrined the legal right to fully insured abortion on demand during the first trimester) and liberalize the West German statute (under which abortion is illegal except under certain circumstances) provoked adamant resistance on the part of conservative politicians. In June 1992, a compromise law was passed by dramatic voice vote. It tied the right to first-trimester abortion to the retention of mandatory counseling and a waiting period, although promising a guaranteed "right to day care" at some point in the future to make these limitations acceptable to feminists. The CDU "liberals," led by Rita Süssmuth, thus were able to appeal to less reactionary voters whereas CDU conservatives promptly filed suit with the Constitutional Court. On May 28, 1993 the German Constitutional Court rejected the law as unconstitutional. As a result, since June 16, 1993, women in the united Germany have enjoyed more restricted reproductive rights than in either preunification state. The ruling was welcomed by Chancellor Kohl and the Catholic Church (Dempsey, 1993; Verlautbarung der Pressestelle, 1993).

### The GDR Women's Movement

In contrast to the other socialist countries of Central Europe and the Soviet Union, the upheaval in the GDR in fall 1989 quickly produced an independent women's movement. After other opposition groups such as Bündnis'90, the Greens, Democracy Now, and the Initiative for Peace and Human Rights resisted women's demands to be heard and represented on such issues as the preservation of abortion rights or a guarantee of minimum gender quotas for party leadership positions, a group of Berlin feminists, the *Fraueninitiative Lila Offensive*, issued an invitation to women's groups and projects throughout the GDR to meet in Berlin on December 3, 1989 at the *Volksbühne* theater to discuss organizing a feminist coalition. Men provided child care and the theater staff donated time and refreshments. An estimated 2,200 women attended, including journalists, writers, entertainers, academics, interested individuals, members of small discussion groups, and representatives of women's caucuses within existing parties (author, participant/observer). They voted unanimously to found the *Unabhängiger Frauenverband* (Independent Women's Association, UFV) whose representatives served on the Berlin Central Round Table, participated in the Modrow Transitional Government, and won two seats in the German Federal Parliament. Although its influence declined rapidly after formal unification took place in 1990, the UFV continues to be active on the state and local level in eastern Germany, and hold seats in the Bundestag (Hampele, 1993).

The rapid consolidation of a women's political coalition was only possible because of the relatively high level of consciousness regarding women's issues in the former GDR and the presence of the beginnings of a feminist movement, in the form of study groups, discussion circles, and women's projects, before the fall of 1989. Most GDR feminist activists date their involvement to a coalescing of small reading and discussion groups, which were unaware of each other's existence in the mid-1970s (Streit, 1991–1992). A number of peace and environmental groups formed at about the same time under the aegis of the Protestant church, although the most famous of these, "Swords into Ploughshares," had been founded in 1962 (F. Schorlemmer, personal communication, June 26, 1990). In 1982, feminist and peace activists joined in a campaign against a new conscription law obligating women to serve in the army in case of national mobilization. Petitions were circulated and meetings were held within the (somewhat reluctant) churches, and the army retreated, leaving in place a network of women's, peace, and environmental groups under the umbrella of the Protestant church (Streit, 1991–1992). This experience of successful opposition to the state apparatus clearly affected East German feminist activists' attitudes toward interinterest group and especially intergender solidarity in sharp contrast to their West German counterparts.

The Center for Interdisciplinary Research on Women (ZIF) at the Humboldt University in Berlin (East), officially opened on December 8, 1990 (author, participant/observer). It is the first—and still only—women's studies center at a university in the former GDR (Dölling, 1992). Despite its founding date, ZIF is not a direct result of the political upheaval of 1989, although those events may have helped university officials to overcome (at least temporarily) their lingering reluctance to accept women's studies as a legitimate discipline. ZIF grew out of a study group composed of women in the social sciences, cultural theory, and philosophy, which had been meeting since 1979 to discuss feminist theory and develop forms of feminist analysis that could be applied in their areas of research and teaching. After years of meeting informally, the group felt that they needed to institutionalize their work to make it "respectable" within their disciplines, and to broaden their contacts to include women with similar interests in other areas. In addition, the group members felt that a women's studies center would help students, faculty, and researchers to overcome their alienation as isolated individuals within separate departments and focus their energies on common projects, activities, and interdisciplinary discussions (Rosenberg, 1992).

Feminist discourse and research on women in the GDR took place under different conditions than in the West. "Double burden" was extensively discussed, as were the construction of gender roles and the social division of labor, but the public discussion of these issues took place primarily in literature rather than in the social sciences and in private, cultural, or educational rather than political settings. GDR scholars performed a great deal of state-funded research on women and the problems of women in society and collected comprehensive data on women. Irene Dölling (1990), a cultural theorist and cofounder of ZIF, argued this research cannot be called "feminist" because it was neither carried out from a "clearly formulated subjective research perspective" nor intended to "place women in a position to act in their own interests" (p. 2). Dölling sharply criticized this body of work even though it confirmed the disadvantaged position of women in society, arguing that it failed to provide any analysis of the causes of observed gender disparities and that the lack of a critical analytical framework ultimately influenced the interpretation of fact. Hildegard Nickel (1990), a sociologist and also a cofounder of ZIF, drew a distinction between "research on women" and "feminist research." She, too, argued that motivation and control of research, as well as content, are vital to a feminist undertaking. The data collected by the state were used by feminist scholars, but their use of them was limited to an internal discussion. Given this restricted access to or publication of certain statistical information, the subjective reflection of GDR life in fiction was frequently used by East German cultural theorists, sociologists, and political scientists (as well as their Western counterparts) as a point of reference to support analyses of women in GDR society (Mallinckrodt, 1987). It is only one of many ironies that many of the "classic" writers of West German feminism were East Germans such as Christa Wolf, Irmtraud Morgner, or Brigitte Reimann.

In addition to the interdisciplinary feminist study group to which Dölling and Nickel belonged, another Berlin circle had gathered around Hannelore Scholz. Eva Kaufmann and Sigrid Lange, professors of German literature at Humboldt and Jena University respectively, regularly taught seminars in women's literature (E. Kaufmann, personal communication, January 22, 1994). Similar groups had gradually formed at most of the universities and several of the research institutes in the GDR. Despite tightening limitations during the last decade on what could be published in the GDR, a small number of feminist scholars had access to Western feminist literature and permission to travel to Western meetings and conferences and to publish articles in Western publications. They passed their experiences on to their students in classes and seminars on women's literature and women's culture within the university system. What was lacking in the GDR was not an awareness of women's issues, which had been a focus of popular literature for at least a decade, but an explicit connection between the individual experience of gender discrimination (especially the double burden of career and family) and a systematic feminist critique, that is a causal analysis of the relationship between individual experience and social structure. This situation changed rapidly in the winter of 1989, as evidenced by the blossoming of women's publications and organizations.

## Egalitarianism Versus Individualism: The Role of Class

In the mid-1970s West German feminist theory focused on women's role in the private sphere using a relatively simple paradigm of women's oppression under an undifferentiated patriarchy (usually referring the specific structures of the bourgeois family and society), and limited itself to a primarily cultural critique (Ferree, 1990; Kulawik, 1991–1992). The main body of West German feminist analysis continues to be structurally handicapped in addressing the issues of class and race, in either theory or practice (Kreile, 1993; Töker, 1993). It has been largely deflected to the study of gender, almost exclusively in the area of cultural studies (Axeli-Knapp, 1992). Although this work is often highly sophisticated, it continues to be limited by its reduction of the "other" to an exclusively male–female polarity and its assumption that "women" constitute a coherent interest group, sharing overriding common goals. Although the analyses of the cultural construction of gender produced from the mid-1980s to the 1990s have often been both insightful and useful, only a small minority of West German feminists (e.g., Haug, Gerhard) have attempted to locate gender discrimination within a larger social framework (Gerhard, 1992).

Broader issues of difference have thus been largely ignored, perhaps out of a reluctance to confront the traces of Nazi racial theories still contained within the definition of "Germanness," as recently demonstrated in the political campaign to abolish the right of asylum. Very strong presumptions of ethnic, cultural, and class homogeneity are largely correct in a movement that is made up almost entirely of educated, middle- and upper class, White women in academic or professional circles. Although "difference" within gender as a major issue in the United States grew out of African-American and White feminists' discovery of their conflicting class and race interests in the late 1970s, difference among women in Germany has been discussed almost exclusively in reference to sexual preference and the question of cooperation or conflict between lesbian and heterosexual feminists (Allen, 1994). The problem of race has only recently been recognized in theoretical work by West German academic feminists ("Frauen," 1993; Gerhard, 1992) and recent meetings with minority women (e.g., in Frankfurt in March 1989) have served more to reveal the depth of the problem than to provide any constructive engagement (Hügel et al., 1994; Walker, 1993). Difference has had virtually no effect on party political women's caucuses, where social stratification effectively excludes lower class women and racial minorities are simply not represented.

Another consequence of the strategic retreat of autonomous feminism into grass-roots projects in the mid-1970s was its widespread depoliticization. The slogan "the personal is political," instead of exposing the highly structured connectedness of the supposedly "private sphere" to the larger political-economic context, increasingly came to mean an exclusive focus on individual rather than social relationships. This trend was reflected in the increasing number of separatist and essentialist groups and projects, which in turn tended to increase homogeneity and like-mindedness.

Even within the relatively ethnically homogeneous majority, differences of class have continued to limit the ability of West German feminists to act effectively as a political or cultural voice for German women. One difficulty is the very German problem of a sharp distinction between *Wissenschaft* (or intellectual pursuit) and *Praxis* (activism). The pressure on feminists within the academy to confine themselves to feminist theory or its analytical applications to history and literature has been intense (Werner-Hervieu, 1992). The same has been true of the academic hierarchy's reluctance to recognize women's studies as a discipline, reinforcing the need for feminist scholars to be, above all, scholarly. Even the limited attempts on the part of American academic feminists to bridge that gap appear to be largely absent in the German university context. Instead, a small number of independent or semi-independent institutes have been founded, parallel to or outside of the university structure (Allen, 1994). This problem is exacerbated by the elitism of the German universities, which remains largely unbroken, and the limited economic and class mobility within German society. Despite the removal of matriculation limits in the 1970s, in response to the student movement, the German education system (which separates schoolchildren into academic and nonacademic tracks in the fourth grade) continues to provide a very effective barrier to any real democratization of university life. The "opening" of the 1970s largely made university education accessible to students from the middle and upper middle class, with little effect on the children of lower middle- or working-class families.

Symbolic recognition that maintains actual exclusion from power exists within grass-roots advocacy groups as well. The majority of these initiatives have concentrated on ameliorating the worst ills generated by social and economic dependence rather than attempts to address root causes. Although women organizers in the grass-roots projects have contact with women from other classes or ethnic groups, these contacts take place primarily in the form of intercession or mediation on the part of higher status women in aid of lower status women. Struggling for legitimacy—and with it recognition and funding—from local government (as noted, autonomous does not mean self-supporting), the centers have tended to reproduce both dependency and social hierarchy through a client–advocate relationship, in which (educated) upper or middle-class German women "helpers" mediate on behalf of working-class or foreign "victims." In the absence of sociopolitical structures that reward outreach organizing, these contacts often take the form of "social work," an interaction that tends to reinforce, rather than break down class privilege and differential empowerment. In practice, higher class women enjoy enhanced acceptance and legitimation in the public sphere (while also assuring themselves paid employment) in their traditional role of "helper of those in distress," affirming rather than deconstructing their own place in the power and status hierarchy.

Even for native Germans, the class segregation of German society together with the German party and parliamentary systems, raise nearly insurmountable barriers to political self-representation. Obstacles to effective action range from the class-segregated educational system to such aspects of cultural capital as accent, vocabulary, dress, and behavior codes. All of these serve as status indicators and gate-keeping mechanisms excluding lower class and minority members of society from access to positions of influence within the power structure. In many cases, class indicators exclude their bearers from even being taken seriously by civil servants, again forcing them to depend on middle- and upper class mediators.

In a recent essay, Christine Thürmer-Rohr (1992) rather brutally summed up the devolution of West German feminism:

> The limitation of a women's liberation movement to a women's movement; the limitation of a women's movement to a women's project movement; the limitation of feminist politics and research to women's politics and women's research; the limitation of cooperation to those who are the same, who think the same, look the same, talk the same and live the same; limitation of an interest in change to self-development and changing oneself; limitation of the concept of experience to the experience of self; limitation of the question of collective guilt to one's own faults; limitation of the critique of patriarchy to the gender relations between white women and white men; limitation of the concept gender relations to sexual relations; limitation of understanding of dominance to the gender hierarchy and sexism; limitation of the critique of dominance to its internal cultural effects.
>
> Excluded from the critique of patriarchy are those forms of dominance which are not sexist, but racist or ethnically based and thus do not affect white women; . . . excluded are those women, who of course live in one's own milieu and are thus in no way distant or invisible, but who fall out of one's own self-definition. What has also disappeared is the overarching goal that feminist politics should contribute to the liberation of all women. (p. 15)

## Class in the East–West Context

The movement of West German feminism over the past 20 years away from its egalitarian and inclusive political goals is not unique. Susan Bassnett's (1992) observations regarding U.S. and British feminism are equally applicable in the German context:

> I would have to acknowledge the power of social stratification . . . and the way in which the cult of the individual militates against mass action. In 1970, the idea of feminist gurus was anathema; by 1975 they were identifiable and today there are classic authors and authoritative thinkers. Feminism has gone straight down the traditional patriarchal road, because British and United States society allowed for so little movement across class and economic lines. (p. 13)

The assumption that "we" are all or mostly White, middle class, and university educated has been a stumbling block for feminist organizing everywhere. Together with a widespread lack of recognition and theoretical analysis of difference it has also seriously handicapped West German feminists' attempts to understand East German women. In addition, the emphasis on consumption of style and outward appearance as the marks of prosperity and sophistication in West German society is so strong that oppositional groups, including feminists, rather than resisting the pressure toward uniformity and display have tended to respond by assuming their own distinctive "cultural identity" costumes. East German feminists, emerging from a nonconsumerist society, did not rely on these characteristic identifiers (hair color and cut, use of cosmetics, style of dress). They were thus judged by West German feminists to be dowdy, old-fashioned, and unsophisticated. One East German feminist responded, less than innocently, by asking why all the West German feminists wore purple diapers around their necks (Indian cotton gauze scarves).

Although the most visible markers in styles of consumption are rapidly disappearing, West German normative assumptions and prejudices continue to hamper communication. Here too, class—as revealed through accent and speech patterns, body language, and social custom—remains a significant barrier. A factor that has perhaps not yet been consciously considered by either the Eastern or Western participants in these encounters is that the early postwar GDR underwent a social realignment for which there is no parallel in West German society. Although the West German university system continued more or less unaffected without major reforms or changes in the professoriat or student body after 1945, the early years of the GDR educational system were characterized by significant upheaval. Many professors, along with other professionals, left the GDR voluntarily because of the changes in the political and economic system, whereas others were removed because of an involvement with fascism too active to be overlooked. Those who stayed, needed for their expertise but also frequently under attack for their politics, fought a losing battle to protect the traditional power and privileges of the German professoriat.

A more radical shift took place in the composition of the student body. Special "Workers and Farmers Faculties" (*Arbeiter und Bauernfakultäten*) were set up to quickly bring students from working-class backgrounds into the universities. This was a deliberate attempt to democratize education and to break the tradition of class elites reinforced by professional and technical training (Author collective, 1987). Although this was essentially a one-time shift, the door to higher education never completely closed to working-class students because of extensive affirmative action programs that continued to "delegate" workers and especially women to the universities. These programs, however, also frequently became a second chance for the children of intellectuals or small-business people who had failed entrance exams or had not been accepted into the college preparatory track in high school for political or ideological reasons and had taken a several-year detour through factory life before returning to a professional career path.

Despite the fact that a new intelligentsia established itself and was generally followed into the professions by its children, neither the first nor the second generation, who composed the faculties of the East German universities, the staffs of research institutes, and the professionals in government and industry before unification, were of predominantly upper class or upper middle-class background, as are their West German counterparts. This unacknowleged class component may account for a good deal of the arrogance and condescension that East German intellectuals perceive in their reception by their West German colleagues. It may also contribute to the nearly universal Western assumption that East German professionals are less sophisticated and/or less well qualified and/or earned their positions through political sycophancy rather than merit.

These differences between Eastern and Western academic feminists have been exacerbated by an even more serious barrier to cooperation: the fact that they are in direct competition with one another for limited (and in most cases shrinking) resources in both the funding for feminist research and the very small number of academic positions available to them. Given the limited representation of women, per se, in the West German academic landscape, a large pool of un- and underemployed Western feminist scholars already exists. The dominant position of West German male professors on the Organization and Appointments Committees (*Struktur und Berufungskommissionen*) restructuring the East German universities and the tendency for the most conservative West German models to be applied in this process give West German academic feminists the competitive advantage of being able to present Western credentials (Dölling, 1994). The Westerners' tendency to emphasize their professional and intellectual superiority, rather than this geographical bonus, is not calculated to endear them to their Eastern sisters.

Under these conditions of both scarcity of resources and competitive inequality, to the degree that women's studies manages to survive in the five new states, it will be dominated by West German feminists. Sabine Grünwald (1992), a philosopher and former member of the Academy of Sciences wrote: "During a short break I began to prepare my 1992 calendar. As I began copying work phone numbers from my 1991 list, I noticed that none of them were still valid, none" (p. 91).

## IN LIEU OF A CONCLUSION

I believe that the failure to decisively challenge what Ostner (1991–1992) called the "incomplete citizenship of women" (p. 87) in West German society derives at least in part from Western feminist acceptance of the liberal individualist model of social interaction, as illustrated by the abortion rights campaign. Extending the definition of individual freedom to include the moral and philosophical position that whether or not a pregnancy should be carried to term is a fundamentally private decision that ultimately can be made only by the woman herself is defensible both philosophically and as a political tactic. However, the same line of reasoning applied consistently leads to the conclusion that the decision to bear a child (as well as the decision not to bear one) is a private matter. Within this logical framework the freedom to choose cannot be divided into a private matter from conception to birth (or some arbitrary point in between) and a public responsibility thereafter. Thus, this line of reasoning ultimately places the entire responsibility for children on the mother—because physical reproduction is not viewed as a social process. In the East, this question had long since been resolved, with childbearing defined as a private choice whereas the resulting children were recognized as a shared social responsibility. Unfortunately, although Western feminists have questioned the exclusive responsibility of the mother, arguing instead for the equal responsibility of both parents for their offspring, they have not effectively or even specifically confronted the fundamental issue of whether children are an exclusively private or a social good.

As a result, the common dogma that small children belong in the home under the care of their birth mother (or, if their birth mother happens to have the resources, under the care of another, usually lower class woman paid to replace her) is still widely accepted in the West. The extended maternity leaves introduced as a pronatalist measure in both German states served to reinforce traditional gender roles and reassert the family as the principal point of social attachment for women. In socially and gender role conservative West Germany, maternity leave is a form of state intervention that, ceteris paribus, reinforces the bourgeois family by fixing children in the home and removing middle-class women from the public sphere, but forces working-class women to return to the labor force by providing only token payments. In contrast, salary replacement maternity leave combined with day care (a form of state intervention that allows women to leave the private sphere and become at least to some degree economically independent) characterized the egalitarian East.

> Why is it, asked ... a Nuremberg feminist, that so many of your women have children, despite free abortion and economic independence? That is an interesting question. It revealed in a nutshell totally different value structures. That a child is only a social blemish, financial burden, and self-catapult out of the life of society has to be explained. That is can also have something to do with love, with unique experience ... The woman from the East remained silent about it on that evening, we had already heard the term "ideology of motherhood." (Nguyen, 1991, p. 37)

A further result of the failure to challenge West German policymakers' underlying assumption that reproduction is a private rather than a social process is that the issue of equal access to the public sphere for women has also been essentially cast as a matter of individual choice. Women who choose to enter the public sphere must also be prepared to adjust to the demands and existing structures of that sphere. Women who choose to have children have thus chosen not to enter the public sphere unless they have the resources to replace themselves in their, by definition, primary responsibility to their children and families. West German law excludes the mothers of small children from unemployment benefits, job referrals, or state job programs unless they can prove that they have day care (Berghahn & Fritzsche, 1991).

Thus the vital issue of the *preconditions* for equal access to the public sphere for women—publicly supported day care and after-school care as well as equal education and nondiscriminatory hiring—which rest on the acceptance of at least a partial social responsibility for social reproduction, have become peripheral rather than central to the discussion of equality. In addition both the institutions and the structural characteristics of the Western labor market and the bourgeois family are too frequently assumed to be immutable:

> The (West) German welfare regime produces its winners and losers. Women winners are those who manage to get married to a steadily employed man, have a happy marriage, and who are content with this trajectory. That kind of life does not represent total dependency. In a capitalist society, staying at home and living on a husband's income incorporates the possibility of restricted independence via personal dependence. (Ostner, 1991–1992, p. 89)

In contrast, many East German feminists (e.g., Dölling, Nickel, Röth) base their critique of the social and cultural expressions of gender (and gender discrimination) on an analysis of the economic and political structures that reflect, support, or depend on gender distinctions. Their analysis does not deny the interrelationships and dependencies between these spheres, but provides a structural framework within which to discuss cause, effect, and interaction. With the removal of external (censorship) limits, the East German feminist approach, far from being hostile to Western gender theory, is quite open to its insights. However, it has no reason to abandon its own analytical orientation toward placing cultural constructs within a political and economic framework. The partial socialization and partial valorization of reproductive labor in the GDR combined with the partial recognition of the role of reproductive labor in the economy remain fundamental and significant differences between the experience of women in the two systems and the approaches of feminists to the problems of equality and emancipation.

Sigrid Lange (1992) described the impact of this disjuncture in the collapse of the East German women's movement in the spring of 1990:

> The women activists obviously intended to solve women's problems, which are actually social problems which had been pushed into the private sphere, on the societal level. They understood the ability to combine motherhood and career, the difficulty of achieving a partnership beyond traditional gender roles, the possibility to live as a single mother, etc. as political questions. However, under the conditions of the Federal Republic, coping with this type of difficulty must appear to be an individual, private problem. (p. 315)

## Some Suggestions for the Future

The previous discussion presents some of the differences in what is broadly defined as culture, the interplay of historical, economic, social, and analytical experiences that continue to separate East and West Germans (feminists or otherwise), and out of which misunderstandings arise. For any constructive dialogue to take place, both Eastern and Western feminists must first produce a much clearer and more nuanced understanding of the complex mixture of emancipatory and conservative gender expectations and identities that developed in the old Soviet-type systems under a set of policies that tended both to expand and reinforce traditional gender roles. A better grasp of actual gender conditions, as well as the recognition that Eastern women had no way of anticipating the less visible aspects of gender inequality in the West, help to make women's initial political responses more comprehensible. Unless this work is to be performed exclusively by Eastern feminists, it will require that Western German feminists overcome their reluctance to examine the practice of the GDR socialist system seriously and that Eastern feminists begin to analyze their experience from a comparative perspective, rather than solely in terms of the GDR's failure to implement its declared socialist goals.

Unfortunately, most of the Western feminist work on women in the former GDR reviewed for this chapter, although focused on Eastern women's experience, continues to exhibit a strikingly normative stance. It is both fascinating and slightly horrifying to see Western feminists who in the past criticized West German policy on women and the family, now defending its practices as reasonable and based on sound economic principles. An article describing interviews conducted with working-class women in the former GDR reads more like a polemic than a sociological study. The author interrupted, corrected, judged, and evaluated her respondents, characterizing several women's belief that the state should provide working mothers with affordable child care as "an indefensible position, since the provision of child care serves as a prime example of the GDR implementing a policy that it could not actually afford" (Beer, 1993, p. 6), an assertion unsupported by any economic evidence. Here, the discussion of the complex of issues arising out of the conflict between childbearing and labor force participation is further confused by a tendency to define as economic in origin structural limitations that many feminists regard as political (Beer, 1993; Maier, 1992).

In another article, the author characterized the different social experience of Eastern women as "lack of social experience," criticized the UFV for "clinging to the notion that common interests exist not only among women but between (leftist) men and women," and proposed that in return for Western women making an effort to understand what Eastern women have lost, "east women could try to refrain from stabbing the West German women's movement in the back too intensely (*nicht allzu massiv in den Rücken zu fallen*)" (Diemer, 1992, pp. 357, 360, 361).

Second, initial attempts at East–West feminist cooperation were doomed by the Western feminist assumption of a common agenda based exclusively on West-defined goals and experience. Eastern insistence upon the primacy of economic issues was dismissed as "not our problem," exposing not only a lack of Western solidarity but a distressing lack of awareness of the structural economic discrimination against women in West German society. This failure can only be addressed by broadening the field of Western vision and action to encompass a common response to discriminatory conditions that are indeed a common problem.

In 1989, East German feminists were eager to learn from the practical experience of their West German counterparts and to acquire skills they were unable to acquire under the former regime. West German feminists, coming from an established women's movement, tended to assume a much lower level of feminist consciousness and sophistication in the GDR than in the West. Although aware of their economic roles, they were generally ignorant of GDR women's relative legal and social independence. GDR feminist activists perceived this attitude as arrogant and as a typically Western attempt to dominate joint projects. In addition, Western feminist reliance on the ideology of individualism has led to strategies concentrated on opening spaces within the existing power hierarchy for a few women, and on attacking the gender definitions and prejudices that keep women out rather than the hierarchy as such. Viewed from a more egalitarian perspective, this approach seems elitist, short-sighted, and, in a climate of structural discrimination against East Germans, self-serving.

As Petra Streit (1991–1992) put it: "GDR women never got around to expressing the contradictions in their history while West German women forget they live in a sick society whose fundamental values they carry around with them in their thinking and behavior" (p. 14). Future cooperation between Eastern and Western women will demand that Western German feminists be willing to reexamine their own status within Western society self-critically, and perhaps endanger their own position of comparative advantage by recognizing and addressing structural root causes that they have in the past preferred not to confront. Eastern German feminists would have to avoid either vilifying or waxing nostalgic about the GDR past. Both Easterners and Westerners would have to confront and reject their stereotypes of one another. Finally, feminist theory would have to become flexible enough to accomodate political economy as well as gender theory, and feminist organizing would have to become broad-based enough to speak across class and ethnic boundaries to the needs of a far larger subset of German women.

If Eastern or Western German feminists are to have any positive effect on the situation of women in the transition process, they must confront the practical and theoretical issues that still divide them. Even given a united and well-organized women's movement, current conditions do not provide a warm climate for the self-determination or economic independence of German women.

## ACKNOWLEDGMENTS

The research reported here was conducted with the support of the American Council of Learned Societies/Social Science Research Council, the Council for the International Exchange of Scholars (CIES)—Fulbright, the German Academic Exchange Service (DAAD), and the International Research and Exchanges Board (IREX). None of these organizations is responsible for the views expressed. I would also like to thank Eva Kaufmann for her critique and support.

## REFERENCES

Allen, A. (1994). Women's studies as cultural movement and academic discipline in the United States and West Germany: The early phase, 1966–82. *Women in German Yearbook, 9*, 1–24.

Author collective. (1987). *Das Bildungswesen in der DDR*. Berlin: Akademie Verlag.

Axeli-Knapp, G. (1992). Machtanalyse in Zwischenzeiten. In C. Kulke, H. Kopp-Degethoff, & U. Ramming (Eds.), *Wider das Schlichte Vergessen* (pp. 205–215). Berlin: Orlanda Frauenverlag.

Bassnett, S. (1992). Crossing cultural boundaries, or how I became an expert on East European women overnight. *Women's Studies International Forum, 15*(1), 11–15.

Beer, U. (1993, August). *Coping with a new reality: Barriers and possibilities for East German women*. Paper presented at the Conference on Feminist Economics, Washington, DC.

Berghahn, S., & Fritzsche, A. (1991). *Frauenrecht in Ost und West Deutschland*. Berlin: Basisdruck.

Bock, G. (1986). *Zwangssterilizierung in Nationalsozialismus*. Opladen: Leske + Budrich.

Braunthal, G. (1990). *Political loyalty & public service in West Germany*. Amherst: University of Massachusetts Press.

Browning, C. (1992). *Ordinary men. Reserve police battalion 101 and the final solution in Poland*. New York: Harper.

*Bundesgesetzblatt*. (1994, February 9). Nr. 6, Teil I, Z5702 A.

Dempsey, J. (1993, May 29–30). Fury as Germany ends east's abortion on demand. *Financial Times*, p. 24.

Diemer, S. (1992). Die Mauer zwischen uns wird immer größer—Anmerkungen zur DDR-Frauenbewegung im Umbruch. In G. Meyer, G. Riegel, & D. Strützel (Eds.), *Lebensweise und gesellschaftlicher Umbruch in Ostdeutschland* (pp. 343–364). Jena: Palm & Enke.

Dölling, I. (1990). Situation und Perspektiven von Frauen-forschung in der DDR. *ZIF Bulletin, 1*(1), 1–2.

Dölling, I. (1994). On the development of women's studies in Eastern Germany. *SIGNS. A Journal of Women in Society and Culture, 19*(3), 739–752.

Duggan, L. (1993). *Production and reproduction: Family policy and gender inequality in East and West Germany*. Unpublished doctoral dissertation, University of Massachusetts, Amherst.

East Germany: Labour market developments and policies in the new German Länder. (1994, December). In *Employment Observatory*, No. 13. Brussels: Commission of the European Communities.

Eberstadt, N. (1994). Demographic shocks in Eastern Germany, 1989–93. *Europe–Asia Studies, 46*, 519–533.

Enders-Dragässer, U. (1991). Child care: Love, work and exploitation. *Women's Studies International Forum, 14*(6), 551–554.

Ferree, M. M. (1990). Gleichheit und Autonomie: Probleme feministischer Politik. In U. Gerhard et al. (Eds.), *Differenz und Gleichheit: Menschenrechte haben (k)ein Geschlecht* (pp. 283–298). Frankfurt/Main: Ulrike Helmer Verlag.

Ferree, M. M. (1991–1992). Institutionalizing gender equality: Feminist politics and equality offices. *German Politics and Society, 24/25*, 53–66.

Frauen gegen Antisemitismus. (1993). Der Nationalsozialismus als Extremform des Patriarchats. Zur Leugnung der Täterschaft von Frauen und zur Tabuisierung des Antisemitismus in der Auseinandersetzung mit dem NS. *Beiträge zur feministischen theorie und praxis*, (35), 77–90.

Gerhard, U. (1991–1992). German women and the social costs of unification. *German Politics and Society*, (24/25), 16–33.

Gerhard, U. (1992). German women's studies and the women's movement: A portrait of themes. *Women's Studies Quarterly, XX*(3–4), 98–111.

Gesetzentwurf der Bundesregierung. (1993, July 21). *Entwurf eines Gesetzes zur Durchsetzung der Gleichberechtigung von Frauen und Männern* [Zweites Gleichberechtigungsgesetz - @.GleiBG]. Drucksache 12/5468.

Gornig, M., Schwarze, J., & Steinhoefel, M. (1990, May 10). Erwerbsbeteiligung und Einkommen von Frauen in der DDR. *DIW Wochenbericht*, pp. 263–267.

Gravenhorst, L., & Tatschmurat, C. (Eds.). (1990). *Töchterfragen. NS-Frauengeschichte.* Freiburg: Kore.

Grossmann, A. (1991). Feminist debates about women and national socialism. *Gender & History, 3*(3), 350–358.

Grünwald, S. (1992). Großer Anlauf—Und nun? In C. Kulke, H. Kopp-Degethoff, & U. Ramming (Eds.), *Wider das schlichte Vergessen* (pp. 87–91). Berlin: Orlanda.

Hampele, A. (1993). The organized women's movement in the collapse of the GDR: The independent women's association (UFV). In N. Funk & M. Mueller (Eds.), *Gender politics and post-communism* (pp. 180–193). New York: Routledge.

Helwig, G. (1987). *Frau und Familie—Bundesrepublik Deutschland—DDR.* Berlin: Landeszentrale für politische Bildung.

Hügel, I., et al. (Eds.). (1994). *Entfernte Verbindungen. Rassismus, Antisemitismus, Klassenunterdrückung.* Berlin: Orlanda Frauenverlag.

Koonz, C. (1987). *Mothers in the fatherland. Women, the family and Nazi politics.* New York: St. Martin's Press.

Kreile, R. (1993). EMMA und die "deutschen Frauen." *Beiträge zur feministischen theorie und praxis,* (35), 123–130.

Kulawik, T. (1991–1992). Autonomous mothers? West German feminism reconsidered. *German Politics and Society,* (24/25), 67–86.

Lange, S. (1992). Frauen aus der DDR im vereinigten Deutschland. In G. Meyer, G. Riegel, & D. Strützel (Eds.), *Lebensweise und gesellschaftlicher Umbruch in Ostdeutschland* (pp. 309–322). Erlangen: Palm & Enke.

Maier, F. (1992). Geschlechterverhältnisse der DDR im Umbruch—Zur Bedeutung von Arbeitsmarkt und Sozialpolitik. *Zeitschrift für Sozialreform.* Doppelheft der Jahrestagung 1991 des Sektion Sozialpolitik der DAS.

Mallinckrodt, A. (1987). *The environmental dialogue in the GDR.* Lanham: University Press of America.

Marody, M. (1992). *Why I am not a feminist. Some remarks on the problem of gender identity in the USA and Poland.* Unpublished manuscript.

Meyer, S., & Schulze, E. (1992). Wendezeit—Familienzeit. Veränderungen der Situation von Frauen und Familien in den neuen Bundesländern. *IFG: Frauenforschung,* (3), 45–57.

Meyer-Renschhausen, E. (1990). Feminist research at German universities? Nearly impossible! Taking stock after ten years. *Critical Sociology, 17*(3), 60–73.

Müller, I. (1987). *Furchtbare Juristen. Die unbewältigte Vergangenheit unserer Justiz.* München: Kindler.

Nelles, U. (1991–1992). Abortion, the special case: A constitutional perspective. *German Politics and Society,* (24/25), 111–121.

Nguyen, A. (1991). Kein Einigland von Schwestern. *Ypsilon, 1*(4), 37.

Nickel, H. M. (1990). Frauen in der DDR. *Aus Politik und Zeitgeschichte. Beilage zur Wochenzeitung Das Parlament, B16–17/90,* 41–42.

Ostner, I. (1991–1992). Ideas, institutions, traditions—West German women's experience 1945–1990. *German Politics and Society,* (24/25), 87–99.

Pickel, A. (1992). Jump-starting a market economy: A critique of the radical strategy for economic reform in light of the East German experience. *Studies in Comparative Communism, XXV*(2), 177–191.

Protzman, F. (1993, October 17). In Germany, the ceiling's not glass, it's concrete. *New York Times*, p. D16.

Riding, A. (1993, December 31). Frenchwomen say it's time to be "A bit utopian." *New York Times*, p. A4.

Rosenberg, D. (1991). Shock therapy: GDR women in transition from a socialist welfare state to a social market economy. *SIGNS, 17*(1), 129–151.

Rosenberg, D. (1992). Women's issues, women's politics, and women's studies in the former German Democratic Republic. *Radical History Review*, (54), 110–126.

Schenk, C., & Schindler, C. (1993). Frauenbewegung in Ostdeutschland—Eine kleine Einführung. *Beiträge zur feministischen theorie und praxis*, (35), 131–146.

Skirmishes. (1994, February 12). *The Economist*, p. 50.

Statistisches Bundesamt (Ed.). (1990). *Datenreport 1989. Zahlen und Fakten über die Bundesrepublik Deutschland*. Bonn: Bundeszentrale für politische Bildung.

Statistisches Bundesamt (Ed.). (1993). *Datenreport 1992. Zahlen und Fakten über die Bundesrepublik Deutschland*. Bonn: Bundeszentrale für politische Bildung.

*Statistisches Jahrbuch*. (1990). Bonn: Statistisches Bundesamt.

Streit, P. (1991–1992). Raising consciousness. *German Politics and Society*, (24/25), 10–15.

Szepanski, G. (1983). *Frauen leisten Widerstand*. Frankfurt/Main: Fischer.

Szepanski, G. (1986). *Blitzmädel, Heldenmutter, Kriegerwitwe*. Frankfurt/Main: Fischer.

Thürmer-Rohr, C. (1992, June 26). Die Apartheid des Feminismus. *Freitag*, (27), 15.

Töker, A. (1993). Eurozentristisches Feindbild oder Kritik am Islam? *Beiträge zur feministischen theorie und praxis*, (35), 115–122.

Turgeon, L. (1989). *State and discrimination: The other sides of the cold war*. Armonk, NY: Sharp.

*Verlautbarung der Pressestelle des Bundesverfassungsgerichtes, Nr. 18/93*. (1993). Bonn: Bundesverfassungs-gericht.

Vermittlungsausschuß erzielt Kompromiß bei den Spargesetzen zur Haushaltssanierung. (1993, December 10). *Deutschland Nachrichten*, p. 4.

Walker, B. (1993). Ohne Titel: Redebeitrag zum Thema "Alltäglicher Rassismus." *Beiträge zur feministischen theorie und praxis*, (35), 91–96.

Werner-Hervieu, G. (1992). Women's studies and feminist research in the Federal Republic of Germany and Berlin (West). *Women's Studies Quarterly, XX*(3&4), 85–97.

Winkler, G. (Ed.). (1990a). *Frauenreport '90*. Berlin: Verlag Die Wirtschaft.

Winkler, G. (Ed.). (1990b). *Sozialreport '90. Daten und Fakten zur sozialen Lage in der DDR*. Berlin: Verlag Die Wirtschaft.

III

# HUNGARY: RESTRUCTURING A SOCIETY AND ITS ECONOMY

Fred L. Casmir

Following the collapse of the Berlin Wall and the unexpected demise of one Communist government in Eastern Europe after another, the resulting euphoria resulted in two serious miscalculations. First of all, it was assumed that after 40 or more years of dictatorial rule, East Europeans would gladly embrace democracy as the guarantor of a meaningful, safe, and happy future. What was overlooked in that reasoning is the fact that the United States had been able to build its own version of democracy on many years of British history, political thought, and experience. When our forefathers decided to build a new nation they were, of course, not immune from often very negative reactions to the proposed form of democratic government. Indeed arguments continued for some time, and still do after more than 200 years, as to what that democracy should be like. Even the possibility of setting up a kingdom was considered in the early days of the U.S.-American republic. It was thus very naive to assume that the countries of Eastern Europe, few with any democratic experience in their history, would face an easy transition from authoritarianism to democracy. What happened is strongly reminiscent of an event recorded in the Old Testament following the people of Israel's flight from Egypt. As soon as the hardships of slavery were left behind and new challenges faced the Jewish people as they tried to make their way through an unknown desert to freedom, the lack of material security and whatever little comfort they had known in the land of Egypt caused them to rebel against Moses' leadership. That syndrome is now well known in Eastern European countries. Leaving behind fear and oppression was one thing; having to face competition, lack of jobs, rapid inflation, and lawlessness was something for which none of the people were prepared.

Coupled with unrealistic expectations in Western countries about easy political transformations was the belief that the answer to the economic problems faced by Eastern European countries was a rapid transformation from a socialistic to a free-market economy. Never having faced such a challenge before, because their own economies had developed step by step over many decades, and unwilling to admit that they had never achieved a totally free-market economy themselves, Western advisers and experts looked for almost instant transformations and success in Eastern European countries as proof of their economic theories.

The results have frequently been bitterly disappointing for all those involved. Western economists and marketing experts found themselves frustrated and personally challenged by their failure to produce rapid change. In some cases they had to face the reality that Eastern Europeans saw value in certain aspects of the socialistic systems they had known, but that Western experts had rejected out of hand. In other cases, they had to face the fact that the economic deterioration in many Eastern European countries was so severe that the very social fabric was threatened and unraveling. Coupled with internal intercultural conflicts in most of the Eastern European countries, and the relentless bombardment with poorly understood concepts and images via the mass media, people began to long once again for the "fleshpots of Egypt" and a feeling of security, at almost any cost.

Outside of developments in Germany, no country appeared to provide better opportunities for providing proof of the superiority of the free-market economy and of democracy than Hungary. Only gradually, as Americans and representatives of Western countries began, firsthand, to learn and understand more about the Hungarian people, their history, and their current struggles, did a more meaningful picture begin to emerge. Although it is impossible in one volume to consider *all* of the interrelated challenges and opportunities Hungary faced, the following chapters provide some insights. By the same token, it needs to be understood that what we learn about Hungary in the chapters by McKinley and by Rohde and Pellicaan has in many cases much broader applicability, and that these insights can serve as a useful means for comparison and contrast to what has happened in other Eastern European countries.

McKinley's work as teacher, or intercultural trainer, is representative of efforts by numerous individuals who are trying to lay foundations for the bridges that must be built between cultures and people. What appears like a relatively simple and straightforward task, based on the *learning* of English as the contemporary language of commerce, soon can become an exercise in frustration as both teachers and students begin to understand that much more is involved than a vocabulary and a syntax. McKinley's insights into how and why people *make sense* of words, and the situations in which they are used, thus is very significant as part of one major purpose of this volume, namely the development of a better understanding of the roles language and communication play in inter- or cross-cultural interactions. Rohde and Pellicaan, two Dutch scholars who have extensively interacted with Hungarians in media and business environments, take us into the world of advertising in Hungary. These authors help us to understand a number of very practical applications in today's Hungarian market-oriented economy, related to the challenges McKinley faced with her students and in her classrooms. Considering some of the most relevant historical developments, today's challenges in Hungary must be understood against the backdrop of images, illusions, hopes, and realities that form the basis for the reactions Hungarians have as they are almost overwhelmed by strange, *new* media messages, which many of them can evaluate only on the basis of the specific preparation their own culture and history has provided.

# 5

# *Hungarian Culture in Communication*

Mary M. McKinley
*The Union Institute*

As a visiting professor at Harvard University in 1981, the Polish author Stanislaw Baranczak (1990) responded to an American colleague's question about whether it was as difficult to find an inexpensive apartment in Warsaw as it was in Boston. His reply, in perfect English, covered the entire process of paying the housing cooperative a lot of cash up front, waiting 12–15 years and, if the regulations haven't changed in the meantime, becoming the proud owner of a place to live. He later says,

> At that very same moment, I was struck by the sudden realization that what I had been saying, perfectly logical as it would have been in Polish, made no sense in English. I had been using the right words and expressions but each of them had somehow missed the point. The coercive state-owned institution whose Polish name I had translated as "housing cooperative" had nothing to do with whatever a "housing cooperative" might mean in America. The posh associations and immediate availability of the American "condominium" had nothing to do with the drab cubicle of concrete that a Pole is lucky to obtain the keys to in his middle age, years after he paid hard-earned money for it. Even the verb "to own," though again a formal equivalent of its Polish counterpart, referred to two distinctly different notions in the American and the Polish contexts. Inadvertently, indeed with the best of intentions, instead of communicating some truth I had created a false image of reality. (p. 222)

With perfect clarity Baranczak has described the problem of communicating across and between cultures, the "million subtle ways in which this adopted language diverges from [one's] innate ways of naming the world or expressing [oneself]" (Baranczak, 1990, p. 222).

English has become the language of commerce throughout Europe and is often the only common language a room full of European business people share. In Central and Eastern Europe, where it tends to be the third or fourth language people know (after the mother tongue, Russian, and German), the use of English is fraught with pitfalls because for the speaker, the experience behind many of the terms is at variance with the strict dictionary definition. Even after terms are defined and people learn to use them properly, anecdotal research and case studies indicate that the concepts the words represent have not yet been internalized.

This chapter draws on my experiences while living in Hungary for three years, teaching graduate business students from 10 Eastern and Central European countries as well as Hungarian business executives. From the elderly doctor who corrected me when I referred to Hungary as part of Eastern Europe ("We are and always have been Central Europe! We are its heart!") to the young city planner who, speaking as if it were recent history instead of 996 A.D., said, "If only Arpad had gone 200 kilometers farther west, we could have been Vienna instead of poor Budapest, always being besieged and occupied by foreigners," the people and their history cannot be prised apart. History informs and shapes both their sense of self and society, and their very culture.

Throughout all of Europe, historical differences between the nations and peoples reflect sociocultural differences and contribute to some of the underlying misinterpretations. The cultural boundaries at times are much more fixed than the geographic borders. A recent study conducted among business managers from five European Community nations (Denmark, England, France, Germany, and The Netherlands) explored cultural variations in the interpretation of the communication process involved in worker participation. The study, first locating each nation on Hofstede's Four Dimensions, then using semantic network analysis to compare managers' interpretations of the key word "participation," found that, indeed, diverse meanings are attached to the word and appear to reflect cultural norms and values (Stohl, 1993). The most striking example is that of German managers who, despite the 1951 mandate of *Mitbestimmung* requiring formalized employee/employer participation on work councils, did not interpret participation as relevant to a formal–informal dimension. As Stohl concluded, "shared interpretations are the foundations on which international agreements are based. The internationalization of business, the emergence of a global community, and the reshaping of Europe all create an environment in which the development of shared interpretations is central to the process of organizing" (p. 114).

Given the difficulties encountered by the shapers of an economically united European Community (EC), whose members share a more common recent history with each other than they do with former Soviet satellite countries, it is critical that the cultures of Eastern and Central Europe be examined. Three of these countries—Hungary, Poland and the Czech Republic—have already been granted associate EC membership. If the present members have communication problems despite the hundreds of jurists and linguists employed to address them, how much rockier will the road be for these fledgling members?

## WAYS OF LOOKING AT THE PROBLEMS

There seem to be as many perspectives on culture and communication and their reciprocal influences as there are communication scholars. One of the weaknesses of the Stohl (1993) study, which she cited as a strength, is that it is based on, and appears to be congruent with, Hofstede's predictions about national cultural/behavior dimensions. Her total sample size was only 20, divided among five nations and selected for fluency in the English language, in itself a limiting factor. As Casmir has already discussed in this volume, there are some serious limitations and risks in applying Hofstede's assumptions wholesale, since such discovered congruencies are "the result of the method applied and not of factors inherent in cultures, individuals, or the situation" (see chap. 2 of this volume).

Fully half of the spring 1993 issue of the *Journal of Communication* was devoted to the symposium topic "Communication, Culture, and Identity." Although loosely organized around the homogenization of national identities or subcultures by global media, all four articles stress the importance of finding new ways of conceptualizing what cultural identity *is* before trying to fit it into current methodological frameworks for the convenience of numerical analysis.

Philip Schlesinger's (1993) "Wishful Thinking: Cultural Politics, Media and Collective Identities in Europe" questions the postmodernist propositions that "neo-tribalism" has created such weak social bonds that we can now all be "just consumers in the shopping mall of culture" (p. 8) and that the individual now exerts supremacy over the nation-state. If this were so, he argued, there would be far more tolerance for strangers, minorities, and outsiders, which is clearly not the case in fortress Europe nor in Central and Eastern Europe.

In a second article, "Latin America: Cultures in the Communication Media," Jesus-Martin Barbero (1993) made a strong case for examining culture through an historical perspective. Academics and administrators, he said, tend to define popular culture either in a romantic sense, "associating popular culture with the authentic ... either pure or contaminated," or in a modernist mode as "a backward, cheap, and degraded form of elite culture" (p. 19). He saw culture as a dynamic, rather than static, linkage between common memory, identity, and physical place.

Two Turkish scholars, Halik Sahin and Asu Aksoy (1993), explored "Global Media and Cultural Identity in Turkey." Describing Turkey as one of the "semiperipheral countries," lacking the institutional and civic mechanisms of developed democracies and the dubious protection that poverty affords Third World countries, the authors demonstrated that the introduction of commercial, global broadcasting in a policy vacuum can have devastating effects on culture and identity.

Once the former state-controlled floodgates were opened via pirate satellite TV in May 1990, the "defining tensions of the Turkish identity, such as ethnic origin, religion, language and group aspirations," were brought into the realm of public discussion (Sahin & Aksoy, 1993, p. 35). Trampled by the parade of previously taboo topics ranging from the Kurdish rebellion to homosexuality, "coherence and consistency became as outmoded as the Kemalist principles upon which the republic was founded" (p. 36).

In summing up the overall positive and negative results of the proliferation of imported television and radio broadcasts, Sahin and Aksoy (1993) concluded that it has had both a homogenizing and a particularizing effect. "Global media have played a key role, on the one hand, in breaking up the unitary national culture by feeding the so-called 'small worlds' of real Turkey into the larger world of 'imagined' Turkey. On the other hand, global media have homogenized differences and particularity across frontiers ... Turkish guest workers in Germany can tune in and become part of Turkish culture" (p. 37).

The fourth and final contribution to the symposium is, perhaps, most relevant of all. If the homogenization of cultures should be expected anywhere in the world, North America is that place. But Marjorie Ferguson's (1993) article, "Invisible Divides: Communication and Identity in Canada and the U.S.," propounds just the opposite. Despite the fact that almost 98% of English language prime-time drama is imported, there remain such strong preferences among the Canadian viewing publics for either Canadian or "country of origin" broadcasts that the "divergent philosophies, values, policies, and organizing principles exist materially and symbolically across the invisible continental divide ... in spite of, not because of the global hold of Video America popular culture" (p. 53).

These four articles, although neither analytical nor prescriptive, represent a range of geographic and conceptual problems encountered in intercultural communication and global media studies.

## A NEW RESEARCH AGENDA

Communication research can no more remain static than the social and cultural milieu it studies. Davis and Jasinski (1993) advocated a radical revision of social research mired for too long in the modernist world view. In an ongoing project, begun in 1990, they have attempted to build a new research agenda based on innovative ways of simultaneously investigating culture, defined as the "production of meaning within communities," and "negotiation of meanings between communities. It may be especially heuristic to focus on meaning-production efforts in groups that are consciously seeking to forge new identities and/or empower members to engage in meaningful action" (p. 145).

Those of us who, as contributors to this volume, are seeking ways to relate our own experiences in post-Communist Central and Eastern Europe to intercultural communication research, have agreed that the standard, microlevel analysis must be broadened to include an understanding of the historical bases for cultural diversity in the region. Davis and Jasinski (1993) concluded that:

> [R]ather than fear the consequences of cultural diversity, we need to embrace it. However, this embrace must be grounded upon understanding, not the naive hope that we will somehow get along. Peace between communities doesn't just happen because the leaders of diverse communities reach rational decisions and declare a truce. It must be created through the development of institutions that enable social capital to be negotiated. Communication research should provide the insight needed to do this work. (p. 148)

## HUNGARY TODAY

There are slightly more than 10 million people in Hungary today, 20% of them in the capital. Budapest is equidistant from Rostock on the Baltic Sea and Genoa on the Ligurian; from Moscow and the Bay of Biscay. The division of Greater Hungary after the signing of the Treaty of Trianon in 1920 reduced it to 30% of its former territory, with 58% of its population suddenly living outside its borders. Yet they are and feel themselves to be Hungarians, not Slovenians, Slovakians, Romanians, Ukrainians, and so forth. At the same time, the treaty left a diminished Hungary unique in Central Europe in that it is 97% ethnically homogeneous. Or is it? The vicissitudes of a thousand years and the expediency of changing one's ancestral origins have created an ethnic blend. With typical Magyar ironic style, a popular weekly magazine printed the following play on words, taking advantage of the fact that the word *ki* means "out" in its declarative form and also "who" in the interrogative. "*Ki, zsido! Ki, cigany! Ki, roman! Ki, bulgar! Ki, slovak! Ki, horvat! Ki, szerb! . . . Ki, Magyar?*" ("Out, Jews! Out, Gypsies! Out, Romanians! Out, Bulgarians! Out, Slovakians! Out, Croats! Out, Serbs! . . . Who is Hungarian?") (Anonymous, 1992).

There also exist generational and regional differences. Old alliances are sometimes stronger than new ones. For example, older Hungarians prefer Austria and Germany to the United States; Romanians divide themselves distinctly by whether they are Transylvanian Hungarians, Schwabian/Saxons, or "Roman" Romanians, inheritors of the glory of the Roman Empire. Within Hungary itself, folkways, religion, and language accents differ from village to village, from age group to age group, creating myriad subcultures.

Compounding the problem is the experience of the past 45 years, which created its own vocabulary and a habit of reading, speaking, and hearing between the lines, while ignoring what is being communicated directly.

## HUNGARIAN HISTORY

To some extent, Hungary is typical of other former Soviet-bloc nations. Denied self-rule for centuries at a time throughout history, they each must now make their own way into the future while trying to recapture the unique cultural histories on which they can build a sense of dignity and pride. Yet for Hungarians "the vision of a 'pure, homogeneous' society, and the overemphasis on natural cultural values are indicators of a lack of social or individual identity" (Miszlivetz, 1991, p. 797). The resurfacing of age-old conflicts, continual references to half-mythical, heroic founders, and the demonizing of minorities could hinder their successful integration into a supranational EC, despite their admission as associate members in December 1991.

### The Highest Compliment: "It's so . . . Hungarian"

The origins of the Hungarian people, the Magyar, may be somewhere in the Central Asian steppes, depending on whether the linguistic or the archeological evidence is accepted. One of the small group of Finno-Ugric peoples, the Magyar and Onogur split off at least 4,000 years ago, driven to seek new territory because of overpopulation in the region. Loosely organized into nomadic hunting and fishing clans by blood relation, the northern branches became today's Finns and Estonians. The Ugrians, including the ancestors of today's Magyars, Ostyaks, and Voguls, spread over the southeastern slopes of the Ural Mountains and into the plains and river deltas. Introduced to animal husbandry by the Persians of the Aral region, the Ugrians incorporated the horse as a sacred animal in their pagan rites. Despite further divisions and millennial separations among the various clans, the words for "horse," "saddle," "halter," and "whip" are today the same in all Ugric languages.

The Magyar tongue, with its staccato rhythm, vowel harmony, and oriental grammatical structure, has always distinguished the Magyar from their neighbors. The word *magyar* itself is derived from *mon* (speak) and *er* (man) meaning "the speakers" as opposed to everyone else who were called *nemu* or "mute." Even today, the word for German in Hungarian is *Nemet* (Hanak, 1991). The Magyar probably became known as Hungarians among foreigners because of their close association with the ancient Bulgar Onogurs, as in *Ungarn, ongroise,* and so on, who were their neighbors in the region of Bashkiria from around 500 to 800 A.D.

Driven further west by the stronger Pecheneg tribes the consolidated Magyar tribes learned about military organization from the Bulgars and, under the leadership of Arpad, conquered the Carpathian Basin between 895 and 896 A.D. They drove the Franks out of Transdanubia, the Moravians out of the northwest, and the Bulgars out of the Great Plain to the south, with frequent raids even farther west against the Bavarians, Lombards, and Germans.

But, ever susceptible to glory myths, the Magyars began to claim kinship with the Huns and descent from the great leader Attila, The Scourge of God, in the late 13th century, nearly 1,000 years after Attila's death. A court chronicler of King Ladislas IV created the entire theory, including the direct bloodline descent of the first king, Arpad, from Attila (Klaniczay, 1985). Politically, this justified Arpad's move into the Carpathian Basin, because he could then claim it as his rightful heritage, and it "proved" that the Magyars had long-standing and unalienable rights to the land.

Seeking ever more powerful alliances, the early Hungarian kings established contact with Western Christianity, culminating in the coronation of the first Christian king, Stephen, in 1,000 A.D. Through missionaries sent by the Pope and the military force of the king, the pagan Magyars were converted en masse to Christianity. The Church, representing an ideological change, also changed the social and political face of the region and helped establish Hungary as a modern feudal state, along with the emerging Bohemian, Polish, and Russian states (Hanak, 1988).

For nearly 250 years, Hungary held its own under increasingly strong kings who were receptive to economic and cultural exchanges with both Byzantium and the Holy Roman Empire. French Romanesque and Lombard architectural styles flourished, Hungarian ecclesiastical elites visited the universities of Paris and Oxford, and marital alliances put Magyar royalty on half the thrones of Europe.

Throughout this period, Hungarian rulers conducted a "conscious and consistent policy of taking advantage of Western Europe's overpopulation to acquire people and the latest achievements of Western civilization" (Sugar, 1990, p. 28). The new settlers were called *hospites* (guests) and included Muslim, Jewish, and Russian merchants, Walloon and Italian vintners, and a great wave of Saxon peasants and German miners from the Rhine region who settled in Transylvania. In exchange for taxes paid in cash, they were granted privileges far greater than the local serfs, including the rights of fair holding, limited self-government, and exemption from customs.

The use of Church Latin and the Roman alphabet gradually replaced the runic script of the Hungarian language, providing a new method of writing the language for the rest of the world. Despite the presence of so many foreign settlers, the spoken Hungarian language was somehow maintained.

The open-door policy was so successful, in terms of the royal economy at least, that King Bela IV invited the pagan nomads of the southeast, the Cumans, in large numbers and sent a Dominican monk to Bashkiria to find and bring back any Magyars still living there. The monk, Julian, found more than Magyars. On the banks of the Volga, he found 100,000 Mongols preparing to simultaneously invade Silesia, Transylvania, and Hungary.

Devastating and destroying everything in their path, the Mongols scoured the Carpathian Basin for 12 months, leaving only remnants of 20%–40% of the settlements standing and barely any survivors. The refusal of Pope Gregory IX and Emperor Frederick II to come to Bela's aid in 1241 marked the beginning of a deeply ingrained belief, borne out again and again through the centuries, that only Hungarians can be trusted to help Hungarians.

The Mongol Invasion, considered the first of the three Hungarian national catastrophes, also marked the end of the longest period of Hungarian self-rule for over 700 years. The throne of Hungary was variously occupied by, bargained for, and stolen by rulers from Bohemia, Bavaria, Luxembourg, Austria, Poland, and Naples for the next 200 years. But by the end of the late 15th century, Hungary had become one of the richest and most powerful Renaissance centers in Europe.

And then the second catastrophe arrived in the form of the invincible Ottoman Turks whose presence and its effects lasted far longer than the Mongol Invasion had.

The king and most of the ruling noble class were slaughtered in the first major battle in 1526, in effect leaving the country leaderless. The Turks occupied and ruled most of the country for the next 150 years, destroying more than half the Christian population and its buildings and institutions. The western slice of what remained of Hungary elected Ferdinand Habsburg as King of Hungary in the hope that his powerful family could stop further Ottoman advances. The Habsburgs, seeing Hungary as a buffer for their own lands and interests, maintained that rule until 1918. The eastern section of Hungary was carved off and became the Principality of Transylvania under its own elected king. Transylvania waged war with both the Ottomans and the Habsburgs for the next century and a half.

Although the Habsburgs were able to reunite the Hungarian lands after the Ottoman Turks were defeated by the Holy Alliance in 1699, they were never able to completely subjugate the Hungarian culture. Inspired by the American and French Revolutions and the subsequent Age of Enlightenment, Hungarian nationalistic fervor rose dramatically in the first half of the 19th century. The War of Independence of 1848, though unsuccessful, paved the way for eventual Habsburg concessions resulting in the Compromise of 1867 and the creation of the Dual Monarchy. German ceased to be the official language of Hungary, although the majority of people above the level of the peasant class found it expedient to know both Hungarian and German. The celebration of the Magyar Millennium in 1896 marked the zenith of Hungarian culture in the arts and architecture, followed rapidly by economic improvement and the rise of world-class musicians, scientists, and writers.

But nationalism was not confined only to the Hungarian people of Hungary. Since the Middle Ages Slovaks, Romanians, Ruthenes, Germans, Serbs, and Croats had lived peacefully within its borders, intermarrying and developing approximately as equals. The 1868 Hungarian Nationalities Law guaranteed them use of their mother tongue and development of separate economic and social organizations. But the reality was that each group was chafing under the domination of, first, Hungary, and, second, the disintegrating Austrian Empire. By 1910, a combination of massive emigration (more than 2 million), high birthrates, internal migration, urbanization, and "Magyarization" of minorities had transformed the demographics of the nation and culture into a more homogeneous, modern industrial state with an ever-growing middle class. The Magyar language and culture were now supreme (Jeszenszky, 1990).

And then the third catastrophe struck, the effects of which are still so immediate in the minds of most Hungarians that the entire culture at times seems suffused with resentment. Dragged into the first World War as part of the Austro-Hungarian Empire, with the assurance of full German military support and, for what it was worth, Bulgaria's, by early 1918 Hungary was torn apart by internal strife, revolution, and counterrevolution. Governments of every persuasion were installed and toppled until one compromise leader, Admiral Miklos Horthy, was elected regent in March 1920. Hungarians are fond of saying wryly that only in Hungary could there have been a monarchy with no monarch, ruled by a naval admiral in a land-locked country. On June 4, 1920 the Treaty of Trianon was signed at Versailles and Greater Hungary was no more.

The loss of territory and people was perceived as unconscionably unfair, especially because it effectively removed 89% of iron production, 84% of forest land, and nearly half the food-processing industry. Sixty-two percent of the railroad network was lost, with treaty provisions strictly limiting the building of new ones (Hajdu & Nagy, 1990).

Interwar Hungary became an economically stagnant, bitterly right-wing country, ripe to be drawn into the orbits of Mussolini and Hitler, who promised—and temporarily delivered—the restoration of Greater Hungary. Once more, Hungary chose the losing side. In June 1941, the Hungarian-style blitzkrieg against the Soviet Union began—mobilized by bicycle and horse-drawn carts (Lazar, 1990). Hitler's decision to spare Vienna by sacrificing Budapest at the end of the war resulted in the near-total destruction of the city, as the last Nazi stronghold. The Allies not only upheld the earlier Treaty of Trianon but they also removed a bit more Hungarian territory, which was given to Slovakia. With the extermination of its Jewish population and mass deportation of its German minority, Hungary became even more Magyarized.

## Stalin's Shadow

The Soviet Army first liberated and then occupied Hungary for the next 45 years. It is still difficult to sort out all the effects that the war and subsequent Soviet occupation had on the culture and society of Hungary. Despite the moderate reforms of 1957 and 1968, two full generations of Hungarians knew no system but a centrally planned, and controlled socialist culture.

It is a well-known joke among Hungarians that for over 40 years the word *szabad*, meaning both "free" and "permitted," also meant "not free" because whatever was allowed was compulsory. A remarkable pair of studies conducted in 1978 and 1982 among a large sample population by the Institute of Sociology of the Hungarian Academy of Sciences attempted to identify Hungarian values. The researchers used a set of questions identical to those asked in a similar study in the United States, in which the participants were asked to rank a set of 18 primary values. Both Hungarians and Americans ranked peace and family security as of first and second importance to them. But Americans ranked freedom third, whereas Hungarians placed much less value on freedom, listing it as ninth in 1978 and eighth in 1982. Kornai (1990) cited the study and suggested a variety of explanations for the difference, including the reassurance of living in a paternalistic society, a sort of cognitive dissonance correction that made living within such a society tolerable by devaluing freedom, and the bias in education and mass media in favor of collective rather than individual good.

One of Hungary's young dissident writers, Miklos Haraszti (1987), in his *samizdat* exposure of the absence of overt censorship once artists and writers are assimilated into the system, discussed the notion of freedom for Hungarians. Ironically titled *The Velvet Prison*, his book describes the relationship between artist and censor as "the two faces of official culture—diligently and cheerfully cultivat[ing] the gardens of art together" (p. 7). In the foreword, George Konrad, a dissident of an older generation, said, "In state socialism, one never talks about the writer's freedom, only about the writer's responsibility. He who talks about freedom is irresponsible" (p. xii). As recently as 6 years ago, and in fact up to 1990, private individuals could not import photocopying machines, which were individually registered with the state and their power cords removed and locked up for the days surrounding the anniversary of the 1956 uprising. Authorization was required to purchase artists' supplies, from paint brushes to movie cameras. It was "forbidden to recite poetry and other literature, play music, dance or mount exhibitions in private apartments, in the street, or in any other unauthorized place" (Haraszti, 1987, p. 92).

## THE CONFUSION OF TONGUES

This section attempts to shed more light on specific examples of the intercultural communication problems an American encounters. Of course, as an American, I bring my own cultural baggage to such experiences. Fisher (1987) noted that Americans tend to be "optimistic people who accentuate the positive, are inclined to see situations in their best light, and are ready to move on to take action on the next problem. So there is a tendency not to brood over mistakes, and in any case it seems unpatriotic to dwell on the negative when the national image is concerned" (p. 30).

### Speech Differences

Patterns of speech cause some noise in communication. Hungarian is spoken in a rhythmic near-monotone, with the stress always on the first syllable. In an interrogatory sentence, the only identifying change is that the voice is raised slightly on the penultimate syllable. Word order is of secondary importance, so it is possible to speak two identical sentences with only the lift of the voice near the end indicating that one is a question. For example, I might say to a librarian (in literal translation), "You have last Tuesday's issue of *Nepszabadsag* among the periodicals," and "You have last Tuesday's issue of *Nepszabadsag* among the periodicals?" (Actually, there is no verb meaning "to have," and personal pronouns are never used with strangers, so the construction would be something more like "To one is last Tuesday's. . . .") A Hungarian speaking English tends to transfer this rhythm and monotone, so it is difficult to guess the speaker's emphasis. To the Hungarian ear, native English speakers are hard to listen to and even harder to understand, because our voices are all over the scale.

### Forms of Address

"The Hungarian language is burdened with several levels of formality. Such linguistic polyphony can be construed as a clear manifestation of chaotic interpersonal relations of a nation bitterly wrestling with changing times and social systems" (Krecz, 1993, p. 6). In addition to the typical formal and informal "you" of European languages, there are two extra levels, subtly indicative of social status, age, and/or gender. Compounding the confusion at all but the most informal level is the fact that it is considered rude or even confrontational to use a personal pronoun, as in "you should." This results in the awkward combination of having to repeat the name of the person one is addressing and forming an impersonal phrase such as "it would be necessary."

Western companies, from IKEA, the Swedish furniture distributor, to every possible American fast-food franchise, are training their Hungarian staff to ignore all of the polite forms and say, in the friendliest tones, "May I help you?" The reactions of most Hungarians range from indignation to outright shock. Not only is the informal "you" being used without permission, but the notion that a younger, socially inferior person could possibly "help" a superior is unthinkable and impertinent.

For 45 years, the automatic greeting "*Kezet csokolom*" ("I kiss your hand") when a man encountered a woman was out of favor in public. Among other reasons, the Hungarians realized how silly it sounded with the addition of the required "Comrade." ("I kiss your hand, Comrade.") With the changes in 1990, the custom was immediately and openly resumed. Archaic as it sounds to an American, there is something charming about small boys interrupting their snowball fights when I walk by to yell, "I kiss your hand, my lady."

## EDUCATION

One of the many residual problems is in the higher education system. The "honor system" is unknown and, in fact, cheating is rampant and tacitly condoned. Hungarian university faculty members explain it in terms of a tradition of beating the system, outsmarting the authorities, and gaining prestige among one's peers for being the best at cheating. Because the faculty all came up through the same system, it is self-perpetuating.

On the other hand, questioning the professor, arguing, or asserting alternative solutions is outside the norm. A visiting faculty member learns quickly not to say, "Are there any questions?" but to have long office hours so that students have an opportunity to get answers privately. Furthermore, having been educated and employed in an authoritarian, socialist system, students cannot be certain what it is they don't understand. When I assigned my graduate business students a marketing case about an American building supply company, one of them wrote that the recession in the United States meant that the government would not be building as many skyscrapers in the cities as usual. It took hours of explanation before he was convinced that private companies can and do build high-rise office towers in the United States, not the federal government.

Once, after a coffee break, my students returned to their seats but I wanted them to remain standing for a simulation game. I raised my arms and said, "Don't sit down yet." Instantly all 26 were on their feet! In an American classroom, I would have expected at least half to remain seated and ask, "Why not?"

### Misinterpretations

Imposition of new management, using American business terms, can increase the difficulties of integrating work groups. At one of the large companies that has been bought by an American firm, the Hungarian managers are frequently exhorted by their new American superiors with standard American motivational presentations. They are told that they must share the "vision of the firm," "be aggressive" in getting new business, and seek "new challenges" in their work, all words used in a positive sense. When the definitions of those words are checked in the Dictionary of Foreign Words in Hungarian (*Idegen*, 1990) we find these meanings:

1. vision
   a) apparition
   b) illusion, delusion
2. aggressive
   a) attacking, conquering (policy)
   b) violent, bullying, pushy
   c) offending, provocative (voice)
3. challenge
   a) provocation
   b) threat

The same group of employees identified three other words as representative of the confusion of values-reflecting vocabularies, in addition to the word *challenge*, which Americans substitute for *problem*. A Hungarian uses the word *problem* for everything from running out of coffee filters to a major devaluation of the currency. This gives Americans the impression that Hungarians only see problems in their work, reinforcing the negative stereotype that Hungarians are naturally pessimistic.

The misunderstanding probably stems from the fact that, linguistically, Hungarian has only one noun that covers all bad situations, *baj*, meaning trouble of any kind, plus the loan word, *problema*. Generally speaking, one of the major differences in our languages is that English is rich in nouns and adjectives, while Hungarian is rich in verbs. What we perceive as imprecise is merely the lack of a word that fits.

Two other concepts that Hungarians find confusing and somewhat incompatible are "mission" and "job rotation." A Hungarian thinks of a mission as some cause, usually humanitarian, that requires lifelong commitment. During a training session, a group of Hungarian managers and a group of their new American colleagues were asked to separately spend an hour writing a mission statement for their joint venture. The Hungarians returned an hour later empty-handed and resentful that they had been put in such a humiliating position. The reason was that earlier in the joint session, the subject of job rotation had been discussed. A Hungarian may change jobs two or three times over a lifetime and a transfer initiated by the company is often perceived as a punishment for being unable to work well with one's colleagues. But these managers had been told that if an American firm fails to move a manager every 2–3 years, it is an indication that the person has been forgotten or is perceived as lacking some valuable abilities. The Hungarians were unable to reconcile the ideas of lifelong commitment (mission) and an employer who would keep forcing them to change jobs and, consequently, could not write a mission statement.

For the foreigner who makes the effort to learn the language, the same problems and pitfalls occur. Many Hungarian words seem innocuous in literal translation while the experience behind the word is quite loaded. For example, *izgato* means "an exciting person," but politically it meant "a rabble rouser," one who incited the counterrevolutionary element. Imagine the shock when the school director's business cards were misprinted with that word instead of the word meaning "director," which is *igazgato*.

Other words that still carry heavy negative connotations include *bureau*, *entrepreneur*, and (although this is changing) *party*.

## Lack of Experience

Because there were two main aims of socialist production—using up resources and keeping people employed—there is a telling lack of consumer or profit orientation, demand analysis, use of historical data for forecasting, and basic market principles. One American manufacturer whose marketing director had been struggling with market share, brand recognition, and shelf space problems for 10 months was mystified when he was told that the company always closes down for 3 weeks in summer so that employees can have a long holiday. "But, if we do that," he said, "the city will run out of margarine." "Oh, no," the employees replied, "the people can buy someone else's margarine."

Assumptions and preconceptions about each others' cultures also inform the interpretation of the words we hear each other use. Americans bring with them the assumption that Central and Eastern Europeans know nothing at all about business and market economies, when they have actually been operating in a highly entrepreneurial environment, that is, the black, gray, or second economy. Hungarians assume that all Americans are wealthy and somewhat naive, interested only in a quick return on investment. A proliferation of English-language newspapers and monthly periodicals has been attempting to help bridge the culture gap, usually in a humorous vein. "Negotiations seem to go on forever, always politely, but without concrete result. I would like an answer; I get a coffee," complained one American businessman who has resided in Hungary for 10 years. He blamed part of the inaction and overzealous courtesy on the part of Hungarian businessmen on their dislike of being condescended to. "When treated like a stupid beginner, don't get angry—offer a coffee." He warned of the reluctance of Hungarian managers to admit they don't have the final say. There are still layers and layers of "bosses" whose scope of authority extends no further than the ability to offer a cup of coffee. If the American waits patiently enough, eventually one gets to talk to the real boss, "who is surrounded by a group of highly polite and extremely quiet people who are described as the colleagues. These people all have jobs, functions, and specialist knowledge and none of them will say a damn thing while the real boss is present" (Finch, 1993, p. 8).

A 1992 survey of local managers and their foreign partners conducted by H. Neumann International Management Consultants and reported in *Budapest Week* indicated that the most persistent problems have to do with their ability to understand and relate to each other. The survey "indicated a high level of verbal understanding between eastern and western colleagues, but significant differences in mentality between the two business cultures" (Nadler, 1992, p. 6). Americans perceive Hungarians as "slow in making decisions, unwilling to take risks, too inflexible, and lacking a 'spirit of adventure.' Eastern managers, for their part, consider their western colleagues 'responsible for difficulties and obstacles in communication' because they do not have sufficient respect for local ways and customs, and they lack a detailed knowledge of the regional market" (Nadler, 1992, p. 6). Hungarians perceive Americans as "imperialistic," "unprofessional," "impatient," and "too Wild West acting—like the people in 'Dallas' " (Nadler, 1992, p. 6).

## GENERAL CONCLUSIONS

Americans of northern European descent are particularly prone to jump to the conclusion that there is a common mindset existing in themselves and their Central and Eastern European contacts. That is not the case. Those coming to this region would do well to investigate the history of the area, its people, and their culture. There is a critical lack of useful information exchange and there is no coordination of information resources for either side that would help ease interactions between Americans and Eastern Europeans. Visiting Fulbright scholars are given a half-day orientation. Hungarians receive many hours of MTV and American programs via cable TV. American educators and corporations, as the recipients of the almost overwhelming Hungarian hospitality, must be particularly sensitive to the communication difficulties and take steps to overcome them. Seminars on the communication aspects of doing business in Hungary should be included with the present finance and accounting offerings. For Hungarians, the many courses now available in "business English" should be taught by English-speaking business people, rather than linguists.

As communications researchers, I believe we have a special duty to continue to investigate and broadcast issues relating to intercultural communication problems, in as many venues as possible. Although the English language will continue to dominate modern international communication, its utility can be deceptive because implicit philosophies, logical styles, moral values, motivations, and historic ethnocentric world views fail to be communicated.

## REFERENCES


Anonymous. (1992, Dec. 26). [A play on words]. HVG, p. 77.

Baranczak, S. (1990). *Breathing under water and other East European essays*. Cambridge, MA: Harvard University Press.

Barbero, J. M. (1993). Latin America: Cultures in the communication media. *Journal of Communication, 43*(2), 18–30.

Davis, D. K., & Jasinski, J. (1993). Beyond the culture wars: An agenda for research on communication and culture. *Journal of Communication, 43*(3), 141–148.

Ferguson, M. (1993). Invisible divides: Communication and identity in Canada and the U.S. *Journal of Communication, 43*(2), 42–57.

Finch, D. (1993, Nov. 1). Doing business the Hungarian way. *The Hungarian Times*, p. 8.

Fisher, G. (1987). *American communication in a global society* (rev. ed.). Norwood, NJ: Ablex.

Hajdu, T., & Nagy, Z. L. (1990). Revolution, counterrevolution, consolidation. In P. F. Sugar (Ed.), *A history of Hungary* (pp. 295–318). Bloomington: Indiana University Press.

Hanak, P. (1988). One thousand years: A concise history of Hungary (Zs. Neres, Trans.). Budapest: Corvina Books.

Hanak, P. (1991). The Corvina history of Hungary (Zs. Neres, Trans.). Budapest: Corvina Books.

Haraszti, M. (1987). *The velvet prison: Artists under state socialism* (K. Landesmann & L. Landesmann, Trans.) (2nd English ed.). New York: The Noonday Press.

*Idegen szavak magyarul szotar* [Dictionary of Foreign Words in Hungarian] (3rd ed.). (1990). Budapest: Akademiai Kiado.

Jeszenszky, G. (1990). Hungary through World War I and the end of the dual monarchy. In P. F. Sugar (Ed.), *A history of Hungary* (pp. 295–318). Bloomington: Indiana University Press.

Klaniczay, T. (Ed.). (1985). *Old Hungarian literary reader*. Budapest: Corvin Kiado.

Kornai, J. (1990). *Vision and reality, market and state: Contradictions and dilemmas revisited* (Hungarian ed.). Budapest: Corvin Kiado.

Krecz, T. (1993, October 28). Social status a matter of semantics. *Budapest Week*, p. 6.

Lazar, I. (1990). *Hungary: A brief history* (A. Tezla, Trans.). Budapest: Corvin Kiado.

Miszlivetz, F. (1991). The unfinished revolutions of 1989: The decline of the nation-state? *Social Research, 58*(4), 781–804.

Nadler, J. (1992, March 10). Western managers bring different ways and an "imperialist manner." *Budapest Week*, p. 5.

Sahin, H., & Aksoy, A. (1993). Global media and cultural identity in Turkey. *Journal of Communication, 43*(2), 31–41.

Schlesinger, P. (1993). Wishful thinking: Cultural politics, media, and collective identities in Europe. *Journal of Communication, 43*(2), 6–17.

Stohl, C. (1993). European managers' interpretations of participation: A semantic network analysis. *Human Communication Research, 20*(1), 97–117.

Sugar, P. F. (Ed.). (1990). *A history of Hungary*. Bloomington: Indiana University Press.

# 6

# *Advertising and the Legitimacy Crisis of Eastern Europe*

Carl C. Rohde
Carsten R. C. Pellicaan
*University of Utrecht*

It is a cliché that Eastern Europe is going through deep turmoil and has to fight all the economic, political, and cultural problems accompanying such a process. However, it is a very important cliché, one that is full of meaning. Moreover, the specific meanings associated with that cliché quickly change over time, as they have done over the relatively short period of the last 5 years. This chapter deals mainly with one European country, Hungary. Using examples from politics and economy as illustrations, the chapter focuses on cultural aspects. On this level, the cliché of Eastern European turmoil can be interpreted on the basis of the *deep legitimacy crisis* through which Eastern European countries are going. This ongoing legitimacy crisis can also be seen as the main factor that caused the collapse of the former Communist regimes. No one believed in them any more and all of a sudden that fact became evident to everyone. A dramatic illustration of the suddenness of this turn of events was provided by Ceausescu, the former Rumanian Communist leader, during his last public speech in front of his monumental residence in Bucharest. The speech was staged in the usual Communist way with enforced "spontaneous" applause and other orchestrated indications of supposed enthusiasm. Halfway through it, however, there became evident some signs of dissatisfaction in the crowd and in a short time the ceremony disintegrated. Television transmitted worldwide what had happened. The legitimacy crisis of Eastern Europe became clearly visible, and the outcome is well known to all of us.

The end of the Communist regimes did not mean, however, that the legitimacy crisis was over. On the contrary, it even deepened. Of course, such crises neither come up nor disappear quickly. The end of the Cold War can be analyzed as a long-term result of the growing sense, both in the West and East, that it lacked the necessary basis in legitimacy for its continuation. From the mid-1960s onward, people on both sides of the Iron Curtain felt the war cost more, financially and socially, than was justified. As Segal (1992) put it:

> While military expansion and economic growth seemed compatible in the first decade of the Cold War, this began to change in the 1960s, with the crisis becoming apparent first in the United States. However, in the United States, the relative autonomy of the state prevented the economic crisis from impacting as dramatically on the state, even as the crisis continues. In the USSR, by contrast, with the state, the economy, and the military integrally intertwined, economic crisis more quickly translated into a crisis of political legitimacy, particularly after the institution of perestroika in the mid 1980s, which facilitated the mobilization of oppositional resources. (p. 5)

This brief summary makes clear how deeply rooted the problems in Eastern countries were before the actual political breakdowns, but it also provides an indication of how difficult it is to solve the ongoing crisis.

To regain legitimacy, not only for the political system but for the whole societal mechanism, new narratives must be constructed that deal with the rebuilding of society, new ways of acting or behaving, new kinds or ways of trust, and a new future. Only in that way can the foundations for new social institutions be laid. In his famous study on legitimacy in modern society, Weber (1968) introduced three different kinds of legitimacy. The question that concerns us is what chances do they have to develop again in Eastern European countries?

The first is called *bureaucratic legitimacy*, and it is based on the appeal of the legality of enacted rules. For Weber (1968), this has been the most stable basis for order in modern society. In Eastern European countries, however, it was the most corrupt form experienced by the people. *Traditional legitimacy* is the second kind. It is based on an appeal to the sanctity of immemorial traditions and to history, and it can be activated and vitalized more easily than bureaucratic legitimacy. Hungary is an example. Its history is full of traumas and defeats, yet it is quite clear that people recognize it as a framework from which to distill new meanings, a new kind of "meaning and explanation." The third is *charismatic legitimacy*. For Weber it is based on an appeal to the exceptional character of an individual who exercises power. Although in Eastern Europe there may not exist one such generally accepted exceptional character to which people would point, a significant part of the Eastern European population accepts, in the abstract, that it does exist. It is both symbolized by and seen as having materialized in all the good new things "the West" can provide: democracy and freedom and, (far) more tangibly, riches and consumer goods. Together, these symbols, images, and goods tell stories of a new future and a new hope, of an *ujness* (newness) that has an enormous appeal. Together they function as a fertile ground for a new type of charismatic legitimacy, not exemplified by a person but by an economic and political system.

In this chapter we stress the important role that the symbols, images, and pictures used in advertising and even packaging play in producing fertile ground for this new charismatic legitimacy. In the West, consumers may have become accustomed or even immunized to the fact that ads are rapidly "zapped" and "zipped" away. In Eastern European countries, however, advertisers must deal with a far more attentive public, one that longs for that Western *ujness* of which the ads speak.

Summarizing, we can describe Eastern European countries as suffering a deep legitimacy crisis. Trying to overcome it, people are torn between embracing the charismatic legitimacy of the "new" things that the West has to offer, and attempting to reach back to the traditional legitimacy of their own historical roots. Advertising plays a major role in this balancing act. During the last few years the attractiveness of this new charismatic appeal can be called almost overwhelming, and advertising was the main stimulus in that process. In future years, however, it is not improbable that we will have to reckon with a reaction against this enthusiasm for the new and its charismatic appeal—and advertising probably will also play a significant role in those developing trends.

Contemporary balancing and polarization processes in Eastern Europe are powerfully impacted by the political and economic situation in all the rest of Europe. The end of the Cold War, the explosive growth of the means of communication, and, of course, the influence of the changes that are summarized under the slogan "Europe 1992" prepared Eastern Europe for becoming a part of such a capitalist *global village*. That term is often used to refer to a world characterized by internationalization, by the evaporation of borders, and by the assimilation of all cultures into a worldwide melting pot. It is seen as a process of cultural convergence that is deeply longed for by many Eastern Europeans, because they thought of themselves as being ready to participate in the entire effort. Enthusiasm even deepened and became the basis for action when global companies started to compete for a strong position in the Eastern European markets. Mergers and joint ventures quickly became normal events in many countries, changing not only economic but social life as well. The images and symbols, pictures, logos, and goods that once represented the Western world are now inviting Eastern Europe to become part of the capitalistic global village based on the attractive aura of "the new." In the last few years internationalism, all the good (i.e., Western) things in life, and the charismatic impact of all that was seen as new came together.

However, this trinity of images and concepts is now in danger of being shipwrecked by the practices and the harsh realities of daily life in Eastern Europe. The diffuse promise of an impressive economic growth, for example, is not being kept. Also, many companies involved in international joint ventures and mergers have discovered how difficult it is to overcome intercultural differences. Cultural value systems are far more difficult to change than the Eastern European enthusiasm for the West had led many to believe. As we have already indicated, it is true that Eastern Europeans are immensely attracted to Western symbols, images, and goods. They love Coca-Cola and McDonald's, they much prefer Western cars to their own Trabants, and they readily embrace Western fashion. But these are only superficial indicators in the process of cultural convergence. At a deeper level, that process turns out not to be very harmonious. In Hungary feelings of anxiety and dislocation have been awakened. There exists a sense that the country is lagging behind and is even being dominated again. Though the process of cultural convergence is deeply connected to the charismatic impact of the new, there is now an awareness that a kind of cultural homogenization is the result. The result is a deepening anxiety over losing identity, both as a person and as a nation.

A common reaction in Hungary is to stress one's own cultural and national roots again. Cultural divergence is, of course, quite the opposite of the trend toward cultural convergence. In the extreme, it leads to internal hostilities, which we can already discern so ominously in the republics of the former Soviet Union and in the former Yugoslavia. In the end, it may produce an inimical attitude toward the West, which promises so much and gives so little.

Until recently, advertising products mainly stimulated the process of cultural convergence. Different strategies that have been used are described in this chapter. However, in changing sociocultural circumstances, advertising symbols and images can also work the opposite way, by encouraging a tendency toward cultural divergence. In such instances, advertising stresses and visualizes what is seen as typically Hungarian, celebrating its uniqueness, thus opposing the domineering symbols of the West.

The balancing and polarization processes that characterize Eastern European countries, which are caused by the deep legitimacy crises in that region, can thus be interpreted as a balancing act between the process of cultural convergence and the more recent tendency toward divergence. As a result, we have set ourselves two goals. First, we describe these polarized tensions that are developing in Hungary. Second, we analyze the role of advertising in this cultural struggle.

## WHY HUNGARY?

When, at the end of the 1980s, glasnost, perestroika, and the destruction of the Berlin Wall seemed to open up enormous new markets, most companies, for several reasons, focused immediately on Hungary. First, Hungary constitutes a small market of about 10 million people; this helps to avoid big risks. A second reason is that Hungary, because of its location in Central Europe, is a crucial link in the chain of commerce between East and West. What is more obvious than to use that linkage and to expand it? Hungary is the gate to Central and Eastern Europe. All adjoining countries, apart from Austria, look to Hungary as an example. In the following pages we repeatedly cite participants in our research programs.[1] As one of our respondents put it, "People of Eastern Europe are coming to Hungary to see the Western products. They have pictures of it, based on what they saw in Hungary. So, the Hungarian market is a bigger market than its territory" (a representative of RSCG Havasi & Varga, personal communication, February 1993). Finally, Hungary has a very favorable tax system, created by the Hungarian government to attract foreign capital and investors to the country. All these reasons make Hungary a good base for companies to start their Eastern European ventures, and a good starting point if one is successful for economically conquering the rest of Eastern Europe. In the short run Hungary has played the role of a laboratory.

Hungary's attractiveness as an experimental market is increased by the fact that the country, though carefully but also more intensely than all its neighbors, had come into contact with the great Western themes of democracy and capitalism, consumer goods, and marketing communica-

---

[1]This chapter is based mainly on two different types of research:

1. We did cultural organizational research on joint ventures between Dutch and Hungarian companies. The differences between Dutch and Hungarian organizations were determined to be profound. We set out to illustrate daily happenings and problems in joint ventures while they are engaged in the process of doing international business. The main themes were: cultural differences, different methods of management and marketing, and the adequacy of communication management.
2. We did research on the biggest advertising agencies in Hungary (O&M, McCann-Erickson, Young & Rubicam, GGK, DDB-Needham, Topreklám/BBDO, among others). The main concerns were with: marketing and media strategies; the attitudes of Hungarian individuals, both toward consumer items and on public affairs; their attitudes toward and the reception of advertising messages; and differences, in that process, between Western European cultures and that of Hungary.

tion. Western advertising campaigns have been a part of everyday life in Hungary longer than in the rest of Eastern Europe. One could get an earlier and more intensive impression not only of the enthusiasm for the advertising images making use of the charismatic impact of what we have termed the new, but also of the more reserved reactions of Hungarians, which are currently being provoked by those same advertising images. That is the reason why we focus on the Hungarian culture in this chapter.

Recent developments in that culture can definitely not be readily used to translate events in the other countries of Eastern Europe. Even though all Eastern European countries shared 40 years of Communist domination, that did not wipe out the cultural differences among them. In fact, these differences may even start to play a more important role again when the recent re-re-valuing of one's own culture, history, and roots continues. Still, the analysis of what moves the Hungarian culture today may shed some light on the current and future developments in other European countries. It is not by accident that Hungary has been assigned the role of a laboratory. However, before we describe current events in Hungary, in its quest for new forms of legitimacy, we must first deal with Hungarian culture in its own right.

## THE HUNGARIAN CULTURE

Since the founding of Hungary in the year 1000 by St. István, Hungarian history is a story of constant oppression. Again and again, periods of resistance and plunder alternated with periods of rebuilding. The Mongols plundered and ruled, as did the Turks, the Austrians, and in the recent past the Russians. Of course, this latest period of oppression is still clearly remembered. After the bloody battles in Budapest between the Germans and the advancing Russian armies, a small, devastated country was left behind in 1945. It was put under a Communist regime, had to refuse Marshall Plan aid, and saw the Russians take what industrial capital was left in the country. From 1948 on only one political party existed, the communist MDP. Political efforts included the takeover by the state of all private property. Banks and industrial or business companies were nationalized. The agrarian sector was reorganized into "collectives." Spies and the police (among them the security police forces *ávo* and *ávh*) reigned, and terrorized everyone. A seemingly innocent demonstration by workers and students on October 23, 1956, openly supporting the Polish Reform Movement, was violently disrupted. Two days later this led to an insurrection that spread all over the country. After 4 days, the heroic yet pointless Hungarian resistance had been broken, just like it had been so many times before.

The Hungarians have a reputation for being "historic losers." If anything shapes their world view, it must be the realization that the last 500 years have been a string of failures and lost battles. The "psychosis of the lost nation" has made the Hungarian people fatalistic; they have learned to live day by day. Hungarians have become a sober people. "The loser always ends up more sober than the winner," says the (in Hungary) well-respected Timor Déry. This could be described as a "basic assumption" of the Hungarian culture (Schein, 1991). Still, Hungarians have a strong attachment to their sad history. History is *alive* for these proud and even chauvinistic people.

Frequently historic heroes, many of whom died dramatically, are being reburied or honored in Budapest's Hero Square. Street vendors' stands continue to sell maps of the Hungary of old. The average Hungarian is frustrated by such unfortunate events as the treaty of Trianon, the riot of 1848, and, of course, the insurrection of 1956. Old traditions are not forgotten and the songs and habits of past days are still alive today. One does not toast with beer because the Austrians did exactly that—very noisily—after putting down the Hungarian insurrection of 1848. Hungarians' attitudes towards the present and the future, which are basic and characteristic of every culture (Adler, 1985; Schein, 1991), stem from dealing with this ambivalent past. History has taught the Hungarian the meaning of irony, and how often there is a good reason occasion for mockery; this mental habit continues. One is open to what the future brings, but one thinks in terms of the past. As for politics, this means that one simply does not believe in it. The election turnout of 1989 was bad and it was not much better in the spring of 1994. As far as the charisma of the new is concerned, however, people are more positive about everything promised by Western companies and their advertisements. Contrary to the Western view of the future, this is not a long-term orientation.

Another basic characteristic of the Hungarian society and culture is that every collective form of "basic trust" is missing. There does not live a Hungarian adult who did not have to learn to live with the Great Lie that the revolution of 1956 was a counterrevolution. Neither is there a Hungarian who did not know that the big lies were indeed just that, lies, and yet they had to keep silent. An important heritage of the Stalin era is the deep-rooted suspicion that "Those who are not with us, are against us." Where the legal rule in the liberal West is "innocent until proven guilty," in Eastern Europe the exact opposite is true. At the same time, there is a large measure of acceptance of the fact that the power in institutions and organizations is unevenly distributed, in spite of the claim of social equality. Elders and those in high places are treated with respect; this is shown in countless forms of courtesy. Yet, behind these expressions of respect and courtesy, resistance and dissatisfaction can be felt. These sentiments are never expressed in the form of public boycotts, but they are constantly present as a sort of passive resentment, nourished and cherished by the Hungarian in his private soul. Although on the one hand honor, respect, and courtesy are part of the Hungarian cultural value system, on the other there also exists a continuous, hidden resistance (Hofstede, 1984). Honor, respect, and courtesy have been made empty words by history, and that is one more indicator of the legitimacy crisis in which Hungary currently finds itself.

In the 1960s, the economic situation in Hungary worsened. This led to a series of reforms in 1968. Alongside badly functioning state industries some breathing room was created for private initiative, and Hungary became one of the best managed economies in Eastern Europe. In addition to the official market there existed a so-called free market. From 1989 on, a number of radical decisions were made. The import of Western products was liberalized, and freedom of the press was taken seriously. The government announced that it was prepared to de-nationalize companies. Less than 2 months later, the first two Hungarian companies were taken over by Western interests. All of this could be interpreted as a serious attempt to create a true market economy and not a socialist market economy, as the Russians called it.

Early reforms have also had their darker side. The enormous inflation forced many Hungarians to take on second and even third jobs to keep the same income level. If one adds to this the already existing, serious problems that the country had in the areas of housing, pollution of the environment, insufficient social security, bad relations with Rumania, and finally feelings of insecurity about the future, it is not difficult to see that we are dealing with a stressed and exhausted people. That fact is illustrated by the prevalence of alcoholism, divorce, suicide, and mental illness. These are all signs of a people under pressure! One may expect Hungarians to score high on the insecurity-reduction dimension Hofstede (1984) deemed such an important characteristic of a culture. Yet insecurity reduction does not characterize the Hungarians to a high degree; they are used to living under pressure. Indeed, they have a long tradition demonstrating that fact. We will certainly not see large crowd demonstrations, because of the disastrous results of the insurrection of 1956. The motto is more likely to be: "We will survive this too." Is this a strange attitude in a country where many people have to fight for what they can get out of life? People do not like to think too much about the future, however, the Western advertising narratives about the charismatic new are very attractive.

There is still too much unfinished business, and the Hungarian is able to deal with the resulting uncertainty in an excellent way. Sociologist Elemér Hankiss (1990) told us:

> Hungarians live in a half-finished country in a half-finished society with a half-finished reform-program and in permanent haste. We live in a country in transition. We never know how long we will have in the future what we have now. How long that which is valid now, will stay so. We are virtuoso on the piano of the different systems.

This *is* a rather exhausting way to live. Additionally, the early reforms have had another unexpected consequence. Not all Hungarians have had the opportunity to find a second job. The uneducated, single parents, the handicapped, and others have missed out. Also many of the aged continue to move down on the economic ladder because of their nonadjusting pensions. Although the windows in the shopping areas are brightly lit by the glamour of a new era, a large part of the Hungarian population is falling below the poverty line. In the past people had no choices, but they were able to buy what they really needed. Now everything you can think of is for sale, but in most households there is no money to buy anything more than necessities. Luxury items are only for a select public, for those who are successfully active in the second and third economy. Five percent of the professional population earns more than 10 times the average month's salary, whereas over 30% of Hungary's citizens are living below the official minimum level of existence. Social security is provided, but here as well people are aware that the gap between the millions of "newly poor" and those who will succeed in the new system will grow ever wider. All of this is causing serious concerns and breeds dissatisfaction. If anything will be left over from the old system, it will be the nostalgic longing for the social equality it provided. The legitimacy crisis in Hungary was deep; it remains deep and will stay that way for some time to come.

## ADVERTISING AS A MAIN MEDIA CARRIER OF LEGITIMACY NARRATIVES

In the contemporary or, as some refer to it, in this postmodern era, the fact that we are living in a media-dominated society cannot be overemphasized. Our world is to a great extent constructed by the media (Thompson, 1992). Revolutions come to us via the media; their success or failure may even depend on the media. The downfall of Communist regimes made that fact quite apparent. As a result, the legitimacy crises in Eastern Europe are impossible to solve if one ignores the dominant role of the media. It is through the media that the narratives come to us with which we construct and readjust our vision of the world, its legitimacy, and the place we occupy in it.

In Hungary, as in other Eastern European countries, the particular role advertising plays in these developments is extremely important. In very appealing ways advertising provides people not only general impressions but also specific clues concerning their world and what it could look like in a few years' time. Advertising implicitly communicates that what it presents is a realistic image of the future of Eastern Europe. In a culture torn to pieces by an ever-present legitimacy crisis, such advertising messages are both quite welcome and impressive. In fact, they are far more impressive than we realize, because we tend to take our own reactions to advertising as a worldwide norm. People in Eastern Europe countries look differently at advertising. It is not that they do not understand, even as we do, the manipulative power of advertising. It would be wrong and superficial to suppose that 40 years of Communism made people naive. However, in Hungary's contemporary cultural crisis, which is characterized by, among other things, an ultimate disenchantment with the world, advertising not only becomes a possible way to "re-enchant" the world (Featherstone, 1990), but it can even function through the media as a main provider of legitimacy narratives. In the autumn of 1993 a new gas station was opened in Prague. The opening festivities were attended by hundreds and hundreds of Prague's residents. This was not because Czechs love to be manipulated, but because in that opening of a modern service station the deprived public saw the ingredients, both material and abstract, that make up the narratives about a different, new future. That event provided the ingredients of a narrative and a future to which people could and wanted to relate.

## Advertising in Hungary

Hungarian advertising history began in Prague in the spring of 1968. In the years to follow concepts like marketing and advertising were introduced because of the growing number of contacts with Western Europeans. As early as 1968, the Hungarian authorities conferred monopolistic powers in the field of advertising on two organizations. The first one, Hungexpo Advertising, focused mainly on external trade and business. The second one, Magyar Hirdeto, monopolized the internal market. Both were huge state-owned agencies, but quite differently organized from their Western counterparts. In those early days, one of them had over 700 employees. However, the creative sector included only 10 individuals. The need for creative communication was almost completely lacking, because employees were never asked to think strategically or to create images and symbols with regard to a certain brand. There were no different brands, and real competition did not exist. The main task of advertising was to let people know that some products were available. That is, sometimes they were available, sometimes they were not.

In 1987 the situation changed significantly. At that time, Hungexpo and Magyar Hirdeto lost their monopolistic power. Other advertising agencies were allowed access to the media and could enter the marketplace. Since then the number of advertising agencies has boomed. However, 20% of the total turnover in Hungary's advertising industry is realized by only seven agencies. All seven have their headquarters in Budapest and are part of international advertising chains. In Hungary this can be interpreted as one indication of the attractiveness of international narratives concerning the charismatic new way of life.

Most of the Hungarians who work in the Budapest offices of international advertising agencies are former employees of Hungexpo and Magyar Hirdeto. In Hungary advertising was not an academic subject taught at a university or anywhere else. Thus, the two original organizations mentioned earlier functioned as the seedbed for the contemporary generation of Hungary's advertising agencies. They educated almost all of the professionals who are working in Hungarian advertising today, and they also created the first springboard for international contacts and learning experiences. The original agencies still play a major role in the Hungarian advertising world. This cannot hide the fact, however, that recent changes in advertising trends are tremendous. Especially the creative aspects are stressed more than ever before. Despite the drastic character of these changes in advertising, as far as strategic thinking, creative input, and a national/international orientation are concerned, most advertising professionals welcome them. Especially when they move into international agencies these individuals are not disheartened but revitalized. As one of our respondents said:

> It was just like a fresh breath of air when we started working at an international company. It wasn't a problem. We didn't feel inferior. There was no collective inferiority complex. We just said O.K., let's start. This is what we have waited for. (a representative of GGK Budapest, personal communication, December 1992)

Thus we can see one more indication of the overwhelming attractiveness and motivational power of the trinity of concepts previously mentioned, which includes internationalization, all Western ideas, and the charisma of the new.

In this section we have described and analyzed the connection between advertising on the one hand, and its function as a provider of legitimacy on the other. However, there is not a direct connection between the two, because the first objective of advertising is always to sell a product. If in that process advertising produces in any way legitimacy narratives, this is a secondary function, as seen from the advertiser's point of view. Such an additional function may be of great importance in the contemporary sociocultural climate, but it is only important after advertising has fulfilled its primary function: the promotion of sales. In the promotion of sales one encounters a few problems that are as basic as they are prosaic, which we discuss in the next section of this chapter. After dealing with those issues we consider in what way advertising may play and fulfill its roles as a producer and provider of legitimacy narratives.

## Practical Problems in a Confused Market

A basic problem for everyone working with advertising in Hungary is that the market barely provides any established distribution channels. Only after such channels are established can advertising practice its trade: recommending goods to consumers. It is only at that point that advertising truly becomes all that we mean by that term:

> The basic problem for all clients is distribution. So the first point is, get your products on the shelves. Because there is no point in advertising unless you have your products on the shelves. And there are a fair number of clients, international big clients that do not have good distribution and do not have their products on the shelves. No matter how much you advertise, it doesn't help and it also creates frustration on the part of the host sellers, retailers, and consumers because they see the products that they can't buy. So, forget all other things. The very first strategy is to have good distribution. (a representative of Topreklám/BBDO, personal communication, January 1993)

A second basic problem in Hungary is that there is nothing like a stable market division. The present polarization of the community creates a lot of confusion; the divisions in the society are becoming extreme. Although there exists an ever-growing lower class, there is only a small upper class, whose buying power keeps increasing. The group at which most advertising is directed in the West, the middle-class, hardly exists in Hungary. One of our respondents noted that "This means that target-group marketing is out of the question. The products that are normally being marketed and advertised for the middle-class could easily be proven to be totally out of place here" (a representative of McCann-Erickson Interpress, personal communication, January 1993). Direct mail, an advertising strategy traditionally used to reach the upper class as well as other consumers, is also still in its infancy in Hungary. That view is supported in another response:

> Direct mail is really pretty unadvanced here. An incredible number of households do not have a telephone. Or the phone numbers are incorrect. With addresses it is exactly the same. Because of that, direct mail becomes

> no more than firing a blank, and it is, therefore, relatively expensive. (a representative of Topreklám/BBDO, personal communication, January 1993)

Under these circumstances most advertising agencies focus their efforts on the young people, as is indicated in this statement:

> We are aiming at the generation who is curious about life, curious about the world. Who want to do well or want to do better than they are doing. Who want to get all the technological things that they've always heard everybody can get in life. Who want to be part of the big scene. (a representative of Ogilvy & Mather, personal communication, January 1993)

So far there exists a tendency in Hungary to write off the older generation, which is not a very desirable development if that society is to be swept up in toto into the new era. However, that approach is based on good reasons, one respondent believes:

> A lot of the older, postwar generations, who are in their 50s, 60s, 70s now, are not really interested now. They are occupied trying to cope with their present-day life. Getting their pension. And be warm in the winter. And get enough food and watch their children grow up. (a representative of GGK Budapest, personal communication, December 1992)

Another respondent told us: "People over 40, 45 years old are dead. Victims of history. Under 25, no problem. In between, so; some do, some don't. It's sad" (a representative of Lintas Budapest, personal communication, January 1993).

More refined instruments to identify target groups as well as valid statistics do not exist. This means that the advertising industry in Eastern Europe, out of necessity, has to work in more random ways than in the West, with, paradoxically, much more deeply felt results than those that are observable in the West. That fact underlies the following reaction: "The funny thing is that one would think that you divide the market and then you fill it up with the brands or the products. It's different in Hungary. You launch products. And this is creating the market division itself" (a representative of McCann-Erickson Interpress, personal communication, January 1993). Though that was not its purpose, this statement illustrates the formative power of advertising and marketing in contemporary Hungary. Together, with marketing in the lead, they are actually shaping a new market. Together, with advertising in the lead, they create lifestyles that did not exist before. Together, with marketing in the lead, they have the potential to establish a new order in Hungarian society. Together, with advertising in the lead, they have the persuasive power to legitimize this new order.

In such a chaotic market it is very difficult for advertising agencies to come up with well-thought-out communication strategies. They lack the data and directives to legitimize decisions. As we have mentioned several times, this situation mirrors the general legitimacy crisis of the Hungarian society in the daily professional practices of advertising agencies. One solution to such problems might be to work on the basis of gut-level feelings and intuitions, believes one respondent: "When we started to work in the Hungarian market, that was in 1990, we mainly determined the positioning of the product and other facts and decisions, by feelings. By feelings only. Feelings still have very great importance, but that is changing slightly now" (a representative of RSCG Havasi & Varga, personal communication, February 1993). Another solution to the problem of legitimate strategy development is to join up with international agencies and adopt their international approach. In recent years this has appeared to be a frequently used, successful solution. As a result, many leading agencies are now joint ventures between a Hungarian and an international agency. Whereas the Western agencies need Hungarians to provide a deeper knowledge of the local language and culture, Hungarians also gain what they need the most: capital and a point of orientation. That this point of orientation results in an international approach and an international perspective should be self-evident. Most international advertising agencies that have set up business in Budapest have done so because of their international clients' wishes for the Eastern European market to be opened up for them in the same consistent way as is true everywhere else in the world. One of those involved in that process believes that "The ultimate goal is to have a pan-European or a pan-Asian or even a worldwide approach. That is what most global clients want. Therefore, they prefer to deal with the same advertising network everywhere" (a representative of Topreklám/BBDO, personal communication, January 1993). It is clear that such an advertising practice supports in large measure the process of cultural convergence. Commercial images are produced that fit an international standard for international goods and that, in this way, contribute to the legitimizing of the charisma of all that is new.

### Advertising as Narratives of the Charismatic New—And How Those Narratives Reach the Eastern European Public

The stories told by advertising can reach audiences via different links in the chains of communication. These are links that have proven effective many times for Western capitalism, following roughly a certain chronological (historical) order (Ewen, 1976; Leiss, Kline, & Jhally, 1986). As the Western advertising industry flows into Eastern European markets, the same links are being used. However, there is no accelerated repetition of the West's advertising history apparent. The Eastern European situation is too hectic; at this moment all links are being tried and used at the same time. Still, the use sequence of links in Western advertising history has some limited applicability and meaning in Hungary's situation today. In the following section we describe how advertising messages reach Eastern European publics.

### The Premature Phase: "Buy Me"

In the Communist era a product was simply a product, it did not have an added value. One respondent familiar with that situation, commented, "For example if a consumer wanted to buy some soup, he could. But if he wanted to buy the same soup, or the same toothpaste some time in the future, he could not do so. He had to buy what was available, and the brand was completely irrelevant" (a representative of Mareco, personal communication, December 1992). Even though the early reforms in Hungary had provided a certain familiarity with concepts such as market and profit, assets and liabilities, prices and labor productivity, more sophisticated concepts such as consumer choice, brand awareness, and brand loyalty were never mentioned. This is not strange in a world in which people were happy to be able to buy anything at all. A function for advertising in such a situation would be to simply communicate the message "buy me."

In the last 3 or 4 years all the large, globally recognized brands have entered the Hungarian market. Apart from the two largest, Pepsi and Coca Cola, which had already been known for 20 years, all others were entirely new, and they were greeted with enormous enthusiasm, as the following reactions indicate: "At the very beginning they were just like forbidden fruits. People only heard about them. They only could dream about them. Then, at last, they also could buy what was not available in Hungary for such a long time" (a representative of DDB Needham Worldwide, personal communication, January 1993). For the very first time the Hungarian consumer had a certain freedom of choice. Yet at the beginning it was an extremely rudimentary freedom of choice. "He always had to buy what was available. Now there was some choice. If it was packed in foreign packaging, with foreign writing on it, he chose that one" (a representative of Young & Rubicam Hungary, personal communication, February 1993). All that was Western stood for high quality. A more refined brand awareness did not yet exist, as one of our respondents mentioned: "In Hungary, when the car market was liberated, and the people were asked 'What kind of car would you like to buy,' most of them said, 'I would like to buy a Western type car.' That was all and enough" (a representative of Lintas Budapest, personal communication, January 1993).

Today all large companies and brands are represented in the Hungarian market, and the competition is deadly, as noted by one of our respondents: "Take for instance a market like petrol stations. Sixteen competitors. Sixteen different brands battling in the same market. You can't find any other country in Europe where more than 5 or 6 different petrol station—chains are sharing the cake!" (a representative of Lintas Budapest, personal communication, January 1993). Consumers are overwhelmed by all the new names and new logos telling their individual stories. Although this is what they have wanted for years, they are now not able to deal adequately with such diversity and complexity because of formerly lacking the same, as indicated in yet another comment:

> It used to be such a simple method to buy a pair of shoes, because a pair of shoes was a pair of shoes and there only was a set number of shoes. You could buy them and they worked and they were warm in the winter. And now they go to the shops and they think, God, what do I buy, what color do I want, which image suits me? (a representative of GGK Budapest, personal communication, December 1992)

Today's Eastern European has to be taught consumer habits and enabled to make choices as an essential part of that total process, insisted one of our research subjects:

> Capitalism has arrived and it is more stressing than people thought. All the Western brands are available in Hungary too. But in the West these brands have personalities, and a history, and an identity—advertising gave it to them. Here they don't. And people do not know how to decide and choose. They are disoriented. There lies a tough job for advertising. (a representative of McCann-Erickson Interpress, personal communication, January 1993)

One thing is clear, advertising that restricts itself to communicating "buy me" is outdated.

### Advertising as Brand Name Communication

At this point, a slightly more sophisticated communication link becomes meaningful, which can be used to aim advertising messages stories at the public more effectively: advertising as brand name communication. In the constellation described previously, it is a necessary step in the communication process. Each brand has to strive for familiarity of its name with the public. Only then can one move the public to buy the brand, now and in the future, suggests a reply to our questions concerning that effort: "I guess you have to put your name everywhere. That is basic. If you want your name to be known, then you have to have it everywhere. With high intensity and with real visibility. On TV, on the radio, on outdoor displays, at presentations in the stores" (a representative of DDB Needham Worldwide, personal communication, January 1993). Procter & Gamble, for instance, is represented in every series of commercials by one of its products. In this way, high visibility is produced.

A few years ago Hungary had 50 billboards. Now it has 5,000; half of those are in Budapest. All larger companies and brands realize that visibility is a necessary condition for continued sales success. Brand name communication is an essential part of the process, because brand name communication adds visibility, and visibility can be seen as a basic form of legitimacy. What is true of positions of power in the abstract, and for the national flag as a concrete symbol also applies to product brands: As they are seen more frequently and become more visible, they legitimize their existence. It then becomes increasingly more difficult to say that they should not be allowed their place in the sun.

One way to use brand name communication effectively is to work as part of a joint venture. That was Sara Lee Douwe Egberts' approach:

> They came in as a Western company and bought the best known Hungarian coffee, Omnia. They did all the advertising together. First Omnia retained the highest name recognition. Then it was displaced by Douwe Egberts Omnia and now it is Douwe Egberts. So now they are the best known. They successfully linked themselves with the best known brand name. Then they took over Omnia, with all the narrative connotations Omnia had. (a representative of Topreklám/BBDO, personal communication, January 1993)

This kind of brand name communication strategy is faced with one danger. The association with the former Omnia, a Hungarian brand, could tarnish the international reputation of Douwe Egberts. On the other hand, it could prove to be an advantage for Douwe Egberts in the future, if or when the sociocultural climate moves from idolizing the international and the Western to a renewed longing for one's own products, and for one's Hungarian roots.

Another, more highly developed communication strategy is the building of a story, or even a legend, around the brand name, in the hope of attaching an attractive image to it. This is what Philips did. It emphasized its past ties with Hungary even though that connection had been broken by the now defunct Communist regime. Philips is using the slogan "old friendship, new quality" to gain familiarity and trust for today from old narrative connotations. Another example is IBM. As a starting point for its first campaign in Hungary it used the given fact that Hungary, just like IBM, found itself at the beginning of a new period of its life. One of those involved in that advertising campaign told us:

> When we started advertising IBM in 1989, we couldn't use the international materials. In Hungary we had to begin a story. Nobody really knew us. There was no underlying legend. And that was the guiding light of our creative people. Because both Hungary and IBM started a new life at the same time, we could develop a campaign in which we said that we were both in the same situation. (a representative of GGK Budapest, personal communication, December 1992)

Such an approach involves more than just adding visibility to the brand name. The legitimizing effect of this type of communication strategy is powerful as well, because the brand name becomes the core around which those stories and symbols are created that legitimize its very existence. More than that, the strategy legitimizes not only the existence of the brand, but also the world from which it comes and to which it belongs. As a result, brand names function as a crystallization point around which all advertising can reinforce the legitimization of the new, or the new way, and its charismatic power.

### Advertising Narratives About Product Qualities

As soon as brand name identification has been established in this way, which is not easy, advertisers usually move to product commercials. One of them informed us: "We try to tell all of our clients that if the company is not known yet in Hungary, we should start with an image campaign and then a product campaign" (a representative of Young & Rubicam Hungary, personal communication, February 1993). In 1993 there were many more product than image campaigns. Now that most brand names are well known and have acquired a definite image, the need for product information has become dominant. The fact that so many new products are being introduced also explains the need for and the current emphasis on product campaigns.

Even Coca Cola and Pepsi cannot do without campaigns that provide more specific product information. The images of these brands are, just like in the rest of the world, very well known in Hungary, as summarized by one of our respondents: "Youth, sports, music, fun, the four basic elements of the images of both Colas are valued everywhere in the same way" (a representative of Ogilvy & Mather, personal communication, January 1993). However, the famous, and in the United States widely used, Ray Charles commercial for Diet Pepsi would totally miss its target in Hungary:

> In most of the world's countries you can find the Ray Charles commercial. But what does that commercial actually say about Pepsi Light or Diet Pepsi? It doesn't talk about what a diet soft drink actually is. It does not tell you what Diet Pepsi is. It does not tell you what the product can mean to you. It shows an image. In Hungary, right now, a commercial like that would not work. Because all that knowledge about diet and "light" soft drinks hasn't been provided here for our consumers. A commercial for a product like this must show what the benefits are; it must be focused on information and less on an image. (a representative of Topreklám/BBDO, personal communication, January 1993)

Another respondent adds the following insights:

> I personally believe very much in product advertising for Hungary now. Not because I like it. I, like so many from Western Europe, prefer the artistic approach and a nice picture. But it just does not work here. People still don't know the new product very well, so, you can't sell it to them purely on the basis of an image. Most of the products are new, like Halvarine. Most of the people think that Halvarine is simply a brand name for a margarine. They don't understand the concept of "half the calories" in that name. And if a customer doesn't really know the product, I wouldn't recommend a very sophisticated advertising approach. In contemporary Hungary sophisticated advertising messages mean that their association with the product is very remote. (a representative of GGK Budapest, personal communication, December 1992)

Naturally, the choice of a specific product campaign depends on which particular business is involved. Insurance products, for instance, as another contributor to our research indicated, represent a very specific and new market in Hungary: "Under Communism everybody was more or less state protected. Now, in a very short time, everybody must become interested in private insurance, which is a completely new concept. That means a lot of explanations in advertising" (a representative of McCann-Erickson Interpress, personal communication, January 1993). On the other hand, for perfumes or candy bars product information used in commercials is very simple, or it may not even be necessary at all. There is yet another reason why product campaigns are generally preferred in today's Hungary. Even if every advertising campaign aims at developing a long-term strategy, the circumstances in Hungary change so rapidly that every long-term strategy, as a result, is partly built on quicksand. Even well-planned image campaigns rapidly become less attractive, and who can say with certainty which image will be successful for which product group or business 5 years from now? The safe way is to closely associate advertising with a given product as is indicated in the following reaction: "Whatever you advertise, if long-term impact is uncertain, it makes sense to show your product" (a representative of RSCG Havasi & Varga, personal communication, February 1993).

Brand name communication and product advertising can be seen as virtually distinct approaches because they emphasize different factors and follow each other most of the time, in the order described earlier. Moreover, the narratives they tell have different legitimizing effects. Brand name communication concentrates on making the brand more visible and better known to the public. It strives, so to speak, for a universal presence; this is its basic legitimizing capacity. Product advertising goes further, because it tells stories that further refine and shape, in an attractive way, the rough, initial information one has first received about a given brand. In this way the stories told in product advertising lift the basic legitimizing capacity of brand name communication to a higher level, which gives it a more distinct character.

## Lifestyle Advertising

In Western Europe lifestyle advertising reached its peak in the 1980s (Rohde & Burghoorn, 1991). It created a new link that advertising narratives could use to reach their audiences. Lifestyle advertising makes use of images of people who are just that little bit wealthier, prettier, and younger than the individuals in the target group. By coupling the product with such images, advertisers try to make the product more desirable. Lifestyle advertising is aspirational advertising and Hungarians are familiar with this type of commercial message as well. Viewers see these commercials broadcast on foreign television, but Hungarian stations use them as well, employing a Hungarian voice-over or a Hungarian application. In Budapest, where there always existed a cosmopolitan and Western orientation, this advertising approach is well understood. A very successful example of commercials featuring the lifestyle concept are recent ones advertising Mazda automobiles. They always feature Trabants, an Eastern European low-quality car, and they use the slogan "If I only were a Mazda," illustrating the aspirational aspect of lifestyle advertising. The Trabant has developed into the most important symbol of the inferiority of the old system. Mazda wants to identify its product as the exact opposite, and as a symbol of all that is new. An expert observer commented:

> The Mazda campaign must have been especially created for the Hungarian market. It is great, because it has irony and it is witty. It is a human story. It does not look down on the people. That's why I am sure the people will love Mazda. It's a voice with which the people can identify. (a representative of GGK Budapest, personal communication, December 1992)

The symbolic impact of the Mazda commercial is even more remarkable, because it does not even include any Mazda product.

Lifestyle commercials are not, however, most representative of today's Hungarian advertising. This type of approach is expected to grow, but it is difficult to estimate what effect that will have, as the following reaction indicates:

> I'm really curious how it will work in Hungary, because I'm not sure people are able to identify themselves already in that way. There are so many things here that change quickly. People have their own identification problems. How are you going to construct a lifestyle with which these people want to identify? (a representative of Mareco, personal communication, December 1992)

It may be possible to build a lifestyle story around a product that will make the Hungarian public look eagerly forward to its arrival even though it will remain far beyond their reach. The key question to ask about a successful lifestyle campaign is, however, how far out of reach should the image of the new lifestyle be? That is exactly the kind of question with which one of our respondents struggled: "We must not create such a big glossy image that everybody feels that it's out of reach. We must develop advertising that communicates that you can become a part of this new lifestyle. The final purpose is: Let people know that they can be a part of it" (a representative of GGK Budapest, personal communication, December 1992).

However, execution of the strategy in specific advertisements can take a hundred forms, as indicated in the following example:

> One very successful product is Wrigley's chewing gum. The commercial shows people walking the beach with a huge pack of gum. Stupid maybe, because there is no beach in Hungary. This isn't anybody's lifestyle in Hungary. Yet the commercial works. It has made Wrigley quite popular in Hungary. (a representative of Topreklám/BBDO, personal communication, January 1993)

All this is really not so remarkable in itself. People in Eastern Europe, just like those in the West, want to identify themselves with images of luxury and the good life. Problems related to more subtle intercultural differences are, however, not always solved. Seven Up, for example, used the slogan "For someone who is a somebody," and most Hungarians did not get the message. Other examples of unsuccessful lifestyle commercials can be cited, for instance: "We made a spot commercial, and the theme was American football. American football is unknown in Hungary. We tested it. They think it is too aggressive a sport. So we had to do a completely new spot" (a representative of Young & Rubicam Hungary, personal communication, February 1993).

Considering all these pitfalls, we would conclude the statement that lifestyle advertising in Hungary is a promising, but risky approach, and one of our respondents expressed the same feeling: "You can hardly predict how it will work out. On the other hand it has the potential to influence the ways in which people think and live" (a representative of RSCG Havasi & Varga, personal communication, February 1993). The last part of that statement makes clear just how great the legitimizing capacity of lifestyle advertising really is. We can consider it the superior vehicle to transmit to the public charismatic narratives about the new way of life. Intercultural differences, however, can play an impeding role, which certainly is the case in Hungary and probably in all former Communist countries. As one of our respondents put it, "Lifestyle advertising differentiates society and the market. This goes right against the essential community view in Communist society that basically everybody should be equal" (a representative of Mareco, personal communication, December 1992).

## *UJNESS* AS THE CORE SYMBOL

Whether it is the more primitive buy me concept, or brand name communication in which the brand name may or may not be surrounded by a series of stories and legends, whether it is advertising focused on the qualities of the product or on the lifestyle of the target group, images and symbols are always generated that at least help to structure reality and the collective fantasy. In fact, they may go even further and actually construct reality. Considering the deprived circumstances of the people living in Eastern Europe, the latter is not unthinkable. The impact of stories told in advertising should not be underestimated.

One key symbol stands out in all the advertising stories mentioned in this chapter, the symbol of newness, or *ujness*. This is not remarkable, because that central message of every advertising story only reflects what people see happening around them every day. The speed with which change follows change in Hungary is enormous, explained one of our contributors:

> Hungary is new and different every day. Something new happens everyday, in terms of consumer expectations, consumer goods, in terms of media, new magazines, new programs on the TV, new channels arriving on the market. What was impossible one week ago is possible today. (a representative of Lintas Budapest, personal communication, January 1993)

All that *ujness* in advertising stories not only illustrates such developments, it underlines and affirms it on a daily basis. Herein lies the basic and powerful legitimizing effect of advertising stories. Under present Eastern European circumstances the legitimizing effect of advertising narratives goes even further. During recent years we have seen that although the *ujness* people saw taking shape around them may have been confusing to them, they were very much attracted by it. Under the old regime, now and then, citizens were permitted to travel, but in addition to those experiences people constantly saw images of the West on television. Then, very slowly, more and more Western consumer goods became available. All this happened although faith in the local economy and politics had long been lost. In such a situation it was only natural that everything international and Western would be identified in the collective experience as "good," and, even more important, as "meaningful." The reasons are summarized in this succinct response to our questions:

> They want to enjoy life now. That's very important everywhere; so it is very important to marketing as well. Their lives are shaped by a new fashion. Shaped over and over in new fashions. That's new, that's absolutely new. This is the one desired future. They love it. They want it. (a representative of GGK Budapest, personal communication, December 1992)

Advertising not only makes use of this collective enthusiasm for *ujness*, it supports it in countless ways by enlisting attractive images and symbols with which it underlines and legitimizes international, Westernizing developments. Such efforts represent the charismatic legitimizing effect of all that is new at its best. In the past, everyone went along with this approach, with Hungarian advertisers leading the pack, as one of them indicated: "Here in Hungary, we have the greatest desire for proving that we are as good as they are in the West. Sometimes you feel that a Hungarian commercial wants to be even more Western than the Western commercials are" (a representative of Topreklám/BBDO, personal communication, January 1993).

## THE DANGER OF A CONDESCENDING ATTITUDE

At the same time, we must not overlook the fact that there is developing a change in attitudes held by Hungarian consumers and citizens toward this highly praised *ujness*. Advertising stories using the Western *ujness* theme time and again are in increasing danger of provoking annoyed reactions. When one communicates the concept of *ujness*, it is easy to be condescending. For example, when the German company Henkel entered the market, they started to broadcast 6-year-old commercials in Hungary. But Hungarian customers knew these old commercials; they had already seen them in years past on international networks. In such situations Hungarian consumers feel that they are considered to be inferior. "Hungarians now start thinking that Western people consider them less valuable and less educated, while, in effect, only the economic situation is different," said one of our respondents (a representative of DDB Needham Worldwide, personal communication, January 1993). Aversion to this kind of condescension can only increase if one considers, among others, a marketing strategy used by Philips in Eastern Europe. That company offered outdated electric shavers on the Hungarian market. Undoubtedly, such an approach resulted in short-term profits, but it can be predicted that it damaged Philips' image in the long run. Moreover, it increased the Hungarian dislike for what was seen as representative of the condescending attitude of the West. To cite another example, whether it is true or not, no one deems it unthinkable that the West dumps bad condoms on the Eastern European market. This illustrates how easily fertile ground can be found for reactions based on what are seen as subtle and not so subtle forms of negative Western displays of superiority.

Advertising images and narratives provoke the strongest resentment when they do not recognize a growing East European aversion to condescending *ujness* communications. Such images and stories often reveal the patronizing attitude of the West in its most concentrated form, according to one of the participants in our research projects:

> When they bring a new detergent on the market, they say in many ways: "You are really, really lucky, to be able to have bought Omo today. Because it is not Hungarian, it's Omo, and it's so much better." In fact, Omo isn't that special. But it is Omo, and the people here are Hungarian. That should be enough to make them feel fortunate to have bought Omo. (a representative of Lintas Budapest, personal communication, January 1993)

Current attitudes within the advertising community still promote such an approach. One respondent's impression is that the international chains that dominate the scene want to stay in control as much as possible:

> A lot of international clients aren't prepared to trust the local countries to do their own thing. That's why there is so much adaptation. They want to be sure that in Czechoslovakia and Bulgaria and Rumania and Moscow people see the same quality work. Quality work according to the standards of Western countries. (a representative of DDB Needham Worldwide, personal communication, January 1993)

Even though this attitude is understandable, it can also confirm for Hungarian consumers their opinion that the West makes no effort to adapt its advertising images to Hungarian requirements. "If you consider commercial breaks in Hungary now, 80% of the material is international, which means 80% is adapted. Only the ending is changed into Hungarian, or the last 10 seconds are in Hungarian, or the voice-over is in Hungarian," one of the participants in our research project explained. It is true that this has not produced a general lack of enthusiasm during the past years for the charismatic impact of all that is new. But, as we mentioned before, things do change in fast in Eastern Europe. Good marketing and advertising should consider that fact, said one of our subjects:

> The people here are not the most bouncy, happy people in the world. But through all their years of difficulties and depression, they have developed and retained their intelligence and a critical eye. With their eyes they look at advertising now. They are perfectly capable of making judgments and evaluations for themselves. They don't need the teacherlike manner of contemporary advertising. To change that is one of our most important jobs, I think. (a representative of GGK Budapest, personal communication, December 1992)

The advertising community is beginning to change. Most of the agencies now employ more Hungarians, and in top positions one can find only one, or at the most two, non-Hungarians. Furthermore, the realization is growing that Eastern Europe has its own cultural roots, and that insight influences organization in the advertising community more and more. One practitioner commented:

> We now have an agency in Prague, one in Warsaw and one here in Budapest. The markets in these three countries are more or less in the same situation. The three departments work very closely together to develop campaigns that fit the Eastern European market. Not only for reasons of cost efficiency, but also because the whole region needs its own advertising. (a representative of Lintas Budapest, personal communication, January 1993)

## A STATE OF REFLECTION: BACK TO THE ROOTS?

Though change never ceases in Hungary, there can be found some clues that its citizens have entered a reflective phase. There are several indications to support that impression: changes in actual buying behavior, reactions to the invasion of Western images and symbols of *ujness*, which are growing stronger, and also the way in which people are reemphasizing their cultural roots as a foundation for national pride. To begin with we provide insights into shifts in actual buying behavior, which were provided by a respondent to our study:

> In the first 7 years of our freedom people bought everything which was Western, just because it was Western. It had very nice packaging and an even nicer promise. But now people are beginning to realize that Hungarian products are sometimes much better. (a representative of Ogilvy & Mather, personal communication, January 1993)

(And much cheaper, we might add.) If Hungarian products still lack nice packaging, especially for fruits and vegetables, it does not follow that their quality is lower than that of their Western import counterparts. That fact is being discovered everywhere, and it is encouraged by near-empty consumer wallets, as the following reaction makes clear: "For example, last year there was a campaign by one of the biggest store chains. They developed a campaign for Hungarian products. And everybody thought that it would be a failure, because who would want to buy Hungarian products. On the contrary! It was an enormous success" (a representative of GGK Budapest, personal communication, December 1992). That reaction only seems like a miracle to those who believe that the charismatic appeal of all that is new, Western, and international continues to shine brightly, making all else seem pale and dull by comparison. This is no longer the case! Take, for example, French wine sold in Hungary, which costs 500 forints for the worst and cheapest kind. On the next shelf one can find Hungarian Tokai, which is far better, far cheaper. Nobody used to want it, because it was Hungarian. One of our respondents claimed, "But now it's changing, I am quite sure" (a representative of Young & Rubicam Hungary, personal communication, February 1993). Naturally, such a shift translates into advertising images as well. "Using an American image is not an advantage here, anymore. During the next 2, 3 years we will have to develop a new media culture, which will adapt to shifts in consumer needs and in the culture itself. That new media culture still does not exist at the moment," is a valuable insight, in that regard, provided by one of our advertising practitioners (a representative of McCann-Erickson Interpress, personal communication, January 1993).

It is true that the sophistication level of the Hungarian public as it reacts to advertising messages is still below that of Western publics. In the West, communication between advertising agencies and publics has been culturally institutionalized in such a way that either one needs only a hint from the other to understand various messages. In that setting even subtle images are immensely informative or revealing. On the other hand, as one Hungarian advertiser observed, ". . . sometimes these commercials are still too sophisticated for the Hungarian audience" (a representative of Ogilvy & Mather, personal communication, January 1993).

This applies, as we have seen, especially to lifestyle advertising. In the West that approach became enough of a cliché to lose much of its effectiveness, whereas in the East it is still new enough so that the whole concept is not yet clear to everyone. But it is wrong to accept the lack of sophistication among Hungarians and to make that state of affairs the starting point for communication policies. There are two reasons for not being satisfied with the status quo. First, Eastern Europe and especially Hungarians are learning fast. Their countries are being invaded by new technologies. A significant part of the population has an almost fanatic interest in that process. Many people in Eastern Europe gain more new information in 24 hours than many Western consumers and citizens do in 24 months or weeks. The following response from one of our subjects is enlightening in that regard:

> I think we are taking an immense leap from where we were, from the very old and the almost redundant. Telecommunication helps us to successfully make that leap. A lot of Western countries want to sell us their best; I guess they get a good price for it. So, hopefully, in about 10 to 15 years this country will probably be more advanced than all the Western countries, because here we have bought the most avant-garde of Western technology. (a representative of GGK Budapest, personal communication, December 1992)

Even though it is a very optimistic view of the future that is being indicated in that summary statement, one thing seems certain, this respondent claimed, "We are not going through the evolutionary stages the West went through" (a representative of Topreklám/BBDO, personal communication, January 1993). Eastern Europe may evolve faster, a lot faster, but also by suffering a lot more confusion. Ultimately the fact must be accepted, that under 40 years of a Communist regime Hungary did not stand still in all areas, and it was not cut off entirely from developments in the West. That means Eastern Europe does have to start all over again from a point where it was 40 years ago.

There is a second reason why we should not take the low level of sophistication in Eastern Europe in regard to advertising as a starting point for the development of communication policies. Increasingly, Western messages are being interpreted as condescending. No matter how subtly Western superiority is communicated as *ujness*, the Hungarian consumer is developing a negative response to it. That in itself is an indication of how fast the level of sophistication is rising among Hungarians when it comes to reactions to contemporary advertising. They get annoyed and turn away, and their awareness of the fact that they are no different *as human beings and as cultural beings* from their well-to-do Western neighbors is increasing. Expectations they have concerning the future, as citizens and as consumers, are the expectations of today's individuals everywhere, and not those of people living in an "underdeveloped" country of the early 1950s. In the view of a growing number of Hungarians the only real difference between the East and the West is income. That view is summarized for us in the following statement:

> Everything is going very, very fast. The Hungarian consumer is joining the Western consumer very fast. However, not in terms of purchasing power. There is a big difference between how much the average Hungarian consumer can spend and what the average Western consumer can spend. Nevertheless, in terms of expectations, both in consumer expectations and in expectations from life in general, they are equal. (a representative of Mareco, personal communication, December 1992)

Put in these terms, the biggest problem seems to be a problem of price. Eastern Europeans want the same things as Westerners do, and they consider themselves to be their equals. Charismatic advertising narratives about all that is new have confirmed their belief that their desires are justified and legitimate; the only problem is that Hungarians cannot afford their dreams. In that situation every hint of Western domination or cultural superiority becomes exaggerated. Seen in this light, Hungarians' aversion to formerly successful *ujness* communications becomes understandable.

The promised happiness, the promised prosperity and riches, are not materializing, which led one observer to comment:

> These are short-term-oriented people. Frustrated people. Don't forget their 40 years of frustration. They want to get the money *now*. Not in 10 years. They have waited for 40 years. And now some people, people from the West, come and say that they must see things from a long-term perspective. What is long term in a Hungarian's eyes? Death! (a representative of Lintas Budapest, personal communication, January 1993)

Outside the area of consumption, Hungarians realize as well what problems have arisen since the escalation of economic and political reforms. "I guess you have to pay for freedom and democracy with crime, don't you, sir?" said a Hungarian taxi driver to me, with all the lack of emotion peculiar to his people.

People are disappointed because they are still in deep trouble. They even feel cheated, because of the advertising messages that painted and continue to paint pictures of the new, the international, and the Western as legitimate images of the future. They ask themselves if they are really happier people because of all the promises made in the name of *ujness*. Is there not more pride and a stronger sense of their own identity to be found in their own history, their own roots? That is the most current question on the minds of many Hungarians. That question could result in a vengeful response. On the other hand, it could fall silent, if under more favorable economic circumstances the charismatic narratives of the new become more attractive again. It is also possible that new advertising formats will be created, new advertising formats that join worlds, Western internationalism, and the roots of the proud Hungarian people. However, that scenario demands a new and different attitude, even a whole new media culture. But, as we stated earlier, that new media culture does not yet exist.

## CONCLUSION

Like no other medium, advertising supplies the images and symbols, and especially the stories or narratives of the Western world with which Hungary has been saturated during the years after the collapse of Communism. Advertising, and especially lifestyle advertising, even seems to have the power to divide society once again. It produces countless narratives, images, and symbols to provide the ingredients for an attempt to supply Hungarian culture and society with a new legitimacy. In this chapter we have called that process the charismatic legitimization of the new. Its major components are internationalization, the Western lifestyle, and *ujness*.

We have, however, also pointed out that there are some signs of change. Charismatic messages about the new have not immediately brought the prosperity and happiness people expected. The power of the message, as a result, has decreased, and the Hungarian people may end up seeking new forms of legitimacy for their society. They may find it is their own history, their own specific culture, their own roots, ever-remembered aspects of their past that are growing more and more attractive. Few advertising narratives in support of this possible development exist so far, but growing dissatisfaction with current advertising messages makes a turnabout not improbable. Until that turnabout becomes a reality, however, advertisers will have to take into account the growing sensitivity of Hungarians to every condescending gesture emanating from the West. Even the slightest hint of a new attempt at colonization will cause Hungarians to react negatively, even though their resistance may not be expressed openly or violently. Such a covert resistance would be in keeping with the history and the traditional, culturally conditioned responses of Hungarians whenever they have been put under pressure by outside forces.

## REFERENCES

Adler, N. J. (1985). *International dimensions of organizational behavior*. Boston: Kent.

Ewen, S. (1976). *Captains of consciousness: Advertising and the social roots of the consumer culture*. New York: McGraw-Hill.

Featherstone, M. (1990). *Global culture, nationalism, globalization and modernity.* London: Sage.
Hofstede, G. (1984). *Cultures consequences: International differences in work related values.* Beverly Hills, CA: Sage.
Leiss, W., Kline, S., & Jhally, S. (1986). *Social communication in advertising: Persons, products and images of well-being.* Toronto: Methuan.
Rohde, C. C., & Burghoorn, A. (1991). *The reception of symbols in international advertising: between universalism and particularism.* Utrecht, The Netherlands: Isor.
Schein, E. H. (1991). *Organizational culture and leadership.* San Francisco: Jossey-Bass.
Segal, D. R. (1992). The transformation of European Communist societies. In L. Kriesberg & D. R. Segal (Eds.), *Social movements, conflicts and change* (pp. 5–). Greenwich, CT: JAI.
Thompson, J. B. (1992). *Ideology and modern culture, Critical social theory in the era of mass communication.* Cornwall, England: T. J. Press Padstow Ltd.
Weber, M. (1968). *On charisma and institution building* (Selected papers, S. N. Eisenstadt, Ed.). Chicago: University of Chicago Press.

# IV

# COMPLEXITIES OF CHANGE: OTHER EASTERN EUROPEAN EXAMPLES

Fred L. Casmir

Eastern Europe, the Balkans, these words often lack any feeling of precision or clear identification. Like so many other umbrella terms they hide more than they reveal. In keeping with the concepts of this volume that culture and history play major roles in the interactions of nations, and that in our contemporary world the impact of media has added another significant dimension to political and economic developments, the contributions to this section are intended to give at least some insight into the incredibly complex intercultural communication challenges the people of Eastern Europe face.

One of the first countries to manifest an internal effort to break with the Communist system, and develop a democratic form of government was Poland. In spite of that fact, internal struggles and external influences, which we have already noticed in the cases of Germany and Hungary, also led to unexpected developments in Poland. "Demassification" is the term Olson has chosen to explore what has taken place in Polish media, as the logical outgrowth of traditional Polish culture. It is instructive to trace developments in Poland from the singular voice of state-controlled media under Communism to the multitude of voices and interests today. Indeed, struggling with the roles, types, and impacts of demassified media is something most East European states have had to do in recent years. Based on firsthand impressions gained during his stay in Poland, and continued interactions with well-informed individuals in Poland, Olson uses the resulting intercultural information base to advantage, as he studies contemporary Polish media.

Bringing a very different background and field of interest to his chapter, Gilder addresses the intercultural challenges faced and the insights gained by someone who has been in Romanian classrooms for a number of years. The firsthand experiences of this author demonstrate not only common challenges faced by anyone who desires to share knowledge or insights with someone from another culture, but they also present us with an opportunity to understand better the internal conflicts and cultural value systems that Romanians bring to the what Gilder calls a "severe transformation process." The limits and the opportunities such a situation provides, especially for a cultural *outsider*, give pause to anyone who approaches teaching, instruction, and training across cultural lines of division with the naive impression *"that all we have to do"* is to be concerned with people and make our insights *available* to them. Gilder's attempt to find a *rhetorical* strategy for his work is only one of many answers individuals had to discover and apply as they find themselves communicating interculturally. It is not difficult to understand why Gilder claims that *"fostering a democratic spirit"* requires the development of skills that go far beyond the sharing of information or language learning.

As we listen to the voice of someone who does not enter our dialogue as a cultural outsider, but rather as someone who was born in Bulgaria, knows its history, and spent many years there, Iordonova carves another facet into our reflections on developments in Eastern Europe. Factors that are often overlooked as we study contemporary developments are the traditional roles, positions, history, and value systems, especially of smaller Eastern European countries that have been caught in a multitude of conflicts for hundreds of years. Most of us know the name of Bulgaria; very few of us know where exactly it is located, or what is significant or important about it. As Iordonova invites us to take a look at Bulgarian media, we are forced to recognize the fact that for hundreds of years Bulgaria has identified itself vis-à-vis other countries or powers, and that that process continues. Iordonova demonstrates how important the media can be in providing insights, but how they function also as a source of distortion for what is happening in our world. We have seen similar influences at play in the case of Hungary, and are thus reminded once more of the fact that those who are fortunate enough to have at least access to a variety of voices and media need to carefully consider how differently history has prepared other people in other cultures to listen, hear, and understand.

Adade's chapter is purposively included here to provide very different insights and reminders of the fact that intercultural communication challenges *inside* a country often make us forget that there are broader and more general challenges to be faced. *Internal* conflicts between ethnic and cultural groups are, of course, evidence of bigotries, hatreds, and historic events that need to be understood if we are to deal with them in an effective way. However, racism is something that has an impact far beyond the internal conflicts in one country or among one people—it is a plague that has infected much of the human race. Adade's firsthand experiences, as an African in the former Soviet Union and now with Russians, remind us of the tragic fact that racism is *not* limited to one nation, one people, or one state. It is a pervasive practice born out of ignorance, fear, the lack of communication between ethnic and cultural groups, feelings of unwarranted superiority, and distorted information as a result of slanted or inadequate media presentations. In reading Adade's chapter it is the striking similarities across political, ethnic, or cultural boundaries that confront the reader with the necessity to find answers to much more than a limited-in-time or -space problem.

Just how deep the roots of misunderstandings, mistrust, fears, and outright hatred go has been difficult for most of us to understand or believe—until the former Yugoslavia, an early deserter from the ranks of Soviet Russian Communism, a country of beauty, great cultural achievements, impressive monuments, "wonderful people," and the Sarajevo Olympics, exploded in an orgy of bloodletting and so-called *"ethnic cleansing."* The question *"who would have thought it?"* became both a confession of ignorance and the perplexed reaction of individuals, outsiders, who had simplistically based their impressions of Eastern Europe on what *they* knew, *they* believed, and *they* experienced. In other words, culture and history were largely ignored in favor of a belief in supposedly significant, positive social, political, and economic changes that could be readily produced in an age of rapid technological advancement and scientific development.

Williams' chapter stands at the end of our search for understanding, because it is a well-documented, carefully reasoned study of what happens when human rights violations become the norm in a bloodbath just as complex as the cultural, historical, ethnic, and religious factors that produced it. Maybe the outcry of the Jewish people *"never again!"* should be globally modified, because of the insights we have gained in this chapter and the others that preceded it, into a determined *"never again shall we be so naive!"*

My own, final chapter is not so much a summary as an attempt to think through the *implications* of what we have learned, and what answers would seem to be required of those of us who seek an intercultural dialogue rather than the continued application of models that have been woefully inadequate. It should *not* be seen so much as an ending, or as a conclusion, but rather as a call for *new beginnings* that make use of the best insights and the best knowledge available to us. After all, the ultimate challenge for social scientists has always been the *meaningful, beneficial application* of what we have learned, not merely the presentation of what we think we understand and know to others like us.

# 7

# *New Democratic Vistas: Demassification and the Polish Media*

Scott R. Olson
*Central Connecticut State University*

In Poland they have a saying: Get two Poles in a room and you will have three opinions. This is a good description of the irony implicit in Poland's democratic vistas. The democratic possibilities are manifold, but its meaning too diversified. To work properly, democracy relies on consensus and majority, something Poland is finding difficult to develop even though democratic institutions themselves are secure. The media now act to increase the diversity of possible meanings, not narrow them. The Polish paradox, then, is perhaps one of too much democracy.

The roots of this paradox can be found in Polish communication styles and traditions, which set the stage for varied and complex textual readings. There are adequate theories to account for the extensive demassification Polish media have engendered, a demassification greater than the removal of Stalinism alone could predict. In short, *telewizja* (television) has created new democratic vistas for Poland, but the horizon stretches out in all directions.

From a cultural standpoint, democracy in Poland is a logical outgrowth of its traditional culture. From a historical standpoint, and particularly in the light of 20th-century Polish history, democracy is precarious, endangered from within and without. There is a history of a quest for freedom and of democracy movements in Poland, from the Kosciusko revolt in the 18th century to the uprisings of the 19th century and the Solidarity movement in the 1980s; all of these sought to redistribute power from the foundations up, in order to make the peasants a citizenry

(Wieniewski, 1981). But this quest for democracy has seldom achieved its goal. Although a measure of freedom and democracy has been attained in the 1990s, it is in some ways a fragile variety, and one unique to Poland. Bogucka (in Maryniak, 1993) pointed out that the alliance to promote democracy between intellectuals, workers, and peasants in the Solidarity of the 1980s has since fallen apart as the workers and peasants have become more interested in increased wages than in economic reform. This is reflected in the 1993 parliamentary crisis that culminated in an election in which a former Communist, Waldemar Pawlak from the Polish Peasant Party, became prime minister (Perlez, 1993b). This party and government have no ties to Solidarity, and they have pledged to slow down the pace of reforms.

Poland is a nearly uncontaminated example of the demassification effect. Demassification means that the dominant effect of the mass media is to decentralize, particularize, and segment society rather than centralize and unify it. It has two domains: the democratization of transmission and the diversification of reception. Its transmission domain has been analyzed by Pool (1983), Brand (1987), and McLuhan and Powers (1989). The reception domain has been examined at the textual level by Ang (1985, 1991) and Fiske and Hartley (1976). Particularly useful concepts in describing textual demassification are textual "poaching" (Bacon-Smith, 1992; de Certeau, 1984; Jenkins, 1988, 1992), oppositional decoding (Hall, 1980; L. Steiner, 1988), and polysemy (Condit, 1989; Fiske, 1987). Demassification has also been observed in the disparity between designed and actual effects of propaganda by White and Pravda (1988) and Mickiewicz (1985). The incipient social devolution has been observed (Howell, 1982; Olson, 1985, 1987) and described theoretically (Olson, 1994b). In Poland, bottled-up voices for liberty were suddenly let loose in a country with a historical love of freedom, democracy, and the rule of law but a tendency to slide into political anarchy, parochialism, fanaticism, and chauvinism.

In order to understand the interplay of communication and democracy in Poland, it is important to first analyze Polish communication culture to see what patterns of communication are unique to it. Second, theories of the relationship between media, meaning, and demassification are examined. Third, these theories are applied to the Polish media and their relationship with democracy. The example of a contemporary Polish political television program is examined in the light of these theories. This exegesis reveals that Poland is truly a country of ironies: Even its demassification takes on a massified form.

Does it make sense to import theory to Poland in order to describe its media? In a sense, of course, a scholar observing primary phenomenon must have theory; things cannot be observed without it. Pure description is impossible. Nevertheless, theory needs to be appropriate to the situation to which it is applied. The theories of demassification used here have been developed by scholars throughout the world, and tested empirically in Western Europe, Africa, North and South America, and Australia; I would argue that they also have some initial applicability to Eastern Europe. At the very least they can provide a way to begin thinking about the relationship between media and democracy in Poland.

## POLISH COMMUNICATION CULTURE

Communication culture is used here to mean the essential principles and values that constitute and are constituted by communication processes. Earlier in this volume, Casmir defines culture as a "human sense-making explanatory tool" with implicit control mechanisms and common environmental interpretations. Bogucka (1981) described culture in the Polish context as an arbitrary and adaptive set of rules; to understand Polish culture is to identify these informal rules, particularly as they manifest themselves in communication. Such rules form the way Poles communicate, and as they are communicated, they reinforce cultural values. In effect, they manifest themselves in most forms of Polish communication, from interpersonal to mass communication, but they are easiest to observe in the mass media. The five most identifiable attributes of Polish communication culture are: the idealization and romanticization of the peasant and the countryside, the love of liberty, Christianity, chivalry, and Western classicism.

Casmir (1992) and Olson (1985) discussed the problems inherent in presuming that nations, cultures, and subcultures are economically and politically contiguous. Frequently, they are not the same thing, which leads to confusion when intercultural communication is being discussed: Is communication between countries necessarily intercultural communication? Can communication within a country be intercultural? Poland is a country, and although it is generally contiguous with the Polish culture, it is not completely so. Not everyone living in Poland is Polish, and Poland's current borders date only from World War II. Lower Silesia used to be part of Germany, and the Poles living there were transplanted from L'vov in the Ukraine, a part of which used to be in Poland. Within Poland there are several ethnic minorities, including Lithuanian, Ukrainian, German, and Russian. Compared with most European states, however, Poland is more of a nation-state; the nation and the state mostly overlap. The attributes of the culture described here do not reflect the sub- or cocultures within Poland except to the extent that they have shaped Polish culture. Neither are these attributes meant to be comprehensive or exclusive; many of these elements can be found elsewhere in Europe. They are a necessary but insufficient beginning point for defining Polish communication culture.

***Peasant Culture.*** Wieniewski (1981) called the first of these attributes, the peasant ideal, "the native element" and saw its roots in the Polish-Slavic ethnicity found in the region. The reverent status conferred on the peasant class is embodied in all forms of Polish communication. The origins of the peasant-centeredness of Polish communication can be found in Venedian culture, which brought peasant crafts and a sedentary agrarian economy to Poland in the second century B.C. Since that time, peasants have come to be known as "the belly of the Polish nation" (Kasprowicz in Wieniewski, 1981, p. 24), which is not surprising because two thirds of all Poles descend from the peasant class.

Romanticizing Polish peasant simplicity in speech, dress, and custom permeates Polish arts and literature. This gives rise to various elements of the culture, each with positive and negative aspects: religiosity, which can sometimes take on a fanatical tone; patriotism and self-sacrifice for freedom, which can occasionally develop into a chauvinistic forms; simplicity, which can lead to oversimplification of complex social issues; and Sarmatian ideals—the love of all things native, which can degenerate into "sarmatism," parochialism or backwardness. Indeed, folklore and ruralness seem to be the primary foundations of Polish traditions and consciousness. The *fin de siècle* author and Nobel prize winner Wladyslaw Reymont described the "savage love of the soil, the pious attachment to tradition, the complete psyche, closely tied to the landscape, the climate and the unchanging cycle of work in all four seasons" (in Wieniewski, 1981, p. 25).

Even the Polish language embodies this native/peasant orientation. Fierce pride in the Polish tongue began with Mikolaj Rej in the 16th century. In Rej's works and in the poems of Kochanowksi, the peasant tradition and village life are romanticized. The language used can be political as well as purely romantic. Under Communism, Polish communication styles began to reflect the country's new political economy. By the early 1980s, language and speech manifested social attitudes: "We didn't 'buy' things, we 'received' them. We would say 'I've received a loaf of bread' (*dostalem chleb*); 'I've received some milk' (*dostalem mleko*). And if it was more difficult to buy something we would say 'caught' (*zdobylem*, literally 'conquered'). 'I've caught a pair of shoes'; 'I've caught a telly' " (Teresa Bogucka in Maryniak, 1993, p. 13). Even in this politicization of speech, however, the romantic peasant tradition is evident, because it truly undergirds all aspects of Polish life and culture. The enduring power of that tradition was evidenced in the 1993 Polish elections, in which the Polish Peasant Party came in second in overall votes (Koza, 1993b).

***Freedom.*** The love of freedom is a second attribute of Polish culture. Stankiewicz (1981) saw the search for liberty as the central feature of Polish history, particularly since the 16th-century "golden age." Roos

(1981) felt that freedom and equality in the form of a social contract were for Polish gentry the political and intellectual bases of Poland. The intellectuals, workers, and peasants of Poland have had strong inclinations toward democracy throughout their history, although there have been few opportunities for expression. The origins of Polish democracy coincide with the origins of American democracy; in fact, General Pulaski, who fought for Polish freedom together with General Kosciusko, also fought in the American Revolution. One outcome of the Kosciusko uprising was the "Uniwersal Polaniecki" proclamation in 1794, which created universal freedom in Poland and gave serfs the right to own property (Wienewski, 1981). Consequently, Polish culture has always been tolerant of political dissent; under the principle of *de non praestanda oboedientia* (roughly, "no surpassing obedience"), for example, citizens in the 16th century could be excused from political obligation to the crown.

Roos (1981) also pointed out that this passion for liberty at times resulted in a *reductio ad absurdum*. Although the goal of these democratic safeguards was the preservation of personal liberty, when they came to be understood in absolute terms, political chaos was the result, including "extreme parliamentarianism with its crippling principle of *liberum veto* (unanimity), the selfishness of the aristocracy, and the unrestrained individualism, fecklessness and lack of loyalty to their king displayed by the gentry" (Stankiewicz, 1981, p. 16). The resulting chaos was always of a political sort, though, and it did not degenerate into social disorder or violence as often was the case in other European nations. Ironically, as liberty led to anarchy, that anarchy weakened Poland, setting the stage for Russian and Prussian conquests (Roos, 1981).

***Christianity.*** A third attribute of Polish communication culture, Christianity, refers, of course, to the influence of the Roman Catholic Church, which was introduced to Poland in 966 A.D. The church fused easily with the native peasant aspects of the culture, and affected many customs and beliefs, primarily through its mixing of piety and patriotism (Wieniewski, 1981). In part, Christianity has been such a tenacious influence in Poland because Polish Christians then and now regard themselves as "the rampart of Christendom" (Stankiewicz, 1981). The essential attributes of Roman Catholicism that can be said to have influenced Polish culture are a belief in hierarchical authority, the reinforcement of a Roman legal system, a bearing that resists moral intervention from outside the church, and particularly the legitimation of traditional masculine and feminine roles (Kohn & Slomczynski, 1990). Hand kissing is only one readily observable manifestation of this gender role differentiation (Bogucka, 1981).

The role of the church in resisting Communism cannot be underestimated. In fact, the church is for many Poles the "bastion of morality" (Bogucka in Maryniak, 1993, p. 13). However, the Roman church has not affected all aspects of Polish life. Intellectuals in particular are much more positivistic and materialistic than the rest of the country, and although there have been Catholic intellectuals, the effect of Catholicism on intellectual life is dwindling (Wieniewski, 1981).

***Chivalry.*** Chivalry is a fourth attribute of Polish communication culture. The medieval kings and queens of Poland are memorialized and enshrined in Wawel Castle in Krakow and elsewhere, and they remain a source of great pride for the Polish people. Many aspects of the culture reflect this. Wootton (1981) described Polish composer Chopin's music as an embodiment of Polish "chivalry and noblesse." Daniells (1981) felt that honor, strength, courtly grace, gentility, and courage as embodied in the Teutonic Knight stories are essentially Polish virtues. Popular entertainment, particularly for children, is dominated by chivalric images as Poles look back to a lost golden age. The Polish national symbol, the eagle, reminds us of the heraldry of chivalric traditions. Polish chivalry is also embodied in the formality of Polish speech (Bogucka, 1981).

***Classicism.*** A final dominant aspect of Polish culture is Western classicism. This refers to the way the dual threads of idealism and realism that are woven through classical literature manifest themselves in Poland. From classical culture, according to Wieniewski (1981), the Poles have gained "individualism, respect for humanity, democratic ideals of equality, individual and national liberty, . . . [and] the Polish ideals of freedom, patriotism, rule of law, tolerance, and democracy" (p. 82). It is because of this Western element that Poles and Polish communication reflect an attachment to the West rather than the East. Poles, after all, are quick to point out that they are a *central* European nation, not an eastern European one.

In summary, then, it is possible to identify the following essential elements of Polish communication culture: the romanticizing of peasant life and culture; a love of chivalry, simplicity, and the land; hierarchical authority; traditionally defined gender roles; individualism; patriotism; and the belief in freedom, equality, and democracy. Although this communication culture is frequently in conflict with itself, it remains true that through a culture's communication rules, its internal logics can be understood best (Bogucka, 1981). In order to understand how these cultural attributes are reinforced in the media and manifested in an explosion of democracy, it is essential to understand media demassification.

## DEMASSIFICATION THEORY

Traditional mass communication theory only considered the massifying effects of the media. Such a process includes the unifying, collective, deliberate, and strategic aspects of media programming. Massification effects include nation building (e.g., Schramm, 1964), propaganda (e.g., Lasswell, 1927), indoctrination (e.g., Grachev & Yermoshkin, 1984), and other "development" agendas (Hornik, 1980). Although some massification effects have been observed under specific circumstances, it would be wrong to conclude that these are the only effects the media can have. Media can have a strong demassification effect as well, acting to disunify and separate, often in an accidental, coincidental, or "guerrilla" fashion. Two types of demassification are commonly identified: first, the democratization of transmission, that is, a decentralization and redistribution of the means by which messages are communicated; second, the diversification of reception, the absence of singular and simple responses in the ways audience members understand and interpret these messages. At the transmission level, the theories deal with participatory democracy, and at the reception level, they consider oppositional decoding, polysemy, poaching, and devolution.

### Transmission

The democratization of transmission is the most frequently studied issue because it is of interest to the commercial and public policy as well as to the academic worlds. It examines how increasing the number of media channels and the amount of information transmitted on them creates greater diversity and democracy; this increased media diversity supposedly brings about "true democracy" by virtue of the breadth of options it allows (Becker & Schoenbach, 1989). The media usually discussed in this connection are computers and television, the former as an example of the demassification of interpersonal media, the latter as an example in mass media. Because these two media are currently converging into one single medium, computers are taking on aspects of mass media and television of interpersonal media. For example, televisions will soon have computerlike operating systems. Because computers have not had the same broad household distribution in Poland that they have in the United States, for purposes of this chapter the democratization of transmission in Poland refers mostly to the television medium.

Historically, U.S. television has had a unifying and centralizing effect on American culture (see Tichi, 1991), however new technologies that provide viewers with greater opportunity to make selections and exert control over programming seem to be changing this. Scores of broadcast, cable, and satellite voice, video, and data channels are now available in the United States. New technological breakthroughs promise the equivalent of 500 channels in the near future, leading President Clinton to speak of an "information superhighway."

It has been observed in the Netherlands (Olderaan & Jankowski, 1989) and Italy (Martini & Mazzoleni, 1989) that increasing the number of available media channels increases time spent in using them. It is not clear, however, that demassifying transmission actually increases democracy. In other words, we cannot be sure that increases in transmission actually result in democratization, or that "more" is necessarily better. Certainly, increasing the number of channels does increase the volume of voices, but it does not necessarily diversify them (Becker & Schoenbach, 1989). Although democratization is a presumed effect of demassifying transmission, it is not an inevitable one. Audiences can reject media diversification as easily as adopt it; frequently, what is "adopted" is the increased viewing of entertainment, not political broadcasts (Bouillin-Dartevelle, 1989; Wober, 1989). To assume that availability of more channels automatically means more democracy is a kind of "magic bullet" or "hypodermic injection" assumption, a theory of media effects long since abandoned (Bineham, 1988; Sproule, 1989). In that connection, it is instructive to remember that Heidegger (1977) suggested that even though we will to master technology, control over it slips through our fingers.

The most familiar argument linking demassification of transmission to democratic systems is to argue that increasing the number of channels and creating opportunities for interactivity increases the participation of citizens in their own democracy, gradually replacing representative democracy with "participatory democracy." Such speculation seems to have inspired Ross Perot's "electronic townhall" vision during the 1992 U.S. presidential campaign (see Elgin, 1991, who advocated weekly or monthly electronic town meetings to track constituent opinion). Most of the participatory democracy enthusiasts write for the popular press (e.g., Naisbitt, 1982; Toffler, 1981), but a few use a more scholarly approach. Rheingold (1991, 1993) particularly emphasized the role of the computer in the media democratization process, as a means of transformation from mass to grass-roots media. Pool (1983) is one of the most theoretically grounded of the demassified-transmission futurists. His argument is that new electronic media technologies, such as electronic publishing and cable television, will be a boon to free speech because they "are dispersed in use and abundant in supply. They allow for more knowledge, easier access, and freer speech than were ever enjoyed before. They fit the free practices of print. The characteristics of media shape what is done with them, so one might anticipate that these technologies of freedom will overwhelm all attempts to control them" (p. 251). Brand (1987), and McLuhan and Powers (1989) expressed similar views. In other words, in a technologically deterministic sense, electronic media decentralize control and diversify the voices in public debate; thus more is assumed to be better. The freedom such decentralization engenders results in more democracy. Landow (1992) looked at technological determinism from a critical perspective, yet similarly concluded that new electronic media will decenter and democratize access to and use of media.

Even the geographic limitations of government may be preempted in an electronic media environment. Although currently "all politics is local," electronic media create communities that transcend specific localities. Godwin (1991), for example, argued that virtual communities that exist in cyberspace will become a potent political force, creating constituencies and "neighborhoods" scattered across the world, linked only by fiber optic wire. This is of course consistent with McLuhan's (1964) concept of an electronic "global village," except that Godwin (1991) envisioned many villages, not just one.

This interpretation of the new media environment is frequently cited by giant telecommunications companies to assuage public fears as they merge with other giant telecommunications companies. However, at the present time there exists no situation in the United States that proves that additional channels means the emergence of more diverse voices. So far, for example, most cable television channels are owned by a few companies, and half of them seem to do nothing but rebroadcast programming seen on others. When Rogers (1988) examined how participatory democracy experiments were actually working, he concluded that although new communication technology does have the potential to create participatory democracy, pilot projects demonstrated it had not succeeded in doing so. Huglen (1993) concluded that the process of mediating democratic discourse acted to squelch alternative voices, because the media want after all to mediate. Although a strong demassification effect as a result of an increase in the number of transmissions may seem feasible, it has not yet happened. In effect, rather than encourage responsible citizenship and democratic participation, media have often had a destabilizing and anarchy-inducing effect on political behavior (see Frederick, 1988).

Another potentially destabilizing side effect to demassifying the channels of transmission is that in the absence of a highly centralized broadcasting authority that closely monitors what is seen in the media, imported programming may begin to replace indigenous offerings. This happens in part because imported television is less expensive than indigenous production, and in part because imported Western programs often have a broad audience appeal. Replacing authoritarian broadcasting with imported broadcasting is not necessarily a step toward democracy. It may be a step toward a global monoculture, or it may be a step toward imperialism (Schiller, 1991). Indeed, demassified broadcasting has often meant more imported and less locally produced programming (Blood, 1989). Either of the alternatives mentioned here endangers nascent Polish democracy. If positive effects of demassifying transmission on democracy are not clear, then, other approaches to demassification may need to be considered. One is the demassification of reception.

## Reception

The diversification of reception has, in theory, a much more intense, predictable, and observable effect than that of transmission. Because of its implicit subjectivity, its relative newness, and its origins in literary theory (Iser, 1978; Jauss, 1982) and the uses and gratifications approach (see Becker & Schoenbach, 1989), however, not many researchers are trying to observe actual audiences actually watching television. Often, scholars infer diverse reception from a close analysis of the media program itself, in part because this approach involves how written and visual texts are read or watched, shared, and interpreted. It eschews the assumption that media audiences are passive receivers and regards them instead as active agents in the production of media meaning. From this perspective, the meaning of a television program is as much a creation of the receiver as of the sender.

For many years, such a personal agency approach to demassification was the only type available to Poles, given the monolithic nature of Polish media. In other words, because the state media system spoke with such a singular voice, if a Pole wanted to hear a different voice, he or she would have to create it him or herself in the process of watching a program with a different intention. The simplest example of this would be ridiculing a state-sponsored broadcast: The intention of the program might be indoctrination, but the viewer could easily use it to resist indoctrination by viewing it in a resistant way. This personal resistance, the subjective construction of alternative and adversarial meanings, was for many years the only available option to Poles who disagreed with the state; their voice would simply have no other channel. As a result, Poland is an interesting context in which to attempt observing the demassification of reception.

It has been observed empirically that as channels diversify, polysemy (the extraction by an audience or reader of multiple meanings from a written or visual text) and devolution (the breakdown of large states into smaller national, ethnic, or tribal political groupings) naturally increase (Martini & Mazzoleni, 1989). The meanings of texts become less fixed, less two-dimensional, less oriented toward what the sender of the text intended it to mean, and become instead more shifting, more polydimensional, and more oriented toward all the different things the reader or viewer infer as they read or watch the text. One advantage to a reception-oriented approach is that it provides an excellent context from which to examine intracultural communication, the way a culture communicates with itself (see Casmir, chap. 1 of this volume; Shuter, 1990).

Oppositional decoding is used by Hall (1980) to explain how some members of a television audience resist the intended meaning of media texts. The analysis of oppositional decoding involves semiotics and hermeneutics, not behavioral methodologies and positivistic empiricism. According to Hall, the manner in which a message is encoded attaches a power relationship to it in addition to its content. There is, then, a preferred, "dominant," and legitimized decoding available to the audience, this being the meaning that is intended by the transmitter (e.g., "buy Coca-Cola" or "be a good citizen and vote"). Essentially, the magic bullet hits the bull's-eye. In the case of American television, dominant decoding would lead the viewer to purchase the products advertised, not question the system, and other acceptance rituals.

Alternative decodings are possible, however. The "negotiated" code occurs when the legitimacy of the dominant code is accepted but somehow not enacted at the personal level. An example might be the desire to buy a certain product, but confusion over brand name or availability. Oppositional decoding, the third possibility, occurs when the audience decodes a message in a manner dialectically contrary to the intended meaning; Political advertising that angers an audience enough to vote for an opponent or not to vote at all would be an example of this, as would be the case with advertising that inadvertently provoked a boycott of the product it was trying to sell. As is demonstrated later, because of the homogeneity of Polish broadcast media, oppositional decoding was one of the only alternative voices in Polish culture until 1990. Polish humor especially used an oppositional tone (Perlez, 1993a).

A second approach to demassified meaning, polysemy, as mentioned previously refers to a diversity of decodings, with many more meanings possible than the three Hall (1980) outlined. There is no general theory of how this occurs, but it was observed by Ang (1985) in her study of how Dutch women interpreted the American television program "Dallas." Noticing the diversity of meanings they ascribed to it, she concluded that:

> ... the dominance of the normative discourses of the ideology of mass culture—as it is expressed in all sorts of social institutions such as education and cultural criticism—has in fact a counter-productive effect on people's practical cultural preferences so that, not through ignorance or lack of knowledge, but out of self-respect they refuse to subject themselves to the prescriptions of the ideology of the mass culture or let their preferences be determined by it. (p. 115)

Liebes (1988) similarly observed the diversity of readings given television texts across cultures by asking representatives of several Israeli subcultures (Arabs, Moroccan Jews, Russian immigrants, and second-generation Israelis) and second-generation Los Angelenos to interpret "Dallas." The range of their interpretations was vast and addressed both the formal and thematic aspects of the program. A brief broadcast of "Dallas" by the Soviet television authority in Moscow in 1991 produced similar polysemy (Gumbel, 1991). Polysemy in Poland would be evident if television programs encourage more than just the dialectical, agree–disagree meanings of oppositional decoding, but many different types of meaning, a multitude of diverse interpretations of what has been said.

A third type of demassified meaning, poaching, is a more proactive form of polysemy, one in which the audience asserts its own control over the meaning of a text. This perspective assumes that audiences have many different levels of narrative textual engagement, from "couch potatoes" who passively receive, to interactors who actively engage. Poaching, a concept that originated with de Certeau (1984), is the process through which media interactors make the narrative text their own by creating their own meanings for it. These are the most dedicated and engaged of television viewers, but they are not content merely to accept what is transmitted. Consequently, because receivers create their own meaning, poaching is both a form of play and a mechanism for organizing experience in meaningful ways (Bacon-Smith, 1992). They co-opt characters and situations from television programs for stories, dramas, skits, conventions, and fanzines, which are semiunderground magazines published by and for the fans of particular music or television programs. The television program "Star Trek," for example, has been "poached" by hundreds of fan-published and -distributed underground magazines that present new, unauthorized, copyright-violating stories about the starship Enterprise. Control of the narrative slips away from its original creators as it comes under the power of its fans. As Jenkins (1992) indicated, "their activities pose important questions about the ability of media producers to constrain the creation and circulation of meaning. Fans construct their cultural and social identity through borrowing and inflecting mass culture images, articulating concerns which often go unvoiced within the dominant media" (p. 23). In the media communities they create, the distinction between observation and participation, between being "outside" and "inside" the text, becomes harder and harder to discern. The essence of poaching is that the audience is aware of its ability to make meaning and actively asserts it, often in direct opposition to the intentions and desires of the program transmitters. Media poaching in Poland would mean that audiences have become sufficiently dedicated to a television program that they create a subculture around it, co-opting it for their own use.

If the different demassifications of reception reflect a continuum, devolution is the highest level of audience assertion of meaning. Oppositional decoding and polysemy describe how an audience diversifies meaning, but they imply no action taken by it; in poaching, the audience is more assertive, co-opting meaning and becoming an alternative meaning factory and distribution system. Devolution, however, involves active, tactical resistance. This usually entails a resistant group setting up their own broadcasting facility or printing press (Howell, 1982; Olson, 1985, 1987). Occasionally, these are "pirate" or "underground" media, communicating illegally. The need among the disenfranchised for a formal, consistent, legitimate alternative voice is powerful; according to Maryniak (1993), "a society under threat creates its own ways of survival through subversion and conspiracy" (p. 13). In observing the failure of Soviet-style propaganda to achieve its intended objectives (i.e., to massify), White and Pravda (1988) and Mickiewicz (1985) lent observational credence to the devolutionary approach.

In the United States, oppositional decoding, polysemy, poaching, and devolution can all be observed. In Poland, oppositional decoding was the predominant tool with which Poles could demassify reception under the Soviet media model. To oppose the indoctrination messages and the "propaganda of success" predominant in the Polish media was easy and inevitable, but until the 1980s such opposition usually remained private, frequently going no further than a close circle of Polish friends, because public opposition could have serious ramifications. It is not clear that under a Stalinist media system polysemy is as possible as oppositional decoding, in part because the forcefulness, linearity, and directness of the Stalinist ideology forces a dialectical rather than polysemic response to the message. It is easier to respond "I disagree" than "here are some alternatives." Oppositional decoding somewhat preempts poaching, because poaching requires initial receptiveness to the means through which the message is manufactured. It is difficult to play when one rejects the rules. Finally, devolution of a legal type was strictly prohibited. As a result, illegal devolution would have been exceptionally dangerous and difficult. Nevertheless, a small Polish underground press did emerge in the late 1970s.

Just as there are problems with the democratization of transmission approach, there are limitations to the demassification of reception. Traditional critical theorists are not interested in it because they feel it does not describe fundamental phenomena. Schiller (1991), for one, found reception-oriented approaches dubious, in part because they deal with particular individual texts, whereas for him any meaningful effects of media come from "the seamless media-cultural environment" (p. 24), one that conditions its audience to accept capitalism. Scholars interested in the role of media as part of lingering imperialism would be interested to note that Radio Zet, Poland's most successful private commercial radio station, operates as a joint venture with a French armaments company (Koza, 1993a). Another problem inherent in reception-oriented approaches is that they are interesting in theory but, given the subtleties of personal agency, are difficult to observe in practice. This explains why reception is more often conjectured about than tested. Reader-response critics get around this problem by doing a careful exegesis of each text, looking for its polysemic potentialities. Until more data are available from Poland, it is this latter methodology that must be used. It can illuminate interesting questions about Polish audiences that could then be observed experimentally.

Existing reception theory indicates, however, that it is reasonable to hypothesize that audiences in Poland have changed in their interaction with the media since the end of the military government and the introduction of democracy. Oppositional decoding should no longer be needed as the dominant demassification response because audiences are instead free to experiment with polysemy, poaching, and even socially sanctioned devolution. In order to understand the potentialities within the Polish audience, it is first important to describe the circumstances of massification and demassification in the Polish media.

## DEMASSIFICATION IN POLAND

The Communist leadership in Poland operated by using a Soviet model of the relationship between democracy and media. That model assumed the utility of a mass society approach. That approach cannot be considered unwavering, though. There have been several interpretations and applications of the model in postwar Polish history, including Stalinism, de-Stalinization, re-Stalinization, and resistance and martial law. What unifies these views is a general belief that television and radio were to be used for shaping pro-Socialist public attitudes. Frequently this meant that alternative points of view were unwanted because they were unnecessary, destructive, and contrary to Socialist ideals. The mainstream of Polish media history since World War II has been a struggle between forces that have sought to massify transmission and those that have sought to demassify it. Until quite recently, the forces of massified transmission prevailed, and discourse was usually confined to an either–or, dominant oppositional mode.

### Stalinism

Stalinization, an extremely massified philosophy of transmission, considered communication and culture a primary avenue for ideology through deliberate socialization, a process of Pavlovian behavior modification.

A. White (1990) described this as the belief that the party can and should modify behavior through cultural enlightenment or *wychowanie*. The persuasive aspect of this is often called the "propaganda of success," because the media presented only that information that made the Soviet system appear successful. However, persuasion was not the only intention of Stalinist media. Another strategy of Stalinist culture was its overt attempts to prevent the genesis of co- and countercultures. This reflected a rather primitive, hypodermic approach to the media, and ignored two decades of research in the West that pointed out that responses to media are varied and complex, as discussed earlier (e.g., Ang, 1985, 1991; Fiske & Hartley, 1976; Olson, 1994b). Under Stalin, the media and other cultural venues were highly centralized and controlled as vehicles of state-sponsored behavior modification and indoctrination. It is still rumored in Poland that the Secretary of the Communist Party had a private daily newspaper printed up for himself that included all the news left out of the papers for the masses.

Stalinist ideological culture did achieve a bit of what it intended, mostly through proscription of alternatives. That which was not explicitly sanctioned was tacitly prohibited, limiting diversity of media and expression; although not necessarily illegal, alternative discourse was always suspect. Opposing explanations and viewpoints were scarcely articulated because the culture did not allow a language for their articulation (A. White, 1990).

## De-Stalinization

Democratization of transmission began in Poland approximately in the mid-1950s with some reluctance when hard-line Stalinism was abandoned as the government's approach to culture formation. However, the mass–demass balance continues to swing like a pendulum until the present time. The de-Stalinization initiative was fueled by Khrushchev's "secret speech" of 1956, in which he quietly advocated moderate liberalization, and the Poznan demonstrations that same year (A. White, 1990). Poland State Television, which was overseen by the State Committee on Television and Radio, had been used primarily to reinforce the sense that Communist leadership had been successful in creating a prosperous, strong, unified Poland (R. Steiner, 1981). By 1956, it had abandoned the behavior modification approach of the Stalinist period.

In a sense, the Communist Party released its control over culture at that time, a process that continued until the late 1960s. In part as a response to this liberation from above, but also due to increased urbanization, a younger population, the broad distribution of television sets, and the availability of Western music, Poles took more control over their own media and they diversified. Consequently, more and different kinds of programming became available (A. White, 1990). Transmission had begun to demassify, yet most responses to media still fell into the dialectic of accepting the dominant or accepting the oppositional code.

## Re-Stalinization

The government temporarily suspended the demassification process in 1968 in response to political unrest, a direct result perhaps of the loosening of controls on cultural activities (A. White, 1990). The television system, which had been a disorganized, technically crude, decentralized experiment, was strengthened and centralized by Prime Minister Edward Gierek in the 1970s as a reextension of the state, described as its "ideological front" (R. Steiner, 1981). That effort was based on the addition of a second channel and government subsidies that allowed almost everyone to afford a television set. Gierek simultaneously did away with regional broadcasting and instead centralized all programming under Central Committee control. Journalists and programmers were ushered toward conformity and compliance. Steiner described some of the ideological strategies used by the government to re-Stalinize the media: information that reflected badly on the state, such as the examination of health policies or standards of living, was forbidden; popular American programs were scheduled so as to discourage attendance at church; and national and international news was presented in a neutral, nonanalytical style.

## Resistance and Martial Law

Resistance to the dominant system, a sort of nascent devolution, began in the late 1970s as an underground press developed. It published opposition papers and ran cultural events outside and in defiance of the state system (A. White, 1990). This had the understandable effect of drawing people away from state-sponsored programs, creating a cultural crisis for the government's architects of meanings and laying the backdrop for the growth of organized resistance to restalinization. Polish leader General Jaruzelski's response was a mix of repression and permissiveness, of darting between Stalinism and liberalism.

The disparity between television representations of abundant food and the meat shortages of the early 1980s created a dissonance that led to open resistance. This occurred in conjunction with the rise of Solidarity, which began to exert its authority over public information after the Gdansk strike of August 1980, which marked that labor movement's rise to power. The communication landscape changed as Poles stopped "receiving" things and began to "take" them, a change in attitude that was even reflected in the language they used (Maryniak, 1993). Control of television became a public struggle. Even as Poles began an underground alternative press, Solidarity began to insist on "freedom of expression and publication," including access to the broadcast media (R. Steiner, 1981). The union did prevail to some extent, gaining access to television for 1 hour of dissenting public opinion on the air and C-SPAN-like broadcasts of Central Committee deliberations. Some of the first programs Solidarity put on the air were a speech by union leader Lech Walensa and a Roman Catholic mass. The union would have preferred more access to television and a radio station of its own.

Solidarity found it difficult to develop its own voice in the media. The Polish state-broadcasting commission was willing, at most, to give Solidarity limited access to the airwaves. The union, on the other hand, wanted complete control over the programs it produced and access to the means of control over broadcasting (R. Steiner, 1981). It is typical that a subordinate culture recognizes that mere access is not sufficient to attain a political voice; control is necessary. The Central Committee was using a strategy of pater/maternalism, whereas Solidarity was using a strategy of communication secession (Olson, 1994a). As was demonstrated by Fiske and Hartley (1976), Fiske (1987), Ang (1985, 1991), and de Certeau (1984), increased access to media releases a diversity of meanings in the audience. Once Solidarity had been granted access to the airwaves, the countercultural Pandora's box had been opened and would prove impossible to close. The theories of polysemy appear correct in this instance: Media in Poland (and the USSR and Hungary) had a demassifying, counter-culture-creating effect during the 1980s (A. White, 1990).

Evidently embodying confusion within the party and government over how to respond to this increasing polysemy, the state responded at first by further liberalizing the media. This reflected in part the philosophy of Jozef Klasa, a journalist with a somewhat liberal reputation, who was installed as broadcasting chief by the Central Committee. Diversity of opinion and opposing viewpoints were increasingly tolerated and censorship diminished. Klaza's policies proved to be a brief experiment, however, and by December 1981 controls were tightened anew, Klasa was removed, martial law declared, and Solidarity was outlawed. The additional imposition of martial law reasserted strong centralized control over the broadcasting media.

In contrast to the broadcast media, the film industry had been relatively free of government control from the decline of Stalinism in 1953 until the imposition of martial law in 1981. The government did control two aspects of Polish cinema, however. First, all scripts needed to be approved by the administration; second, the government acted as distributor of films after they were completed. These restraints, moderate compared to those on broadcasting, resulted in the censorship of few films. However, martial law represented a return to rigidity, even for this relatively unhampered cultural medium. Independent film units were disbanded and strict controls over the information presented in all media was reclaimed by the government (Michalek & Turaj, 1988).

## After Communism

After the first free elections in 1989, and perhaps in reaction to the oppressive structure of Stalinist media formulations, culture in Poland had to become "spontaneous and small-scale" (A. White, 1990, p. 16). Under Stalinism, the state tried to control all aspects of citizens' leisure time. As Stalinism faded away, leisure time came to be more and more under the control of the individual. This freedom allowed a resurgence of traditional Polish values and ideals, and as they asserted themselves, time became further unstructured. In a sense, leisure time became "free" time.

There are now many more media channels available and they function as "new media" as far as democratization is concerned (Becker & Schoenbach, 1989). Almost all voices are tolerated, consistent with the Polish love of liberty. Videotapes of all varieties are widely available in local shops. The comics industry, which had been heavily influenced by government intervention, exploded, spawning many small independent publishers (Thompson, 1993). The parliament has changed Polish law to allow competition for state-owned radio and television, and one television and four radio stations have been granted licenses to provisionally begin broadcasting. One of the radio stations, Radio Zet, is the largest in central Europe, and has about 30% of the audience share in Warsaw, second only to the state's Radio 1. Zet will soon be broadcasting nationwide, and has even broadcast into other European states such as Lithuania. It grosses about Zl 100 billion, approximately $5,200,000 (Koza, 1993a).

The commercial television station, Echo-TV in Wroclaw, is supported through advertising. It runs local news and many dubbed Western television shows and movies. It is a devolutionary institution, because it single-handedly created its own rules, devolving the formerly centralized Polish economy. Following its model, a commercial television station has since opened in Russia (Dawtrey, 1993). Privatization has become a centerpiece of Polish post-Communist economic policy ("Mass Privatization," 1993), resulting in a demassification of ownership that initially decentralizes control and could potentially democratize transmission, at least in comparison to Stalinism. Ironically, though, advertisements on television for luxury items may be creating a level of resentment against capitalism and capitalists that the Stalinist media machine never achieved (Remnick, 1993).

Solidarity regarded freedom of information as essential to Poland's social evolution (R. Steiner, 1981). Now that the forces of Solidarity have prevailed, secession is no longer the objective. Polish leaders are trying to nurture principles of democracy, but helping them take root is proving more difficult than many expected under Communism. Democracy was a clearer objective before it was possible than after it became attainable, in part because:

> life in the underground was very simple: there was a single end to be achieved through one uncompromising effort. It was black and white: good and evil were clearly defined . . . The people who once saw the ends in simple terms continue to seek simple solutions. They want to achieve things quickly . . . It's as if the complexities of life haven't penetrated the minds of [the leaders]. They still haven't realized that building is much slower and less spectacular than victory at the barricades. (Teresa Bogucka in Maryniak, 1993, p. 13)

In other words, transmission has been demassified, but has not proven the panacea it was hoped to be. Whereas many Poles were unified in their dislike for martial law, its absence makes it difficult to stick together. Now there are many more voices in the chorus, and they are not often in harmony. In fact, the 1993 elections in Poland exemplify the electoral anarchy that free elections have wrought. No party received more than 21% of the vote. The party that received the most votes, the Democratic Left Alliance, is in fact a coalition of 28 groups, the party of former prime minister Suhocka received only 10%, and over 36% of the votes were for parties that received less than 5% of the total (Koza, 1993b). This is similar to the 1991 elections, in which over 200 parties stood for election (Newman, 1993). This is certainly reminiscent of past parliamentary anarchies in Poland.

Poland's post-Communist chaos is not unique, but given the relative homogeneity of Poland, it is an interesting phenomenon that cannot be accounted for on ethnic or linguistic grounds. Instead, Polish culture, somewhat like American culture, seems inherently to encourage diversity of reception, so political heterogeneity grows out of common cultural traits. Yet this diversity of reception demassified at a different rate than transmission: Diversified reception began before demassified transmission "allowed" it through oppositional decoding of Stalinist programming, but true polysemic response did not become widespread until after access to the media increased. Perhaps some democratization of transmission is necessary to invigorate polysemy. Indeed, democratized transmission has had the effect of "atomizing" the Polish people (A. White, 1990) and has been shown elsewhere to create political anarchy (Frederick, 1988).

Clearly, though, the failure of Soviet-style propaganda alone does not explain demassification in Poland. The atomization of Polish public opinion also had cultural roots. Polish communication culture sets the stage for the decentralization of information and meaning. The romanticizing of peasant life and culture creates a situation in which the media frequently use imagery and ideas representative of that life, a trend quite different from the Soviet industrial model. Under Soviet influence the peasant way of life was targeted for elimination through collectivization and other processes, although these efforts ultimately failed. The enshrining of peasant life can be divisive, however: It creates a tension between urban and rural, traditional and modern, intellectual and uneducated, Eastern European and Western European. Similarly, the love of chivalry, simplicity, and the land is used to reflect Polish nationalism and patriotism where loyalty to class and party dominated previously. However, these changes create divisiveness as well among Poles. Although hierarchical authority is ordinarily acceptable to Poles, it has to be perceived to be moral and domestic. Soviet hierarchies did not fit that description, and resistance to them was natural. In their absence, domestic politicians are generally respected, but there remains some distrust of their motives and techniques.

Polish Catholicism, always resistant to Communist leadership, is no longer in an oppositional position but in a dominant one. Although it usually exerts a powerful unifying force on the country, it has recently acted to drive wedges between intellectuals and the rest of the nation. The belief in freedom, equality, and democracy are also great unifiers, but in Polish history, these often led to nonviolent political anarchy. In short, both internal and external forces pushed Poland toward the democratization of transmission and reception. Polish communication culture inclined Poland away from massification, and since the removal of Soviet mass culture, the pressure for further demassification remains.

However, until elections were held and a civilian government formed, Poles had essentially two choices for their reception of media messages: participation in the dominant code or, more likely, oppositional decoding. There was little opportunity for polysemy or poaching. As described earlier, the behavior modification approach of Stalinist texts did not allow much diversity of interpretation. It can be concluded that this situation is now changing. Data about reception in Poland are difficult to obtain, and they are perhaps best received through interpretation and exegesis of media texts, a method often used in the West. Nevertheless, some generalizations about the Polish attitude toward cultural texts can be asserted historically. One such generalization is that public mistrust of media messages remains, even though Stalinism has passed. Another generalization is that public participation in cultural enlightenment has diminished, whereas consumption of television has increased (A. White, 1990). Both of these factors have had the effect of creating an environment ripe for polysemic reception.

The television program "Polski Zoo" is an excellent example of the democratization of transmission and reception in Poland. If as MacBean (1975) argued, theory always arises from an individual text, then this is the ideal text to assist with understanding the relationship between media meaning and democratic vistas in Poland. The program is on once a week, for 10 minutes, with a subsequent rebroadcast. It spoofs Polish parliamentary politics. Polish and international politicians appear on the program to debate the pressing political matters of the day as animal puppets in a Polish zoo, speaking in humorous rhymed couplets. These animal caricatures function as a metaphor for the political philosophy, physical appearance, and the communication style of the politician they parody. Some faces are fairly familiar to an outsider: Former prime minister Suhocka is portrayed as a llama, former president and intellectual Masowiecki as a turtle, U.S. President Clinton as a ram, and Polish President Walesa as a lion. Representatives from scores of Polish political parties are similarly embodied. Olesky, a former Communist, is a dinosaur; Pawlak of the Peasant Party, elected prime minister in 1993, is an ox; Michnik, a journalist, is a fox. Representatives of 16 different political parties are represented as goats, moose, ducks, gadflies, koalas, birds, boars, mice, rats, devils, crows, bees, beavers, and other animals. Amidst the manifold political parties and democratic anarchy that make up contemporary Polish parliamentary politics, there is even a "Beer Drinker's Party." The head of that party is portrayed on "Polski Zoo" as a gorilla in a beer-icon T-shirt.

An interesting episode was Number 89, broadcast the week after President Walensa dissolved Suhocka's parliament in June of 1993. It was an interesting moment in Polish history and for the show, because the potential anarchy of Polish politics exploded into kinetic anarchy. The episode began with an empty parliament as politicians scrambled to keep power and privilege:

*Guard*: It's spooky in the high chamber today; only the moose is busy.

*Chrzanowski* (Moose, National Christian Union, Speaker of the Parliament): I am closing everything down.

*Guard*: What are you doing here?

*Cleaning lady*: I'm only cleaning.

*Geremek* (Goat, Democratic Union): There is no applause in the high chamber.

*Tusk* (Donald Duck, Liberal Democrat): Where are the fights?

*Hall* (Conservative Party): Where are the debates?

*Olesky* (Dinosaur, Social Democrat, Former Communist): Our salary has been taken away!

*Korwin-Mikke* (Gadfly, Union of Realistic Politics): So were the fax machines!

*Cleaning lady*: Why look, there's a pale-looking member of parliament at the door.

*Maciarewicz* (Movement for the Republic): Dear lady, please let me in for a second.

*Cleaning lady* (seeing several animals at the door): Who are you? An audience?

*Maciarewicz*: I left my folder in there.

*Olszowski* (Koala, Movement for the Republic): I left my voting card.

*Cimoszewicz* (Social Democrat): I left my Parliamentary Privilege of Immunity.

*Kaczynski twins* (Centrum Agreement and Supreme Chamber of Control): And we left our own heads.

*Bielecki* (Liberal Democratic Congress): I left some bills to be passed.

*Olszowski*: And me—I left complete and detailed plans for decommunization.

In this scene, a guard and a cleaning person were left in control, as former Communists scurry to protect their lost privileges. Centrist politicians complain that they had completed perfect plans for reform that were on the verge of passage, only to have them locked away in the empty chambers. It proved easy for these animals to agree because they had been locked out, even though the zoo was closed (the parliament was dissolved) because it had reached an impassable stalemate.

A bit later in the episode, the animals comment on having been closed out of the zoo by the king of the animals, the Lion (President Walensa):

*Moczulski* (Bird, Confederation for Independent Poland) and *Kwasniewski* (Boar, Social Democrats): We wanted to give the Llama (Suhocka) a lesson.

*Suhocka* (Llama, Democratic Union, prime minister): I had some doubts myself. I saw the Lion's tricks coming.

*Pawlak*: He gave us a lesson instead.

This scene showed a fascination not just with political personalities, but with the parliamentary strategies and tactics they use. In a corollary fashion, the scene identified the political process as the source of the chaos. It also showed that no one, not even Walensa, was above criticism on "Polski Zoo."

Later in the episode, there was even a fascination with the role of the media in the political process when journalists are portrayed as magicians:

*Miodowicz* (Bee, Trade Union Party): And meanwhile, in Krakow, a congress of crystal gazers has gathered.

*Wizard 1*: Hey, media, telepathic media, occultists, wizards—please look kindly on our yard.

*Miodowicz*: What awaits us: prosperity or poverty?

*Wizard 2* (gazing into crystal): I see, I see clearly . . .

*Miodowicz*: What?!

*Wizard 2*: I see darkness.

*Wizard 1*: Dangerous times are coming for politicians!

This was an interesting scene, one with the media commenting on themselves in the media. In spite of the humor of the situation, the television medium recognized its role as another political estate, a part of a system of checks and balances, as well as an actor in the democratic drama, which it had not been prior to demassification of transmission.

The program is phenomenally popular in Poland, and is in fact the centerpiece of many Polish family evenings. If one considers the fact that many Americans do not even know their own vice president, it is surprising that a show using sophisticated political parody could be so popular in Poland. American attempts at animated/"animalized" television political humor, such as Stephen Spielberg's "Capitol Critters," have been short-lived. The ratings of such programs have been insufficient to warrant more than a few weeks' run.

"Polski Zoo" embodies all aspects of Polish communication culture, even its self-contradictory nature. In its spoofing of the bureaucratic wranglings of the Polish parliament, it romanticizes peasant simplicity, yet in embodying Walensa as a lion, or benevolent despot, it reflects a love of chivalry. Hierarchical authority is thus reinforced even as it is parodied. Gender roles also retain their traditional Polish characterization. The only female character in most episodes is former prime minister Suhocka, who is portrayed as a diminutive llama, and President Walensa's wife, as a mouse. The raging individualism of the many small Polish political parties is the subject of frequent sarcasm, but the show assumes that the audience will respond to it subjectively. One is struck by the high level of the show's sophistication and literacy. The rhymed verse that is used not only parodies politics but the classics (Damocles, Cicero), history (Solidarity, Romanov Russia), contemporary culture, international relations, pornography, economics, and even Mike Tyson.

The show is at once patriotic and unpatriotic, in the way flag burning is for American free-speech absolutists. A flag burner burns the flag to assert a First Amendment right to do so, an irony given that the process of burning it is a criticism of the country that gives them that right. Similarly, "Polski Zoo" has little respect for any politician (except perhaps Walensa), yet respects and takes seriously the principle engendered in the fact that the politicians allow it to disrespect them. Consequently, it reinforces the belief in freedom, equality, and democracy, yet it depicts the political system as being in a chaotic shambles. Even the title, "Polish Zoo," implies the anarchy to which unfettered democracy can lead.

The sheer scale of Polish politics, with its myriad parties representing minute political agendas, is a kind of political anarchy, an anarchy homologous to "Polski Zoo" 's own anarchy. So, interestingly, even though "Polski Zoo" has the mass-audience popularity normally associated with massification, it embodies the demassification of Polish politics and the decentralization of reception that is parallel to what Ang (1985) and Shekwo (1984) found in their studies of European and African audiences' interpretations of "Dallas." Polish politics is no longer the bipolar dialectic of oppositionally decoding Stalinism. Today it is a postmodern hodgepodge of perspectives, none of them sacrosanct, all of them suspect. This is fertile ground for polysemy, in part because communication not only represents, but constitutes. In representing anarchy, it engenders anarchy, at least at the level of the generation of meaning. The constitutive nature of communication leads to a meaning diversity that Stalinism could not allow by virtue of its attempt to centrally control the formation of culture. Indeed, it is only in the presence of a "continually modifying nature of communication [that] there is a great diversity to communication, or in our interpretations of it. Given that we cannot resort to experience outside our communication to validate our interpretations, then the possibilities are endless . . . There can be as many descriptions as we, in our participation, are capable of generating" (Penman, 1992, p. 245). Because audiences read mass media in many different ways, even phenomenally popular television programs can have a diversifying effect. Such is the case with "Polski Zoo." That program indicates that Poland seems to be at a stage of rapid transmission expansion, at least to the extent its economy allows, with polysemy developing ever more fully and the possibilities of poaching and devolution on the horizon. Poland has come to this state in an extremely short time.

## CONCLUSIONS

The demassification of transmission and reception in Poland has created a diversity of democratic vistas and a multiplicity of voices that confront that country with a postmodern incoherence as well as a reassertion of its historical anarchic traditions. Education for democracy may be one response to this dilemma, but it seems unlikely that it will be resolved any time soon in Poland. The elites and intellectuals (such as Masowiecki), now disaffected but once a part of Solidarity, are reluctant to press for democratic education because most peasants and workers are happy with the state support they are given. In essence, all communication between the workers and the intellectuals has been cut off (Maryniak, 1993). As shown throughout this chapter, theories of demassification seem, at least initially, to be applicable to Poland. Perhaps, as theory-guided observation and description continues in Poland, these media theories can be adapted to see how they can help to explain the Polish political and media situations.

Yet a comparison of the trials and tribulations faced by nascent democracy in Poland with those in Russia gives room for optimism. In Russia democracy has been unattainable, even for "democratic" President Yeltsin, who permanently banned 13 newspapers and the television program "600 Seconds" during the weeks after the constitutional crisis of October, 1993 (Whitney, 1993). *Pravda*, the official newspaper of the Communist Party, was disbanded and its name forbidden. Ironically, the Russian President has banned opposing viewpoints in the name of national security and democratic reform. The conceptualization of a free press, which is so common in the West, and its essential nature in the cultivation of democracy, is officially discouraged in the former Soviet Union. Even a newspaper as "balanced" as *Tambov Life* has been threatened for running opposing viewpoints alongside columns written by Yeltsin. Its editor, Vladimir Biryukov, has said "the so-called democrats, whom I don't view as democrats, see things the way they want to . . . but the new ruling party is based simply on personal loyalty to the president" (Ignatius, 1993, p. A1). Most Russians are pessimistic about the prospects of their country ever becoming a democracy (Remnick, 1993). Clearly, democracy's relationship to the press in post-Soviet Russia retains a distinctly Soviet flavor that I have not found in post-Soviet Poland.

Of course, some aspects of Stalinism remain. Poland's commercial radio stations, for example, were forbidden by the broadcasting council to cover the parliamentary elections. In anarchic fashion, they did so anyway (Koza, 1993a). As White and Pravda (1988) and Mickiewicz (1985) demonstrated, Soviet-style controls over the press failed to achieve their desired objectives. That created a situation in which Polish citizens were compelled to decode information oppositionally, and that produced increasing pressure on media channels for more diversity. However, the failure of Soviet-style propaganda alone does not explain demassification in Poland. The existing, prevalent Polish communication culture set the stage for the decentralization of information and meaning. Yet, many Polish cultural principles have had a dual effect. What is particularly interesting about Poland is the degree of its internal political chaos in spite of, not because of, cultural diversity. Poland is an exceptionally homogeneous country, and yet since the reemergence of democracy, Poland's political arena is, if anything, too diverse. The foundational cultural elements discussed in this chapter unify Poland on the one hand because they are commonly shared, but diversify it on the other hand because each contains the seeds of divisiveness. Poland is truly a land of ironies and as media transmission and reception demassify, these ironies are compounded. Perhaps the traditional Polish saying should be amended: Get two Poles and a television set in a room, and you get a multitude of meanings.

## ACKNOWLEDGMENT

The author would like to thank Eva Wolenska of Central Connecticut State University for help in translation.

## REFERENCES

Ang, I. (1985). *Watching Dallas: Soap opera and the melodramatic imagination*. London: Methuen.

Ang, I. (1991). *Desperately seeking the audience*. London: Routledge.

Bacon-Smith, C. (1992). *Enterprising women: Television fandom and the creation of popular myth*. Philadelphia: University of Pennsylvania Press.

Becker, L., & Schoenbach, K. (1989). When media contact diversifies: Anticipating audience behaviors. In L. Becker & K. Schoenbach (Eds.), *Audience responses to media diversification* (pp. 1–27). Hillsdale, NJ: Lawrence Erlbaum Associates.

Bineham, J. (1988). A historical account of the hypodermic model in mass communication. *Communication Monographs, 55*, 230–249.

Blood, R. (1989). Australia: Hollywood goes down under and outback. In L. Becker & K. Schoenbach (Eds.), *Audience responses to media diversification* (pp. 267–280). Hillsdale, NJ: Lawrence Erlbaum Associates.

Bogucka, G. (1981). *A contrastive analysis of Polish and American cultures: Implications for Polish-English language teaching and learning*. Unpublished doctoral dissertation, University of Pittsburgh, Pittsburgh, PA.

Bouillon-Dartevelle, R. (1989). Belgium: Language division internationalized. In L. Becker & K. Schoenbach (Eds.), *Audience responses to media diversification* (pp. 51–70). Hillsdale, NJ: Lawrence Erlbaum Associates.

Brand, S. (1987). *The media lab: Inventing the future at MIT*. New York: Viking.

Casmir, F. (1992). Third-culture building: A paradigm shift for international and intercultural communication. In S. Deetz (Ed.), *Communication yearbook, 16* (pp. 407–436). Beverly Hills, CA: Sage.

Condit, C. (1989). The rhetorical limits of polysemy. *Critical Studies in Mass Communication, 6*(2), 103–122.

Daniells, R. (1981). Sienkiewicz revisited. In W. Stankiewicz (Ed.), *The tradition of Polish ideals* (pp. 166–187). London: Orbis Books.

Dawtrey, A. (1993, October 18). First commercial Russian news station bows. *Variety*, p. 36.

de Certeau, M. (1984). *The practice of everyday life*. Berkeley: University of California Press.

Elgin, D. (1991). Conscious democracy through electronic town meetings. *Whole Earth Review, 71*, 28–29.

Fiske, J. (1987). *Television culture*. London: Methuen.

Fiske, J., & Hartley, J. (1976). *Reading television*. London: Methuen.

Frederick, H. (1988). Media strategies stifle democracy in Central America. *Media Development, 2*, 32–37.

Godwin, M. (1991). The electronic frontier foundation and virtual communities. *Whole Earth Review, 71*, 40–42.

Grachev, A., & Yermoshkin, N. (1984). *A new information order or psychological warfare?* Moscow: Progress Publishers.

Gumbel, P. (1991, July 3). Moscow nights: Dallas makes it to Soviet television. *The Wall Street Journal*, p. A1.

Hall, S. (1980). Encoding/decoding. In S. Hall, D. Hobson, A. Lowe, & P. Willis (Eds.), *Culture, media, language* (pp. 128–138). London: Hutchinson.

Heidegger, M. (1977). *The question concerning technology and other essays* (W. Lovitt, Trans.). New York: Harper Torchbooks.

Hornik, R. (1980). Communication as complement in development. *Journal of Communication, 30*, 10–24.

Howell, W. (1982). Bilingual broadcasting and the survival of authentic culture in Wales and Ireland. *Journal of Communication, 32*, 39–54.

Huglen, M. (1993, November). *The electronic town hall: Technology and pseudo-participatory democracy*. Unpublished paper presented at the Speech Communication Association national convention, Miami, FL.

Ignatius, A. (1993, October 18). Settling accounts: In Russian provinces, Yeltsin's supporters stifle the opposition. *The Wall Street Journal*, p. A1.

Iser, W. (1978). *The act of reading: A theory of aesthetic response*. Baltimore: Johns Hopkins University Press.

Jauss, H. (1982). *Toward an aesthetic of reception*. Minneapolis: University of Minnesota Press.

Jenkins, H. (1988). Star Trek as rerun, reread, rewritten: Fan writing as textual poaching. *Critical Studies in Mass Communication, 5*(2), 85–107.

Jenkins, H. (1992). *Textual poachers: Television fans and participatory culture*. New York: Routledge.

Kohn, M., & Slomczynski, K. (1990). *Social structure and self-direction: A comparative analysis of the United States and Poland*. Cambridge, MA: Basil Blackwell.

Koza, P. (1993a). Business: Zippy Zet. *Business Central Europe, 1*(5), 25.

Koza, P. (1993b). Politics and economics: What's left? *Business Central Europe, 1*(5), 13–14.

Landow, G. (1992). *Hypertext: The convergence of contemporary critical theory and technology*. Baltimore: Johns Hopkins University Press.

Lasswell, H. (1927). *Propaganda technique in the world war*. New York: Knopf.

Liebes, T. (1988). Cultural differences in the retelling of television fiction. *Critical Studies in Mass Communication, 5*(4), 277–292.

MacBean, J. (1975). *Film and revolution*. Bloomington: Indiana University Press.

Martini, P., & Mazzoleni, G. (1989). Italy: A broadcast explosion. In L. Becker & K. Schoenbach (Eds.), *Audience responses to media diversification* (pp. 255–266). Hillsdale, NJ: Lawrence Erlbaum Associates.

Maryniak, I. (1993). Teresa Bogucka: The politicians sing along. *Index on Censorship, 22*(1), 13.

Mass privatization program takes off. (1993, September). *Eastern European Business Bulletin*, pp. 1, 4.

McLuhan, M. (1964). *Understanding media: The extensions of man*. New York: McGraw-Hill.

McLuhan, M., & Powers, B. (1989). *The global village: Transformations in world life and media in the 21st century*. New York: Oxford University Press.

Michalek, B., & Turaj, T. (1988). *The modern cinema of Poland*. Bloomington: Indiana University Press.

Mickiewicz, E. (1985). Political communication and the Soviet media system. In J. Nogee (Ed.), *Soviet politics: Russia after Brezhnev* (pp. 34–65). New York: Praeger.

Naisbitt, J. (1982). *Megatrends: Ten new directions transforming our lives*. New York: Warner Books.

Newman, B. (1993, September 20). Ex-communists take the lead in Polish vote. *The Wall Street Journal*, p. A10.

Olderaan, F., & Jankowski, N. (1989). The Netherlands: The cable replaces the antenna. In L. Becker & K. Schoenbach (Eds.), *Audience responses to media diversification* (pp. 29–50). Hillsdale, NJ: Lawrence Erlbaum Associates.

Olson, S. (1985). *Devolution and indigenous mass media: The role of media in Inupiat and Sami nation-state building*. Unpublished doctoral dissertation, Northwestern University, Evanston, IL.

Olson, S. (1987). The struggle for autonomy. *Journal of Communication, 37*, 189–190.

Olson, S. (1994a). Strategies and tactics of communication empowerment: Toward a descriptive tautology. In A. Malkiewicz, J. Parrish-Sprowl, & J. Waskiewicz (Eds.), *Social communication in the transformation process*. Wroclaw, Poland: Instytut Nauk Ekonomiczno-Spolecznych Politechniki Wroclawskiej.

Olson, S. (1994b). Television in social change and national development: Strategies and tactics. In A. Moemeka (Ed.), *Communicating for development: A new pan-disciplinary perspective*. Albany: State University of New York Press.

Penman, R. (1992). Good theory and good practice: An argument in progress. *Communication Theory, 2*(3), 234–250.

Perlez, J. (1993a, November 7). How many comics can fool Poland's rulers. *The New York Times*, p. A6.

Perlez, J. (1993b, October 15). Leftist leader is named prime minister of Poland. *The New York Times*, p. A6.

Pool, I. (1983). *Technologies of freedom: On free speech in an electronic age*. Cambridge, MA: Belknap-Harvard.

Remnick, D. (1993). Letter from Moscow: The hangover. *The New Yorker, LXIX*(39), 51–65.

Rheingold, H. (1991). Electronic democracy: The great equalizer. *Whole Earth Review, 71*, 4–11.

Rheingold, H. (1993). *The virtual community: Homesteading on the electronic frontier*. Reading, MA: Addison-Wesley.

Rogers, E. (1988). *Participatory communication technology and democracy*. Unpublished paper presented at the World Academic Conference of the Seoul Olympics 88, Seoul, South Korea.

Roos, H. (1981). The Polish nobility in pre-revolutionary Europe. In W. Stankiewicz (Ed.), *The tradition of Polish ideals* (pp. 85–112). London: Orbis Books.

Schiller, H. (1991). Not yet the post-imperialist era. *Critical Studies in Mass Communication, 8*(1), 13–28.

Schramm, W. (1964). *Mass media and national development: The role of information in the developing countries*. Stanford, CA: Stanford University Press.

Shekwo, J. (1984). *Understanding Gbagyi folktales: Premises for targeting salient electronic mass media programs*. Unpublished doctoral dissertation, Northwestern University, Evanston, IL.

Shuter, R. (1990). The centrality of culture. *The Southern Communication Journal, 55*(3), 237–249.

Sproule, J. (1989). Progressive propaganda critics and the magic bullet myth. *Critical Studies in Mass Communication, 6*(3), 225–246.

Stankiewicz, W. (1981). Introduction. In W. Stankiewicz (Ed.), *The tradition of Polish ideals* (pp. 11–22). London: Orbis Books.

Steiner, L. (1988). Oppositional decoding as an act of resistance. *Critical Studies in Mass Communication, 5*(1), 1–15.

Steiner, R. (1981). The struggle for Poland's airwaves. *Channels, 1*(4), 24–26.

Thompson, M. (1993). Polish comics industry tries to rebuild. *Comics Journal, 161*, 38–39.

Tichi, C. (1991). *Electronic hearth: Creating an American television culture*. New York: Oxford University Press.

Toffler, A. (1981). *The third wave*. New York: Bantam.

White, A. (1990). *De-Stalinization and the house of culture: Declining state control over leisure in the USSR, Poland and Hungary, 1953–89*. London: Routledge.

White, S., & Pravda, A. (1988). *Ideology and Soviet politics*. London: Macmillan.

Whitney, C. (1993, October 15). Permanent ban for thirteen Russian newspapers. *The New York Times*, p. A7.

Wieniewski, I. (1981). *Heritage: The foundations of Polish culture*. Toronto: University of Toronto Press.

Wober, J. (1989). The U.K.: The constancy of audience behavior. In L. Becker & K. Schoenbach (Eds.), *Audience responses to media diversification* (pp. 91–107). Hillsdale, NJ: Lawrence Erlbaum Associates.

Wootton, C. (1981). Frederic Chopin and the Polish ideal. In W. Stankiewicz (Ed.), *The tradition of Polish ideals* (pp. 150–165). London: Orbis Books.

# 8

# *Turning Personal Experiences Into Social Reality: Communication as a "Third-Culture-Building" Tool in the Romanian Classroom*

Eric Gilder
*Social Science Center*
*Soros Foundation for an Open Society, Romania*

*For Cristina Mihailescu (1958–1995)*
*Colleague and friend*

## AN AMERICAN RHETORICIAN MEETS THE REALITIES OF ROMANIA

When I was unexpectedly called in the fall of 1992 to teach social sciences in Romania, I gathered what information I could on the pragmatics of living in a country that, however rich in resources, had gone through a traumatic, even "demonic" recent history, and was only now coming to terms with the "revolution" or "events" of December 1989.[1] Upon arriving at Otopeni airport in September of 1992, the first thing I noticed were the terminal army guards wielding AK-47s. Despite this forbidding first image, I was well received by my university hosts. The students I taught seemed most eager, and the physical hardships I faced were less than I had been led to believe.

But, soon, warning signs appeared that all was not well with the society: A neighbor, of what was called "peasant-worker" background,

[1]On the 21st of that month, the despotic ruling couple of Romania, Nicolae and Elena Ceausescu, were deposed and assassinated by mysterious captors, and fighting between government and military factions continued for some days. At the time, the revolution was called the "Christmas miracle," but now the miracle has been tarnished by authoritarian government action and lack of structural reform. For example, the government of Ion Iliescu called out miners to quell student demonstrations in the same manner in which the previous regime would have approved; inflation was eating away at already meager salaries; corruption and cronyism continued apace (Verdery & Kligman, 1992).

was ready to beat me for a malfunctioning phone in my apartment that interfered with his; taxicab drivers and waiters were often willing to cheat unsuspecting American visitors; people with grotesque deformities were in the subway begging coins; "friends" often appeared, later to seek unspecified "favors"; many official promises and contracts were subsequently open to retraction; government officials often had to be bribed to perform their duties. In sum, very little trust in the system exists in today's Romania, and what trust there is can be found primarily within families and among friends. Many Romanians view their society as being "in transition." They see it as going from order to a Hobbesian jungle of chaos.[2] As a visiting professor, I possessed both a certain traditional social status that helped me in official settings, and a cultural heritage that attracted curious students. However, although university students are still very much a social elite in Romania, and are, therefore, better situated to benefit from social change than many members of the general populace, they are also disillusioned.

As Lazar Vlasceanu (1992) of Bucharest state university observed, students had been the vanguard of the revolutions throughout Eastern Europe. They were committed and eager agents of change in the year following the revolt in Romania, but "the period of euphoria did not last very long . . . [for] a whole range of contradictions had begun to appear" (p. 35). As he explained in more detail:

> *Disappointed by the political struggle for power and by the slow pace of change in some quarters, students have entered into a period of passive resistance to the political events and of apathy with regard to what has been going on in their own institutions.* This trend has been accompanied by the revival of social skepticism . . . and of strong critical attitudes or simply indifference towards the newly established structures. Many students have adopted very practical attitudes towards their present and future lives. *The aggravating conditions of living, the growing unemployment problem among young people, the unclear prospects for the future economic development of the countries in question, and the few opportunities for travel and for making contacts abroad* are among the justifications frequently invoked by students for their skepticism and practicality. (p. 35; emphasis in original)

Romanian society is definitely undergoing a severe transformation process, with many "traditional" social norms being called into question along with the failed economic structure. Furthermore, it is debatable

[2]Close interpersonal relationships are distinguished from formal functional relationships in many ways, one being the varied forms of the Romanian "you," *dumneavoastra* (formal) and *tu* (informal). Once you are received into a circle of friends, creative possibilities open; many things once impossible become possible.

whether these transformations are leading to organic, structural change or whether they are only artificial and superficial. As Mihailescu (1993) noted, despite Romania's struggle toward the development of a "market economy" and political pluralism:

> ... more than ever we live under the sign of paradox. The freedom we have long sought is ours, but we do not know what to do with it or how to handle it. Some of us try to turn our backs on the past and to live for the future only; such people are often called opportunists. Others cling to the past, not out of fidelity and nostalgia, but because they are powerless and have nothing else to cling to. Others struggle with day-to-day existence, too busy and anxious to care about political nuances; still others seek revenge for past injustices.
>
> The common memory still inevitably determines the way we think and feel. The big and little myths ... survive, only in transmogrified form. Where we once spoke about the "new man", the "new golden era", and the like, now we write, speak and even shout about "responsibility", "democracy", "pluralism", "consensus", the "new European homeland", etc. and, less loudly, about "opportunism", "cowardice", "*langue de bois*", "revenge", "forgiveness", and so on. We live in a society whose daily backdrop or presupposition is still one of antagonism. (pp. 2–3)

In this period of committed cynicism on the part of the general population and students in particular, I wonder how I can simultaneously understand the daily challenges my students face and still honestly entice them to embrace impractical liberal university studies. As many a democratic theorist would attest, the achievement of a civil society requires the creation and sustaining of a self-knowing social agent, uniting the creative force of an individual's intuitive convictions with the logical pluralism of sound thinking upon a trusted social stage. As I stated elsewhere, we first:

> ... speak with each other because we care enough about some topic, on an intuitive level, to "risk confrontation" with others—to sally forth and say our piece. Secondly, once we care enough to speak of some [personally] perceived experience, we are compelled to employ the social construction of language to create an imperfect evaluative image of our [perfect] inward vision. For [each one of] us, there may be one beautific vision, but for all of us there are many fallen visions.... From this subtle interplay of our affective and logical selves, a social ethos is created across time, a "socius" that is inevitably pluralistic in its makeup. (Gilder, 1992, p. 354)

But to rightly persuade my students into abandoning their cherished societal prejudices (and in my case my own) in the classroom dialogue is a great responsibility that challenges my pedagogical philosophy and practical teaching skills to the fullest. For in asking them to join me in the process of building a "third culture" of meaning creation, I am asking them to risk, to possibly become estranged from their own culture. Academics in America are often used to this process (cf. Weaver, 1964), but for a Romanian student to take the chance could be more costly. Anti-intellectualism runs strong here; by questioning premises too much, one can be easily castigated as "not a true Romanian," that is, finding oneself accused of "cosmopolitanism," and lumped in the public's mind with other undesirable populations: gypsies, Jews, homosexuals, and so on. Facing such complexities of my task, I seek to call upon the theoretical aid of Williams (1983a, 1983b), Burke (1945), Aristotle (1960), and Kelly (1955) to assist me in constructing an appropriate philosophy and methodology of teaching.

## PERFORMING THE "OFFICE" OF PEDAGOGICAL RHETORIC WITHIN ROMANIAN CULTURE

I have been pondering the role of a meaningful philosophy of teaching and the practice of humane studies in Romania. In that process, I have come to see the challenge facing me as a rhetorical one. The central questions to which I return are, how do we come to "know what we know," how do we come to know *how* we know, and how much freedom do we possess in applying our knowledge to social structures in the realm of action? As Kenneth Burke (in Nichols, 1989) noted, "teaching is an office of rhetoric" (p. 324). Therefore, I believe that adequate answers to these questions require consideration of philosophy and ideology, the role of the private self within a social role, as well as an understanding of the larger culture in which *both* teachers and students live. As Williams (1983a) observed, there is great tension between the "primitive feeling" of group solidarity and individual distinctions in a society undergoing structural change (such as Romania today). However stressful, this tension is a necessary creative component to social development, argued Williams:

> Solidarity, as a feeling, is obviously subject to rigidities, which can be dangerous in a period of change. The command to common action is right, but there is always the danger that the common understanding will be inadequate, and that its enforcement will prevent or delay right action. No community, no culture, can ever be fully conscious of itself, ever fully know itself. The growth of consciousness is usually uneven, individual and tentative in nature. (p. 334)

What is needed to achieve constructive social acts of meaning creation between the creative individuals and groups of solidarity within a changing society is language. Ever since the days of Babylon, teachers have sought to achieve common meaning, so that a culture could come, albeit imperfectly, to know itself through the diverse life experiences of persons that construct it. As Williams argued, pluralistic discourse is central to communal progress:

> A culture, while it is being lived, is always in part unknown, in part unrealized. The making of a community is always an exploration, for consciousness cannot precede creation, and there is no formula for unknown experience. A good community, a living culture, will, because of this, not only make room for but actively encourage all and any who can contribute to the advance in consciousness which is the common need. Wherever we have started from, we need to listen to others who started from a different position. We need to consider every attachment, every value, with our whole attention; for we do not know the future, we can never be certain of what may enrich it; we can only, now, listen to and consider whatever may be offered and take up what we can. (pp. 334–335)

I believe that Williams would agree with Burke on the centrality of the "office" of rhetoric in achieving such a pedagogy of progress. Burke (in Nichols, 1989) argued that it is our common use of language that makes it possible for us to cooperate as humans, to build civilization. Through language we can achieve an empathic *identification* with others, which, if successful, can lead to a *consubstantiation,* that is, becoming one with them. Remembering Hitler's mesmerizing powers, such a communion can have both healthy and pathological forms, however. Given the ambiguous state of social reality in Romania, I posit that the optimistic humanistic assumption undergirding much communication and educational theory (that essential differences between persons and cultures can be done away with in large part if we can only remove misunderstandings of terminology or field-dependent language [Toulmin, 1958], or equalize political power differences between communicators [Habermas, 1984]) is too simplistic. The inherent imperfections of coming into consubstantiation with the "other" requires a theory of communication that is ironic. Burke's theory of identification incorporates such irony, for it realizes that although language inevitably imprisons each one of us in its divisive hierarchical structures, it can become the tool of our communal liberation, if employed creatively. Sorin Hudac, a student in my seminar, made a most interesting point concerning the seminal role that language plays in assisting us in distinguishing between creative and destructive forms of consubstantiation. Discussing the varied forms of nationalism in Romania, Hudac (1993) argued that the avoidance of pathological forms of nationalism requires an appeal to the higher consciousness of humans, the collective "super-ego." But, he stated:

> . . . for this procedure to work *requires* that language, the source of "norms" for the culture, has to be a discriminating element by definition . . . in our personalities. Only by such socially-constructed "norms" can the source of violence and expediency in ourselves (and in the culture collectively), the "id," be constrained by the representations of others' higher interests. With language being assigned to such a central role as the ordering element in society, favoring one [language] over others constitutes, I believe, a cultural nationalism that is good and necessary.
>
> On the other hand, mere political-economic nationalism is destructive because of its tie to the collective "id" of a people. While some wealth is obviously necessary (such as land) for a nation to exist, the collective "id" can become all too easily represented in the form of a conquering army, taking over other peoples and nations exploiting them for greedy motives, even to the point of killing them. As suggested above, only the discriminating power of language, rightfully employed, can assist a nation in avoiding this mistake. (p. 6; emphasis in original)

Thus, I believe that Burke's comprehensive theory of rhetoric and society, however difficult to summarize in a short chapter, can be most useful in understanding the construct of nationalism and communication in Romania now. Thankfully, Burke's dramaturgical schema of the communicative/educative process is not too complex. Any language activity, Burke (1945) claimed, can be analyzed in relation to five sites, or locations, on a dramatic stage: act, agent, scene, agency, and purpose.

Act is central to Burke (1945), for it is the possibility of intentionality that makes us human, and separates us from the lower animal orders. Basically, Burke claimed that although mere motion can coexist with action, the two are not similar. Motion occurs throughout the natural world, but to act requires symbolic action. Agent is the human actor who carries out the act in Burke's theory, whereas scene is the specific time and place of the action that, in part, structures and controls its performance and outcome. Any act requires a means or agency (which is the medium that the agent employs to commit dramatic action) as well as a purpose, the conscious or subconscious motivations that prompted the actor to perform the intentional act.

Burke (in Nichols, 1989) linked his dramatic theory of the communicative process to an "ongoing conversation," or dialogue, between actors separated by time and or place. For example, what I am doing in my teaching in Bucharest today is part of a social discourse incited by the historical acts of the previous regime upon the scene of Romanian society, which, given my professional training and personal hopes, I believe can be improved by creating a communion of minds within an increasingly pluralistic culture.

## Education as the Agency of Nationalism and Ideology in Romania: A Description of Scene

In line with Gramsci's (1957; see also Joll, 1978) and Williams' (1983b) conception of intellectual activity *as an ongoing process* that occurs across time, within a concrete situation, and that assumes contradictions, I expect that the emergent intellectual ideology of Romania is open to rhetorical intervention. Specifically, the old determining structures that defined a socially appropriate "civil education" during the Communist era can now be thought of (somewhat ironically) as the traditional ideology in the East European context. Western ideas, especially in a scene becoming dominated by the material lures of a market economy, are presently competing against renewed nationalistic ideas for ideological dominance. Such a struggle between tradition and modernity is not new in Romania, however.

Romania has been and still is a predominantly agricultural society, with a large peasant population and a small socially-aware governing elite. Placed as it is between the great Oriental and Occidental powers, the land that is Romania has been ruled in turn by Romans, Hungarians, Turks, Austrians, Germans, and Russians, with true political independence from outside forces a rarity. Nevertheless, the concept of a unique Romanian culture has survived via its language. As Pilon (1992) stated:

> Romanian nationalism dates from the eighteenth century, particularly in Transylvania. Its linguistic idiosyncrasy—a Latin island in the Balkans—helped to distinguish the nation from the Hungarian, Slavic, and the German ethnic groups surrounding it. . . . [The] rediscovery of a distinguished cultural/linguistic heritage led to the petition known as *Supplex Libellus Valachorum* sent to Emperor Leopold, whereby the Romanians asked the Hapsburg ruler to grant them the same rights as those enjoyed by others in the province of Transylvania. (p. 49)

Important to note, however, Pilon observed that this plea for independence was made by and for the elite of Romania, the "bourgeoisie, higher clergy, and intellectuals, definitely not the peasants" (p. 49). In such a situation, academics had become reluctant agents of power, all the while claiming the impotency of being mere agencies of national solidarity. Not surprisingly, therefore, education in Romania has tended to be a servant of nationalistic sentiments, a sentiment that, in the post–World War II period, was merely clothed (in varying degrees) by the ideology of Marxism-Leninism. (For example, the first university in Romania was founded in 1860 in Iasi by one of the founders of the new state of the

Union of the Romanian Principalities, Union Prince Alexandru Ion Cuza [1820–1873].) According to Sadlak (1990), "the inauguration itself was considered as an act of creation of the 'national university' and as an important confirmation of the newly acquired statehood" (p. 4). Although academics in the pre-Communist period sought and won (via the Education Act of 1932) some measure of freedom and autonomy from nationalist politics (by citing their philosophy that the academy "is not only a school whose task is to prepare future professionals as needed by the state. Its function is much more important than this. Most of all, it is the flaming source of culture whose destiny is to spread light and truth" [Sadlak, 1990, p. 15]), academic autonomy was short-lived. First weakened in the immediate pre–World War II period by Romanian government efforts to curtail fascist student political activity, academic autonomy was destroyed by the Soviet-dominated "people's education" philosophy of the 1945–1965 period.

Through the 1950s, a Soviet model of educational policy was followed, which made higher education into a practical unit for providing industrial manpower. During this period the responsibility for schooling was shared between the Education Ministry and various industry ministries (Sadlak, 1990). In the vision of the Romanian Communist Party First Secretary, Gheorghe Gheorghiu-Dej, the liberal-bourgeois idea of education was to be replaced with an education model that sought to create a people's intelligentsia, drawn from the working class and party membership. Students were obliged to study dialectical materialism as much as their primary subject, leading to the birth of a compliant professional class that would, as Sadlak stated, "express the unity of professional endeavor with obedience to the Party's teaching in professional and social activities, as well as in private life" (pp. 24–25). Due to state repression, there was little organized opposition to these policies, in that more than 70 academics were imprisoned at the time for political reasons, and many students were required to abandon their studies.[3] Far from being an independent light for truth, universities were part and parcel of the new Socialist state, doing those tasks assigned to them by the government. According to Sadlak, the content of studies during this period was "subject to scrutiny from the point of view of its 'usefulness'—economic as well as ideological" (p. 36).

By 1965, education in Romania was reformed to meet the economic and political needs of a new regime that was interested in increasing political independence from Moscow. Because of this drive for inde-

[3]From 1945 to 1965, although the total numbers of students enrolled in various technical schools and "worker academies" grew to a high of 81,206 students in 1957, the percentage of university students in the population declined (Sadlak, 1990).

pendence by the new leader of the Romanian Communist Party (RCP), Nicolae Ceausescu, a certain liberalization and modernization resulted in Romanian education. For example, expansion of educational polytechnics and pedagogical institutions (to fulfill the expanded instructional demands created by a new 8 years' schooling requirement) occurred, and ideology was downplayed in favor of expertise. "In the beginning, the academic policy of the Ceausescu regime, like in other fields, was generally met with approval and hope" (Sadlak, 1990, p. 38). Romanian historian Vlad Georgescu (1984/1991) observed that:

> under several fairly enlightened ministers of education, [in the years 1968 to 1972], there was progress, modernization, and some openness in education, with less weight being given to Marxism and more to the hard sciences and technical fields. Russian disappeared almost entirely from schools and universities, to be replaced by English, French and German ... equally innovative changes were permitted in the social sciences, with sociology and history enjoying an "unexpected renaissance." (p. 251)

Cooperation with the West in technical, social, and linguistic matters followed (Sadlak, 1990). These actions increased the support of the Party by intellectuals, a group usually independent of it. Forty-three percent of all teachers and a "slightly higher percentage of university teachers" (p. 39) became members of the Communist Party, as compared to 15% of the general population, stated Sadlak.

However, this supposed support of the RCP by intellectuals was often more a result of cynical careerism, and less a heartfelt conscious embrace of Communist ideology. The brutal censorship and repression of the early postwar years gave way to an insidious self-censorship. "This mechanism of totalitarian 'self-restraint'," Sadlak (1990, p. 39) stated, showed why it was possible for the RCP to have such control over academic agenda, so that the academy did not challenge the Party, "even when its vital interests were undermined" (p. 39). In addition, under the Education Law of 1968, the Education Ministry was (for the first time) placed directly under the institutional control of the Central Committee of the RCP. This rigid centralizing control was extended over the universities by 1972.

In the mid-1970s, economic difficulties required Romania to draw back into the CMEA (Council for Mutual Economic Assistance) orbit against the wishes of the Party leadership. This move hurt Romania's much-valued political independence and international prestige. As Almond (1991) noted, during the Communist reign:

> Success in foreign policy, and the prestige which it confers, have been of much of immense importance to Ceausescu. Romanian propaganda remorselessly proclaims every meeting held between the *Conducator* and

> foreign leaders, with pride of place given to evidence of his acceptance by Western statesmen as a valued partner, even a friend. (p. 303)

When he was forced back into the arms of the Soviet economic sphere, the nationalism of the Ceausescu regime took a pathologically suspicious turn, and what little reform had occurred in the social sphere was forgotten. Indeed, the regime sought to turn more to the extreme examples of the few totalitarian nations left in the world: China, the Central African Empire, and North Korea. Almond (1991) gave a telling example of Ceausescu's mindset at the time:

> At a press conference with Western journalists in July 1988, the wag of the regime, Stefan Andrei, representing Romania at the Comecon summit in Prague, expressed all the contempt and loathing of his boss for the idea of *glasnost* when he turned to his interpreter, saying he did not understand the word and needed a translation. Ceausescu's reorientation of Romania's trade towards the Soviet bloc over the past few years has, as a result, put him in an awkward, contradictory position. . . . (p. 305)

According to Almond, early reports of the growing nepotism and subsequent "grotesque cult surrounding his personality—and more recently, that of his wife, Elena—made jokes about 'socialism in one family' almost obligatory in the few reports on the country which appeared, usually filed from abroad" (p. 279). These telling reports, however, were ignored by Western leaders until Ceausescu's strategic uselessness in the new world order was made plain. When he was finally abandoned by the West as a preposterous, self-aggrandizing ruler, Ceausescu turned away from an (always weak) policy of international communistic solidarity toward a more charismatic Italian-style, nationalistic fascism. Turning more and more inward, the ruling family of Romania only trusted itself, and educational policy suffered. As Sadlak (1990) observed, "a policy of austerities and political restrictions with regard to the functioning of . . . academic life in general, became more and more persistent" (pp. 48–49). With ever-increasing intensity, the Ceausescu family came to strictly control Romanian social and educational life. The educational establishment became Elena Ceausescu's private domain. Established academic bodies of previous international reputation (e.g., the Academy of the Romanian Socialist Republic) lost what influence they formerly possessed to her organization, the National Council of Education and Science (Sadlak, 1990).

Under directives of the National Council, all basic scientific research was halted in favor of applied industrial research. Research in the humanities could only function if it was given, "sometimes quite artificially" a practical relevance to what can be called a cult of industrialization and systemization (Sadlak, 1990, p. 54; see also Almond, 1991). In the later periods of the

Ceausescu's rule, Sadlak noted, "higher education was treated instrumentally and only as an executioner of the policies and tasks set for it by the Ceausescu's and their cronies in the communist party, government and academia" (p. 55). This focus of public scholarship on glorification of the Stalinist notion of "one nation, one party, one leader" forced those intellectuals who wished to remain free either into the study of applied sciences, or to esoteric studies of formalism and aestheticism in literary fields (Sadlak, 1990). Reflecting this destructive effect of ideology, the humanities and social sciences suffered from the shift of students toward applied engineering and architecture, with 30%–40% of students in the mid-1970s to over 70% of students by 1989 studying applied sciences (Sadlak, 1990; World Bank, 1992). As Sadlak remarked, "no other European country experienced such a displacement" (p. 60) of intellectual capital. Therefore, by 1985, only 10.6% of students graduating from higher educational institutions had earned humanistic or natural science degrees.[4]

Of course, the return to ideological and economic emphases affected student's lives. Under a policy that viewed education research and production as a unitary process, university and polytechnic faculties were often required to function as state research "factories," with faculty and students contributing 60%–80% of their workload to such mandates (Sadlak, 1990). Combined with a rampant anti-intellectual climate in which, for example, typewriters had to be annually registered with the police, and given an education policy that sought to create "worker-intellectuals," university student enrollment declined (Sadlak, 1990).[5] That was to be expected, because those students that remained in the universities had to take studies they did not desire, work in factories and farms instead of studying, and, if they spoke out, they had to fear repercussions from coworkers and bosses or the dreaded political police, the *Securitate*. Therefore, few academics and intellectuals openly opposed the regime before 1989, and the few demonstrations that did occur, such as a student protest in Iasi in 1987, were quickly and brutally repressed (Sadlak, 1990).

---

[4]Although pre-Communist Romanian education had a decidedly theoretical and literary bent, during the Communist era the country had produced more applied engineers than anything else, for this was what a regime bent upon building vast prestige projects and products demanded. Today, the apparent educational demand is for training in the similarly pragmatic and hard-nosed aspects of business, finance, and corporate law. Sadly, humane studies might suffer under the new structures as they did under the old, this time for economic, rather than overtly political reasons.

[5]After a peak in enrollment in higher education in 1980–1981 (192,769, 83% full-time, with 8.2% of the students being foreigners), by 1985–1986 this population declined to 100,040, 63% full-time, with 17% of the students being foreigners; by 1990, this figure improved somewhat to 164,507, of which 94,952 were full-time (Sadlak, 1990; World Bank, 1992). Sadlak observed that there were roughly the same number of Romanian full-time students in 1990 as in the early 1960s.

This is why the revolution of 1989 took everyone by surprise. As Georgescu (1984/1991) observed, in the 1980s, "... as the Ceausescu regime approached its twenty-fifth jubilee, its rule appeared stable, and the leadership displayed greater determination than ever to perpetuate its policies and enforce its ideological values in defiance of the reformist trends at work in other countries in the Soviet sphere" (p. 278). Its fall in December 1989 struck many Romanians as a miracle, "the miracle of December" (Calinescu & Tismaneanu, 1991). Referring to the poet and dissident Mircea Dinescu's statement on Romanian television on December 22, 1989, that "God has turned his face toward Romania again," Calinescu and Tismaneanu stated:

> It is remarkable that normally skeptical, freethinking Romanian intellectuals should resort to such theological language. The sincere, intelligent need for religious terms and metaphors ... measures how deeply traumatic the character of Communism in Romania was, particularly in its last, grotesque, terrifying, and indeed demonic years, during which Ceausescu ran the country as a virtual concentration camp. Other metaphors—psychological metaphors of madness, for instance—have also been used and misused in trying to explain what will, in the life of individual Romanians as well as of the nation as a whole, remain ultimately unexplainable. (p. 279)

## Description of the Current Romanian Scene and Contests Over the Emergent Ideology of Education

Today, following the 1989 revolution, the social fabric of Romanian society is badly frayed, or even torn. According to the World Bank (1992):

> Because life under the Nicolae Ceausescu Government had been so hard, Romanians held high hopes about reform. The first year of changes did not bring a rapid rise in living standards, however. Like her reforming neighbors ..., Romania suffered a decline. GDP [gross domestic production] per capita fell eight percent. Inevitable confusion surrounding the disappearance of command structures, the collapse of the CMEA trading arrangement, and disruption cause [*sic*] by rapid changes in relative prices were factors that all contributed to accelerating inflation, economic stagnation, and widening macroeconomic imbalances. (p. 1)

One reflection of this decline is the abysmal health indicators in Romania, which are currently among the lowest in Europe.

Such economic crises generate ill effects in the political culture as well. As Gilberg (1992) observed, the transition to a democratic society in Romania has been hindered due to: (a) a lingering legacy of authoritarianism, (b) continued distrust of opposition parties and programs, (c) harassment of political opponents to the regime, (d) appeals to old, nationalistic, antiminority, and xenophobic attitudes, and (e) an administrative structure still under the shadow of Ceausescuism. Because of this, political discourse in Romania has been strongly influenced by nativist forces of both the right and left, leading to, as Gilberg stated, the:

> ... great deal of nastiness in political discourse that now pervades this system; lacking in Romania is the notion of "unity in diversity" and the respect for others and their political and socio-economic goals that must be present in a pluralistic democracy. There is a great deal of evidence that much of this inflammatory rhetoric is, indeed, accepted by the general public of Romanian ethnic origin. And that is certainly a bad omen for the process of democraticization in this unfortunate country. (p. 91)

Examples of this social acceptance of symbolic violence are demonstrated, Gilberg claimed, by the increasing physical attacks against gypsies, the growing existence of anti-Semitic rhetoric, and the growing influence of a Ceausescu cult, encompassing many persons of the still-powerful security apparatus.

And the academics are guilty too: Given their historical role in Romania's elite culture, academics had been tempted in the Ceausescu years to support the regime, either covertly or overtly. According to Sadlak (1990), "the lack of organized opposition [in the days before 1989] generated important problems in re-construction and the moral renewal of higher education. In fact, only a small part of university teachers and academics reproach themselves for not criticizing earlier the communist regime's policies" (p. 67). It is just such duplicity among the so-called agents of change that has increased the difficulties of societal transition in Romania in comparison to the other formerly Communist countries.

In spite of this pervasiveness of duplicity and careerism among educators, there exist agents of change within the school structure who can objectively assess the current challenges. Researchers at the Institute of Educational Sciences, Bucharest (1993) argued that both the principles and the targets of educational policy are confused in today's Romania, in seven specific ways:

1. There is no clear education policy governing reform efforts.
2. Little systematic knowledge exists about the current educational situation.
3. There is little knowledge of the philosophical and practical education options available to Romanian policymakers.
4. Shortages of motivated and qualified teachers and administrators are severe.
5. Reforming agents have to struggle against a still rigid and centralized administrative structure.

6. There are still many persons who sincerely believe in the Socialist planning paradigm, but it has become dysfunctional.
7. Finally, and perhaps most important, there is little money to fund needed changes.

The educational system reflects this systematic chaos. Although overall educational attainment of the general population is high (85% of secondary-age children are in school), there is no reliable measure of educational quality (World Bank, 1992). Moreover, only 10% of those who are 20–24 years of age are in higher education. That is the lowest number of students in Central and Eastern Europe, for the Organization for Economic Cooperation and Development (OECD) average is more than 30%. Although the total number of university students has increased only slightly above 1980–1981 levels (to 236,000 in 1993), the antiquated state university system cannot meet the demand, particularly in the newly popular economic, law and social science faculties. Therefore, since the revolution, a large number of private universities have appeared. At first operating without state accreditation, private institutions meeting minimal criteria have been granted provisional accreditation under 1993 legislation, subject to a formal review procedure over the next 5 years (Minstry of Education, 1994). This last fact indicates that, amidst all of this turmoil and uncertainty in the society, young Romanians do see that education is a vital tool for personal and social advancement. In the words of the World Bank (1992), Romania:

> ... will need citizens capable of performing the civic duties required for democracy—formulating judgements on policy issues, choosing candidates, and demanding service from government. It will need employees and entrepreneurs capable of exercising initiative and responding to events—including the loss of a job and the need to switch sectors or retrain. The education system will now have to be responsive to an electorate, and to a market economy. (p. 89)

Seeing mediated visions of Western democracies as exemplars of development, many students agree with this finding, at least in part. To the minds of other students, however, this prescription by the World Bank for reform begs the question, that is, whether or not Romanians wish for a capitalistic market economy and the Western European political system. As detailed previously, there remain in Romanian society and culture strong residues of both the Communist and pre-Communist authoritarian eras.

With all of these contradictory social demands, it comes as no surprise that the dominant oppositional and alternative ideologies of society that inform any definition of liberal education are in flux. As the Institute of Educational Sciences in Bucharest (1993) observed:

> Each historical period, each regime or government, is making certain options: for some specific goals, for a certain society pattern, a certain development model, certain norms of social behavior. Such fundamental options, defined as postulates, as explicit or implicit principles, refer either to the global society, or to a certain activity sector. They represent, in fact, *the policy* in the respective field: the economic policy, the cultural policy, the human resources policy, etc. As far as the *education policy* is concerned, it has two major elements: the principles and the targets (objectives) of the educational system. (p. 2; emphasis in original)

Repair of the Romanian civil society will come with, Sadlak (1990) claimed: (a) the complete de-ideologization of studies, (b) the "re-discovery of . . . positive experiences in teaching and research" (p. 70), (c) adherence to principles of university autonomy, and (d) the return of the culture to its European roots. But, as Sadlak warned, Romanian history has demonstrated that "system-wide modifications" (p. 71) in higher education have had unseen consequences. Given this observation, starting the process of reform with the individual students and teachers would seem more promising, as suggested in point (b). Romanian history, however, shows clearly that social structures affect the thinking of individuals; individual choices are structured in part by historical conditions.

### Education of Students as State Agencies: Loss of a Humane Emancipatory "Will to Power"

Due to an educational preparation that demanded much skill at simple recall, but little corresponding skill in analytical/critical thinking (i.e., synthesis) abilities, many college-level students in Romania are deficient in argumentation (World Bank, 1992). Even the best students are often trained in ways that emphasize theory recall over and divorced from practice. A student (well trained in literature and philosophy), stated, "The pupils' levels are very unequal, and the good ones strive encyclopedically at highly theoretical matters. . . . This would be wonderful, if they could furthermore be introduced in social life, to apply knowledge" (B. Moise, personal communication, November 1993). He argued that when the typical student is confronted with new educational demands, problems of initiative appear.[6] This lack might be explained by the fact that students formally attend 30 hours of classes a week. Moreover, during

[6]When a survey by the Romanian National Commission (1991) on university students' opinions of educational reform in Romania was performed, a surprising finding (in the context of this study) was revealed when the students were asked, "Which of the socio-human disciplines do you think might best help you to enhance your professional competence, as related to your education line?". The choices given were: psychology, sociology, pedagogy, philosophy, ethics, logic; 63% answered primarily "logic."

the 1980s, whole fields of study were eliminated, such as psychology, sociology, and pedagogy, due to political reasons (World Bank, 1992). In addition, like many of their professors, a majority of students also are having to work full-time in addition to their studies to support themselves, due to a lack of state subsidies.

Not surprisingly, the teachers are confused as well. At a recent conference on civic education in Timisoara, Romania, which I attended, it became clear that, in this age of uncertainty, no teacher knew what was really the *purpose* of a "democratic" educational process. Just as important, the *agencies* of change in the society outside of school, especially the mass media, were overpowering the role of educators, thereby becoming an *agent* of a "dominant" ideology in Eastern Europe, whether the messages are Western marketing or governmental propaganda. Therefore, the *scene* upon which education has to function in Eastern Europe in general and Romania in particular is not a favorable one, given social, political, and economic realities.[7] Adding to these challenges is the isolation of Romania's teachers, with most of them being cut off from Western contact for 20 years. Thus, few teachers here know how to assist their students in becoming integrated social *agents*, possessing the knowledge and wisdom to *act* in the democratic society. For social change to occur from the individual level up, individual students and teachers need to be able to construe alternatives for their own lives.

## THE DEVELOPMENT OF AN EMPATHIC APPROACH TO SOCIAL LEARNING IN A "COMMUNITY OF SELVES"

Clearly, the societal agenda Romania, as well as the other Eastern European nations, face in their transition to democracy is complicated by the fact that, before the newly formed formal democratic structures of governance can have any real effect, a democratic social ethos needs to be created. Given a historical scene dominated by, among other factors, a paternalistic state, the political exploitation of nationalism, and abuses of human rights, the crucial process of developing *informal* democratic folkways and mores will not come easily. Change needs to occur on both the institutional level, as outlined by Pusic (1993), and in pedagogy, as detailed by Aviram (1992). Despite their different emphases, both authors

[7]Although Romanian universities have a large supply of faculty (about a 1 : 15 teacher–student ratio), the physical setting is poor. There is little classroom space or modern equipment, and instructional materials, including textbooks, are scarce. Indeed, in my own experience, I find that even the chalk often does not work on the chalkboards!

claimed that any such process must, first of all, actively deal with real-life issues and concerns. An "objective," value-free approach will not work; rather, a social vision of the "good life" must be clearly defined. Second, it must develop, particularly in students, the critical skills and "morality of the heart" (Shelton, 1990; see also Booth, 1974) that will foster the formation of a democratic spirit. I believe that a pedagogical theory and approach based on such an empathic pluralistic philosophy and rhetorical-dialogical methodology will assist Romanians in beginning their long walk toward a better life.

In my experience in teaching (both in Romania and in the United States), I have found that by embracing the philosophy of constructive alternativism as articulated by Kelly (1955), I have been able to tentatively develop a theoretically sound, yet practical pedagogical approach that answers this social need for societies "in transition." With the aid of my social psychology students I currently teach in Romania, I have sought to apply and refine a "pedagogy for pluralism" from within the philosophy of constructive alternativism.[8] From 1993 to 1995, we have been exploring the philosophical grounds of construct psychology as applied to the study of minority populations and lifestyles in modern Romania.[9] The approach we offer possesses the following important characteristics: (a) a grounding of empathy and care as embraced by Casmir and Asuncion-Lande (1989), Broome (1991), Shelton (1990), Mestrovic, Goreta, and Letica (1993); (b) an argumentative logic drawing upon the rhetorical proofs of Aristotelian (Aristotle, 1960) theory and Platonic definitions of Weaver (1989); (c) an emphasis upon social dialogue as elaborated by Gramsci (1971; see also Joll, 1978) and Freire (1968/1970); leading to, finally, (d) a socially grounded ethical testing of knowledge grounded upon the categorical imperative of Kant (1785, 1797/1983).

---

[8]Members of my English-language social psychology class (1993–1995) at the Romanian College of Arts and Sciences, "Gheorghe Cristea," Bucharest, who have in class discussions and projects assisted me with the development of this chapter are: Gheorghe Costea, Gicu Firu, Mihaela Hudac, Sorin Hudac, Bogdan Moise, Ina Morarescu, and Eduard Rebegea. Many thanks are also due to my American colleagues, John Ely and William Stearns, and the always engaged and engaging students in our advanced team taught sociology reading group. With their sincere intellectual and personal friendship over the past few years, many unknown visions have become known to me.

[9]Being the products of a relatively homogeneous culture in a state that still practices nationalistic politics, Romanians often have difficulty in showing empathy with those populations they define as different, and/or inferior, such as gypsies, Hungarians, Jews, Arabs, feminists, gay persons, and so forth. Perhaps this difficulty is a result of an accident of place; Romanians have historically seen themselves at victims of foreign "cosmopolitan" invaders. Thus, the urge to find scapegoats among members of denigrated categories in this time of economic difficulty is often irresistible. To determine the validity of this judgment, my students are currently applying their knowledge developing survey questionnaires to ascertain the Romanian public's construing of social deviance.

## First Things: The Philosophy of Constructive Alternativism and The Psychology of Personal Constructs

The philosophy of constructive alternativism challenges humans to construe the world in such a way that allows for the dignity and freedom of human choice, however limited that choice may be by physical, cultural, or social elements. As Kelly (1955) stated, philosophical constructivism "emphasizes the capacity of the living thing to represent the environment, not merely respond to it" (p. 8). In other words, the cognitive mental structures each *individual* generates in response to environmental stimuli are what govern that human's behavior and not the reverse. In proposing his psychological theory of personal constructs based on this humanistic foundation, Kelly was advancing a theory of psychology based on creative anticipation, in sharp contradiction to behaviorist and Freudian psychologies (Bannister & Mair, 1968). Although past events give us templates with which to compare present events, the choices we make are strongly influenced by what we predict will occur in the future if we follow a certain path of action. Monaghan (personal communication, October 10, 1990) stated it best: "We think and act according to what we expect to happen."

Although Kelly (1955) gave great weight to individual construings of reality, it is important to realize that he construed the individual as a human socialized within society, a person with both personal and social selves. Drawing from this insight, Mair (in Bannister, 1977) suggested the usefulness of conceiving each person in a society as being a "community of selves":

> Perhaps it is easiest to introduce the idea of "self as if a community of selves" by referring to . . . a community of two persons. Most of us have probably, at some time, found ourselves talking or acting as if we were two people rather than one. We talk sometimes of being in "two minds" about something, part of you wanting to do one thing and part wanting to do something else . . . To consider oneself . . . as two people rather than one-self can make it possible for us to pay attention first to one of the "people," and then to the "other" one. In this activity the person can be encouraged to ignore, for the moment, one of the "selves" and "get inside" the other. From this vantage point of being inside" [another] it is sometimes possible for the person to sense more fully some of the hopes and fears, values and plans, concerns and confusions of this "other person." (p. 130)

Mair's "multiple selves" model (in Bannister, 1977) serves to add an intrapersonal dimension to the "third culture" paradigm that Casmir and Asuncion-Lande (1989) and Broome (1991) described, making the gaining of that elusive culture somewhat easier. Casmir and Asuncion-Lande explained how such a third culture is created:

> Though beginning with contrasting perceptions and behaviors, two individuals, through their interaction, create a unique setting for their interaction. In the conjoining of their separate cultures, a third culture, more inclusive than the original ones, is created, which both of them now share. Within that third culture, the two can communicate with each other more effectively. Thus, a third culture is not merely the result of the fusion of two or more separate enitites, but also the product of the "harmonization" of composite parts into a coherent whole. (1989, p. 294)

However, achieving this ideal state is not a simple matter; each party to the third-culture-building dialogue must take special care and responsibility in the process. Broome (1991) argued that each participant in the conversation should understand what a worthy definition of empathy is. To him, intercultural empathy must be based on the following:

1. It must be "dynamic and provisional"; that is, it must be satisfied with an imperfect knowing.

2. The communication meaning that grows from such dialogical sharing should be interpreted from within the actual context, an interpretation that leads not to the mere reproduction of another's intent, but the creation of new knowledge as a result of the synthetic merging of individuals' subjective-meaning constructions.

3. Such a relational empathy results in the creation of a third culture wherein persons from different cultures can communicate in a communicative sphere that is created by themselves.

To perform this social construction, each student is required to realize the diverse "community of selves" within him or herself, and to thus accept differences in others. Such philosophical pluralism assumes the notion that although reality exists, we cannot see it well alone, and therefore need to engage in dialogue with multiple selves both intrapersonally as well as interpersonally to come to a more complete understanding (cf. Booth, 1979; Hardwig, 1973). Although I therefore attempt to begin laying the foundation of an epistemic third culture in the classroom, I then amplify the need to take the construct into the outside world. To make the principle clear, I draw a cone on the blackboard, and situate three sites around it: point A, above it; point B, below it; and, point C, to the side of it. Then I ask the students, "What would a person at each of these sites see of the cone?" The person at point A would see a circle; the person at point B would see a point; and, the person at point C would see a triangle. Then I ask, "Which person would have a 'correct' view [of the cone]?" After some discussion, it becomes evident to my students that whereas all of these hypothesized individuals see what they see, each person in the example is unable to perceive the totality. Within this imperfect frame of reference, I then claim with Kelly (1955) that each person is a "social scientist" who actively seeks to understand and act in the present by anticipating the future, a prediction that is tied to past experiences. In short, I argue that most persons act reasonably, *given the options they can construct from reality as they see it*. Although I agree with Williams (1983a) that our free choice in life is limited by sociocultural requirements for group solidarity as well as physical limitations of time and place, we have much cognitive freedom to choose how we will react to our environment.

Therefore, participants in communicative encounters share both similarity in their human sense limitations and inductive grounding to experiences *and* essential differences of both ascribed and acquired social distinction. Derrida reminds us that this paradox of similarity and difference reveals the limits of both communication and philosophy, that is, our individual conception of the "ideal" that structures our culture-bound behavior is not a realizable social imperative. For in this mediated world especially, we are doomed to live in what Pierce called "secondness," that is, there is always a part of another's materiality that is beyond our conceptualization (Cornell, 1992). In sum, society is an inherently imperfect human symbolic creation that we experience not only as lone agencies or parts of scenery, but as creative, communal actors struggling against that which cannot be known.

Along with the observations of Kelly (1955), I also draw upon the classic rhetorical proofs of logos, ethos, and pathos associated with Aristotle (1960) in describing human communicative behavior. I posit that we seek to logically make sense of the world as shown in Kelly's aforementioned theory; we, furthermore, intuitively respond to these perceptions of our logos via our emotions, or pathos. The creative tension caused by the dialectical relationship between these intrapersonal forces is then reflected in the interpersonal social actions of our character or ethos. The actions of our ethos encompasses both our personal selves and social roles, roles that structure how we analyze, or come to understand the specific event in front of us, and synthesize, that is, make social generalizations from that event.

## Application of Pedagogical Model

Whenever the students and I have a social "text" to analyze, whether it be a book, an essay, or another person, we use the described model, both individually and collectively, in the following fashion. The first two steps I construe as basically focusing on individual, analytical construing processes, and the two later steps as centering on the social, synthetic-creating construing processes.

I first ask them each to assess their intuitive response to the subject; that is, what is their personal experiencing of the "reality" presented to them, based on a construing of their pasts, the sense they make of their present situation, and how they anticipate the future? This question allows the students to better understand their feelings toward the "other," as well as how this intuitive response to a situation in the present is based on their individual experiences in the society. Once the students know how they feel about the other, I then pose the question, "how do you think this other person would feel about you, given what you just said?" The goal sought by these questions is, first, the attainment of a state that Black (1965) called pure perception so that the student is then able to know if he or she is practicing an honest relational empathy with another. As Broome (1991) stated, relational empathy does not require similarity between persons. He claimed, *"although similarity of constructs may aid in understanding, similarity is not essential in order for empathy to characterize the intercultural communication encounter"* (p. 243; emphasis in original). Indeed, for educators as myself to assume that there *should* be such similarity between Romanians and Americans can be tragic in its consequences for individuals in a culture, given that each has its own "survival process" (Casmir & Asuncion-Lande, 1989, p. 290). An intercultural educational process that hopes to produce individually liberating, yet socially conscious humane action on the part of individuals must, then, embrace the inherent tensions between "irreconcilable horizons" (Broome, 1991, p. 243). In sum, the third culture must be a product of negotiation between equal partners in dialogue, not the winnings of a rhetorical victor, the goal being the joint creation of a shared common ground for the reconstruction of meaning.[10]

Next, I then have the students try to construct a logical form of their vision. The purpose is to have them become aware of the argumentative structure of the claims they make about the subject. To assist in this task, I ask each of them to write a credulous reconstruction of the subject's point of view, written as if a friend of the subject wrote it. I then request the students to write a third-person description of themselves in the same way. Next, I ask the students to compare these "biographies," with the charge to locate the superordinal and core constructs presented in each document (explicit and implicit), and the order of the construct hierarchies revealed. By this procedure, I wish to assist them in discovering how an other, on the surface seemingly very different from themselves, can often be very much like them in essence, particularly given our common jour-

[10]I am reminded of Booth's (1988) "decalogue" for would-be rhetorical critics in which he stated that the first responsibility is for the reader to attempt to reconstruct the meaning of the author so that, ideally, the author would recognize the reconstruction as his own. In this way, much "useless controversy" over authorial intent could be avoided.

ney as humans through a life cycle seeking meaning (Kelly, 1955; Turnbull, 1985).

Once the intuitive ground and the logical structure of a student's viewpoint toward the "text" is laid out, then I ask each student to become a disinterested reader of his or her own thoughts. To help the process along, either I (or other students) play the role of the interacting reader, asking the author to clarify, explain, and expand the arguments made. Often, disagreements over interpretations of the subject will surface, thereby providing an operative definition of dialogical pluralism. By this method, the claims made by any particular student begin to make the transition from untested private opinions into a reasonable discourse that is suitable for the public forum. The individual's arguments will now have to be able to stand the test of confrontation and survive intact or be subject to modification (Brockriede, 1974; Tussman, 1960). With the aid of an adaptation of a fractional communication model employed by Monaghan (1968, March), I am able to then assist my students in construing their arguments within nine analytical categories created by factoring the three classic rhetorical speech forms (forensic, deliberative, and epideictic) with the three argumentive forms as defined by Weaver (1989) (definition, analogy, and circumstance). By this methodology, elements of historical "factual" events, present policy concerns, and social values within a given society are rhetorically considered in light of the way individuals think about them. Furthermore, the question of how much power students believe they possess to affect policy on specific issues is also opened for consideration.

At this point in my discussion, I often ask the students how the social structures of language, customs, or politics limit what my students (and I) are able to conjure up, say, or do in the social realm. I encourage my students to reflect upon varied social myths, or unstated taken-for-granteds that structure thoughts in a culture. Intercultural comparisons and a communal judgment of their applicability can profitably be made at this point. In Foucault's (1972/1981) terms, I ask what discourses are allowed by a culture and what discourses are silenced, and what are the ethical implications of "opening the silences" within and between culturally distinct societies?

Finally, if the argument made by a student has stood up to scrutiny and the solutions offered for remedy seem reasonable the class as a whole, then there is one final question to ask, which parallels issues raised by Kant's (1785, 1797/1983) "categorical imperative": What if the vision offered became general practice in the society? This question helps us to see both the personal and social implications of theory and practice in social sciences; it brings theorizing "down to earth." After all, Romania has been wrecked in the recent past by Ceausescu's attempt to impose his ideal personal vision of the "multilaterally developed society" upon a public that he did not consider to be made up of his equals. Western teachers, steeped in our own ideology of market capitalism, need to be culturally sensitive so as to avoid imposing a new "tyrannizing image" of society upon a highly stressed social order (see also Weaver, 1964).

## CONCLUSIONS

By the use of Kellian psychological theory as placed within an Aristotelian and Burkeian philosophical frame, I have demonstrated how students and teachers function as colearners in the third-culture-building process of dialogue. Whatever the pedagogical benefits of such a teaching approach to a particular student or class, in the volatile context of the Balkans, there is a much greater social benefit to be gained. By implementing such a paradigm on the social stage, the logical desire of theorists to generate universal, abstract concepts is controlled by constant reminders to "embrace the particular." As Mestrovic et al. (1993) argued, if such an understanding of culture could have been employed by Western policymakers the tragic violence of Yugoslavia might have been avoided. Similarly, foreign advisers need to respect the reasonable desires of the Romanian people in this time of change, for they need to be the authors of their own future social narrative; it cannot be profitably ghostwritten.

## REFERENCES


Aristotle. (1960). *The rhetoric* (L. Cooper, Trans.). New York: Meredith.

Almond, M. (1991). Decline without fall: Romania under Ceausescu. In G. Frost (Ed.), *Europe in turmoil: The struggle for pluralism* (pp. 279–321). Glenview, IL: Greenwood.

Aviram, A. (1992). A humanistic higher education programme. *Higher education in Europe, 17*(3), 99–112.

Bannister, D. (Ed.). (1977). *New perspectives in personal construct theory.* London: Academic Press.

Bannister, D., & Mair, J. M. M. (1968). *The evaluation of personal constructs.* London: Academic Press.

Black, E. (1965). *Rhetorical criticism: A study in method.* New York: Macmillan.

Booth, W. C. (1974). *Modern dogma and the rhetoric of assent.* Chicago: University of Chicago Press.

Booth, W. C. (1979). *Critical understanding: The powers and limits of pluralism.* Chicago: University of Chicago Press.

Booth, W. C. (1988). The English teacher's decalogue. In W. C. Booth (Ed.), *The vocation of a teacher: Rhetorical occasions, 1967–1988* (pp. 90–102). Chicago: University of Chicago Press.

Brockriede, W. (1974). Rhetorical criticism as argument. *Quarterly Journal of Speech, 60,* 165–174.

Broome, B. (1991). Building shared meaning: Implications of a relational approach to empathy for teaching intercultural communication. *Communication Education, 40*, 235–249.

Burke, K. (1945). *A grammar of motives*. New York: Prentice-Hall.

Calinescu, M., & Tismaneanu, V. (1991). The 1989 revolution and the collapse of Communism in Romania. In V. Georgescu (Ed.), *The Romanians: A history* (pp. 279–297). Columbus: Ohio State University Press.

Casmir, F. L., & Asuncion-Lande, N. C. (1989). Intercultural communication revisited: Conceptualization, paradigm building and methodological approaches. In J. A. Anderson (Ed.), *Communication yearbook 12* (pp. 278–309). Newbury Park, CA: Sage.

Cornell, D. (1992). *The philosophy of the limit*. London: Routledge.

Foucault, M. (1981). *The archaeology of knowledge and the discourse on language* (A. M. Sheridan Smith, Trans.). New York: Pantheon. (Original work published 1972)

Freire, P. (1970). *Pedagogy of the oppressed* (M. B. Ramos, Trans.). New York: Continuum. (Original work published 1968)

Georgescu, V. (1991). *The Romanians: A history* (M. Calinescu, Ed.; A. Bley-Vroman, Trans.). Columbus: Ohio State University Press. (Original work published 1984)

Gilberg, T. (1992). Romanians and democratic values: Socialization after Communism. In D. N. Nelson (Ed.), *Romania after tyranny* (pp. 83–94). Boulder, CO: Westview Press.

Gilder, E. (1992). Uniting the alpha and omega of critical discourse: A Kellean rhetorical analysis of W. C. Booth as "career author." Doctoral dissertation, The Ohio State University.

Gramsci, A. (1957). *The modern prince and other writings* (L. Marks, Trans.). New York: International.

Habermas, J. (1984). *The theory of communicative action* (Vols. 1 and 2; T. McCarthy, Trans.). Boston: Beacon.

Hardwig, J. (1973). The achievement of moral rationality. *Philosophy and Rhetoric, 3*, 171–185.

Hudac, S. (1993, November). *Nationalism: A struggle between the collective "id" and the collective "super-ego" of nations*. Paper presented at the meeting of the Civic Education Project seminar on nationalism in Romania and Central Europe, Iasi, Romania.

Institute of Educational Sciences. (1993). *The reform of education in Romania: Conditions and prospects*. Bucharest: Author.

Joll, J. (1978). *Antonio Gramsci* (Modern Masters series). New York: Penguin.

Kant, I. (1983). *Ethical philosophy* (J. W. Ellington, Trans.). Indianapolis: Hackett. (Original works published 1785 and 1797)

Kelly, G. A. (1955). *The psychology of personal constructs: Vol. 1. A theory of personality*. New York: Norton.

Mestrovic, S. G., Goreta, M., & Letica, S. (1993). *The road from paradise: Prospects for democracy in Eastern Europe*. Lexington: University Press of Kentucky.

Mihailescu, C. (1993). *Education, culture and the post-totalitarian state*. Unpublished discussion paper, Institute of Educational Sciences, Bucharest.

Ministry of Education. (1994). *Romanian state education: Realities and goals*. Bucharest: Author.

Monaghan, R. R. (1968, March). A systematic way of being creative. *Journal of Communication, 18*, 47–56.

Nichols, M. H. (1989). Kenneth Burke and the new rhetoric. In J. L. Golden, G. F. Berquist, & W. E. Coleman (Eds.), *The rhetoric of Western thought* (4th ed., pp. 319–332). Dubuque, IA: Kendall/Hunt.

Pilon, J. G. (1992). *The bloody flag: Post-Communist nationalism in Eastern Europe (spotlight on Romania)*. New Brunswick, NJ: Transaction.

Pusic, V. (1993). Intellectual trends, institutional changes and scholarly needs in Eastern Europe. *Eastern European Politics and Societies, 7*(1), 1–13.

Romanian National Commission. (1991). *Trends in Eastern Europe and their impact on higher education: The student–professor relationship*. Bucharest: UNESCO.

Sadlak, J. (1990). *Higher education in Romania, 1860–1990: Between academic mission, economic demands and political control* (Special Studies in Comparative Education No. 27). Buffalo: State University of New York, Graduate School of Education, Comparative Education Center.

Shelton, C. M. (1990). *Morality of the heart: A psychology for the Christian moral life.* New York: Crossroad.

Toulmin, S. E. (1958). *The uses of argument.* Cambridge: Cambridge University Press.

Turnbull, C. (1985). *The human cycle.* London: Triad/Paladin.

Tussman, J. (1960). *Obligation and the body politic.* London: Oxford University Press.

Verdery, K., & Kligman, G. (1992). Romania after Ceausescu: Post-Communist Communism? In I. Banac (Ed.), *Eastern Europe in transition* (pp. 117–147). Ithaca, NY: Cornell University Press.

Vlasceanu, L. (1992). *Trends, developments, and needs of the higher education systems of the Central and Eastern European countries.* Bucharest: UNESCO.

Weaver, R. M. (1964). *Visions of order: The cultural crisis of our time.* Baton Rouge: Louisiana University Press.

Weaver, R. M. (1989). "Language is sermonic." In J. L. Golden, G. F. Berquist, & W. E. Coleman (Eds.), *The rhetoric of Western thought* (4th ed., pp. 304–317). Dubuque, IA: Kendall/Hunt.

Williams, R. (1983a). *Culture and society: 1780–1950* (2nd ed.). New York: Columbia University Press.

Williams, R. (1983b). *Keywords: A vocabulary of culture and society* (rev. ed.). New York: Oxford University Press.

World Bank. (1992). *Romania: Human resources and the transition to a market economy: A World Bank country study.* Washington, DC: Author.

# 9

# *Media Coverage of Bulgaria in the West and Its Domestic Use*

Dina Iordanova
*University of Texas at Austin*

## MEDIA COVERAGE OF BULGARIA IN THE WEST

Media coverage of Bulgaria? It is a nonexistent item in the West. Scattered reports appear now and then on such topics as the unpaid parking tickets of employees at the Bulgarian United Nations mission in New York,[1] Bulgarian Parliamentarians mistaken for shoplifters in Minnesota,[2] the expulsion of Vladimir Zhirinovsky from Bulgaria in December 1993,[3] or to report the December 1991 TV hoax involving bogus reporting of a fatal

[1]This subject was touched on in a number of publications, the Bulgarian mission being a favorite to reporters—see Willens (1993a, 1993b), Roth (1993), and Clark (1993a, 1993b). It was reported that the Bulgarian U.N. mission owes $187,000 in unpaid 1992 traffic tickets (Clark, 1993a), and that "... in the shadow of the U.N. itself, Traffic Officer Adeyi found a car from the Bulgarian mission—number four on the naughty mission list" (Roth, 1993). Bulgarian attaché Kostov reportedly said: "We are not willing to pay because we are diplomats. This theme is nasty because it breathes unkind foreign feelings" (Willens, 1993b).

[2]See "Store Regrets" in *Chicago Tribune* (1991) and "Do Not Travel to Minnesota" in *Svoboden Narod* (1991).

[3]See "Zhirinovski Makes Private Visit" (1993); *UPI* reports "Russian Ultra-Nationalist" (1993), and "Bulgarian President calls" (1993), and *Reuters* reports from Sofia "Zhirinovski Proposes Plan" (1993), "Bulgaria Expels" (1993), and "Zhirinovsky Leaves" (1993); "European doors slammed" from *The Globe and Mail* (1993). Tim Judah (1993) of *The Times* reported: "Mr. Zhirinovsky was overheard telling a Russian Embassy official that he should call the Bulgarian president and tell him he is a scum. He takes better care of Russian prostitutes in Bulgaria" (p. 26).

nuclear accident.[4] British writer Julian Barnes's *The Porcupine* was widely reviewed in 1993. This book was considered noteworthy because it was based on documentary material of the fate of Bulgaria's dictator Todor Zhivkov. The *Bulgarian Umbrella* murder of writer George Markov in 1978 is another among the few references to Bulgaria in the Western media, as is the alleged plot to assassinate the Pope in 1981.[5] Money laundering, drug smuggling, trading in arms and heroine (involving such mysterious organizations as Kintex) are also on the agenda.[6] Other than the examples cited here, Bulgaria has received little attention from the Western media.

Maybe it is this absence from Western media content that leads to frequent references about Bulgaria in various other contexts. It is a well-known fact that because of restricting clauses in their contracts, George Harrison, Bob Dylan, and Tom Petty could not reveal their identities when they started recording together. Thus the cover of their first *Traveling Wilburys* album (1988) states that Wilbury Record Company is a subdivision of the Trans-Wilbury Corporation of *Bulgaria*, which is used as fictitious, fake name for the record label. To give another example, the "Texas satire king" Kinky Freedman suggested during a 1991 show in Toronto that someone should call the Bulgarian embassy in order to get a "large *Bulgarian* masseuse" (Howell, 1991, p. D1). As yet another example, back in the forties Sam Goldwyn, on learning that a script he had acquired featured lesbian characters, is said to have replied, "Well, we can always call them *Bulgarians*" (Smith, 1993, p. C5). This anecdote

---

[4]In an article entitled "Nuclear Joke Not Amusing," *The Washington Times* reported on December 23, 1991:

> A joke on a student-run Bulgarian TV program about a nuclear accident triggered hundreds of panicky telephone calls to the station. The bogus report Saturday on the student program "Ku-ku" said an accident had occurred at the plant and that the president would address the nation. Authentic-looking footage of what appeared to be emergency measures was shown. The hoax was disclosed 50 minutes later. Reports later in the day said that angry viewers mobbed the creators of the program outside the TV studios, but police prevented any injuries. (p. A2)

[5]The list of publications relevant to support this statement is as long as 26, the most recent ones being *Federal News Service* of March 2, 1992, *Nassau and Suffolk Edition News* of June 9, 1991, and *PR Newswire* of April 4, 1991. On these issues see also *The Bulgarian Umbrella*, by Kostov (1988).

[6]Another 26 media reports on these issues are available. It is remarkable, for example, that the only two times *Forbes* magazine features Bulgaria for the past 5 years was about money laundering (Fuhrman, 1989) and about the Bulgarian arms-trading company Kintex (Fuhrman, 1993). Some other publications on these issues are the ones by Sudetich (1990a, 1990b) and Bonner (1994a, 1994b) at *The New York Times*, by Marcus (1993) at *The Jerusalem Post*, by Zdroj (1993) at *The Washington Post*, and by Judah (1990) and Boyes (1991) at *The Times*.

provided the title for 1987 Kaier Curtin's history of the emergence of gay and lesbian characters on the American stage (Curtin, 1988).

Larger American research libraries maintain online indexes to periodical articles published since 1988 in academic and popular publications like *The Economist* and *Time* and in newspapers like *The New York Times*. When a search was conducted using the online index at the Perry-Castañeda Library of the University of Texas at Austin in February 1994, using the title/keyword *Bulgarians*, 16 titles were retrieved, whereas the same search with title/keyword "Poles" retrieved 213 titles, *Czechs*: 92, *Hungarians*: 44, *Slovaks*: 42, *Albanians*: 50, *Yugoslavs*: 45, *Romanians*: 42. Another title/keyword search hit 150 titles containing the word *Bulgarian*, as opposed to 882 titles containing the keyword *Polish*, 501 titles matching the word *Hungarian*, 483 for *Czech*, 214 for *Romanian*, 194 for *Slovak*, and 186 for *Croatian*, outnumbering only Albanian, with 106 titles. The word *Bulgaria* is present in 254 titles, as opposed to *Bosnia* in 1,752, *Poland* in 1,460, *Yugoslavia* in 1,184, *Hungary* in 844, *Czechoslovakia* in 640, *Czech Republic* (for the brief period of its existence as a separate country) in 92, *Slovakia* in 93, *Romania* in 520, *Croatia* in 381, again only to surpass *Albania* with 250. In the *Business Periodicals Index*, a search for title/keyword *Bulgaria* hits 275 matches, while *Poland* hits 1,720, *Hungary* 1,119, *Czechoslovakia* 598, plus 88 for the *Czech Republic* and 53 for *Slovakia*, 356 for *Romania* and 151 for *Albania*.

If we compare the results of these searches for Bulgaria and Hungary, which is approximately the same size country[7] and where no special events like the Yugoslav war or the separation of Czechoslovakia have taken place to induce more coverage, the ratio for coverage of Bulgarians versus Hungarians is 2.75 times more in favor of Hungarians. The word *Hungarian* is mentioned 3.34 times more often than *Bulgarian*; *Hungary* is mentioned 3.32 times more often than *Bulgaria*; and Hungary is covered 4.07 times more often in business periodicals than Bulgaria.[8]

A similar, and even wider search can be conducted through the state-of-art computer database Lexis/Nexis, which includes records from all types of major Western mass media (newspapers, telegraph agencies, and major TV networks). Searching on Lexis/Nexis makes it possible to retrieve all reports where a given keyword is mentioned in the textual body.[9] For the keyword *Bulgaria*, 27,396 stories were found—as opposed to 68,672 stories for *Hungary* (which is 2.5 times more); 14,150 for *Albania*; 36,198 for *Romania*;

---

[7]Hungary has a somewhat larger population and slightly smaller territory. The population of Bulgaria is 8,870,000, whereas Hungary's is 10,334,000. The surface of Bulgaria is 42,823 sq. miles, that of Hungary is 35,919 sq. miles.

[8]One should also keep in mind that these are purely quantitative comparisons, leaving the qualitative dimensions of the context entirely out of the discussion.

[9]The search was restricted to articles appearing between March 1992 and March 1994.

109,501 for *Poland;* 24,753 for *Slovakia;* 30,351 for the *Czech Republic* and 50,515 for *Czechoslovakia. Bulgarians* was found in 14,735 stories, while *Hungarians* appeared in 52,895 (3.59 times more). No stories were found in the search for keyword combination of *Bulgarians/Europe* as opposed to the combination *Hungarians/Europe* which was featured in six stories.

## BULGARIAN MEDIA REPORTING WESTERN COVERAGE

At the same time, if one studies the Bulgarian media reporting of Western coverage of the country, one is left with a different impression: namely, that Bulgaria and its efforts to overcome a Communist legacy are being discussed actively in the West, and that the West carefully watches the country with concern for its fate.

The geographical, political and sociocultural isolation of Bulgaria is clear from the point of view of the West, but the Bulgarian audience cannot feel it. Bulgarians, with access primarily to their own media, do not know to what extent they are excluded from Western news coverage. "The world is looking at us" is a leading theme in all Bulgarian-language print and broadcast media, no matter to which political force they have affiliation. Every political power group is eager to demonstrate that its efforts are leading to wider recognition and attention to the country by foreigners, and that it is the one that will promote Bulgaria and give it prominence among the nations of the world. Thus acknowledgment by "the world" is used as a synonym for "approval," to justify the actions of various politicians. Because "looking at us" is commented on so often, no matter that in most cases the conclusion is that actually "no one looks at us," the very presence of the question provides the frame for political discourse.

The media are doing their best to claim the involvement of Bulgaria in many international initiatives, although that fact may be difficult to demonstrate—at least if poor coverage in the foreign media is any indication. Subjects like the involvement of a Bulgarian military contingent in Cambodia,[10] strict enforcement of the embargo against Iraq and Serbia,

[10]The abundant media coverage of the deployment of Bulgarian troops within the U.N. contingent in Cambodia illustrates well to what extent the appreciation of the West is wanted and expected. The coverage on Bulgarians in Cambodia always implies that this presence attracts the attention of the international community, which looks at us carefully and appreciates our efforts to keep up with the international requirements. An example is the newspaper article by Kornazhev (1993) in which the author interpreted the untimely withdrawal of Bulgarian troops as a Communist conspiracy aimed at damaging the image of the country as a cooperative force in the international arena. He wrote: "The new authority, which we are trying to build for our country within the international democratic community would thus collapse and we would find ourselves again in the company of these same states of which we are trying to emancipate ourselves" (p. 7).

Bulgaria being admitted to membership (usually only as an associate member, but the specific meaning of the term is never explained in the media) of this or that international organization, or that Bulgaria was visited by one foreign politician or another, are indicative of that approach. Some Bulgarians may suspect that their country is not among the major interests of Westerners. Still, they can reassure themselves by believing that, even if the Western audiences are poorly informed and have no understanding of their concerns, powers that be (leaders) in the West do know everything about them. They feel assured that their interests are on the agendas of intelligence agencies and corporate think tanks, thus turning a blind eye to the possibility that those institutions may also depend on the media, or that, rather, they quite often use the presence (or absence) of coverage in the media as an excuse for specific operations.

The monthly publication of the Open Society Foundation of Sofia, *Letter from Bulgaria* (funded by George Soros), which is designed to inform Bulgarians living abroad of recent developments in their country, is a prime example of this approach. The newsletter features a chronology of current events that usually span a 2-month period. Major events are often omitted; however one can find a large variety of reports illustrating how intensive the contacts of Bulgaria are with the "outside world." Stories include information about a folklore ensemble of children from Gabrovo departing for a tour in Southern France; a report about six Bulgarians taking off for Antarctica to participate in mining development along with representatives of 24 other countries, to secure a lasting Bulgarian presence on that continent; and coverage about a factory, Burya, in Gabrovo that received a contract from Germany for 5,000 ladies' pajamas.[11]

At this point, the question is: Why is all this so important to Bulgarians? Do the Bulgarian media create and perpetuate such an illusion in a conscious fashion?

On the one hand, the answer is no, because what is reported reflects actual Western media coverage. This is probably due to the fact that any scattered reports in the Western media are carefully translated and used by Bulgarian sources. If a short editorial on the post-Communist reality of Bulgaria appears in some major newspaper in the West, that fact is reported the next day in all major Bulgarian newspapers, as well as on radio and on television. Thus the public is left with the impression that "the world is looking at us," "the world is watching us," and "the world knows and cares about us."

[11]*Letter from Bulgaria*, Nov./Dec. 1993, No. 28-9. Sometimes these reports develop into more than mere reporting. For example, see the following: "The troupe of the Kyustendil Drama Theater returned from Bossilegrad. There they performed 'Little Red Riding Hood' by Charles Perrault for the children of Bulgarians of this city, located in our Western outlying parts, which was left beyond Bulgarian borders after the peace treaty of Neuilly" (p. 4).

On the other hand, such re-reporting takes a particular publication or broadcast item out of the context of the media agenda of the source country, and invests this item with a far greater significance than it originally had. In the Western newspaper the story about Bulgaria would have appeared as a small item on the international news pages. Its re-reporting in Bulgarian media, however, moves Western coverage to the front page, and moves major events in the originating country of the coverage to highly visible places on the relevant international news pages. Because coverage of Bulgaria abroad is reported as a major event within the country, the natural conclusion is that such importance is also being attached to it within the media context of the country in which it originates.

## RARE CONSENSUS

That one should provide extensive coverage of the media image of Bulgaria abroad is one of the few matters on which there is complete consensus within the conflict-torn Bulgarian media. All political forces, including the ones that emerged in post-Communist times, would like to exploit to the utmost the attention the West pays to the country. That attention can be used as a sort of validation and justification of their efforts toward shaping the post-Communist political climate of the country.

This consensus has its historical reasons and justification.[12] A part of the Ottoman empire for nearly five centuries (1396–1878), Bulgaria is proud to have preserved its Slavic/Orthodox heritage. The emancipation of the country, however, did not occur as a result of independent effort, because the national uprising of 1876 failed. The country was liberated as a result of the Russo-Turkish war of 1877–1878 and its fate was decided by the big European powers at a series of subsequent international conferences. Toward the end of 19th century the consciousness of predetermined dependency of the country on the big powers became a major feature of Bulgarian national ideology. In this context, the notion of a genuinely caring big power gains extreme importance. It is usually paired with the opposite one—the concept of a big power with suspicious interests at stake. The nationalist ideologues of Greater Bulgaria always have played with these concepts, preaching for finding a big power to support the effort of Bulgaria to compensate the territorial losses it has suffered as a result of preceding international conferences at which other big powers have disposed of the fate of the country. All involvement of

[12]Concise and useful information on the geography, history, and culture of Bulgaria can be found posted on the Internet (Newsgroup No. 2997—soc.culture.bulgaria).

Bulgaria in the 20th-century wars and all its alliances in wartime can illustrate the infatuation with the big caring power: the Bulgarian part in the Balkan Wars (1911–1913); in World War I (1914–1919) as an ally of Germany, and in World War II (1940–1944) as an ally to Germany again and with Bulgarian forces occupying the Macedonian regions of both ex-Yugoslavia and Greece.

After World War II Bulgaria was awarded as a sphere of influence to a new caring power, Russia. It is not by chance that it gained eventually the nickname of "16th Soviet republic." After the collapse of communism in 1989, however, it was clear that at least for a while Russia was no longer an option, and that there was only the West to turn to. Both politicians and media in Bulgaria find it of extreme importance to maintain the impression that the West is paying attention, no matter to what extent this attention is fact or fiction. Admitting that the West does not care but tends to marginalize the country in this period of vital changes, could trigger extremist nationalist tendencies. The nationalist cause would then have very good reasons to call for noncompliance with Western-imposed standards in pursuit of specific national interests and for disregarding the requirements of the international community, which requirements will be revealed as manifestation of the hypocritical interests of big powers.

This is generally why at this moment Bulgarian media do their best to ensure the audience that the country is not marginalized. It is essential to maintain the impression that the West appreciates any effort Bulgaria would make toward cooperating with the international community. The task of suppressing a possible bitter realization of the fact that the country is neglected by the big powers in the West is carried out mostly by the media. One of the major directions in which this concept takes shape is the public debate in the media regarding the chances of the country's "return to Europe."

## RETURN TO EUROPE

In the Bulgarian case the issue of that "return" is often being formulated as "joining Europe." Bulgarians believe that they are destined to always be someone's satellite, and that the only relevant issue is whose satellite they would like to be. This is articulated by essayist Evgenia Ivanova (1992) who wrote that:

> There is a theory according to which the Balkans in general (and Bulgaria in particular) is the bridge between the East and the West, between yesterday and tomorrow. A bridge or passage. It seems that the destiny of the

> Balkans and of Bulgaria is to be an eternal bridge or passage. . . . The world press, inasmuch as it deals with Bulgaria, describes her as "an island of peace in the Balkans." It is similar to exotic squared: the first level of exotics is the idea that the Balkans are an arena of blood baths, cruelty and terror; the second level of exotics is that there is no bloodshed and no terror in Bulgaria. A third level is also possible: "Bulgaria is in the Balkans." (p. 73)

Further, Ivanova (1992) noted, "Bulgaria was always a province: of Byzantium (11th–12th century); of the Ottoman Empire (14th–19th century); of Russia, Germany and the Soviet Union virtually throughout the 20th century. Whose province shall we become next? Of Europe or America?" (p. 73).

Thus Ivanova (1992) was clearly outlining today's directions of the political interests in the country. What is really at issue, however, is whether Bulgaria itself will choose whose province it is to become—or if it will be the province of another country at all. The eternal illusion is that if one is ready to let oneself be taken over, there always will be someone interested in taking advantage of that fact.

"Return to Europe" is actually a major feature on the agenda of all East European countries. However, Bulgaria's chances are far more remote, both because of its geographical location and of its sociopolitical situation to rejoin Europe than the countries of "Mitteleuropa" (Central-East Europe). Well-known Bulgarian historian Andrey Pantev (1992) wrote:

> Today we are facing the undeserved unique chance to re-claim our earlier significance given that we not only understand what is going on, but will also be able to foresee with a minimal political intellect what is going to happen in the near future.
>
> If we stay a condemned eternal European periphery in times when many other countries which do not belong to Europe in a geographical sense are already Europeanized, depends also on whether we will be able to overcome the archaisms of the old Balkan nationalism and to invent, adapt and make compatible to the new times a different approach and principle for our national goals. (p. 3)

All political forces in Bulgaria use the concept of Europe as a political slogan in one way or another. The "Road to Europe" was even the name of a reformist caucus within the former Communist Party. The slogan with which the new post-Communist political formation Union of Democratic Forces (UDF) competed in the elections in 1990 was also about Europe—according to it the country would join Europe as soon as the UDF was elected to power.

How problematic a return to Europe might be is a substantial part of the post-Communist sociopolitical discourse. "A return to Europe implies that Europe existed in the same form at the time of departure as it does today, on the eve of the return," noted Misha Glenny (1990) in his *The Rebirth of History* (p. 216). That idea is seldom considered when dealing with the claim of Central East European countries that they have shifted back to the cultural sphere called Europe.

In the case of Central East European countries—no matter how often it is questioned and disputed—this return is the subject of an ongoing discussion. Concrete steps to be taken by Bulgaria toward realization of that goal are much more problematic, however.

Certainly, Europe is no longer what it used to be "at the point of departure" (Glenny, 1990), that is, at the time when the Eastern Bloc left it. If, in the case of Central East European countries, the return can take place only after restoration of some features of the status that existed at the time of the "departure" from the rest of Europe, a reevaluation of what constitutes the new unified Europe must be developed. Reestablishing a cultural and social space for Mitteleuropa, including the return to, reentering, or joining Europe by Bulgaria requires an utterly different conceptualization of the point of departure. There are several such possible, but incompatible, scenarios for a reconstruction that would serve Bulgaria's present need to claim a place within the conceptual boundaries of Europe.

First, there is the potential reconceptualization of Europe as a fragile area living under the permanent threat of an Islamic invasion, which needs to be shielded by the southeast Balkans. In that scenario Bulgaria would be an essential player. Second, there could be a reassessment of the spheres of influence negotiated at the end of World War II at the Yalta conference—a redrawing of the maps in which the West would reclaim the entire Soviet sphere "en bloc." It would result in a package deal, from which countries like Bulgaria, to which no one lays claim, would benefit. Third, one might possibly find a West European power whose interest in the Balkans is underrepresented. That power might be provided with access to the southeast corner of the Balkans (Bulgaria), thus gaining validation, legitimizing the claim that Bulgaria is part of Europe. Although this is a very abstract scenario, it is nonetheless being considered. There is also a fourth possibility, which may be closest to reality, but which is less desirable for Bulgaria's politicians—an ongoing attachment of the country to Russia, continuing the long tradition of sattelitism in the spheres of culture, politics, and economics.

Each one of these four incompatible scenarios is promoted by the Bulgarian media and in each case Bulgaria's image abroad is used in a specific way.

## Islamic Invasion

Bulgarian historians, who also serve as national ideologists, make it a major stake for Bulgaria to serve as a shield for Europe, protecting it from an always-imminent Islamic invasion—a role that Europe is expected to understand and appreciate.

Bulgarian print media generously provide space for numerous articles by or interviews with historians, who speculate on the topic of the historical ties of Bulgaria to the European tradition. They are preoccupied with proving the place of Bulgaria in Europe by especially focusing on concepts such as the proto-Renaissance, a pictorial style manifested mostly in icon painting, which they see as a specifically Bulgarian contribution to European culture around the 13th century. Its progress was brutally interrupted by the Ottoman invasion at the end of the 14th century, thus cutting the ties with the western part of Europe and leading Bulgarian culture away from the general European track of development. The point here is to prove that Bulgaria was a cradle of European culture and that its history is intrinsically connected with Europe's development. Interestingly enough, at the same time historians take pride in matters that actually separate Bulgaria from the West European cultural tradition—the fact that it adopted the Cyrillic alphabet, and did not accept Roman Catholicism. Here one can note an attempt to interpret the concept of European culture more broadly, thus asserting one's own cultural values.

The history of the country, which was conquered by the Turks in 1396, but managed to preserve its specific Slavic cultural and national identity throughout five centuries, until 1878, when its European identity re-emerged, is stressed repeatedly. The Ottoman yoke is considered to be a major interruption in the development of the country as a part of Europe. Its legacy is considered to be a major impediment to the fulfillment of the nation's Euro-centered goals. Pantev (1992) noted that, "We are situated on the border between the Christian and Islamic civilization, but we are also on the border between the modern world and the world of traditional societies" (p. 3).

If Europe needs Bulgaria once again as a shield, that would undoubtedly restore the country as a part of the European cultural realm. Thus, stressing present-day European fears of a possible invasion by Islamic fundamentalism becomes essential to Bulgarian nationalist ideologues. Today's Bulgarian authorities officially distance themselves from the oppressive policies directed against the country's Turkish minority since the mid-1980s. Yet, it is a commonly shared idea that Bulgaria can be important to Europe only if it finds itself in the way of another Islamic penetration of the continent. As a result, no matter how abstract, the scenario of such an invasion is being debated again and again. Bulgaria is the place from which Muslim mercenaries might penetrate into the former Yugoslavia to fight alongside Bosnian Muslims. Bulgaria is the place from where oil supplies mysteriously reach the Serbs. Bulgaria is the country that appears on TV maps only if there are reports about the conflict brewing around the former Yugoslav Republic of Macedonia. Within the country itself there still exist nationalistic tensions in Turkish-populated areas, and numerous references in the media hint that the so-called Movement for Rights and Freedoms, controlled by ethnic Turks, plays a treacherous role in Bulgaria's politics.

The coverage of today's ethnic Turks' migration patterns perpetuates the impression that a takeover is imminent. There is also an abundant amount of material dealing with the alleged fears of the West of an Islamic invasion. In Bulgarian newspapers, for example, one can often read comments hinting that the West is actually so reluctant to interfere in the Bosnian war because interfering would mean protecting Muslims, who are more to be feared than protected.

## Package Deal for the East Bloc

Geographically Bulgaria is a part of Europe, but it exists outside the European semantic space. As a result, Bulgaria's role in Europe has always been questioned. Always an isolated country, Bulgaria actually profited to some extent from the existence of the Communist East Bloc because that guaranteed it the company of Central East European countries such as Czechoslovakia, the eastern part of Germany, Hungary, and Poland, which had always been seen as parts of Europe. In the 1990s, as that East Bloc dissolved, primarily into two major areas, Central East Europe and the Balkans, Bulgaria was to some extent excluded from European territory. Its location beyond Belgrade makes it appear, from a Western perspective, to be Europe's ultimate south eastern boundary.

Seen in this context, a potential "package deal" transferring the entire former East Bloc to Europe is a solution not only acceptable but desirable to Bulgaria. It is another question whether such an option is really available. The return of Bulgaria to Europe or its desire to enter Europe implies not only the existence of Europe in the same form as it existed at some earlier point, it also requires a package deal transferring *all* countries of the East Bloc into that new Europe. Today Bulgarian politicians often make statements for the media equating the situation of their country to the one of the other East European states. Bulgarian ambassador to Canada, Slav Danev (1993), for example, repeated old clichés from Communist times, implying solidarity with other comrades of the former Bloc, when he wrote, "Like all the other countries of the Eastern European bloc Bulgaria discarded the totalitarian regime and enthusiastically took the way of building a democratic society based on a market economy" (p. 24).

For decades, Bulgaria has been automatically equated with countries such as Czechoslovakia, Hungary, and the GDR (German Democratic Republic). However, Bulgaria today does not have the same chances for integration into Europe as these other countries. Although earlier Central East-Europe and the Balkans had just been geographical descriptions that did not stand for different and incompatible political entities, the total dissolution of the East Bloc became an incontrovertible fact with the Bosnian war.

No matter that the formation of new entities such as the new economic union of the Central East European countries (the Vyshegrad group) are being reported in the Bulgarian media, there is no public discourse on what they mean to Bulgaria. A brief visit by then vice president Dan Quayle in 1992, and his formal address, consisting of a few sentences directed to Bulgarians, were glorified by the media to such an extent that one could be left with the impression that the event was equal to a presidential visit of the kind the Czech Republic had experienced. At the same time, scattered reports can be found in Bulgarian media covering the extensive visa requirements for Bulgarians that countries like the Czech Republic and Hungary recently introduced. These are hardly sufficient, however, to make it clear that Bulgaria is no longer in the same "league" as those states. Of course, another reason why the package deal scenario cannot work is the fact that each one of the Balkan countries is trying to distance itself from the others:

> It is known that Bulgarians can never complain of a lack of enemies (things are different with friends); but the ones, who in the larger part of their new history are considered to be the real, notorious enemies, in spite of temporary flirts and even alliances, are their NEIGHBORS. The reason being that, at the very moment of starting a life at his own political home, the Bulgarian finds out that he is surrounded by his own kind, unreleased brothers on each side, objects of attention to (of course) their NEIGHBORS. He has been fighting with all of them at one time or another. (Mishkova, 1992, p. 82)

Because of their geographical proximity to Central Europe, countries like Romania and Yugoslavia would also have to be part of the package. But they are clearly not included in the Bulgarian concept, thus invalidating the entire idea. Bulgaria's goal of becoming part of Europe always implies a vision that contacts with Central or Western Europe can be developed while totally ignoring the existence of what are considered to be unworthy neighbors, with whom one not only does not want to be identified, but does not want to be even distantly associated. In the Bulgarian media one can find numerous reports, for example, dealing with the efforts of Bulgaria to make sure that the embargo against the Serbs is being enforced, since the river Danube, Bulgaria's northern border, is the route by which many of the alleged supplies reach the Serbs. Media reports always mark the extent to which the Bulgarian economy is affected by the embargo, but never neglect to mention the appreciation of Western countries for the embargo support Bulgaria provides.[13] Thus the impression is maintained that the West is paying attention to Bulgaria, looking beyond its unworthy neighbors, Yugoslavia and Romania, and that it appreciates the significant efforts of Bulgarians.

### Who Is Interested in Bulgaria?

The third scenario implies identifying some Western power that would be interested in strengthening its presence in the Balkans. Bulgaria would offer it access to that strategic part of Europe, and would receive political and economic support in exchange. The only question is, which nation would that be? It is common consensus that England traditionally has neglected Bulgaria. That is a fact, although Bulgarian historians like Lyudmilla Zhivkova, daughter of former President Todor Zhivkov and herself a former minister of culture, wrote her PhD dissertation in the 1970s dealing with relations between Bulgaria and the United Kingdom. Germany, allied with Bulgaria both during World War I and World War II, looks like a very attractive partner to Bulgarians. There is a consensus that, theoretically, the Germans would be supportive of the Bulgarian cause, but that they could not back up their support with any substantial financial contributions. Because of its recent reunification, the attention of Germany is focused on the economic development of the former East Germany, and, as a result, significant economic support could hardly be expected from that country.

In this context, quite unexpectedly, France and Spain come into focus for Bulgarians: France—because of its desire to consolidate Francophone countries against the cultural invasion of America; Spain—because of the fact that the exiled Bulgarian monarch lives and is quite active there, while enjoying the support of the Spanish crown.

---

[13]See "Bulgaria Is Affected the Most" in *Otechestven Vestnik* (May 31, 1993). Two articles on the topic can be found in only one issue of the newspaper. The editorial on page 1 reads: "If we consider it more closely, this way the U.N. is punishing Bulgaria no less than the former Yugoslav republics. This is why it is quite natural for the world community to reward us for the losses suffered. The compensation should have financial, not ethical dimensions." On page 4 one reads: "Bulgaria will have the support of France and Portugal. Both these countries-members of the EC will present a plea for our country to the European Community so that we could be compensated for the losses suffered from the Yugo-embargo" (translated from the Bulgarian by Dina Iordanova).

***Francophonie.*** In January 1994, Bulgaria applied for full membership in the community of Francophone countries, and President Zhelyo Zhelev took part in the two last meetings of that organization in Paris and Madagascar. There are other examples of Bulgarian interest in such a relationship. A music festival, "Francofolies," was staged in 1993 in Blagoevgrad, a city located in the Bulgarian part of Macedonia. Furthermore, some interesting "statistical" data appeared in the media to prove that about one third of Bulgarians have some level of fluency in French—which represents a "scientific" basis for Bulgaria's claim that it is a natural member of the Francophone group. These claims led to increased tension with Romania, which has also applied for full membership in the same organization. The Bulgarian media have published a number of articles to prove how inappropriate Romania's claim to be considered a Francophone country is, compared to Bulgaria's. The fact that Romanian is a Romance language, whereas Bulgarian is a Slavic one, is considered to be irrelevant. One relies on the notion that France would want to have its interests in the Balkans better represented than Romania could do, and thus would admit Bulgaria into its circle of allied and supported countries.

As far as Spain is concerned, it is expected to demonstrate interest in Bulgaria because of that country's current discussion of the possible reestablishment of a monarchy. The Spanish King, Juan Carlos, visited Bulgaria in 1993, an event covered extensively by the Bulgarian media. The coverage of this visit represents only a small part of the abundant stories that the media devote to the more general topic of the restoration of the monarchy.

***Monarchism.*** The topic of monarchism has two dimensions: a narrow one—related to the Bulgarian Czar in exile, Simeon II, and a broad one—dealing with the potential restoration of the monarchy in Bulgaria in general.

Simeon was born in 1937 and became Czar in 1943, after the untimely death of his father, Boris III. He was dethroned in 1947. Since then he has lived in the West, mostly in Spain, and has never returned to Bulgaria. But he would not mind returning, it seems. Bulgaria is currently undergoing a leadership crisis, and restoring a monarch with a Western-education-and-Western-ties looks very attractive from the perspective of many people within that country. Bringing Simeon back, however, would mean bringing back the monarchy as an institution, something that encounters strong opposition in many political circles. A suggestion was made that Simeon could be brought back to Bulgaria as president of the republic, which clearly indicates that there is more interest in his personality and his Western connections than in the restoration of the monarchy itself.

Simeon, however, seems reluctant to discuss any option other than returning in his capacity as monarch. He claims he has never ceased to be Czar of the Bulgarians, because his dethroning, in the 1940s, was unlawful. He tours Western Europe and often delivers lectures or keynote addresses at different monarchist gatherings, developing his views on the contemporary role of monarchies into a thoroughly philosophical concept. Thus he has secured for himself a lasting presence in all the Bulgarian media. Some of them feature special interviews or articles on him; some just go along with the common tendency of paying attention to anything in the West that would somehow relate to Bulgaria.[14]

Whereas King Mihai of Romania was refused access to Romania when he arrived at the Bucharest airport in 1992, Simeon does not even try to come to Bulgaria. But the visits of his sister and mother became major popular events, with active involvement on the part of the media. Public-opinion polls indicate that a large percentage of the Bulgarian public considers Simeon to be a Bulgarian (even though his grandfather, Ferdinand, is of Austro-Hungarian descent, his mother is Italian, his wife is Spanish and his children were born in Spain and educated in the West). The belief of many is that once he has returned, Simeon will influence Spain to support Bulgaria economically. Supposedly, Spain also wants access to the Balkans like everyone else in Western Europe, especially because it presently does not have any direct involvement in Eastern Europe. There are at least five Bulgarian parties promoting the idea of restoring the monarchy: the Democratic Movement for Constitutional Monarchy, the "Enlightenment" Society, the Natural Monarchist Party, the Monarchy-Conservative Union, and the Rousse-based union "Kingdom of Bulgaria."

Simeon does not disappoint his supporters and promoters. When asked in an interview if he sees the Balkans as part of a bigger Europe his answer was:

> Certainly, yes. It does not matter what is our geographical location, it does not matter that sometimes people think of us as pseudo-Asians or half-Turks, we are simply there and we do exist. I sincerely believe that up-to-date communications, up-to-date technology and a truly new re-distribution of the European wealth and technologies will let us witness a new industrial revolution. (Koburggotski, 1993c, p. 1)

[14]See coverage in *Democratsia* ("H. M. Simeon," 1993), an interview on the matter with the Bulgarian ambassador to the United Kingdom Ivan Stanchov (1993), articles by Y. Valchev (1993) and G. Lozanov (1993), and numerous interviews with the monarch himself (Koburggotski, 1993a, 1993b, 1993c, 1993d). The Czar's name is used as an attraction to readers even in a book review of *The Bulgarian Brides*, a new novel by Spanish author Eduardo Mendicutti dealing with the lives of bisexual immigrants from Bulgaria ("Czar Simeon Is Mentioned," 1994).

This is exactly what the Bulgarian public wants to hear: Bulgaria is in Europe, and there is implied a possible redistribution of European wealth. Thus, no matter how unrealistic, the monarchy-Spain scenario is still very much on the agenda of the Bulgarian media when they promote foreign images of their country for domestic use.

The fourth scenario, the Russian one, is not so popular with the public, but it is gradually receiving more and more attention in the media.

## Russia + "Natural Markets" = Natural Allies

Economic links to the Soviet Union and Comecon, the old communist trade bloc, were vital to the Bulgarian economy—76% of Bulgaria's exports were going to countries in that bloc. With the dissolution of the East Bloc and the loss of Russia's markets, the Bulgarian economy suffered severely. This loss might have been compensated for if new markets for Bulgarian goods had appeared, but that did not happen. That is why more and more often one can see the Bulgarian media lamenting the loss of markets and suggesting that one should do something to regain them. In May of 1992, during a short visit, U.S. envoy Lawrence Eagleburger was approached by a number of Bulgarian journalists on the subject of America's willingness to purchase Bulgarian goods, and to send them as humanitarian aid to Russia. Thus the traditional market ties would be put in place again, only the payment would be coming from a different, solvent source.

The interest of Russia in the Balkans grows in tandem with the growing isolation of this area from the West. Openly expressing interest in the deployment of troops in the former Yugoslavia, the Russians have reintroduced their presence into south-eastern Europe. Bulgaria again is within the realm of Russian influence. And, willy-nilly, the media develop the scenario of reinstating Bulgaria in the Russian sphere of influence in an active manner. A new weekly, *Russia Today*, had its successful start in early 1994. It is a Bulgarian language digest of materials from the Russian print media which enjoys growing popularity among Bulgarian audiences. Its very existence is more than telling provided that not so many new periodicals can find a niche at the oversaturated print media market of 1990s Bulgaria.

In his March 3, 1994 address for the National Day of Bulgaria, President Zhelev explicitly stated that in spite of the fact that Bulgaria will still pursue a "foreign policy orientation towards Europe, towards integration into European structures, towards the Atlantic system of security, the Republic of Bulgaria does not renounce the historical and cultural values that bind us to Russia, such as our common Slavonic roots, the alphabet introduced by Cyril" (Zhelev, 1994).

It is difficult to say at this point to what extent the fourth scenario for foreign reorientation of post-Communist Bulgaria is viable, but talk about it becomes more and more immanent. Although there is some information in Bulgarian media about undercover diplomatic activities of Russians, it normally appears as a refutation of rumors rather than as a report of facts. As a result, the public is left confused as to at what these alleged Russian envoys actually aim. The Bulgarian Telegraph Agency ("Russian Ambassador Denies," 1994) reported that, "The Russian ambassador to Sofia described as speculative statements in the Bulgarian press that one of the purposes of the 19th–22nd February visit in Bulgaria by State Duma Chairman Ivan Rybkin was to mediate in the partitioning of Vardar Macedonia between Belgrade and Sofia." Western agencies are more unambiguous in making hints about the new power spheres in the south-eastern part of Europe. The British Broadcasting Corporation reported that "Istanbul daily says USA has abandoned Balkans to 'Russia's influence' " (1994); let's not even mention the new map of Europe drawn by Zhirinovsky in early 1994, according to which Bulgaria gets a great deal of the new adjacent territories and which was widely publicized by the media in the West.

More and more, Bulgarian media cultivate the realization that the fourth scenario, although not the most desirable, is the most viable one. More and more they acknowledge both the absence of coverage of Bulgaria from Western media and from Western scholarly publications. And, because the belief that Bulgaria should definitely be a province of a bigger power is as strong as ever, Russia appears more and more in the forefront of the agenda for affiliation. That Bulgaria is virtually being ignored by those in the West is finally being admitted and commented on by the Bulgarian media. More and more people now realize how poor the image of Bulgaria is in the West.

## IMAGE OF BULGARIA IN THE WEST

Numerous scholarly and quasi-scholarly books dealing with the revolutions of 1989 and their aftermath were published in the West in the early 1990s. These books usually start with analyses of the situation in Central Europe, and go further to discuss the Balkans (Hoffman, 1993; Laufer, 1991; Slater, 1992). Normally, Bulgaria is mentioned, but the special circumstances of the country are rarely explored in detail. If efforts are made to include a chapter on Bulgaria, it usually focuses on one issue about which the author has managed to gather some information. Nationalism, for example was the only issue worth discussing for John Feffer in his journalistic *Shock Waves* (1992). In his scholarly *After the Fall: The Pursuit of Democracy in Central Europe* Jeffrey Goldfarb (1992) included a chapter on Bulgaria. In it he resorted to popular journalism, explaining for more than 10 pages to his readers how uneducated Bulgarian academics looked to him during his 3-day visit to that country in 1990, and how excited he was to meet even one who was an exception to the general ignorance. That kind of approach—visiting Bulgaria for a couple of days, while on a trip to the "real" East European countries, and then reporting the impressions one has gathered while passing by—is widespread. Such authors conduct a few interviews with Bulgarian officials, and thus become overnight "experts" on Bulgaria. One example is the publications of researchers affiliated with the University of Georgia's James M. Cox Jr. Center for International Mass Communication Training and Research (Hester & Reybolds, 1991; Hester, Reybolds, & Conger, 1992). Frequently, the names of Bulgarians discussed in other reports are misspelled. Bruce Litte's chapter in the *Handbook of East European Films and Filmmakers* is a prime example. Some names are mentioned twice in the index, both times misspelled, and with different spelling errors.

Another approach to Bulgaria is just to "skip" that country. If one can only say superficial things, it is better to say nothing, goes the reasoning. In a number of collections of articles covering developments in East European countries there is no chapter at all that deals with Bulgaria (see, for example, Brinton & Rinzler, 1990). But because the country is on the map of the region studied, the editors try to explain why it is not covered. Chris Corrin (1992), for example, claimed that she was unable to find any information or anybody who would prepare a chapter dealing with the situation of women in Bulgaria; as a result it was excluded from the book she edited entitled *Superwoman and the Double Burden*. She wrote, "Had it been possible to include studies on Romania, Bulgaria and Albania this would have been welcomed, but no such studies were available to us when compiling the present work. . . . In Bulgaria and Albania change has been slower than elsewhere, and women have fewer opportunities within these countries to change their situations" (p. 1).

Similarly, in *Spring in Winter*, the editor wrote: "The absence of a particular Bulgarian chapter in this book is an omission which I acknowledge and regret" (Prins, 1990, p. xxi). In *The Magic Lantern*, Timothy Garton Ash (1990a) provided a viable explanation: He omits Bulgaria from his account of the revolutions of 1989 simply because he was not a witness to the events there and did not feel confident enough to judge the situation. In his earlier *Uses of Adversity*, Bulgaria is not mentioned a single time (Garton Ash, 1990b). Neither is it mentioned in Andrei Codrescu's (1990) *The Disappearance of the Outside*.

The real image of Bulgaria in the West is one of a forsaken "backyard of Europe." When considered by Western scholars, any uniqueness of the situation in Bulgaria goes unnoticed. Whereas the countries of Central East Europe are being analyzed in academic books, Bulgaria is merely being "covered." That "coverage" always appears somewhere toward the end of the index. Although Western mass media fail to provide coverage on Bulgaria, that trend is made worse by academics who, instead of analyzing, just mention the country, possibly in the hope of compensating for what has not been done by the mass media.

## RECEPTION OF BULGARIANS ABROAD

Even if the Bulgarian media were to stop perpetuating an incorrect image of their country in the West, and would in this way stop creating wrong impressions among the Bulgarian audiences, one basic fact remains: even if the country is forsaken and neglected, the people have a vitality that could potentially produce for them a good reputation abroad.

There is a special technique that is sometimes used by reporters, that is, when the media cover the opinions *others* have of *us*. For example, the opinion of a German farmer who had hosted a group of Bulgarians for agricultural training was that "Bulgarians have the reputation of hard working people, on whom one can rely. Unlike the uptight Germans, Bulgarians are well-balanced people" ("Eight Bulgarians," 1993, p. 25). The very fact that the question, "What is the reputation of the Bulgarian abroad?" is being asked and has been answered on numerous occasions may gradually help to create a clear and well-defined reputation of Bulgarians for the people of other nations, thus helping to validate the image that the nation has of itself.

As a result, ultimate hope rests with Bulgarians living abroad, who can prove that theirs is a nation of survivors. Media attention in Bulgaria is beginning to focus more and more on such cases. Interviews with Bulgarians who have lived abroad for some time, or who are now citizens of other countries, are featured by all media. Most often these are Bulgarian women who have married foreigners and at some point have started small businesses of their own—fashion designers, for example. They usually have Western-sounding family names and during visits to their native country they reside in the expensive new hotels post-Communist times brought into existence. Such reports provide portraits of émigrés who have succeeded in establishing themselves abroad, as a feature of the post-Communist media. Similar success stories also feature people who have recently left the country: for example, the CNN anchorwoman Ralitsa Vassileva, and young theater directors Ivan Stanev in Germany and Boris Velchev in Canada (Stefanova-Peteva, 1994). A Bulgarian newspaper, reporting on the tragic fate of David Koresh's followers, did not forget to mention that the Branch Davidians sect was founded back in the 1930s by a Bulgarian, Victor Hutev ("Museum of Branch Davidians," 1994). No matter that there is no clear-cut Bulgarian diaspora, the Agency for Bulgarians Abroad in Sofia is an important institution whose work is extensively covered by the media. Bulgarians abroad are the potential target of a number of publications that are written in English and that originate in Bulgaria, like *Bulgarian Quarterly*, *The Insider*, and *Balkan Media*. They probably will never enjoy the popularity of *The Prague Post* or of the *Budapest Review of Books*, but they still do exist in spite of the fact that the number of subscribers is small and that the Western librarians have serious doubts if these periodicals will survive.

Quoting connections with the West when talking to representatives of the media is a form of legitimizing oneself within the Bulgarian cultural and political sphere. George Ganchev, leader of an organization called Bulgarian Business Bloc, has mastered that approach. During the January 1992 presidential elections he won almost 17% of the votes. Ganchev is a former fencer and stuntsman who emigrated to the West in the early 1970s, has lived in Britain and the United States, and has been earning his living in the world of show business. Ganchev returned to Bulgaria in the late 1980s, right at the time when the political changes began. He pronounced himself leader of the Bulgarian Business Bloc and declared his intention to compete in the presidential elections. Shortly thereafter he launched a fierce self-promotional campaign, which included activities like singing his own songs on TV, giving numerous interviews to reporters, and citing an abundance of connections to Western multimillionaires in the entertainment world, who were described either as his former in-laws, or as drinking buddies. The message Ganchev was addressing to Bulgarians was: "Vote for me, because I will help you to enter Europe. I have the best connections there, because my connections are not just business ones. These people are personally indebted to me." Ganchev was described by the Western media as a "dark-horse candidate." *The New York Times* compared him to Poland's Stanislaw Tyminski and called him "a joke candidate" ("Candidate With U.S. Citizenship," 1992). *France Presse* called his campaign "largely humorous" (Sergieva, 1992), and *The Times* ("Stand-off," 1992), described him as a ". . . thoroughly Westernized outsider, who ran a cheerful campaign on a platform of unity and capitalism telling voters that they would never rejoin Europe if they were 'nasty, poor and ugly', and that he would help them to become 'confident, rich and optimistic' " (p. 40). Still, Ganchev remains one of the most popular personalities in Bulgarian politics, favored by the media and enjoying a good reputation.

## CONCLUSION

The marginalization of Bulgaria in this period of transition will certainly have an impact on future events and developments. What I have tried to make clear in the preceding pages is the fact that no matter how different political forces would like to shape the future of Bulgaria, all of them are interested in maintaining the impression that they enjoy the backing of the West—which is supposed to prove to the Bulgarian public that their cause is being appreciated and supported by the rest of Europe and the world. The media promotion of this backing of and interest by the West in Bulgaria is seen as being vitally important, because it is believed that it will lead to an actual intensification of exchanges, even at the cost of a less-than-adequate intercultural communication perspective. Even if Western coverage of developments in Bulgaria were to become scarcer, the media of that country would continue to compensate for that lack of interest, and the isolation of the country from the rest of the world would go as unnoticed within the country itself as it has until now.

## REFERENCES


Barnes, J. (1992). *The porcupine*. London: Picador.

Bonner, R. (1994a, January 27). Arms for the revolution: The Bulgaria connection. *The New York Times*, p. A3.

Bonner, R. (1994b, January 30). Bulgarian hunts criminals of Communist era. *The New York Times*, p. 15.

Boyes, R. (1991, October 15). Skeletons rattle police closet. *The Times*. p. 27

Brinton, W. M., & Rinzler, A. (1990). (Eds.). *Without force or lies: Voices from the revolution of Central Europe in 1989–1990: Essays, speeches and eyewitness accounts*. San Francisco: Mercury House.

Bulgaria expels Russian ultra nationalist leader. (1993b, December 28). *The Reuters Library Report*.

Bulgaria is affected the most [Trans. from Bulgarian by Dina Iordanova]. (1993, May 31). *Otechestven Vestnik* (pp.1 and 4).

Bulgarian President calls Russia's Zhirinovsky a fascist. (1993, December 29). United Press International.

Candidate with U.S. citizenship blocs clear victory in Bulgaria. (1992, January 14). *The New York Times*, p. A2.

Clark, K. (1993a, December 13). Diplomatic scofflaws ordered to pay N.Y. parking tickets. *The Houston Chronicle*, p. 12

Clark, K. (1993b, December 5). Envoys may learn how mean N.Y. streets are: diplomatic immunity hits stop sign. *Chicago Tribune*, p. 23

Codrescu, A. (1990). *The disappearance of the outside: A manifesto for escape*. Reading, MA: Addison-Wesley.

Corrin, C. (Ed.). (1992). *Superwoman and the double burden. Women's experience of change in Central and Eastern Europe and the former Soviet Union*. London: Scarlet Press.

Curtin, K. (1987). *"We can always call them Bulgarians" (The emergence of lesbians and gay men on the American stage)*. Boston: Alyson Publications.

Czar Simeon is mentioned in a novel about homosexuals [Trans. from Bulgarian by Dina Iordanova]. (1994, February 14). *168 Hours*, p. 46.

Danev, S. (1993, June). Bulgaria. *Diplomat and International Canada* (p. 24). Ottawa: Ministry of Foreign Affairs.

Do not travel to Minnesota [Trans. from Bulgarian by Dina Iordanova]. (1991, April 3 ). *Svoboden Narod*, p. 3.

Eight Bulgarians to train in agriculture in Germany [Trans. from Bulgarian by Dina Iordanova]. (1993, August 13). *24 Hours*, p. 25.

European doors slammed in face of Zhirinovsky. (Germany refuses visa, Romania angry; Russian envoy apologizes to Bulgaria). (1993, December 30). *The Globe and Mail.* p. 1.

Feffer, J. (1992). *Shock waves. Eastern Europe after the revolutions.* Boston: South End Press.

Fuhrman, P. (1989, April 17). The Bulgarian connection (money laundering in Bulgaria). *Forbes*, p. 40.

Fuhrman, P. (1993, May 10). The heart of illegal trade (Bulgarian arms-trading company Kintex). *Forbes*, p. 42

Garton Ash, T. (1990a). *The magic lantern: The revolution of '89 witnessed in Warsaw, Budapest, Berlin and Prague.* New York: Random House.

Garton Ash, T. (1990b). *The uses of adversity: Essays on the fate of Central Europe.* New York: Vintage Books.

Glenny, M. (1990). *The rebirth of history. Eastern Europe in the age of democracy.* London: Penguin.

Goldfarb, J. (1992). *After the fall: The pursuit of democracy in Central Europe.* New York: Basic Books.

Graubard, St. R. (Ed.). (1991). *Eastern Europe ... Central Europe ... Europe.* Boulder, CO: Westview Press.

H. M. Simeon does not intend to stay in the shadow [Trans. from Bulgarian by Dina Iordanova]. (1993, September 6). *Democratsia*, p. 1.

Hester, A., & Reybolds, L. E. (1991). (Eds.). *Revolutions for freedom: The mass media in Eastern and Central Europe.* Athens: University of Georgia Press.

Hester, A., Reybolds, L. E., & Conger, K. (1992). (Eds.). *The post communist press in Eastern and Central Europe: new studies.* Athens: University of Georgia Press.

Hoffman, E. (1993). *Exit into history: A journey through the new Eastern Europe.* New York: Viking.

Howell, P. (1991, October 15). Country music's Groucho rides warped sense of fun. *The Toronto Star*, p. D1.

Istanbul daily says USA abandoned Balkans to Russia's influence. (1994, March 5). *BBC Summary of World Broadcasts.*

Ivanova, E. (1992). East-East. *Bulgarian Quarterly, II*(3/4), pp. 73–81.

Judah, T. (1990, August 2). Sofia's 'dirty tricks' department offers to help trace terror arms. *The Times*, p. 28.

Judah, T. (1993, December 30). Russian fascist leader barred from Germany. *The Times*, p. 26.

Koburggotski, S. (1993a, June 30). I would not like to return to Bulgaria as a tourist [Trans. from Bulgarian by Dina Iordanova]. *Duma*, pp. 1–6.

Koburggotski, S. (1993b, June 24/25). The irrefutable truth is that since August 28, 1943 I am Czar of the Bulgarians [Trans. from Bulgarian by Dina Iordanova]. *Noshten Trud*, p. 3.

Koburggotski, S. (1993c, April 23). Monarch of the future [Trans. from Bulgarian by Dina Iordanova]. *Korona*, p. 1.

Koburggotski, S. (1993d, September 8). My patience in waiting for the throne comes to its end [Trans. from Bulgarian by Dina Iordanova]. *24 Hours*, pp. 1–3.

Kornazhev, T. (1993, August 13). This could have developed into an international blunder [Trans. from Bulgarian by Dina Iordanova]. *24 Hours*, p. 7.

Kostov, V. (1988). *The Bulgarian umbrella. The Soviet direction and operations of the Bulgarian secret service in Europe* (B. Reynolds, Trans.). New York: Harvester.

Kovachev, R. (1993, September 7). Why return to Russia? [Trans. from Bulgarian by Dina Iordanova]. *Noshten Trud*, p. 2.
Laufer, P. (1991). *Iron curtain rising: A personal journey through the changing landscape of Eastern Europe*. San Francisco: Mercury House.
Lozanov, G. (1993, September 7). Is there a place for the Czar in our hearts? [Trans. from Bulgarian by Dina Iordanova]. *Express*, p. 7.
Marcus, R. (1993, April 25). "Mystery man" denies "Forbes" allegations of arms smuggling to Croatia. *The Jerusalem Post*, p. 4.
Mishkova, D. (1992). "Allies-scoundrels": From the history of Bulgarian national stereotypes of their neighbors. *Bulgarian Quarterly, II*(3/4), 81–109.
Museum of Branch Davidians opens in Texas [Trans. from Bulgarian by Dina Iordanova]. (1994, Feburary 26). *24 Hours*, p. 23.
Nuclear joke not amusing. (1991, December 23). *The Washington Times*, p. 12.
Pantev, A. (1992, June 12). The chances of contemporary nationalism [Trans. from Bulgarian by Dina Iordanova]. *24 Hours*, p. 3.
Prins, G. (Ed.). (1990). *Spring in Winter—The 1989 revolutions*. New York: Manchester University Press.
Roth, R. (1993, December 1). The free ride is over for diplomatic autos in New York [Broadcast]. *CNN News*.
Russian ambassador denies Duma chairman on secret mission. (1994, March 5). *Bulgarian Telegraph Agency*.
Russian ultra-nationalist ordered to leave Bulgaria. (1993a, December 28). *United Press International*.
Sergieva, V. (1992, January 13). Zhelev fails to win majority in first presidential vote. *Agence France Presse*.
Slater, T. (Ed.). (1992). *Handbook on East European films and filmmakers*. New York: Greenwood.
Smith, S. (1993, April 27). Gays proudly leading the band into mainstream theater. *The Toronto Star*, p. 15.
Stanchov, I. (1993, September 7). If Simeon comes back, after the euphoria is over, he will be destroyed [Trans. from Bulgarian by Dina Iordanova]. *Standart*, p. 1.
Stand-off in Sofia. (1992, January 14). *The Times*, p. 40.
Stefanova-Peteva, K. (1994, January 24). Boris Velchev amazes the Canadians with Stefan Tzanev [Trans. from Bulgarian by Dina Iordanova]. *168 Hours*, p. 47.
Store regrets calling Bulgarians shoplifters. (1991, April 1). *Chicago Tribune*, p. C3.
Sudetic, C. (1990a, September 6). Confrontation in the Gulf: East bloc to sell masks to Saudis. *The New York Times*, p. A20.
Sudetic, C. (1990b, August 2). Evolution in Europe. Bulgaria to share arms export data. *The New York Times*, p. A6.
Valchev, Y. (1993, June 30). The rulers tie up the best with the life and the ideals of their people [Trans. from Bulgarian by Dina Iordanova]. *Otechestven Vestnik*, p. 4.
Willens, P. (1993a, September 17). Diplomats Pummeled. *States News Service*.
Willens, P. (1993b, September 23). Senators fed up with diplomats abusing privilege. *States News Service*.
Zdroj, B. (1993, April 24). Eastern Europe's "merchants of death" elude U.S. sting: Officials criticize customs service operation aimed at Poles for showing our hand. *The Washington Post*, p. A21.
Zhelev, Z. (1994, March 3). Zhelev urges good relations with Russia in National day address [text of speech broadcast]. Sofia: *Bulgarian radio*.
Zhirinovsky leaves Sofia for Moscow. (1993c, December 29). *The Reuters Library Report*.
Zhirinovsky makes private visit to Bulgaria. (1993, December 26). *Agence France Presse*.
Zhirinovsky proposes plan to stop Bosnian fighting. (1993a, December 26). *The Reuters Library Report*.

# 10

# *Africa, the Kremlin, and the Press: The Russian Soul Comprehending and Communicating the African Spirit*

Charles Quist Adade
*University of Windsor*

Contemporary Russia is riddled with ethnic, racial, linguistic, and territorial conflicts. Although much is known about ethnic and territorial cleavages, our knowledge of racial attitudes—especially in relationship to Black peoples—is extremely limited. This chapter traces the historical and cultural background of racial attitudes and prejudices in Russia with Africa as the point of reference, and the role of the press in communicating, shaping, reinforcing or perpetuating these attitudes and prejudices, and argues that ethnocentrism rather than ideology informed the nature of intercultural communication in Russia before and after Communism. Two hypotheses form the basis of our discussion:

1. The ethnocentric "blood" is thicker than the ideological "water," in other words, the more ethnocentric a culture is the more it will dismiss, trivialize, and marginalize Africans.
2. "There are no permanent friends; only permanent interests in politics."[1]

The chapter also explores the extent to which the changes in the former Soviet Union that led to the end of the Cold War and the subsequent demise of Communism influenced intercultural communication during and after the rule of the architect of the changes, Mikhail Gorbachev. The

[1]This hypothesis is borrowed from Lord Palmerston's famous dictum.

research covers the periods between the immediate Gorbachev era and the post-Gorbachev era (i.e., the Yeltsin post-Communist era 1985–1993).

## THE "BLIND" FORCES OF HISTORY AND CULTURE IN INTERCULTURAL COMMUNICATION: AN ATTEMPT AT A CONCEPTUAL ANALYSIS

The scientific-technological revolution has led to an information boom and also turned our planet into what Marshall McLuhan called the global village. Although the global village has made us more interdependent than ever before, the information boom has created difficulties of mutual comprehension. In a single day, we are literally assailed by a hurricane of events. Even in one single country the number of events are so overwhelming that its citizens are hard-pressed to keep track of all of them. The problem is complicated when it comes to the international arena, where the simultaneous and successive flow of happenings in all parts of the globe makes it humanly impossible to follow every single event.

We are handicapped by time, distance, and other factors. We are compelled to depend on the mass media for our global information. But ethnic and racial stereotypes and prejudices become new stumbling blocks to complete comprehension of the information we receive, as we have no time for personal inquiry and verification, not forgetting, of course, that media people too are themselves constrained in their work by their own stereotypes and prejudices. As I argue, the media do not necessarily create these stereotypes, but they play no small part in shaping, reinforcing, and entrenching stereotypes and attitudes.

It is in this light, therefore, that the role of the international communication media in shaping intercultural attitudes and feelings assumes enormous importance. Their role in molding, educating, and mobilizing people for good or bad ends remains unchallenged. The role of the mass media in influencing the feelings and perceptions of the people on international issues becomes even greater, considering the diverse cultural norms, beliefs, and practices of peoples in different parts of the world.

Successful communication between people of different cultures hinges on the mutual understanding between partners. Mutual understanding is a two-sided phenomenon: the understanding of the aims, motives, and attitudes of the partners which, can help in coordinating actions and lead to the acceptance of these aims, motives, and attitudes. Mutual sympathy, respect, and friendship may then become possible. The development of mutual understanding is, of course, an intricate process that presupposes the perception of external features of the individual, their correlation to personal traits, and the resulting interpretation, on the basis of acts and assumed aims (Sherkovin, 1985).

The content of intercultural perception depends, to a large extent, on the subject of perception. Each of the partners strives to interpret the other's behavior, including his or her motives. Because in real life people are often unable to correctly perceive the motives of behavior of others, or because they possess inadequate knowledge of them, interpretations are based either on the strength of previous experiences or the analysis of their own motives that would have guided them in a similar situation. A series of experimental studies (Adorno, 1950; Kon, 1967) have shown that attitude plays a significant role in the process of interpersonal perception. It is especially so in the formation of the first impressions about an unknown person based on previously acquired information (Sherkovin, 1985).

Whereas prejudices often are the result of first impressions and may be transient, stereotypes are formed over a longer period of passive interaction or incomplete socialization. Stereotypes—oversimplified and stable images of people—are based on limited previous experience and the desire or need to draw conclusions on the basis of such limited experience. Stereotyping has as its consequences two phenomena, on the one hand, an oversimplified process of mutual cognition, and on the other, the emergence of prejudices. If impressions are based on previous negative experiences, then they are inevitably negative.

Racial and ethnic stereotypes, like ethnocentrism, are universal phenomena. Limited information about individual representatives of a certain ethnic community gives rise to prejudiced opinions about an entire community, group, or nation. Adequate understanding by people of each other is hampered by stereotypes and prejudices. On the other hand, communication in groups united by their activities over a long period of time can contribute to a better mutual understanding, drawing people closer because of their similar "emotional background" (Kon, 1967).

A considerable amount of research has been devoted to assessing the influence of mass media on attitudes and opinions. Results have tended to show that social attitudes, including prejudice, are relatively resistant to influence by the media. It appears that people select what they read and what they view, and they tend to avoid communications that they consider to be unacceptable. Individuals are selective in what they perceive as well as what they remember.

According to Klapper (1960), the mass media are much more likely to reinforce existing attitudes (whatever the attitude and whatever the "message") than to change them. Attitudes may be expected to be particularly resistant to change when they are supported by strong group norms or the prevailing cultural milieu. In particular, the mass media play a major part in defining for people what the important issues are and the terms in which they should be discussed. This is the agenda-setting role of the mass media (McCombs & Shaw, 1981). Lang and Lang (1966), specifically focusing on the agenda-setting function of the media observe: "The mass media, forced attention to certain issues. They build up public images of political figures. They are constantly presenting objects suggesting what individuals should think about, have feelings about" (p. 466). Cohen (1963), for his part, noted that the press "may be successful much of the time in telling people to think, but it is stunningly successful in telling its readers what to think about" (p. 120). Although the mass media may have little influence on the direction or the intensity of attitudes, it is hypothesized that the mass media set the agenda for political campaigns, influencing the salience of attitudes toward political issues (McCombs & Shaw, 1981).

Soviet media coverage of the release of Nelson Mandela offers a good insight into the agenda-setting function of the media. When Nelson Mandela in 1990 was freed after 27 years of incarceration by the South African apartheid regime in February 1990, Soviet television ran a mere 30-second report on that historic event at the very end of its major evening news program. The sports news of the day was considered more newsworthy than the release of one of the world's most famous prisoners.

*Izvestiya*, the mouthpiece of the Soviet/Russian parliament, did not carry a single story on Mandela's release. Instead, it ran a story by its Southern African correspondent about threats by White South African nationalists to kill Mandela if he were freed. *Pravda*, the chief organ of the CPSU (Communist Party of the Soviet Union) did carry the story, but it was a four-paragraph, long dry, noncommittal political profile, on page four buried below a commentary on the new Soviet–U.S. relationship.

Meanwhile, Mandela's release had the media in the West and the Third World going into a frenzy. Television programs included several hours of profiles, interviews and background features, whereas newspapers ran full-page spreads dealing with the ANC (African National Congress) leader. Why did the Soviet press largely ignore the news of the release of the man, head of the ANC whom the Soviet press had for years touted as a friend of the Soviet Union and the ANC as a most progressive liberation movement?

## COURTING AND "PLATONIC" FRIENDSHIP IN THE PRISM OF TIME: THE *NASHI* IDEOLOGY

Over the years, Marxist-Leninist propagandists set the agenda for the mass media in the Soviet Union. Africa, and the Third World in general, were projected as allies in the "struggle against Western domination." The apartheid issue fit well into the propaganda pattern as long as the West was seen as providing the props for the South African racist regime. However, since the mid 1980s, when Mikhail Gorbachev began his perestroika/glasnost reforms, the old-time Marxist-Leninist state ideology gave way to "new thinking" which saw a new rapprochement with the Western "imperialists." The favorable press, the ANC, and indeed many so-called progressive movements in the Third World that were around in the preglasnost Soviet Union did have a positive influence on Soviet public opinion, even if it was superficial and short-lived.

There is no extant serious research in the Soviet Union to determine Soviet public opinion as regards the ANC and other Soviet-supported Third World liberation movements, owing principally to the prohibition by the Communist Party of opinion surveys of this kind. However, stories by Third World students about their various encounters with Soviet citizens during the pre-Gorbachev era reveal that the Soviet public was at least tolerant of these movements and countries with a so-called socialist orientation (Adade, 1985). A number of African students have recounted incidents when they had to introduce themselves as Black Cubans, in order to win the favor or friendship of Soviet acquaintances. Those who came from the so-called capitalist Africa were treated like other foreigners from the West; that is, they were seen as spies or potential enemies of the USSR. Thus some of them had to introduce themselves to Soviet citizens as coming from friendly "socialist-oriented" countries, in order to either gain favorable reception or avoid hostile reactions.

A Ghanaian student who was confronted by a hostile Soviet youth-gang had to identify himself as coming from Mozambique, which caused the gang leader to simply say: "*Nashi*," meaning "he is one of us." The student was left unharmed. But luck did not smile on him the next time when he was confronted by another gang. This time the student introduced himself as coming from Cuba, but when he was asked to speak Spanish, he began to stammer. The response was immediate: He was beaten and his clothes weres stolen from him.

Even in the lecture halls and classrooms, Third World students from "fraternal" countries, or who belonged to "progressive" organizations and liberation movements, were treated differently from those from "reactionary, capitalist-oriented" states. It was common knowledge among Third World students that lecturers tended to be more friendly to students considered to be *nashi*, that is, coming from satellite states of the Soviet Union.

There is little doubt that the *nashi* perception, contrasted with the enemy or spy identification of African and other Third World students in the minds of the Soviet citizenry, was largely the result of mass media messages. The use of various descriptive terms and stereotypes, as well as the tone employed and the significance attached to specific events and stories emanating from various countries by the mass media, determined how the Soviet people related to different countries and different citizens.

Agenda setting by the mass media in the Soviet Union was fairly easy due to the party-controlled, monolithic press system. Because there were practically no alternative sources of information or media channels, it was relatively easy for the media gatekeepers in the Soviet Union to control the flow, quality, and quantity of information, and also to decide when and how news stories were made available to the public. For example, news stories about "socialist-oriented" African countries painted a picture of absolute harmony of the leaders of such countries with all policies of the Soviet Union. As a rule, most stories included a quotation from an African statesman heaping praises on this or that Soviet policy (Asoyan, 1987). This friendly image of the "African socialist" did not fail to register in the perception of the Soviet citizenry, even if the results were only momentary. At the same time, a different image, based on stereotypes recycled by the media, was that of Africans who did not fit the *nashi* description; it was the image of real or potential enemies.

## CARVING INTERCULTURAL IMAGES: THE ROLE OF THE MASS MEDIA IN COMMUNICATING AND REINFORCING STEREOTYPICAL IMAGES

Any discussion of the roles of and relationships of the mass media and intercultural communication is ineluctably linked with peoples' attitudes and public opinion. If the media do influence events, they rarely do so directly, but rather through the way people are encouraged to think (McQuail, 1972).

Communication can take place successfully between people who share common frameworks of interpretation. Individuals in society or culture need to have similar meanings for the same symbols, and a common way of thinking about things before they can effectively communicate. Our perceptions are structured by the mental categories which are made available to us for making sense of our world. As a result, the sense we make of our world depends largely on our cultural environment. Each national culture expresses itself in a way that asserts normativeness, gives vent to expression, encourages thought, and permits action. As McQuail pointed out, individuals are consumers of culture as well as of information. Culture is thus both cognized and communicated (Gerbner & Siefert, 1989).

Attitudes, on the other hand, are a state of mind, behavior or conduct regarding some matter as indicating opinion or purpose. The terms *attitude* and *orientation* are often used interchangeably. Attitudes help individuals relate to and understand their environment without necessarily having much empirical knowledge about it. We can define attitudes as a predisposition to react to a given thing, situation, or idea in a given way.

Hartman and Husband (1974) pointed out that past research into attitudes commonly concentrated on differences in attitudes between people and groups; the interpretive frameworks within which such differences occur were either taken for granted or glossed over. Whenever racial or ethnic prejudice is involved, this emphasis is likely to produce a tendency to seek the origins of prejudice in the personality of the individual, or in the immediate social situation rather than in the cultural or social framework (Hartman & Husband, 1974). Such an approach is evident in the so-called *Colour and Citizenship* survey (Rose, 1969), which led to the misleading conclusion that intense prejudice is a phenomenon rooted in the personality of the individual, a type of solution to the inadequacies of undetermined personality (Deakin, 1970).

But prejudice is often not merely the result of personal pathology or social strain; it may be built into a given culture. Hartman and Husband (1974) argued that British thinking about people of color, which was influenced by that country's colonial past, constitutes a built-in predisposition to accept unfavorable beliefs about such individuals. The beliefs and values that serve to define this thinking are related to a particular social and industrial history and are well embedded in British culture. Only when such an underlying cultural predisposition to prejudice has been taken into account do variations in prejudice and how they relate to other factors make sense (Hartman & Husband, 1974).

## THE RUSSIAN VERSION OF AFRICA'S "TARZAN" IMAGE: FROM CZARISM TO COMMUNISM

It is tempting to say that because Russia has no colonial history in Africa, Russian thinking about Africans may be different from British thinking, because it is not influenced by a colonial past. It is equally tempting to draw the conclusion that Russian Orthodox religious ethics, as opposed to British Protestantism, may produce different thinking about people of color. Although it is true that Czarist Russia's imperial quest did not extend beyond its backyards in the Caucasus and Central Asia, and that Imperial Russia did not take part in the scramble for and partition of Africa by its Western counterparts, Russian culture has many factors in common with British and European culture. In fact, as Likhachev (1991) noted, Russian culture has been greatly influenced by the West:

> From the beginning in the history of the three peoples possessing a common origin—Russians, Ukrainians and Belorussians—their neighbors have played an enormous role. . . . In the north it was the Scandinavian peoples, the Varangians (an entire conglomerate of peoples that included the future

> Danes, Swedes, Norse, and "English"). In the South of Rus the chief neighbors were the Greeks, who lived not only in Greece proper but also directly bordering on Rus, along the northern shores of the Black Sea. Then there was a separate conglomerate of peoples, among whom were also Christians and Jews. (pp. 3–4)

Peter the Great is quoted as having said that Russia was a kind of undeveloped Europe, "therefore I order us to be regarded as Europeans" (Pleshakov, 1992, p. 14).

Russian culture is a White culture. As is true of British culture, there is a built-in predisposition to accept unfavorable beliefs about people of color. In the case of Russia they are its dark-skinned former subjects living south of the Russians in the Caucasus and Central Asia. Included are also a small number of African slaves brought to Abkhazia, on the Black Sea coast, by Arab slave traders, as well as individual Blacks including Abraham Hannibal, the grandfather of Russia's greatest poet, Alexander Pushkin, actor Aira Oldridge, and various sailors and ship captains who lived in Imperial Russia at one time or another (see Khanga, 1993). Some Soviet scholars have attempted to explain the Russian attitude toward Africans and people of African origin as more of a benevolent paternalism than racial prejudice (Davidson, Olderogge, & Solodonikov, 1966). But what these apologists for Russian racism tend to forget is that paternalism is merely the reverse side of the same racist coin. Racism is racism, no matter the name or guise it takes. Although anti-Black sentiments did not reach the height of anti-Semitism, which resulted in various pogroms in Imperial Russia, the seeds of current anti-Black hatred were sown long ago. Not even the Soviet-style Communist attempt to build a multiracial society after the demise of the Czarist empire could wipe out racism among Russians. Russification of the southern subjects begun during the times of the Czars and continued during the Communist era under the guise of *sovietization* and the "politics of internationalism" (Khabibullin, 1989), were the products of Russian racist thinking. It is the "Great Russian nation's" chauvinistic attitude toward the Azeris, Armenians, Chechens, Ingush, Tartars, Tadjiks, Georgians, Uzbeks, and others, that resulted in a reverse racism (Russophobia) from the former, which since 1986 has led to seemingly inexorable interethnic vendettas plaguing the former Soviet empire.

Although Russia's links with Africa date back to the 18th century-Czarist empire, the links were limited to Abyssinia (modern-day Ethiopia), and parts of North and South Africa (Davidson et al., 1966; see also Tains, 1992). Broader interaction with Africa began only after the World War II. Although in the 1930s the Communist Party of the Soviet Union (CPSU) had invited some members of the South African Communist Party (SACP) to study at the Lenin Institute for the Peoples of the Orient, it was only after the death of Stalin that the largest number of Africans began to arrive in the Soviet Union. These were mostly students, and diplomats and their families, who under Nikita Khrushchev's Third World policy came to the Soviet Union during the "thaw" years. It must also be mentioned that a small group of African Americans, who fled racism and the Great Depression in the 1930s, made homes in the Soviet Union. However, many of them were compelled to leave their new-found "safe haven," when they became victims of the Stalinist purge during the late 1930s and the early 1940s (Khanga, 1993).

Competition generated by large-scale immigration into an area leads to more negative attitudes. Competition (real or imagined) may serve to activate or intensify the existing cultural tendency to view people of color people negatively (Hartman & Husband, 1974). Here again it is tempting to say that because Russia has never been known as a home for large numbers of African immigrants,[2] attitudes toward Africans among the average Russian Soviet citizen may be less prejudiced than in the West. There has not been any serious extant research work on the level of Hartman and Husband (1974) into Russian Soviet attitudes towards Africans and people in general. The data we do have are the results of opinion surveys conducted mainly during the first 5 years of Gorbachev's glasnost policy.

One such survey, conducted in 1989 among Moscow schoolchildren, revealed a high degree of prejudice toward Africans. Only 16% of the children believed that "Africans are human beings like we are." Moreover, only one schoolboy said that Africans are good and kind. A year earlier, a similar poll conducted among 860 Moscow residents by the Moscow-based All-Union Centre for Public Opinion Studies showed the following: Only 37% of Muscovites believed Africans are hard-working; as few as 23% of the respondents considered Africans to be attractive; 65% said Africans are poorly developed; only 15% believed Africans are intelligent; 65% said they would never approve of wedlock between their close relatives or friends and Africans; 55% responded negatively to the question, Would you like to get acquainted with and befriend a "dark-skinned African"?; 59% of the Muscovites said they are indifferent to Africans, whereas only 25% said they have any kind of sympathy for Africans; 12% harbored antipathy against Africans, yet only 7% of the respondents had ever had any interaction or contact with Africans. Nearly the same scores applied to perceptions of African Americans. The corresponding figures for the perception of Europeans were as follows: hard-working,

---

[2]The largest number of Africans to have emigrated to Russia are the African Abkhazians numbering about 50 families. Other sources put their number before the World War I at 500. They are believed to be African slaves who were brought to the Black Sea Coast in the 16th, 17th, and 18th centuries by the Arabs. When Abkhazia became part of Russian in 1918, some of them fled to Turkey. The rest remained in Russia.

80%; attractive, 74%; developed, 83%; intelligent, 66%; about wedlock—66% Muscovites said they would give the nod to a marriage involving their close relatives or a friend with an European, and 67% would approve of acquaintanceship and friendship; 59% said they have sympathy for Europeans, 37% were indifferent whereas only 1% felt antipathy (*Le Nouvel Observateur*, 14, 1988). Another survey conducted by this author in 1991 among Russian students and professors, as well as Western exchange students, at various St. Petersburg institutions of higher learning produced similar results. Remarkable in these results was the fact that the majority of the polled Russian students said they had warmer feelings for White South Africans than for Black South Africans (Adade, 1993).

The African/Black experience as represented in the Soviet media carried all the connotations of racism found in the American West. They depicted alien cultures and peoples who are less civilized than the Russia's, people who "stand lower in the order of culture because somehow they are lower in the order of nature, defined by race, by color, and sometimes by genetic inheritance" (Hall, 1992, p. 13).

The prevalence of images and stereotypes about people of color in the Soviet/Russian mass media are at best implicitly derogatory. This may be gauged from the existence of a number of traditions in cartoons, jokes, and photographs. Such themes and images are to be found in poetry, rhymes, idioms, and literature. In Russia, early examples of images and stereotypes about Africans, and people of color in general, can be found in travelogues and essays by explorers, historians, and anthropologists (Davidson et al., 1966). For example, a film produced by Lenfilm (the Leningrad/St. Petersburg film board), based on the accounts of Russian/Soviet writer Vladimir Nabokov, portrays Africa as populated by wild, prowling man-eating beasts. Although the film is purported to be about the bravery of Africans, nothing in it suggests that. Human beings are practically absent. The only Africans featured are a group of barefooted women in a bamboo-thatched cottage.

Jokes and Russian/Soviet poetry include their share of derision and denigration of the African. One popular joke is about the dilemma of a Russian wife, who on delivery found out that her child was Black. Fearing the reaction of the Russian husband, she asked the doctor to "invent" a reasonable explanation. The doctor, of course, could not come out with a plausible explanation. But as he was discussing the case with the *babushka* hospital cleaner, the baby's father appeared in the hospital. The following conversation ensued: Babushka (Russian for granny or old woman): "Did you clean your chromosomes before having an affair with your wife?" Husband: "No." Babushka: "You see, that's why your baby is Black!"

Visual information plays a key role in helping people form ideas and perceptions about other people. Generally, Russians, like other White people, perceive the African continent based on a narrow set of stereotypical ideas that have been built up over a long period of time through photographic and other visual presentations in the media. A film shot in the 1930s, called *Circus*, although meant to demonstrate the superiority of socialism over capitalism, also highlighted Soviet feelings of paternalism toward Africans. A section of the film includes the statement: "In our country we love all kids. Give birth to children of all shades of color. They can be Black, White, red, even blue, pink. . . ." However, another segment includes the following: "Intermarriage between the Black and White races is a racial crime." Significantly enough, the latter message did not fail to have an impact on the Soviet audience. In a 1992 Russian television talkshow, a participant repeated that phrase. To show that the message was a result of seeing the film *Circus*, the show's producer used archival footage, specifying the segment of the film that the woman participant was parroting. Textbooks, used in the lower grades, were written to infuse compassion for Blacks in students, yet the racist undertones were clear. A textbook published in 1967 uses stories of racial abuse of African Americans, claiming that a Soviet young pioneer saved a young Black slave. She was said to have bought the slave for a mere 5 rubles from capitalist "sharks" at a slave auction in the United States. The paternalism is difficult to disguise. A White (Russian) girl infused with "Communist compassion," and fired by the ideals of a Soviet civilizing mission, rescues a helpless Black victim. A familiar picture is thus drawn: Blacks are the objects of infinite white benevolence, which is "the White man's burden."

Other messages were even more explicit. A poem by popular Soviet poet Chukovsky is one of the many examples that can be cited. One stanza reads, "Kids, never on earth must you go to Africa/In Africa, there are gorillas/In Africa, there're huge crocodiles/ They'll bite you." A television cartoon portrays the Black man as being on the level of beasts of the jungle. Such truncated and stereotypical presentations of Africa have led to widespread prejudice. African students have complained that Soviet citizens often asked them questions or made comments like: "Do you have houses in Africa?"; "You must be brave to cohabitate with snakes and lions." The students claimed that some who questioned them thought that they arrived in Russia half-naked in loin cloths, only to be provided with clothing at Moscow's Sheremetyevo International Airport by compassionate Communist party officials.

Even more telling is the Russian attitude toward African-Russians.[3] Several cases of racial stereotyping, abuse, and threats were reported in an interview I conducted with African-Russians and their mothers for a video documentary film. Here is an excerpt of the interview: Lena (a

[3]African Russians are the children of mainly African students and Soviet Russian mothers who, for various reasons, their departing fathers left behind in the former Soviet Union.

mother): "To my neighbors, I'm a prostitute because the child is Black and a Black man comes here. They don't want to clean the bathroom because they say I have AIDS. Once a Black man comes here I have AIDS. Morally, it is difficult when every day they tell you that you are a prostitute just because you love someone with a different skin color. On the streets, they point fingers at my child, they call her names. baby negro. . . ." (see also Simmons, 1991).

## THE RUSSIAN ETHNOCENTRIC "BLOOD" TURNS OUT TO BE THICKER THAN THE SOVIET COMMUNIST IDEOLOGICAL "WATER"

Experiments carried out by Hartman and Husband (1974) in selected British schools showed that fear of being deprived of jobs, housing, and other social amenities by immigrants of color made school children see Blacks in negative terms. According to Hartman and Husband, children who lived in areas of low immigration relied perforce more heavily on the media for their information about people of color than others did. Media-supplied information carried the inference of conflict more than that received from other sources. As a result these children were more prone to think about race relations in terms of conflict than were those from "high"-contact areas, even though they (those in low-immigration areas) live in places where the objective conditions for intergroup competition or conflict are absent. It would seem, Hartman and Husbans contend that whereas *attitudes* are responsive to the characteristics of the local situation—that is, the extent of immigration—interpretive frameworks or ways of thinking, are heavily structured in areas where there are few immigrants.

It is not difficult to see a similar pattern in the Soviet Union, an area of low immigration, even though one may be tempted to see the seemingly innocuous and predominantly paternalistic and friendly tone of the Soviet media vis-à-vis Africa in the preglasnost era as devoid of references to conflict. Glasnost era conflicts between Soviet youths and African students in several Soviet cities (Asoyan, 1987) were explained by the Soviet media on the basis of competition for scarce resources.[4] However, Soviet reports

[4]Conflict between African students and Soviet youths were in most cases generated by the "envy factor" over Soviet girls. Before the end of Communism, a good number of Soviet women befriended African students, in spite of hostile public reaction. But that shrouds the real raison d'être. African students, like their counterparts from other Third World countries, enjoyed a higher living standard compared to the average Soviet citizen, thanks to the roaring shadow market in imported foreign goods. They returned from vacations in the West with fashion goods and electronic gadgets, bought in most cases from accumulated meager supplementary allowances from their governments and earnings from vacation jobs, for sale on shadow market. Many Soviet youths, and indeed a good portion of the adult population, were made to believe through media propaganda that the Soviet government also gave African students hard cash besides ruble stipends.

about Africa were predominantly about the seamy side of the African reality. Africa was painted as a continent in permanent crisis and Africans as desperately in need of Soviet assistance. The media and politicians never tired of portraying the ex-USSR as a big-hearted "Big Brother" lavishing *besvosmezdnaya pomosh* ("free or disinterested assistance") in line with Marxist-Leninist humanitarianism on "poor and defenceless peoples of the developing world struggling against capitalist subjugation and neocolonialist blackmail" (Zevin & Telerman, 1991, p. 86).

Historically, the Soviet media have painted a rather simplistic, idealistic, and exotic picture of Africa. A well-known poster, popular among Soviets before perestroika, summarized it all: It depicted a muscular African man inside a map of Africa who had broken a hefty chain that had been fastened around his hands and feet. The inscription on the famous poster read: "*Svoboda Afrike*" ("Freedom to Africa"). Ostensibly, this was meant to elicit the sympathy of Soviet citizens for the African freedom cause. But this mercy eliciting and paternalistic propaganda was carried out hand-in-hand with hate mongering. For instance, although kids were taught to have compassion for Africans, poetry and cartoons directed at young people painted the Soviet version of Tarzan images of Africa, as noted earlier.

The Soviet political bureaucracy, during the immediate preindependence era in Africa in the late 1950s and early 1960s, preached that Africans would be better off by breaking the chains of colonial subjugation and Western dependence. But they would be even better off if they chose the Soviet road to socialism (Asoyan, 1987). Images and propaganda replaced reality, and the media told Russians that with Soviet moral and material assistance[5] Africans were breaking the fetters of imperialist domination and capitalist exploitation.

However, it was not the destiny of the "exploited" and "subjugated" in Africa, but the scoring of ideological points in the Cold War that was of primary concern of the Kremlin's propagandists. The net effect of this propaganda was the identification of Africans as part of today's problems in Russia and other member states of the Commonwealth of Independent States (C.I.S.) today. The speed with which the new Kremlin leaders have called for the payment of what the *Moscow News* (1991) termed "Africa's secret debts" ("Sekretnie dolgi Afriki bivshemy Sovietskomy soyuzy," p. 15) following the demise of Communism in the former Soviet Union is indicative of the spuriousness and shallowness of Moscow's commitment to the African cause. The result—a boomerang effect of Moscow's paternalistic propaganda—is a backlash against Africans. It is easy to under-

---

[5]Recent research (see *New African* 1992, p. 35) revealed that over 89% of the 13.9 billion rubles debt owed by various African countries to the former Soviet Union was in the form of arms deliveries "to defend socialist gains."

stand why, as Russia now finds itself in economic turmoil, Africans have become the convenient scapegoats.

## The End of the Honeymoon: From Platonic Friendship to Progressive Disengagement

Many Russians, upset and threatened by the apparent economic dislocation in their country, began to find scapegoats in the Kremlin's African policy. As the media and the apparatchiks continued to attack Soviet policy in Africa, ordinary Russians began to repeat a question the Deputy Director of the Moscow-based Africa Institute, Alexei Vasilyev (1990) posed in an article in *Izvestiya* entitled: "Why Do We Need Africa?" The main grievance, mainly carried by mainstream media with either left or right political trappings, as well as the neo-Communist press, is that scarce Soviet resources were "generously" thrown away in Africa and other parts of the developing world in the frenzied chase for ideological fraternity and spheres of influence during the Cold War era. One critic said: "We gave to Africa without receiving anything in return." To him, Africa had nothing to offer Russia, continued relations was therefore unprofitable: "We have nothing to lose by cutting our ties with these backward countries but our chains of implacable aid" (Tarutin, 1991, p. 4). In an *Izvestiya* article entitled "Africans Want to Work With Us But We Do Not Need the Dark Continent," the author summed up these sentiments thus: "Enough is enough. After all we saved them from starvation, we healed them, we educated their military officers, bureaucrats, doctors, engineers and agronomists" (Tarutin, 1991, p. 4).

Vasilyev's (1990) article was an attempt to answer the glasnost era critics, and ostensibly to diffuse the current anti-African mood in the country. "We have something to give to Africa and Africans have something to give us in return" (p. 5), he argued. In a passionate appeal for Russia's continued cooperation with African countries, Vasilyev enumerates a number of achievements by Africans in science, culture and economics. In the absence of such information, he contended, it is not surprising that Soviet citizens should regard Africans as having nothing at all to offer their country. "It is ridiculous to underrate the contribution of Africa to human civilization," he stressed and offered a word of advice to his fellow countrymen and women: "Many of our compatriots must overcome the psychological barrier in their relations with Africans banish from our minds the racist and confusing official slogans we learned at childhood" (p. 5).

In the late 1950s and 1960s, the USSR projected itself as a magnanimous do-gooder and godfather for newly liberated countries in the developing world. It offered liberal scholarships to thousands of Third World youths to enroll for higher education in Soviet universities and colleges. Soviet propaganda proclaimed that the USSR was offering humanitarian and "fraternal" assistance to eliminate the dire consequences of colonial rule and save the peoples of the newly liberated countries from neo-colonialism. In reality, however the Soviet Union was busily recruiting future Communists. The Patrice Lumumba Friendship University in Moscow was built for the express purpose of training Third World technocrats, but the Kremlin knew it was also possible to groom in it the future agents of socialism.[6]

A West African journalism student once wrote in Leningrad's *Smena* newspaper that he had arrived in the Soviet Union with a rather naive conception of Soviet people and their society. As an aspiring Marxist-Leninist, Tarun (1989) had "swallowed every nice thing" he ever heard about the "friendly and compassionate Soviet people, their flourishing culture and their progressive, racism-free country" (p. 3). Back home in Africa, he had rejected out of hand any allusions to racism or xenophobia in the USSR as Western-orchestrated anti-Communist propaganda. However, it did not take long for his illusions to be totally destroyed: "During my early days, when I had yet to understand the Russian language, I mistook the invectives and cat-calls shouted at me in the trams and other public transport as 'slogans of solidarity' in support of the oppressed peoples of South Africa, since in most cases their gestures were accompanied by a raised fist, something that looked like the victory salute of the African National Congress (ANC)" (p. 3). However, soon it dawned on him that, "[he] was an object of ridicule and racial slurs and not that of sympathy" (p. 3). In the heady years of revolutionary messianism, when Soviet propaganda told Russians that they were performing a humanitarian duty by extending assistance to Africans in their just struggle against neocolonialism and imperialism (Brezhnev, 1972), solidarity slogans could indeed be heard from ordinary Russians. The first batch of African students were met with cheers and slogans of solidarity on the streets of Moscow. The initial reaction of Soviet people to what Leningrad University lecturer Valentine Vydrin termed "the Black wave" was that of benevolent amazement (see Umar, 1989). A West African minister of state, himself a former student in the USSR in the mid-1960s, said elderly women who had read Harriet Beecher Stowe's *Uncle Tom's Cabin* openly wept when they first saw the first Black students in Moscow's trams and subways (Adade, 1985 ).

---

[6]It is estimated that nearly 500,000 African specialists received their training in the Soviet Union during the past 30 years (Fokeev, 1991). In 1988 there were as many as 13,000 African students in various parts of the Soviet Union. By 1992, the number had whittled down to 8,000 as the government slashed scholarships.

That is no longer the case. The collapse of Communism has changed the slogans of solidarity to cries of disenchantment; the cheers have changed to jeers at African "parasites" as living conditions deteriorate. A Ghanaian mining student in St. Petersburg narrated an incident that took place in 1991, when he was physically prevented by an old woman from picking up a loaf of bread in a grocery store. He was standing behind the old woman in a bread line in the store. After the old woman picked her own bread, she stood in front of the student with outstretched arms, preventing him from picking up the loaf of bread. At the same time she beckoned her compatriots standing behind the Ghanaian to move past him and take the bread. "Can you imagine that an old lady, someone like my grandmother would prevent me, her grandson, from picking bread? But if I had tried to push her, they would all have pounced on me and beaten me up. . . . because everyone you meet here hates you."[7]

Before glasnost, hatred for people of color was suppressed by the totalitarian system. The mass media were instructed to educate the masses that racism or ethnic hatred had dissolved as part of the "new socialist consciousness" and that it was only in the *nespravdiliviy, dikiiy zapad* ("unjust, wild West") that Black people were lynched (Davidson et al., 1966, p. 46). To show the superiority of socialism over capitalism, Soviet television was saturated with images of homeless, unemployed Blacks lining up at the Washington kitchen soup or the dole in London. Meanwhile, the numerous cases of racially-motivated attacks and murders of Africans in the ex-Soviet Union went unreported.

The tone of media reports about the plight of Africans on the African continent and in the Diaspora was one of sympathy and solidarity. Deliberate efforts were made to solicit the mercy, goodwill, and support of the Soviet citizenry for the "defenceless victims of capitalist injustice" and "neo-colonial plunder" (Fokeev, 1991, p. 34). But the truth was that it was not the miserable living conditions of Africans and people of African descent that was the concern of Soviet politicians and journalists. They had a more important concern—the scoring of points in the East–West ideological confrontation during the Cold War.

Ironically, it was in the former Soviet Union's south-central Asian and Caucasus regions, which were populated by non-White peoples or *Sovietskie negri* (Soviet negroes), as they were derogatively called by Russians,[8]

---

[7]The student narrated his experience to me in an interview for my video documentary film on African Russians, *The Ones They Left Behind: The Life and Plight of African Russians.*

[8]The clampdown on nationals from the former Soviet southern republics in the Caucuses and Central Asia in the aftermath of Yeltsin's recent (October 1993) bloody confrontation with his opponents in the former Russian parliament, as well as the ongoing (December 1994) invasion and occupation of the rebel Chechnya Republic by the Russian armed forces are manifestations of the bad-blood that has existed between Russians and their former subjects.

where the boomerang effects of the "mercy-soliciting" propaganda on behalf of Africans had a devastating effect. Anti-Black sentiments are stronger here than in the rest of the country. Armenians, Azeris, and Georgians, themselves looked down upon as "second-rate citizens," vent their spleen on Blacks as an outlet to soothe their feelings of inferiority in a society that has grown highly racist, in spite of 70-odd years of Communist rhetoric about racial harmony. Black students in these republics have been sneered at, called names, abused, attacked, and even murdered on racial grounds. Following requests by Black students, African embassies prevailed upon the Russian educational authorities not to send their students to some of these former Soviet republics.

Among Russians the boomerang effect of Communist propaganda resulted in an aping of Western racists. With Soviet-style Communism discredited, many Russians have come to regard anything that communist education taught them as lies or half-truths. Strange as it may sound, the new logic is: If there is racism in the West, then racism is not as bad as communist educators would want us to believe. Imitating Western examples is common today in an effort to overcome a feeling that Russians are second-rate Whites. Public ridicule of Africans by young and old alike serves not only as a form of psychological relief, but also an attempt to bolster their self-esteem.

## GLASNOST ERA CONFESSION AND SELF-CRITICISM

Africans and their continent have long been a fruitful source for "bad news" in the Western mass media. Adverse coverage that deliberately or unconsciously capitalized on Africa's real or imagined weaknesses since colonialism has been common theme (*The Image of Africa*, 1964). Even a cursory glance at today's Western news media shows that coverage has not undergone any radical shift from the colonial tradition of image distortion of Africa. Hand-in-hand with attempts at denying Africa any contribution to human civilization whatsoever, the dominant international media in the West now present a one-dimensional image reflecting what has come to be called the coup-famine syndrome. In many of today's Western media, Africa is seen as a terminally blighted continent of paralysis and chaos. What has been written about less, however, is how the media in Communist and post-Communist Russia, did and continue to cover Africa.

The extinction of Communism in Russia and Eastern Europe has led to the appearance of extreme right-wing ideologies. Nationalistic, anti-Semitic, and even fascist ideas hitherto suppressed by the authoritarian system are reemerging. Their influence on both society and in the press is growing. In the former Soviet Union (FSU),[9] the ideas of the national chauvinists and fascists have been aired in mass media and in parliament. They consistently fault the FSU's policies in the Third World in general and in Africa in particular. In several articles in the mainstream press, conservative politicians and journalists (on the left-wing/right-wing political and ideological spectrum) have found a scapegoat in the Kremlin's Africa policy. For example, a member of the Russian Parliament complained in the *Literator* newspaper that the former Communist leadership "wasted precious Soviet resources on peoples who have only begun to call themselves a people, who have just descended from the palm trees, and have only managed to pronounce the word 'socialism' " (Travkin, 1990, p. 1). Of course, the current mood could easily be explained away as a result of the economic crisis in the FSU, but as I have demonstrated, there are currents that run far below the surface of economic distress and the resultant scapegoating. We may have to dig deeper to find the real causes. For instance, what explains the Soviet/Russian media's propensity, during the Cold War era, to paint a picture of Africans as *bednie rodstvinki*, "poor cousins," exploited and subjugated by the imperialist and neo-colonialist West, who have to be salvaged by a magnanimous and compassionate USSR? What lies behind the Soviet/Russian version of the "white man's burden"? The media's portrayal of Africa as the (Russian) Communist man's burden was informed more by ethnocentric, paternalistic, and even racist urges than a Marxist-Leninist ideological inclination.

Even during the Cold War years, the Soviet media were saturated with negative images of Africa. Pictures emanating from the continent were predominantly those that reflected the seamy side of African life. The blame for Africa's *otsalost* ("backwardness") was, as a rule, squarely put on Western imperialist and neo-colonialist plunder. Where something positive was shown, it was almost always to show the positive and modernizing effects of the Soviet "civilizing mission," such as the construction of Soviet-assisted projects in a "socialist-oriented" country.

During the preglasnost years, whenever the Soviet media painted a picture of continent of permanent crisis, it was done to show the negative influence of Western presence in Africa. Africans were often shown as "innocent" victims of Western capitalist exploitation and imperialist "blackmail," who needed the express and "selfless" assistance of the "socialist-internationalist" Soviet Union. The USSR, it was proclaimed, has always been on the side of the oppressed nations, giving moral and

---

[9]The December 12, 1993 parliamentary elections in which Vladimir Zhirinovsky's neo-fascist Liberal Democratic Party won the majority of the seats in Russia's new legislature (the Duma) is an indication of the growing influence of right-wing extremists.

material aid to the national liberation movements (Gromyko, 1985). Yet, despite several decades of Marxist-Leninist internationalist education, which was based on racial harmony and the brotherhood of humanity, a large number of Russians harbor racial antipathy against Africans.

In his article "About the Black Colour Without Exaggeration," Asoyan (1990), who was for a long time a Soviet journalist specializing in Africa and is currently Russia's ambassador in Botswana recounted numerous incidents involving African students in the Soviet Union to illustrate the abiding, antiquated stereotypes the average Soviet holds about Africans, their race, skin color and geographical origin. He wrote: In our age of cosmic means of information transmission and moreover, when we have a correspondent in every African country, when we lead many countries in the volume of books and films about Africa, our internationalist education has practically not done away with our racist stereotypes (p. 4). Asoyan blamed the mass media for weaving a web of stereotypes around Africans. The mass media, even under perestroika and glasnost, he charged, continue to portray Africa as no more than an "exotic, undeveloped continent, which is struggling with superhuman strength against the forces of neocolonialism, with our help" (p. 4). Asoyan (1990) contended that, "Under the conditions of our difficult existence, this generates anger and indignation" (p. 4) from the Soviet citizenry, who see Africans as lazy hangers-on. According to Asoyan, a medical doctor wrote to him complaining, "It turns out that we continue to help build their countries, teach and clothe them. What compensation shall we get from them?" (p. 4).

Asoyan (1990) also quoted letters by African students to Moscow newspapers, a majority of which were not published, to demonstrate the psychological trauma these students, especially those from sub-Saharan Africa, undergo while pursuing their studies. The letters complain of constant taunting, ridicule, humiliation, and stigmatization. In cafeterias, on the streets, in public transport, in dormitories they are jeered at, fingers are pointed at them, and racist slurs like *obeziana* ("monkey") and of late *SPID* (AIDS) are hurled at them. One letter quoted an African student as saying he had to play a curious psychological game to save his skin when he was confronted by a group of hostile Russian youngsters. During the encounter, he pretended he was an African American. This resulted in more positive reaction by members of the youth gang, who soon began to ask questions about Stevie Wonder, Michael Jackson, and other African Americans. Asoyan also quoted the famous South African trumpeter Hugh Masekela, who during a tour happened to visit the Patrice Lumumba Peoples' Friendship University in the Soviet capital: "The chaps live under horrible conditions. They told me they are called 'monkeys' " (p. 5).

Soviet anti-African prejudice and dislike are attributed by Asoyan (1990) to "low levels of culture and deficit of truthful information about the people of other nations" (p. 5). The result is a clash of reality with distorted and idealistic views of Africa. "Africans, after all, are not what we took them for; with all their drawbacks and stereotyped manners . . . This also reflects our traditional relationship with foreigners. For those who are ahead of us, we use one yardstick. For those who are poor, another" (p. 5).

In a more recent article, entitled "Red and Black," a Russian journalist agreed with the assertion that Russia is a country of racists. She recalled several incidents in Moscow during which her compatriots cast aspersions on Africans for the simple reason that they have dark skin color. She recounted one such incident: "Recently, I saw in the metro [underground train] a woman with her five-year old child. The kid was crying. The woman was trying to calm him down. Then she set eyes on 'a dark-skinned uncle.' Pointing at the African at the other end of the train, she told the child: 'You see, if you continue to cry this Black man will take you away' " (Deeva, 1992, p. 3). Continuing, she wrote: "Several scenes like this one add some pleasant varieties to our lives. But behind the jokes and laughter, we think and forget that 'the Black uncle' is by no means the cardboard placard depicting the typical [personalities/races], the chocolate-white-yellow trio. They [Africans, the subjects of the jokes and laughter] also think about us. Their opinion about us is: 'The USSR is a country of racists' " (Deeva, 1992, p. 3).

These examples are not of particular importance in themselves, but they serve as "an index of widespread familiarity with" (Hartman & Husband, 1970, p. 435), if not acceptance of the images of Africans Russians carry. It does become disturbing to find this kind of image intruding itself into the media's handling of current events concerning Africans. As a result, elements of cultural legacy that are "at best *ethnocentric* and at worst racist" (Hartman & Husband, 1970, p. 435, emphasis in original) come to influence reactions to and interpretations of events in Africa.

Hartman and Husband (1974) pointed out that such a tendency may most clearly be seen in newspaper-headlines and in editorial cartoons, "where the use of phrases or images will evoke a similar set of associations and meanings in virtually all members of the society to whom it is directed. Such usage makes it possible for a complex point to be crystallized *unambiguously* and memorably in a few words or a single picture" (Hartman & Husband, 1970, p. 435, emphasis in original). For a long time Russian journalists have used the expression "the Dark Continent" to describe the African continent. In fact, hardly any article is written about Africa without the use of this favorite term. Journalists accompanying former Soviet Foreign Affairs Minister Eduard Shevardnadze during his first visit to Africa, filed reports without accompanying pictures. Moscow's Central TV coverage did not include a single shot of visits that took him to countries like Nigeria, Angola, and Namibia. Instead of photographs, a blank map of Africa appeared on the screen, as though to reaffirm the familiar picture of a "backward" Africa exemplified by sunshine and crocodiles. Pictures would have shown the Foreign Minister being welcomed at modern airports by African officials in limousines or attending state banquets in high-rise buildings that match or even exceed similar ones in Soviet cities in modernity and architectural beauty (see Kossowan, 1990).

## "AFTER ALL, WE'RE RACISTS. . . ."

Coverage of African news by the Russian mass media, like that of their western counterparts, has included more than its share of negativity, neglect, and omission. Glasnost era self-critical articles have thrown light on the sloppy and stereotypical character of Soviet journalism dealing with Africa. An article that appeared in the *Moscow News* in 1986 by Davidson, Russian expert on Africa, noted, "Our journalist, more often than not, presented a one-sided picture of Africa. According to them, once Africa throws off the chains of colonialism, then everything will be fine. And should they decide on building socialism, then all problems will be well-nigh automatically solved" (p. 6). Davidson further wrote: "We know about the Flemings, the Welsh. The Scots number five million. We know about their epics, music, their dress. Very few [Soviet] people know what ethnic groups live in Nigeria, a great African power with a population of nearly 100 million" (p. 6).

Another article published by *Literaturnaya Gazeta*, stated that for most Soviet writers and journalists, writing about Africa "is as easy and simple now as it was 25 years ago" (Asoyan, 1987, p. 14). A common recipe exists for them:

> Mix a little bit of exoticism with the struggle against imperialism; add a few fine words by any African in praise of socialist countries and presto! an article is ready. For those who have never visited Africa, there was a different recipe: "Describe the stormy continent from your Moscow office. Cut to the required size an article from a Western newspaper. Dilute the texture of a more successful article written by your compatriot. Add a quote from a mythical dark-skinned friend and an article is born." (Asoyan, 1987, p. 14)

Asoyan added, "To the overwhelming majority of Soviet journalists and writers, Africa today is still the Africa of the pre-independence era: the same myth-ridden, exotic Africa with its awesome jungles populated by prowling, man-eating lions and crocodiles" (p. 14). During the Cold War era, Russian journalists, he continued, described such "maniacal and demagogic" African leaders as Idi Amin of Uganda, Macias Nguema of Equatorial Guinea, and Jean Bokassa of the Central African Republic as "military men with patriotic feelings" (p. 14) when in fact they were murderers who butchered thousands of their own people.

It is pertinent to mention here that at a particular point in the Soviet-African relationship during the 1970s, the Kremlin's Africa policy came to be swayed by the school of thought within the Soviet hierarchy that the USSR should devote its energies in Africa largely to military regimes—particulary those controlled by radical leaders. The continent, it was noted, had a high percentage of governments under military rule or at least dominated by military elements. Moreover, a substantial number of these governments evinced a resolve to introduce major social transformations in their countries and a willingness to establish strong ties with the USSR (Albright, 1987).

Self-criticism by glasnost and postglasnost era journalists does not mean an improved coverage of Africa. What has changed, though, is the old Communist-style ideological "packaging" of the news. Some Soviet commentators have faulted Stalinism and its latter-day manifestation—neo-Stalinism or Brezhnevism—as the cause of the poor Soviet coverage of Africa in the preglasnost years (Tains, 1992). Nothing can be further from the truth. The root of the problem lies elsewhere: in the culture. Neither Stalinist nor Marxist-Leninist ideology can be blamed for the stereotypical and one-dimensional presentation of the African reality. As we show later on in this chapter, news from Africa came to be interpreted within the "old" familiar framework, or in terms of the existing images, stereotypes, and expectations of the prerevolutionary and preglasnost years. The framework and expectations either originated in the Russian culture or they originated in the news and passed from there into the culture. This situation is one of a "continuous inter-play between events, cultural meanings and news framework" (Hartman & Husband, 1970, p. 436), despite the radical changes in ideological orientation and expectations in Russia.

## THE MORE GLASNOST, THE MORE "GLOSS-OVER-NOST" OF AFRICA

The poor coverage given to Mandela's release mentioned earlier was not an isolated case. It is a common trend in glasnost-style and post-Cold War era journalism in the former Soviet Union, now called the Commonwealth of Independent States. This was evident in a 1991 survey of some former Soviet publications (Adade, 1993). The survey showed that marginalization of Africa during the past 8 years had reached grotesque proportions. Perestroika and glasnost in international news coverage applied only to Europe, North America, and some parts of Asia. In addition, the survey revealed that marginalization of Africa increased with the pace of glasnost. The main stereotypes employed by Soviet journalists to describe issues involving Africans in the world context underwent drastic changes. In 1985, Africa's problems were attributed to factors such as "birthmarks of capitalism," "imperialist intrigues," "hostile bourgeois propaganda," "U.S. expansionist policies," "a plot against Africa," and similar concepts. In 1990, these stereotypes disappeared from the lexicon of Soviet journalists. Terms like "solidarity," "disinterested aid," "proletarian internationalism," and "socialist fraternity" (Popov, 1990, p. 36), which were still employed in 1987 to describe Soviet-African relations, understandably, disappeared in later years. In their place, new terms such as "universal human values," "global cooperation," and "deideologization of inter-state relations" came to be used. Yet another remarkable change during the period under review was the gradual toning down of paternalism in Russian writing on Africa. In addition, the "Soviet socialist experience" is no longer recommended as a recipe for good governance in Africa.

It was clear from the survey (Adade, 1993) that the loss of interest in Africa by the Soviet/Russian press coincided with the period of the Kremlin's progressive disengagement from the continent.[10] Not surprisingly, this was also the period of East-West rapprochement and the eventual ending of the Cold War. Ironically, however, the further the Soviet/ Russian press trudged on the road to full-blown democracy, the less interest it showed in Africa.

All this is logical, if one considers it from the point of view of the Gorbachev reforms that were inaugurated in the spring of 1985 to "give socialism a human face," but that turned out to be an anti-Communist revolution. As the Soviet state ideology fell asunder under the new thinking ideology, Soviet journalists, like the rest of the intelligentsia, appeared to be groping for a different vision of the world as a whole. Thus the old image of Africans had to be recast to suit the "nonideological" new Russian vision.

---

[10]My survey of the glasnost press showed that coverage of foreign news did not decrease during the 6 Gorbachev perestroika years. On the contrary, more countries and regions left out of the orbit of Soviet press coverage suddenly came to be covered regularly. Coverage of the countries of Southeast Asia, the so-called tigers, has more than trebled. It must be noted here that foreign news in general was very much restricted in the preglasnost era. The study also showed that whereas *Newsweek*'s coverage of Africa and Latin America remained more or less stable in 1985 and 1990, *Novoe Vremya*'s coverage of the two continents dropped to less than half for the same period.

Coverage of Africa now does no more than merely catalogue ad infinitum the familiar banes and woes of the continent: the world's highest infant mortality and adult morbidity rates, the lowest life expectancy, the threats of population explosion, AIDS, and famine. Although in the past such reports would surely have been spiced with accusations of Western complicity or international finance capital pillage (Gromyko, 1985), recent reports do not look for external culprits. Most articles now put the blame on Africans themselves. For instance, Tarutin (1991) in an article in Pravda entitled "We Are Africans in a European Home," wrote that Africans wasted the "solid" amounts of Western credits through bad management and corruption, and that tiny Belgium produces more goods than the whole of Africa taken together. Characteristically, other objective factors, like the lopsided international economic order that is so skewed against most developing countries or the fact that the Belgian farmers receive more than the African farmer for the same amount of work, are glossed over.

But the new marginalization (Africa, of course, has always been marginalized and trivialized by the Soviet media, as indicated earlier) has also something to do with the new Eurocentrism engendered by Gorbachev's so-called new-thinking. New-thinking, which claims to have its roots in "universal human values" (Gorbachev, 1988, pp. 3–4) has turned out to be rabid Eurocentrism and even racism, for the political bureaucracy and the "new" media. For journalists and politicians, new-thinking and universal human values do not extend beyond the "common European home" and North America.

When Gorbachev, the ex-Soviet leader, commenced his reforms, his team set out to fashion a brand new foreign policy, which became increasingly Western oriented and pragmatic. The new planners of Soviet policy in Africa announced that they were shedding the ideological ballast of their policy in Africa (Popov, 1990). Soviet-African relations, like relations with other parts of the developing world, were now to be based on Lenin's injunction: "More economics, less political/*ideological* trivialities" (emphasis mine).

During the 6-year Gorbachev rule, this injunction was followed to the letter as the Kremlin gradually cut aid and support for its allies. The argument, started by Gorbachev himself, was that the Soviet Union got itself bogged down in useless ventures in Africa, always gave and received nothing in return for its ideological investments. Politicians and the media, both right-wing and left-wing, have made capital of "generous" and "disinterested" aid given to African and other Third World countries ever since Gorbachev raised the issue in a speech in Minsk, the Belorussian capital, during the early years of his reforms.

## POST-COMMUNIST GLASNOST AND AFRICA

But the issue was raised to a crescendo after the botched August 1991 coup, when the so-called democrats led by Russian Federation President Boris Yeltsin took the reins of power. Events in the wake of the demise of Communism have proven that if the Communists and their media were friendly but patronizing, and even solicitous in their approach to Africa, the democrats and the new press appear largely disinterested, condescending, and even racist. Communists had prided themselves on offering "free" and "generous" aid to Africa, and never got tired of drumming home to the Soviet citizenry how the Soviet Union was performing its "Marxist" internationalist duty by assisting poor, Africa countries in their "just struggle against western blackmail and exploitation." The democrats, on the other hand, chose a less pompous, yet infamous role. They lost no time after taking over from the Soviet Communists, in giving full rein to their suppressed racist sentiments. They have used the mass media to air not only their loss of interest in Africa, but also their anger at and disdain for Africans in the fullest expression of glasnost.

Before and after the failed coup in August 1991, Boris Yeltsin was on record as having said that socialism should have been experimented with in a small African country and not in the huge Soviet Union.[11] By his statement, the Russian leader implied that Africans are nothing but guinea pigs who could be experimented on. To go as far as Africa to find a subject for Yeltsin's analogy, when there are as many small countries in Europe or in his own Russian Federation (which is made up of over 80 tiny tribal and ethnic groups), points not only to the condescending and dismissive attitude towards Africans, but also to the blind chauvinism and racial bigotry of Russia's new leaders.

For Russia's new political bureaucracy and the media, using Africa as a metaphor for poverty, backwardness, and hopelessness, has become a fad. Lambasting the former Communist leadership for "wasting" Soviet resources in Africa became a vote catcher and applause drawer at political gatherings and in parliament. In 1991, Vladimir Zhirinovsky, founder of the Liberal Democratic Party of Russia, returned from a visit to the United States to tell Russians that he was appalled by the huge presence of Blacks and Asians in New York. According to him, America's current problems were rooted in the large concentration of people of color in that country.

---

[11]Yeltsin made the statement for the first time during his presidential election campaign in the Urals in June 1991. His speech was reported unedited by the *Mayak* radio station. The print media and television edited out "Africa." He repeated the same statement during an interview soon after the August Communist revanchist coup was foiled.

Fascists too have been given access to state media in what seems to be a calculated attempt by the new leaders to use the media to scapegoat Africa. In April 1992 a program on the state-owned Central Television had fascists openly expressing their resentment against Africans, and Blacks in general.[12] This is hardly surprising, considering the fact that Russia's so-called new democrats differ very little in their attitude towards blacks from those of the motley, national-chauvinistic, and fascists groupings now mushrooming all over Russia. Most of them were yesterday's Soviet-style Communists, who despite their public preaching about the brotherhood of man and racial harmony under Communism, nurtured and spread racism, anti-Semitism, and ethnic hatred among the Soviet citizenry.

Excluded from this attitude is South Africa. It is now referred to as a land of eternal spring, an African el Dorado, "a corner in Heaven," (Ustimenko, 1991, p. 6) and "Heaven for Whites" (Dubrovskiy, 1991, p. 3). It is reported on liberally, and described in glowing terms. The press now traces Russia's historical links with the racist regime as dating back to the Anglo-Boer war when Russian soldiers were said to have fought on the side of the Boers against the English (Nalbandyan, 1991). The ANC has been referred to as the "world's richest" liberation movement, and calls to cut aid to it have been made in the state media including *Izvestiya* (Pilyatskin, 1991). The injustices of the apartheid system, the pet topic for Russian journalists during the Cold War era, are hardly mentioned in recent reports.

From all indications, the new Kremlin leaders seems less interested in the ANC than they are in the White minority regime in Pretoria. Nor do they appear concerned about the prospects of majority rule under an ANC government in the future. An *Izvestiya* article warned Russia's new democrats, most of them yesterday's Communists and staunch supporters of the ANC, not to throw the baby away together with the tub water. "The ANC will play an influential role in post-apartheid South Africa, issuing export and import licences. And soon, the South African Foreign Ministry is likely to be headed by a black, and that country's future ambassador to Russia may be black too, possibly an ANC man" (Tetekin, 1992, p. 5). But to many Russians, pragmatic considerations about where

[12]Several participants in the popular Russian TV program "Tema" (Theme) did not shy away from their racist sentiments. One said in reply to a question, that he would emigrate to South Africa should the future president of Russia be a Black man. According to him it is easier to fight Blacks in South Africa. Russians he claimed are too soft. Taking a cue from the mainstream media are the fledgling fascist alternative media. The St. Petersburg *Otechestvo* wrote in its February 1992 edition: "American blacks, who earn five dollars per hour wages could come to our country and pose as millionaires and take liberties with our girls and contaminate the Russian blood" (p. 4).

today's bread and butter come from weigh more than anything else; its business is with the White minority if that will bring much-needed assistance. Tomorrow will take care of itself. A Moscow entrepreneur summed it all up when he told an *Izvestiya* reporter: "Good white guys came from South Africa with excellent and lucrative proposals. Later they offered goods. Should I refuse them because the ANC or the U.N. is against apartheid?" (*Gemini News Service Bulletin*, 1991, p. 4).

If under Communism the media and politicians singled out the White minority out for castigation for perpetrating atrocities against the innocent Black majority, now the blame is shifting to the Black majority for unleashing "Black" terror against whites and "senseless" Black-on-Black violence. If in the past compassion was expressed about the miserable living conditions of the Black majority, now that sympathy is shifting to the White minority. An article in *Izvestiya* captured this shift in sympathy: "In the past 20 years, the wages of black miners went up by 67 per cent, while those of their white counterparts fell by 24 per cent. For black education, the South African government earmarked 3.3 billion Rands and in 1992, 4.5 billion Rands. Each day 11 classes are built. Education for black children will be free while that for white kids will be paid by their parents" (Chaplina, 1992, p. 12). The *Znamya Yunosti* also portrayed the White minority as the victims of the transition process: "Life is becoming increasingly difficult for the whites as more and more blacks take on jobs which were reserved exclusively for them [whites]" (Dubrovskiy, 1991, p. 3).

## SUMMARY AND CONCLUSION

This chapter explored the roles of, and relationships between intercultural communication and the media in the shaping of Russian-African relationships before, during, and after Soviet-style Communism by analyzing the cultural-historical and politico-ideological factors behind the formation, reinforcement, and dissemination of specific images of Africans in the Russian media. The following conclusions were drawn:

1. The physics and the dynamics of superpower relations determined Soviet press interest in African events. So did the dictum: "In politics there are no permanent friends, only permanent interests."

2. The ethnocentric blood proved to be thicker than the ideological water.

3. The Russian media lost interest in Africa as soon as there were no longer ideological points to score against the West. Had Mandela been

released even 2 years earlier, the Soviet press would have given his release an entirely different coverage. It would have been yet another victory for Communism.

4. Africa became increasingly marginalized as the political and economic reforms advanced in Russia.

5. The paternalistic nature of former Soviet propaganda concerning USSR-African relationships that led to an anti-African backlash, which sought to wrongly scapegoat Africans as "part of the problem," now seems to undergird news coverage of the continent, with the exception of South Africa.

6. With the Communist Party no longer setting the agenda for the press in the wake of the demise of Communism, previously subdued anti African prejudice has been given more transparency. In today's Russian media, words such as solidarity, *antifascism*, *antiracism* and *internationalism* have fallen into disrepute. These "virtues," formerly dictated by the Communist Party but never wholeheartedly accepted by the people, have now become vices.

The stereotyped, one-sided, and oversimplified presentation of African problems distorts the African reality and hence the perception of Russians about Africans. Russians see the continent of Africa as an embodiment of eternal chaos, political instability, primitive culture, civil disorder, corruption, and exotic and barbarous customs. Paternalistic propaganda of the Soviet era has made Russians see Africans as lazy hangers-on and parasites.

One of the ways to attempt to temper this negative perception with a more benign image is through intercultural interaction, and a more responsible use of the mass media. However, with the new Russian leaders eager to cut all links with Africa (several embassies have been closed and scholarships have been virtually eliminated), Russians are likely to continue to wallow in ignorance and will likely be further removed from the African reality. The danger is that if there should develop another opportunity for broader interactions, it would require starting from point zero. When the first opportunity presented itself for broader interaction with Africans during Soviet rule, Russians were largely discouraged from doing so. That problem continues and has increased.

## ACKNOWLEDGMENTS

Special thanks to Dr. Marlene Curthbert and Dr. K. Ansu-Kyeremeh of the Department of Communication Studies, Dr. Tanya Basok of the Department of Sociology and Anthropology, and Dr. L. D. Majhanovich of the Department of Classical and Modern Languages, all of the University of Windsor, for reading the original manuscript and making corrections and useful suggestions.

## REFERENCES

Adade, C. Q. (1985, August 16). African students in the USSR. *African Times*, pp. 8–9.

Adade, C. Q. (1991, January). No glasnost for Africa. *New African*, *291*(16), 24–25.

Adade, C. Q. (1993, October–December). Russia: After the Cold War: The ex-Soviet media and Africa. *Class and Racism*, *35*, 86–93.

Adorno, T. W. (1950). *The authoritarian personality*. New York: Harper.

Albright, D. E. (1987). *Soviet policy toward Africa revisited*. Washington, DC: Center for Strategic and International Studies.

Asoyan, B. (1987, November 7). Afrika uzh tak daleko. *Literanturnaya gazeta*, p. 14.

Asoyan, B. (1989, August 7). Sgushennoi krasok. *Komsomoslkaya pravda*, p. 4.

Belyaninov, K., & Molchanov, D. (1992, August 14). Cherno-belaya logika, Cushestvuyet li rasism v Rossii? *Izvestiya*, p. 3.

Berker, S. L., & Roberts, C. L. (1992). *Discovering mass communication*. New York: Harper Collins.

Brezhnev, L. I. (1972). *Following Lenin's course*. Moscow: Progress Publishers.

Chaplina, N. (1992, October 19). Zebra po imeni YuAR. *Chas pik*, p. 12.

Cohen, B. C. (1963). *The press and foreign policy*. London: Princeton University Press.

Davidson, A. B. (1986, August 28). The dark continent and us. *Moscow News*, p. 6.

Davidson, A. B., Olderogge, D. A., & Solodinikov, V. G. (1966). *USSR and Africa*. Moscow: Nauka Publishing House.

Deakin, N. (1970). *Colour, citizenship and British society*. London: Panther Books.

Deeva, E. (1992, January 2). Krasnoe i chernoe. *Moskovskyi Komsomolets*, p. 5.

Dubrovskiy, A. (1991, July 18). Beliy rai? *Znamya yunosti*, p. 3.

Edelstein, A. S., Ito, Y., & Kepplinger, H. M. (1989). *Communication and culture: A comparative approach*. New York: Longman.

Fokeev, G. (1991). Afrika v chem nash natsional'nyi interes? *Aziya i Afrika cegodniya*, pp. 32, 34.

*Gemini News Bulletin*. (1987, November). p. 8.

Gerbner, G., & Siefert, M. (1989). *Communication & culture: A comparative approach*. London: Longman.

Gorbachev, M. S. (1988). *Perestroika i novoe myshlenie dlya nashei straniy i vsego mira*. Moscow: Progress Publishers.

Gromyko, A. A. (1985). *Aktualnie problemi otnoshenii s strannami Afriki*. Moscow: Progress Publishers. See also Izvestiya (1992, October 20), p. 5.

Hall, S. (1992). Race, culture, and communications: Looking backward and forward at cultural studies. *Rethinking Marxism*, *5*(1), 13.

Hartman, P., & Husband, C. (1974). *Racism and the mass media*. London: Rowand and Littlefield.

Hawk, B. G. (1992). *Africa's media image*. New York: Praeger.

*The Image of Africa: British ideas and action*. (1964). Madison: The University of Wisconsin Press.

Khabibullin, K. N. (1989). *Natsional'noe camosoznanie i internatsional'noe povidenie*. Leningrad: Lenisdat.

Khanga, Y. (1993). *Soul to soul: The story of a black Russian family 1865–1992*. New York: Norton.

Klapper, J. T. (1960). *The effects of mass communications.* London: The Free Press.
Kon, I. S. (1967). *Sociologia lichnosti.* Moscow: Nauka.
Kossowan, B. (1990, July 27). Soviet press still hard on Blacks. *The Times,* p. 9.
Lang, K., & Lang, G. E. (1966). Functions of the mass media. In B. Berelson & M. Janowitz (Eds.), *Public opinion and communication* (pp. 455–472). New York: The Free Press.
Likhachev, D. S. (1991). Russkaya kul'tura v sovremennom mire. *Novyi mir, 1,* 3–9.
McCombs, M., & Shaw, D. L. (1981). Function of the mass media. In M. Janowitz & P. Hirsch (Eds.), *Reader in public opinion and mass communication* (pp. 127–137). New York: The Free Press.
McQuail, D. (1972). *Sociology of mass communications.* Middlessex, England: Penguin.
Johannesburg demenage Moscou. (December 14, 1988). *Le Nouvel Observatuer.*
Nalbadyan, Z. (1991, December 11). Russkie v Yuzhnoi Afrike. *Trud,* p. 7.
Ne yezhai, dazhe esli nado. (1990). *Respublika, 3,* 15.
Pilyatskin, B. (1991, November 23). Zakriyvayutsiya 9 posoltsv. Pochemy ne 50? *Izvestiya,* p. 10.
Pleshakov, P. (1992). The Russian dilemma. *New Times, 2,* 14.
Plehakov, K. (1992). The Russian tragedy. *New Times, 9,* 9–11.
Popov, Y. (1990). *Asiya i Afrika cegodnya, 4,* 36.
Rose, E. I. B. (1969). *Colour and citizenship.* London: Oxford University Press.
*Secretnie dolgi Afriki bivshemy Sovetskomy Soyuzy.* (1991, December 20). Moscow News, p. 15.
Sherkovin, Y. A. (1985). *Social psychology and propaganda.* Moscow: Progress Publishers.
Simmons, A. M. (1991, December 2). Black like Misha and Yelena. *Time,* p. 40.
Tains, S. (1992, January 31). Negri v Rossii. *Nizavisimaya gazeta,* p. 8.
Tarutin, E. (1991, February 3). Afrikantsi khotyat s nami rabotat'. No nam ne nuzhna chernaya kontinenta. *Izvestiya,* p. 4.
Tarun, S. (1989, April 1). Ya innostranets. *Smena,* p. 3.
Travkin, N. (1990, December 1). *Literator,* p. 1.
Umar, M. K. (1989, September 11). How Blacks fare in the USSR. *African Concord,* p. 21.
Ustimenko, O. (1991, December 13). A byili zloveshimi eti tri bukviy—YuAR. *Sovietskiy sport,* p. 6.
Vasilyev, A. (1990, October 20). Pochemy nam nuzhna Afrika? *Izvestiya,* p. 5.
Zevin, L., & Telerman, V. (1991). Razvivayushie stranni v nashei ekonomicheskoi strategii. *Svobodnaya mysl, 18,* 86.

# 11

# *Probing Cultural Implications of War-Related Victimization in Bosnia-Hercegovina, Croatia, and Serbia*

Donald E. Williams
*University of Florida*

Analyzing the book, *Small Town Philosophy*, by Radomir Konstantinovic, a respected Serbian theoretician, Knezevic (1992) interpreted the depiction of the character of Serbian national consciousness. Identifying enduring tribal fealty as the sustaining force of small-town mentality, he associated this consciousness with the attitude it reflects toward acts of violence when effected for corporate cause. Crucial to the rationale for these acts is the premise: "Violence against another person [should] not be experienced as violence against an individual, but rather as violence against the member of an enemy tribe. The violent have nothing against the individual. . . . Just as the violent see in themselves not individuals but rather the will of their whole collective, so too they see in their victim the entire enemy collective" (p. 213).

People culturally moored in the concept of tribal primacy do not perceive images of individual persons, but dichotomously of either people with the same tribal identity or with the identity of the enemy. By preordainment, the individual "melts" into the tribal entity and consequently "is never the executor of his [sic] own will but the 'personification' of the general, tribal will" (Knezevic, 1992, p. 210).

Whatever solidity is assigned to this divining of a central postulate for the programming of Serbian conscience, its vitality was suggested in an observation made in mid-1992 by a reserve captain of the Serbian army in active military service in the conflict convulsing Bosnia-Hercegovina, Croatia, and Serbia. After he had raped and beaten a Croatian woman in a detention camp at Omarska in northwestern Bosnia, he evidently experienced disturbing pangs of remorse and offered an explanation to her for his behavior. According to her testimony, he said, "Our *nationalities* are at war" (italics added; Nizich, 1993, p. 164).

Military might attributed to Serbian forces starkly manifested in Bosnia-Hercegovina and Croatia, two of the widely recognized states that had comprised the former Yugoslavia, beginning in the summer of 1991 and continuing into 1995. In response, various sectors of the world community reacted, after an initial period of incredulous bewilderment, with compassionate concern. The United Nations, spurred by both formal and informal entreaties from its member nations, proceeded to muster its multifaceted strength to defuse this volatile situation that, potentially, could trigger a calamitous military confrontation among nations. Gradually, from many countries, convoys transporting humanitarian aid were dispatched to thousands of Bosnian and Croatian people unable to provide necessities for themselves. A special team of envoys sponsored by the United Nations, meeting as official sanctions were enforced, diligently explored innovative alternatives designed to restore peace as equitably as possible in this Balkan area now in internal chaos. All the while, the myriad of tragedies attendant to war multiplied as the armed forces of established governments, newly conceived insurgent governments, and resolutely committed paramilitary groups, battled with each other over a wide territory. Disputed territorial claims constituted the primary proffered justification for total war. In great rage, and in the names of their nationalities, people have massacred and plundered across the mountainous and coastal land of the South Slavs.

Acts of war, for the purpose of waging battle through military deployment, are not traditionally or currently categorized as being criminal, as abhorrent as this thought may be. Masterminding of war, however, includes no license for combatants to engage in any and all behavior in their war-waging campaigns against their declared enemies. Representatives of national governments convened in recent times as the frightening barbarisms of modern technological warfare became more apparent. In good faith they developed rules of war that were to be adhered to by all military forces. Having deliberated the limits of warring activities, an impressive number of signatory nations pledged to abide by and enforce these solemn declarations.

Violations of these limits on belligerency constitute war crimes; their perpetrators are criminals. At stake is the concept of human rights. Committed in the full fury of war, willful acts violating these rights are classified separately from battle activities; they are categorized as crimes against humanity.

Various acts regarded as violations of humanitarian law have been methodically codified by international tribunals. Since World War II, conventions, protocols, declarations, covenants, and accords have been endorsed by many nations in order to protect human rights. Among the crimes against humanity occurring under the aegis of war are acts such as these: forcible displacement of civilians from militarily controlled areas; taking of civilians as hostages for exchange of captured military personnel; detention of prisoners of war as well as civilians in prisons and camps with inhumane living conditions; pillaging of towns and cities as residences and other buildings are looted by members of military forces; deliberate obstruction of delivery of humanitarian aid destined for civilians under siege; harassment and intimidation of civilians living in militarily administered areas; institutionalized mutilating, raping, and psychological or physical torturing of persons; targeting for attack individual or groups of civilians, concentrations of population, hospitals, and objects or places having cultural and religious significance; compelling of prisoners of war or civilians to serve as human shields in confronting enemy attack; summary execution or mistreatment of captured civilians or combatants (Nizich, 1992).

According to Donnelly (1989), rights inherent in a life of dignity, upholding the values of humanity, have "a strong claim to relative universality" (p. 122). To substantiate this claim, R. S. Clark (1990) cited the precedent of a central conclusion of the historic 1946 trial at Nurenberg, at which the leading officials of Germany's Third Reich were found guilty of war crimes: "The Nuremberg Charter and Judgment firmly established the basic concept of a crime against humanity as a crime under international law" ( p. 198). Writing in 1977, Weissbrodt maintained that "The International Bill of Human Rights has attained such broad acceptance in the international community that a government cannot violate basic human rights without some fear or exposure" (p. 298). In 1992, it could accurately be stated, "The universal tenets set forth in international human rights and humanitarian agreements are not political issues open to compromise, negotiation, or arbitration" (Nizich, 1992, p. 166).

## THE SCENE: THE FORMER YUGOSLAVIA

The reality of armed strife in the former Yugoslavia, dramatically spiraling since 1991, has particularly claimed the riveted concern of nongovernmental organizations. Their single purpose is to detect and document violations of human rights so that persons charged with this criminal conduct can subsequently have their alleged guilt adjudicated in courts of law.

The land of Yugoslavia was contoured in the Balkan area of Europe by international planning councils in the destabilized aftermath of World War I. It was sustained for over three decades from the 1940s to 1980 during the autocratic regime of the people's charismatic folk hero and political leader, Josip Broz Tito. After his death, the region steadily disintegrated, unable or unmotivated to grapple further with deepening schisms. Bosnia-Hercegovina, Croatia, Macedonia, Montenegro, Serbia, and Slovenia were the countries, along with the autonomous Serbian provinces of Kosovo and Vojvodina, that had been originally forged into the political state called the Socialist Federative Republic of Yugoslavia. (This Yugoslavia of past years should not be confused with the recently formed Federal Republic of Yugoslavia, which is based on an alliance between two states, Serbia and Montenegro. References herein to Yugoslavia are to the republic founded in the post-World War I period.) Approximately 10 years after Tito's death, they individually resumed their national lives as sovereign states in a menacing, volatile environment. The territory of the former Yugoslavia was thus divided into these six independent republics and two provinces; the new configuration, with its awesome problems, was quickly accorded the uneasy attention of the world. Encouragingly, all these "new" states "agreed to honor the obligations of the former Yugoslavia under the Geneva conventions" (Meron, 1993, p. 129).

After the death of Tito, Yugoslavia had "simply vanished" from the consciousness of major world powers (Doder, 1993, p. 3). By the 1990s, this area had suffered from "years of scholarly neglect and delusion" (Banac, 1993–1994, p. 174). Beginning in 1991, as war terror was made vivid to the world by television, successive plans for restoration of peace were proposed, guardedly endorsed, and then retracted. Responding in alarm, the world placed in sharp focus the death spectacle of the fragile Yugoslavia of decades past, as its peoples vented their furious wrath on one another.

The composite of Yugoslavia, as well as the different cultures of the former state's components that now function as separate sovereign identities, are being more and more illuminated as the phenomenon of painful rebirth of nations evolves. In East Central Europe, during the 1980s, against a backdrop of continuous political realignments through the centuries, the "summa of the nationality question" was reflected in "the enduring contest between national homogenization and national diversity, between assimilationism and pluralism" (Banac, 1991, pp. 146–147). Of all locales in Eastern Europe, no country reflected this problematic matrix more than Yugoslavia, widely regarded culturally and nationally as the most diversified country in the region. The tension between the drive to blend disparate cultural identifications and the striving to effect political monism provides a basis for understanding why latent national ideologies surfaced and eventually burgeoned here (Banac, 1991).

The homogenization of Yugoslav peoples had been the actuating motive for Tito. In 1952, cognizant of the crest of the anti-Stalinism wave in the country, he depicted his goal of a "firm, monolithic state and the amalgamation of nationalities": "I would like to live to see the day when Yugoslavia would become amalgamated into a firm community . . . of a single Yugoslav nation, in which our five peoples [Croats, Slovenes, Serbs, Macedonians, Albanians] would become a single nation. . . . This is my greatest aspiration" (quoted in Banac, 1991, p. 156).

This amalgamation of nationalities continued, tenuously, for over 40 years. However, after his death in 1980, the formula for unity that Tito superintended "could not survive without his persona and total authority. . . . The glue that held the federation together was gone" (Doder, 1993, p. 14). The key to understanding the Yugoslav state has always been in its parts, never in its whole. "Only an untrained or complacent observer could see something permanent in such a contrived country" (Banac, 1993–1994, p. 174). Permanence can be found in the historical states comprising Yugoslavia and in their persevering, distinct "ideologies and mentalities" that were passionately devoted to the ideal of upholding the concept of inviolable nationhood on an individual self-conscious basis (Banac, 1993–1994, p. 175). Yugoslavia had been created as a country, but nothing like a true national culture could be created simultaneously.

During Tito's tenure as the head of the Yugoslav government, the political consensus of the country was based on Leninism. It is commonly acknowledged that "this arrangement was the necessary basis for the industrialization of an essentially peasant society and for inaugurating a socialist democratic order" (Magas, 1993, p. 218). Even as the country metamorphosed, the value heritage of the people, grounded in "peasant culture and peasant civilization," rather invariably held firm (Podunavac, 1985, p. 49). The most powerful element of this heritage manifesting in the political culture was its confirmed freedom-loving tradition (Podunavac, 1985).

Inherent in the exodus from the countryside beginning in the 1920s was the transfer of this venerated feature of the area into the centers of population. Life in the industrialized cities "became increasingly dominated by a *palanka* [i.e., small-town] mentality. . . . Instead of the provinces becoming citified, the cities became countrified, in effect turning into bigger *palanka*" (Job, 1993, p. 67). Census data as recent as 1985 indicate that a significant majority of citizens in the major cities of Yugoslavia were "still by origin from the village with strong ties to traditional cultural models" (Podunavac, 1985, p. 55). The agricultural/industrial transformation in the post-World War II years had been one of the quickest in history. Between 1948 and 1984, the agricultural population had decreased from 67.1% to 16.7%. These relocated citizens "remained linked to the soil in many ways" (Curtis, 1992, pp. 89–90).

In this economic transformation was also a triumphing and unreconstructed oral tradition, an intrinsically atavistic cultural force. Analyzing ingrained provincialism in the country, Konstantinovic concluded that the area's "true folk values and culture" (quoted in Job, 1993, p. 66) sponsor "the tyranny of local cultural establishments and the idolatry of the national self" (Job, 1993, p. 66).

Listening to songs being sung by Yugoslav soldiers in the early 1960s, songs rising "from the tortured depth" of the country's tragic past, Cvijeto Job (1993), a career diplomat who had served in the United Nations as Deputy Permanent Representative of Yugoslavia, observed, "I was despondent that our vaunted 'socialist revolution' had not really penetrated those primitive layers of our national psyche" (p. 48). Much of the enduring oral tradition of the country, he explained, embodies "fervent folk poetry—epic and romantic" (p. 65). In verse and in song, this poetry chronicles "the grieving of the South Slavs at their fate, the denouncing of foreign conquerors, and the extolling of their own nobility, their heroic deeds, their sacrifices for the honor and liberty of the people" (Job, 1993, p. 65). Enmeshed in the public mind, this poetry is studied in every school. Enshrined in both spoken and written word, it enjoys currency generation after generation. This vibrant folk literature is "often taught literally as history, without much effort to separate poetic license from true events. . . . The cult of revenge, the self-pity and self-praise—all are left unchallenged" (Job, 1993, p. 65). Folk myths, articulated in paeans of tribute and philippics of vituperation censuring labeled enemies of the past, carry messages regarded by cultural analysts as comprising "some national genetic code" deemed as immutable rather than malleable (Job, 1993, p. 64).

Nurturing this cultural stance and propagating it throughout the area is the aura of eminent authoritarianism. According to Job (1993), this central matrical factor provides "fertile soil for bigotry" (p. 66). As a result, by the oral tradition in the area of the former Yugoslavia, folk myths are almost unlimited in their effects: "The dominant objective of scholarship, education, literature, and journalism is not truth but how best to support and advance nationalist myths [of this self-lauding culture]. That culture cannot tolerate any admission that its own people, or any part of it, committed crimes. It is an 'intellectual' life where ethnic identity takes precedence over scholarly integrity" (Job, 1993, p. 63).

Permeating this ethnic-oriented cultural scene incorporating sparse elements suggesting sources capable of generating cohesiveness is a thwarting cultural polyvalence. As Yugoslavia's five cultural groups alternately commingled and fractionated, their extraordinary heterogeneity caused clashes between traditional and acquired loyalties and preferences, differentiating rather than melding these peoples. New orientations were disadvantaged as the prevailing polyvalence circumscribed or de-established them. As a consequence, insofar as societal enhancement was concerned, periodic voids and cultural interregna occurred (Podunavac, 1985).

Additional life realities mitigated against realizing the Yugoslav goal of monistic continuity. For centuries, people living in the entire Balkan area have been denied extended periods of time to experience recovery, stabilization, and objective distance from the past. Rather than experiencing intermittent seasons of reflection and projection, the area has been recurrently agitated by disruptive quarrels, shattering the spirit and cultural stability. Without benefit of adequate respites, compensatory mechanisms have been resorted to, such as "chauvinist manipulation, nationalist chicanery, paranoid fears, and the demonization of others" (Job, 1993, p. 64).

### Entrenched and Nourished Ethnicity

In the restored individualized states that once comprised Yugoslavia, inherited and reinvigorated cultural norms serve to set nation against nation philosophically, politically, economically, and religiously. In Serbia, for instance, a national renewal had been evolving for years; this Yugoslav state had been acclaimed by itself (and reluctantly by its sister states) as being the centerpiece in the former republic. Magas (1993), having traced for 12 years the impending unraveling of Tito's state, contended in 1992, "Yugoslavia was doomed either to become a Greater Serbia or to fall apart. Yugoslavia thus did not die a natural death; it was destroyed for the cause of the Greater Serbia" (pp. xiii–xiv). Conventionally and currently, the popular culture of Serbia magnifies the heroic qualities of its people, carefully preserving "the myth of Serbs as innately the most magnanimous of people, straightforward and hospitable, naive and brave, and perpetually the victims of Albanians, Croats, and many others" (Job, 1993, p. 62). In Job's opinion, this myth had been so well galvanized that "to question any part of the Serbian nation's history, admitting that its people ever committed less-than-sterling deeds, is considered unacceptable, even treasonous" (p. 62).

According to Doder (1993), Serbia nurses "a wounded self-righteousness" and is obsessively preoccupied with the past; he described a primary Serbian national motivation as being "a sense of victimization," which coacts with a "sense of just grievance" so thoroughly shared by the people that it provides "a political force of its own" (p. 15). By the 1990s, the credo of nationalism in Serbia provided the template of the new religion.

Furthering this incipient nation-fever was the extraordinary memorandum issued to the public in 1986 by the prestigious Serbian Academy of Arts and Sciences, condemning the perceived presence of "Serbophobia" in the central government of Yugoslavia. In this hallmark document, the Academy "urged Serbs to pursue their national interests" (Doder, 1993, p. 15).

Significantly, in 1989, as national enthusiasm solidified in expanded compass, a group of Orthodox Christian Church leaders proposed an ecclesiastical-national program for Serbia:

> History once again asks the Serbian State and the Serbian Church to gather their people everywhere, both those within the county and those scattered throughout the world. History asks that the cause of this people's future be served by a final overcoming of all our accursed divisions and migrations. . . . All Serbs must know today: The higher interests of the Fatherland at this moment override all of our political, ideological, regional, and other divisions. (Banac, 1991, p. 160)

Enriched by heritage, recommended by the intelligentsia, blessed by decree of the Serbian Church, the spirit of nationalism became the lodestar for Serbian people, both those who lived in Serbia and those who lived outside its mapped borders. Slobodan Milosevic fired this national consciousness as the elected and reelected President of Serbia, beginning in 1989. Brown (1991), who was affiliated with the Rand Corporation, provided the following assessment of Milosevic as a public speaker identifying himself with the Serbian diaspora throughout Yugoslavia: "To compare his speeches with those of any of his Yugoslav contemporaries was like comparing night and day. . . . His demagogy lay in his ability to stir audiences by depicting the problems that worried them, but without suggesting solutions that even remotely took into account the complexities of the situation" (pp. 228–229).

As foundation and source, the spirit of nationalism gives Milosevic's political strength its stamina. As he has discussed topics of "Serbia's place in the world, of its struggles, of its enemies, of its needs," he has provided for his people "one continuous celebration" of Serb nationhood (Ramet, 1991b, p. 96).

Typical of his efforts to identify strongly with the national aspirations of the Serb people was the public speech he presented in April 1987, in the ethnic-torn, Albanian/Serbian province of Kosovo. On this occasion, he asserted a warrant for the founding of a Greater Serbia: "The establishment of the full national and cultural integrity of the Serb nation, irrespective of the republic and province in which it finds itself, is its historic and democratic right" (Magas, 1993, p. 201).

Kosovo, even though it now languishes in extreme poverty, is symbolically regarded as "the real jewel in the Serbian crown" (Ramet, 1991b, p. 99). The fact that it was the heartland of the medieval Serbian kingdom has been woven into Serbian consciousness as one of the most supportive myths of the scattered nation. The impact of this myth is made all the more durable by repeated references to the legendary 1389 Battle of Kosovo (Ramet, 1991b). In this decisive battle, Serbian armies were devastated by the invading Turkish troops. This epochal military victory ushered in the centuries-long, despotic Ottoman rule over the crushed Serbian populace. Not only did the Kosovo battle come to be regarded as "the cataclysmic event that led Serbs into captivity," but the driving myth that it engendered became "the touchstone of the Serb national character—its disdain for compromise, its messianic bent, and its firm belief in the meaninglessness of loss and the promise of restoration of Serb glory and might" (Doder, 1993, p. 16). Captivated by the enthralling theme of a Greater Serbia, a dream to be undauntedly striven for now rather than at some future time, stalwart Serbs faithful to the goal have become "obsessed with the myth, which calls on them to avenge the injustice of Kosovo and teaches them that no sacrifice is too great for the ultimate good cause of the Serbs" (Doder, 1993, p. 16).

As catalyst for his people's mental images of nationalist grandeur, Milosevic has steadily enlivened this controlling myth in his public speeches, as he did when he spoke to a large assembly of people on the fields of the Battle of Kosovo in 1989, when the 600th anniversary of the hallowed battle was commemorated. He was speaking to all Serbs when he proclaimed on this momentous occasion, "Nobody will beat you again" (Doder, 1993, p. 16). Speaking to those who might contemplate assaulting the Serbs, he warned, "There can be no understanding of the Serbs without fathoming those sentiments" (Doder, 1993, p. 16).

So implacably have the nationalistic sentiments of Milosevic registered with his people, that the center for the nation's intellectuals, the Serbian Academy of Arts and Sciences, hailed him as "the greatest personality in Serbian history" (Magas, 1993, p. 263). Frequently addressing mass rallies, Milosevic has become known as "the voice of Serbian nationalism" (Djilas, 1993, p. 83). In 1993, David Owen, Cochair of the Conference on the Former Yugoslavia, designated Milosevic as "the most important figure in the whole region" ("The Future of the Balkans," 1993, p. 9).

In the former Yugoslavia, such ethnocentric fervor knows no bounds; it thrives widely. In Croatia, after the inception of Yugoslavia as a state, there was unwillingness to accept what was interpreted as an impending Serbian supremacy. Ultimately, this Croatian response was regarded by some as being the primary cause for the disablement of the confederation (Brown, 1991). After a liberal enthusiasm in the early 1970s had been quenched by Tito, Croatia, whose intellectuals "more than in any other Yugoslav republic set the pace of political life," entered a two-decades hibernation period of "brooding introspection" (Brown, 1991, p. 233). Even within its own geographical borders, Croatia began fearfully to envision a Serbian design to acquire a more viable political footing in the sizable Serbian communities in the province (Brown, 1991).

Threat from without, and even more threat from within, deeply injured the Croatian psyche. Much had been done "to perpetuate the myth of

Croats as congenitally more just, civilized, cultured, and democratic than almost any other people, especially Serbs" (Job, 1993, pp. 62–63). Their sustenance also comes from religious faith. The culture-sponsored association between religious affiliation and a sense of nationhood is not only widely countenanced but consciously reinforced by the Croatian political leadership. In keeping with this societal norm, the Croat National Union party headed by President Franjo Tudjman, tried to "perpetuate the illusion" that the dominant Roman Catholic Church endorsed its rule (Ramet, 1991a, p. 263).

In its precedential multiparty election of May 1990, the Croatian electorate chose as leaders the candidates of the National Union Party. It has been referred to as the "most Croat of parties," one that reflects a distinct national ideology (Banac, 1992, p. 181). Unequivocally, President Tudjman's party set as its primary political goal the realization of the foundational aspiration of the people of the republic of Croatia: "Uncontested, nontransferable, nonsuperannuated, and indivisible sovereignty of the Croat people" (Banac, 1992, p. 181). In Croatia, in Serbia, nationalism became the keystone in the restructuring of the area's pattern of states.

Microcosmically, Bosnia-Hercegovina replicates the macrocosm of the former Yugoslavia more than any of the other reconstituted republics. The country is "a crossroads of peoples, cultures, and religions"; it is all the more unique because in its national configuration, there is no majority (Mrdjen, 1993, p. 119). The Muslim population, the largest contingent in Bosnia, represents the legacy of Turkish domination. It has long been associated with the Serbs, the Croats, and the Bosnians, in working together to effect a coalesced, centralized governmental structure.

The continuation of territorial integrity for Bosnia-Hercegovina is particularly vital to the Muslim population. As masses of citizens of contrasting ethnic backgrounds flee or are transported to areas in the other republics where their individual ethnic groups reside, the Muslims "have no other republic to which they can go" (Mrdjen, 1993, p. 121). The pressing practicality of this situation necessitates that Bosnian Muslims find their future where for centuries they have claimed their home.

In August 1991, the fury of war engulfed the region. "Ethnic cleansing" soon became a battling strategy resulting in members of ethnic minorities living in certain geographical areas being forcibly displaced or killed. In Croatia, this relentlessly carried out tactic produced approximately 300,000 refugees in its first year (Magas, 1993). In Bosnia, a country "totally unprepared for war" (Magas, 1993, p. xix), where the aggression of Serbs had the impact of a blitzkrieg and where the policy of eliminating ethnic variability was more determinedly perpetrated, victims numbered almost 2 million within a 6-month period (Magas, 1993).

Although assaults and counterassaults became commonplace among the Croatians, Muslims, and Serbs, onslaughts by Serbian forces claimed the most attention and castigation in the world press. Mass terror among the people targeted as enemies was graphically depicted when it became apparent that the primary object of military actions by the Serbs was the population itself. Cultural emblems, "architecture of cities and villages, . . . churches and graveyards, . . . archives and academic institutions, . . . museums and galleries," were directly damaged and destroyed (Magas, 1993, p. xx). It seemed as if the Serbian forces were intentionally trying to eradicate the whole historical presence of their specified antagonists. Magas, assessing the reality of the aftermath of Yugoslavia, charged that those providing leadership for the Greater Serbia Campaign are enforcing a "scorched-earth policy" in order deliberately to annihilate cultures contrasting with the Serbian culture and existing within shared social, and geographical environs.

Thus, as the political units formerly comprising Yugoslavia fervently value and protect their individual identities, the attractive beacon for charting their multiple paths is pluralistic, not consolidated, existence. In the vanguard of ideals held by all these cultural groups, which are historically accustomed to volatile relationships, is bold, flinty nationalism. Brandished chauvinism has spawned blatant ethnocentrism and resolute attachment to one's nation-by-heritage.

## The Detection Work of Helsinki Watch

Entering this bitterly complicated morass as the horrors of war in the former Yugoslav territory registered in world consciousness was the nongovernmental organization, Helsinki Watch (HW). Formed in 1978, HW exists to monitor compliance with internationally recognized provisions protecting fundamental human rights. Concentrating its efforts for the most part in the countries of Eastern Europe (Livezey, 1988), it maintains, as of 1993, a constant presence in former Yugoslavia, "detailing abuses as they occur" (*Human Rights Watch World Report 1993*, 1992, p. 204). HW personnel shared with the world community their motivating concerns:

> What is taking place in Bosnia-Hercegovina is attempted genocide—the extermination of a people in whole or in part because of their race, religion, or ethnicity. This is the gravest crime known to humankind. . . . Negotiators often appear to be neglecting the human rights of the people of Bosnia-Hercegovina in the interest of signing a peace accord. . . . Helsinki Watch fears that peace in Bosnia-Hercegovina—and, indeed, throughout the former Yugoslavia—will warrant the description by Tacitus in *The Agricola* of how the ancient Romans in Britain "created a desolation and called it peace." (Nizich, 1993, pp. 2, 4)

The charged setting in which HW works—Croats versus Serbs, Serbs versus Muslims, Muslims versus Croats—is one of internecine tragedy in monolithic magnitude. Spanning the melange of "bewildering and abrupt alliances and counteralliances" is the seemingly intractable "twisted madness of Yugoslav fratricide" (Brock, 1993–1994, p. 159).

Acting in accordance with the principle that these infamous crimes are perpetrated by individuals, thinking and acting by their own will, HW, in August 1993, boldly published information connecting individual people with specific acts of criminal behavior:

> In this document, Helsinki Watch, a division of Human Rights Watch, presents summaries of eight cases that, with immediate investigation, will be strong candidates for prosecution. Helsinki Watch identifies 29 possible defendants by name, links each defendant to specific crimes and, in turn, enumerates potential violations of the pertinent law. . . . Five of the cases charge Serbs with offenses, two charge Croats, and one charges Muslims; the allegations span the spectrum of war crimes offenses, from gang rape to genocide. The accused range from the lowest prison guard to the former Yugoslav Minister of Defense and the Chief of Staff of the Yugoslav National Army. . . . Further investigation under the auspices of the United Nations will individualize what is now too often seen as collective guilt. (*Prosecute Now!*, 1993, pp. 2–4)

Emphasizing its intent to pin culpability on specific individuals who committed acts deemed to be criminal, HW designed and followed an investigatory methodology that could serve to undergird evidence derived. Two imposing volumes, published in 1992 and 1993, constitute the primary reports of the investigations of war crimes in the area presented by HW thus far. Wiseberg (1992), editor of the *Human Rights Tribune*, quarterly publication of the Human Rights Internet with headquarters at the University of Ottawa in Canada, referred to the 1992 fact-finding report as "the most extensive documentation compiled to that date about violations of the laws of war" (p. 8). Volume II is similarly highly informative.

The many interviews of various people in many locations were conducted in keeping with specific guidelines. Interviewers solicited direct testimony from victims of abuse or from witnesses to abuse, preferring to give them no advance notice of the discussions. They tried to obtain as recent testimony as possible, from people who were not "practiced in giving statements to interviewers" (Nizich, 1993, p. 5). Interviewees, speaking in their native languages, were interviewed in private by people fluent in these languages. HW also assured all those making use of its reports, "If we subsequently obtain information suggesting that . . . testimony set forth . . . is in fact not reliable, we will publish that information at once" (Nizich, 1993, p. 6).

## SHAPING THE *PRIMA FACIE* CASE FOR GUILT

In its publications, HW presented the collected data as evidence of violations of human rights. HW recognized that no finders of fact are excused from reasonable expectations as to what marks believable evidence. Evidence is a substantive phenomenon; evidential substance serves to confirm what is factual. In demonstrating reality, evidence provides the momentum by which reviewers' judgments can move from particulars to a consolidating claim or conclusion.

### Criteria for Screening Evidence of Human Rights Violations

In proceedings before international tribunals, as in civil law procedures, the person who states a claim assumes the burden of proving it. If this burden is not carried successfully through evidence and reasoning, there will be cause to reject the contention (Sandifer, 1975). As Perelman and Olbrechts-Tyteca (1969) explained, the articulating of elements constituting facts "endows these elements with a *presence*" in the minds of the message receivers, and "presence acts directly on our sensibility" (p. 116). That which is "present to the consciousness assumes thus an importance that the theory and practice of argumentation must take into consideration" (Perelman & Olbrechts-Tyteca, 1969, p. 117).

Writing about the problem of confirming reality through evidence, Ayer (1972) stated, "An event occurs or it does not. There is nothing in between" (p. 55). In finding a fact, however, a pragmatic directive is given in the American Law Institute Model Code of Evidence, because the demonstration of absolute certainty is rare: "Finding a fact means determining that its existence is more probable than its nonexistence.... All that the trier [of fact] can do is to find where the preponderance of probability lies" (Ramcharan, 1982b, p. 5). Discussing judicial procedure as it relates to matters of international law, Ramcharan (1982a), held that cogency itself depends "largely upon general considerations of probability" (p. 79). The standard of proof that should be applied by fact-finding bodies, he advised, should be "a balance of probabilities—probability in this sense may be defined as an evaluation of the likelihood of a past event having happened" (p. 78). Is it more likely that a designated event did occur, or is it more likely that it did not occur? On this question, discerning interpretation of reality pivots.

Likelihood of occurrence is a cumulative precept. Adducing evidence demonstrating a claim is a communicative task requiring plural units, not a single instance. "When particular phenomena are invoked one after the other, we are inclined to regard them as examples.... On the other hand, the description of a single phenomenon is more likely to be taken as a mere item of information. . . . Merely putting an event in the plural is of significance" (Perelman & Olbrechts-Tyteca, 1969, p. 351). In offering evidential support in the plural, the investigator of fact should select cases "in such a way that the representative character of the samples taken from reality is guaranteed" (Perelman & Olbrechts-Tyteca, 1969, p. 355).

HW investigators have repeatedly attested to their serious interest in marshaling valid, believable evidence when making claims that human rights have been and are being outrageously violated. Investigators are intent on basing their findings on direct evidence (Weissbrodt & McCarthy, 1981). According to Weissbrodt and McCarthy (1982), "There is nothing which convinces the outside world so much as the statement: 'We were there and we saw' " (p. 190). These authorities on fact-finding procedure also maintained that the supplying of "corroboration [of evidence] is the most significant and commonly-used method for determining the reliability of human rights information" (Weissbrodt & McCarthy, 1981, p. 70).

Consideration of reasonable and proper mustering of evidence of human rights abuses becomes all the more instructive for HW personnel as criticism mounts of media coverage of war in the former Yugoslavia. For instance, it has been charged that the media in this area purposely practice "advocacy journalism" (Brock, 1993–1994, p. 153). In the beginning of this war in 1991, the *London Times* appraised the reporting from the war zone by noting, "As the desperate attempts to win the hearts and minds of Europe grow, the claims become wilder, the proof skimpier" (quoted in Brock, 1993–1994, p. 161). Recognizing such criticism of the media, Brock, political editor of the *El Paso Herald-Post*, writing in *Foreign Policy*, thoughtfully urged approximately 2 years later that because "the role of international public opinion" is central, it is "critical that the news media report with precision and professionalism" (p. 172).

HW representatives, desiring to make clear the difference in the quality of their reporting from that referred to in the mass media, capitalized on what they believed to be the justified weight of their collected evidence, although remaining wary of assigning undue weight to it. They emphasized that the evidence they had compiled was not only crucial to their noteworthy task but also indispensably timely: "Evidence of war crimes disappears daily and witnesses and survivors scatter across the globe. Unless the international community acts now, any elaborate legal machinery developed to try war crimes will fail; the evidence needed to utilize that machinery will be nowhere to be found" (*Prosecute Now!*, 1993, p. 2).

Of special significance was the readiness of HW representatives to disavow evidence that, to them, lacked validity. The following entries from HW's two published volumes illustrate this discriminative screening of evidential materials: (a) "HW has also received reports that Serbian civilians may have been executed in the municipalities of Sarajevo. However, to date we have not received any evidence that would confirm such reports" (Nizich, 1992, p. 50); and (b) "[Citizens formerly detained in Serbian camps] frequently allege that prisoners were transferred to camps which remain unknown to the international community and the International Committee of the Red Cross. HW has not been able to verify these allegations" (Nizich, 1993, p. 12).

### Helsinki Watch Documentation of War Crimes

Evidence found to be acceptable by HW personnel was presented within a general format of placement considerations having sequential order. Prior to presenting data and conclusions from their investigations, HW representatives provided overviews. In that way, there was progression from background to the elements comprising the scene that the background framed. Human acts were situated within detailed settings marking reality.

The amplification methods of narrative and description were similarly used to provide contextualization of evidence. The following example illustrates this usage:

> En route to Kozibrod, the Serbs captured 30 to 50 villagers, including women and handicapped and elderly persons, from the Croatian villages of Struga and Zamlaca. The insurgents forced their captives to walk in a long column, shoulder-to-shoulder, with their hands held high, in front of the advancing Serbian insurgents. The villagers were used as human shields for approximately 6 hours until a village defender threw a hand grenade and the captured civilians scattered. One of the hostages, a 75-year-old woman was killed. According to hostages interviewed a week after the assault, their houses were ransacked and robbed by the Serbian insurgents and several hostages were beaten, including a 20-year-old woman who lost three teeth. In addition, in front of the hostages, Serbian rebels abused and humiliated three Croatian police officers who surrendered, and then forced them to run, shooting and killing all three. (Nizich, 1992, p. 239)

The chronicling and description of episodes foster the registration of reality in the minds of those reacting to the evidence. People and their activities are imaged; life as it proceeds during a specific span of time is sensed. Although personal presence cannot operate as a factor of perception, mental projection into a scene activates that scene, which can now be internalized. To narrate and to describe human events in detail is to suggest the legitimization of their occurrence.

The reporting of individual instances augments this contextualization of evidence. By their particularities, these instances of testimony can be interpreted by message receivers as verifying reality. Directing the receivers' attention to unique and time-based episodes, HW reporters cited instances portraying human interactions in realistic vignettes. The revealing nature of personalized testimony becomes apparent as victims and eyewitnesses relate minute details of their experiences involving enemy assaults. The testimony of two women from the village of Zaklopaca in the municipality of Vlasenica in Bosnia-Hercegovina depicts believably a scene of summary civilian executions. The first woman related the following:

> I was taking my cows to pasture when I saw the Cetniks [typically members of Serbia's extreme right-wing political faction operating on a paramilitary basis]. I immediately went into my house from where I saw that three Cetniks had gotten out of the car and others were entering the village on foot. About 100 Cetniks came from the direction of Zalkovik. Each Cetnik had two AK-47s, ammunition strapped across his chest and belt and all were dressed in JNA [Yugoslav Army] uniforms but had a Cetnik symbol on their hats. Many wore gloves on their hands and stockings over their heads. They broke off into groups that started going from house to house. (Nizich, 1992, p. 52)

According to the second woman:

> After they killed my husband, we let out a scream and they sprayed our house with bullets and then machine-gunned the entire village. They kept shooting for several minutes all over the village despite the fact that no one was shooting at them. (Nizich, 1992, p. 53)

Grim portrayal of reality was similarly provided by individual witnesses recounting multiple instances of abusive acts they had observed of Serbian occupation forces. As one survivor related, "I watched Serbian soldiers burn houses in Nedjeljiste—300 meters away from our positions. They have mined all the houses in the village; I have seen it with my own eyes" (*Abuses Continue*, 1993, p. 30). A second witness recounted the following:

> ["Perhaps the only surviving eyewitness" of a summary group execution in Snagova Selo reported what happened after Serbian soldiers had discovered a group of villagers hiding in a woods.] I was standing close to the fence of this garage. Thirty-eight were killed there. . . . My wife was killed along with the rest of them; she was pregnant. My other daughter was killed and so was my mother; they had all been standing close to me. . . . I saw them falling. . . . The corpses were all around me. The bodies were riddled with holes. . . . [A soldier] said that our village is number 90 to have been "cleansed." (*Abuses Continue*, 1993, pp. 35–36)

> In the village of Glogava, a woman testified about a Serbian attack. The soldiers went from house to house forcing people to come out and then they gathered men and women on the street, in the center of the village, close to the mosque. There were about 500 people. They separated four men from our group and they started to question them a bit further away from us. They killed one of the men . . . and then the other one. . . . I saw it with my own eyes. Then they started to kill other people—I watched them—they were shooting from guns and pistols. . . . They forced our fellow villagers, Muslims, to burn our houses. . . . The soldiers brought about 50 people in front of the mosque; they lined them up beside the bank of the river. The people were forced to put their hands behind their heads. The soldiers started to shoot. . . . They did terrible things to them. . . . I saw it all. They put the music on, so while they were doing all these terrible things, the music was playing. (*Abuses Continue*, 1993, pp. 36–37)

As one eyewitness after another testified, "I saw," "I heard," the scenes of reality acquired *presence*. Recorded in the published reports, this type of witnessing vicariously enables the receivers of the messages to perceive unfolding episodes, moment by moment. The realities depicted are devoid of obscurities; referents-in-life symbolized by the words employed become infused with specific identity.

Evidential materials, appearing individually, stand alone and are appraised accordingly; when they are expanded into the plural, they are endowed with greater believability. Purposely, HW evidence compilers provided basis for the reviewers of the evidence to experience the heightening effect of corroborative support for the claims of human rights abuse.

This instance of HW reliance on corroborative evidence illustrates its usage. An August 1991 incident occurring in Pecki, Croatia, was reported as follows: "After the village of Pecki (population 374) was occupied by Serbian forces, four Croatian men were killed when they returned to the village to feed their livestock. Three of the men appear to have been tortured prior to their execution" (Nizich, 1992, p. 278).

Corroboration of both the torturing and the killing was provided by medical doctors from the Department of Pathology and Cytology at Sisak Hospital and the Department of Anatomy at the Zagreb University School of Medicine who performed autopsies on the bodies of these three men. They found that one man "was shot and stabbed repeatedly, most probably with bayonets. His left arm was amputated, probably with an ax" (Nizich, 1992, p. 278). It was recorded that hand axes were probably used to kill the other two men, the skull of one of them being "fractured after his head was held firmly to the ground while heavy blows were inflicted with a blunt object" (Nizich, 1992, p. 278). The third man, 70 years old, "died as a result of multiple gunshot wounds" (Nizich, 1992, p. 278).

A notable feature of the primary evidence recorded by HW is its forceful specificity. In all evidentiary materials, exactness is of the essence.

The distinctive nature of this evidentiary property in HW's data is illustrated here through examples.

On February 13, 1992, in a long letter to President Franjo Tudjman of Croatia, Jonathan Fanton, HW Chair, and Jeri Laber, HW Executive Director, documented violations of the laws of war attributed to Croatian military sources. On page after page in the letter, the circumstances constituting the violations, along with their precise dates and places, are chronicled under topic headings such as summary executions, torture, and mistreatment of people held in detention.

Citing a pathologist at the Military Hospital in Belgrade as the source of their information, Fanton and Laber presented the details of the massacre of Serbians that occurred during the previous December in Gospic:

> Twenty-four bodies—15 men and 9 women—were found burned near the villages of Siroka Kula and Perusic. . . . Five more bodies were found nearby. . . . All the victims were shot. Several who apparently did not die from the gunshot wounds were brutally executed. One person . . . appeared to have been stabbed in the back by a knife; a second individual was hit above the eye with either a bayonet or an ax; a third person (a woman) was shot in the head at close range; a fourth individual appeared to have had his skull broken by a heavy, blunt object. The bodies were then thrown into a pile, doused with gasoline and set on fire. (Nizich, 1992, p. 315)

They reported what a Serbian man held captive in a hotel in the village of Marino Selo, along with approximately 20 other men, told of his experiences:

> Four of the Croatian Guardsmen would get drunk frequently and beat all of us. . . . They would take some of the captives out of the cell and tell them that they were going to be exchanged. They were taken outside and we heard gunfire. Those taken from their cells never came back. The Guardsmen who killed them made us bury the corpses. I buried seven men [six of whom he identified by their names]. (Nizich, 1992, p. 316)

In a similar letter, dated January 21, 1992, HW officers provided for Slobodan Milosevic, Serbia's President, and Blagoje Adzic, Chief of Staff of the Yugoslav People's Army, a full discussion of violations of humanitarian law based on a mass of accumulated data. Affirming that these violations were committed "by the Serbian government and the Yugoslav Army" (Nizich, 1992, p. 274), HW associated these data with "very serious and credible reports" (Nizich, 1992, p. 276).

Specific places were accorded precise identity, not only in terms of their locations but also in terms of the particular happenings in them, thereby separating them from all other places. Illustrative of this type of evidence was the report filed by HW, written on the basis of interviews with eyewitnesses:

> On November 18, at approximately 7:15 a.m., the Yugoslav Army and the Serbian paramilitaries launched a mortar and artillery attack against the Croatian village of Skabrnje.... At 11:00 a.m., a Yugoslav Army tank reached St. Mary's Church in the center of town and fired a mortar at the main door. Serbian paramilitaries then sprayed the church with machine gun fire and one paramilitary took up position in the bell tower and shot at the village from the tower [The report notes that 41 civilians were killed.]. (Nizich, 1992, pp. 282–283)

Another HW report contained specific details about a Yugoslav Army attack on a hospital:

> During the course of three days, from September 14–17, Osijek hospital was hit 56 times by mortar shells, 21 times by tank shells, and 17 times by rockets from multiple rocket launchers. The hospital was also hit by bullets from light weaponry. During one attack a 38-year-old nurse was killed and two doctors were wounded. Most of the hospital wards, including the intensive care unit, were damaged during the attack. (Nizich, 1992, p. 295)

In addition to these precise statements forwarded to the highest government officials in Serbia and Croatia, numerical tabulations of human rights abuses characterize the two volumes published by HW. One report tabulates the members of individual families killed by Serbian paramilitaries in a village massacre:

> On May 16, 1992, at least 83 Muslims were summarily executed ... in the village of Zaklopaca. At least 11 children (ranging in age from 6 to 16) and 16 elderly persons (over 60) were among those killed, according to eyewitnesses to and survivors of the execution [Individual families are then listed by name, with the number of members killed in each family: 30 from one family, 9 from another, 8 from another, etc. These numbers were based on HW interviews of eyewitnesses and a list of victims compiled by volunteer workers at Zagreb's mosque who consulted with survivors.]. (Nizich, 1992, pp. 50–51)

Devoting extensive attention to the provision of specific informative details as evidence of war crimes was proffered, HW personnel stressed that they were consistently endeavoring to document crimes committed by all parties to the conflict, not restricting their investigations to the acts of those representing only one ethnic, religious, or national group.

Throughout the second volume of compiled evidence of war crimes published in 1993 by HW, documentary materials are classified under the headings, "Abuses by Muslim Forces," "Abuses by Croatian Forces," "Abuses by Croatian and Muslim Forces," "Abuses by Serbian Forces."

Determined to be equitable in their coverage of abuses constituting grave breaches of international humanitarian law, HW staff members unequivocally declared, "All of the parties to the conflict have committed such crimes and all should be held accountable and prosecuted for their abuses before impartial tribunals that afford the protections of due process of law" (Nizich, 1992, p. 198). At the same time HW conclusively stated, "The overwhelming number of crimes are being committed by Serbian forces in Bosnia-Hercegovina which are carrying out a policy of 'ethnic cleansing' in systematic fashion" (Nizich, 1992, p. 198).

Writing in January 1993 to Boutros Boutros-Ghali, Secretary General of the United Nations, HW Chair Fanton underscored the significance of this HW opinion: "The actions of the Serbian forces conducting sieges of several communities in Bosnia . . . are exactly those that are forbidden by . . . requirements of international law" (Nizich, 1993, p. 404).

HW provided the basis for perceiving Serbian military forces effecting their ethnic cleansing policy as their foremost instrument in waging war. Comprehensively designed and methodically carried out in small compass and in large, this Serbian policy can be regarded as embodying the genesis, raison d'être, and goal of intensive armed combat waged by Serbian forces. Progressively, from the beginning months of the war, the displacement of non-Serbs by Serbian troops has accelerated, "thereby producing larger swaths of 'ethnically pure' areas" (Nizich, 1992, p. 74). As ethnic cleansing has become an absorbing strategy on all fronts of the war, "trust among the various ethnic and national groups has eroded and members of each group have sought to escape to areas controlled by their own group" (Nizich, 1992, p. 75).

HW also imputed, in general, the institutionalizing of rape as an instrument of war to Serbian more than to Muslim and Croatian military forces (Nizich, 1993). Recognizing that the crime of rape can and does often occur in situations involving military occupation, HW was also cognizant of the fact that the commission of this tortuous crime can represent aberrant, individually motivated behavior. When the act becomes group encouraged and group condoned, however, when it is resorted to in a campaign of terrorization, it can become a weapon of warfare. HW maintained this crime has not only become systematized, but a leading factor in accomplishing the objective of ethnic cleansing: "Whether a woman is raped by soldiers in her home or is held in a house with other women and raped over and over again, she is raped with a political purpose—to intimidate, humiliate, and degrade her and others affected by her suffering. The effect of rape is often to ensure that women and their families will flee and never return" (Nizich, 1993, p. 21).

As a further substantiation of this rationale, Nixon (1993) commented on the assigning of invariant identities to the genders:

> Women are often assigned symbolically crucial roles as reproducers of the nation under the aegis of nationalistic impulse and as upholders of its innermost values. Women may thus serve in a double sense as the bearers of the nation, carrying in their wombs the hope of perpetuity while also incarnating national values.... They come to mark the borders between ethnicities. Thus, ethnic biology, ethnic culture, and ethnic territory converge in their beings.... They are ... weighted down with symbolic responsibilities as guarantors of homeland, ethnos, and lineage.... Mass rape is, among other things, organized insemination, men's way of interfering with the lineage of the enemy. (pp. 16–17)

The concept of male conquest, a degrading motivation commonly associated with the crime of rape, can be expanded to imply potential ethnic conquest. Competing ethnic identities are detested and inferentially obliterated as women are physically subdued. As a case in point, a Muslim woman living in Sukovac testified that during interrogation at the police station, she was beaten and raped for bearing Muslim children (Nizich, 1993). Self-identity was commonly revealed by rapists, as if to testify to their conquering of victims. A Muslim woman detained in a high school in Doboj expressed shock when recognizing two of her rapists as being Serbian medical doctors with whom she had worked, even though they wore black stockings as disguises over their faces. The first physician she recognized was a man whom she had known for 10 years. The second physician, also an acquaintance of the victim, said to her, "Now you know who we are. You will remember forever" (Nizich, 1993, p. 218).

For ethnic identity to be figuratively erased, a new identity needs to replace it. As a Croatian woman testified about her treatment at the Omarska detention camp, she reported that she was told by an officer of the Serbian army before he raped her, "I needed to give birth to a Serb—that I would then be different" (Nizich, 1993, p. 164). Another Croatian woman who had been repeatedly raped at Obudovac by Serbian soldiers testified, "It was their aim to make a baby.... They would say directly, looking into your eyes, that they wanted to make a baby" (Nizich, 1993, p. 215).

As a consequence of this philosophical programming, the crime of rape is embedded in the infrastructure undergirding the cross-currents characterizing the daily life of war in Bosnia-Hercegovina. Evidence abounds. According to the findings of HW, "rape appears to have been rampant and an accepted mode of behavior for Serbian soldiers in the municipality of Foca. In one case, a commander was aware of, and initially condoned, the gang rape of several women" (Nizich, 1993, p. 242). In a detention center, formerly a high school, sexual abuse was commonplace. A Muslim woman detained there testified: "This type of scenario occurred every night. I was held in the high school for 10 days, and every day I was raped. Some of the men who came to take us away and then rape us were familiar to me; others I had never seen before" (Nizich, 1993, p. 248). Another Muslim woman detained in the same place testified: "I was raped every night during my stay in the sports hall. The men who raped me were always different—the same man never raped me twice" (Nizich, 1993, p. 249). Later, a gynecologist, who examined women who had been detained in the Foca area in mid-1992, confirmed they had been raped; some were impregnated, others "suffered uterine or ovarian complications as a result of their abuse" (Nizich, 1993, p. 253).

The number of rapes occurring in situations integrally related to war activities, such as territory occupation, people displacement, and forced detention of citizens in locations under the close surveillance of military troops, cannot be precisely documented. The factual evidence that has been recorded arguably suggests, however, that this vile crime against women is widespread to an appalling degree. HW cautioned that more investigative work must be completed before the extent of sexual abuse against women in the former Yugoslav states can be accurately determined. HW warned that inflated estimates at this point "unfortunately may contribute to an eventual backlash which could undercut the seriousness of the abuse if the high numbers cannot be substantiated" (Nizich, 1993, p. 23).

Working within the contrasting cultures of former Yugoslavia, speaking to the people comprising them, while also addressing the world community regarding the duty to safeguard axiomatic human rights, HW representatives strive to marshal substantive evidence of systemic violations of these rights. They have methodically communicated extensively confirmed and corroborative data that warrant adjudication of these grave charges by a duly appointed tribunal not only commissioned but activated to execute that task.

To confirm their claim that war crimes have in fact been committed on a wide scale to effect the military goals of governmental and paramilitary agencies to devitalize and eliminate scorned ethnic populations, HW personnel have cogently demonstrated the continually experienced reality in the now-disintegrated Yugoslavia. This well-supported depiction is infused with an aura of *presence* in the consciousness of people who contemplate it. The claim posited by HW advocates appears to be more probable than alternative interpretations. Unless well-grounded rebuttal is forthcoming, the claim of HW personnel garners additional credence.

## PROBING SEQUEL TO CULTURAL IMBROGLIO

Even though its investigation of war crimes in the former Yugoslavia is continuing, HW, in publishing the current version of its report, maintained that "at the very least," it has competently provided "*prima facie* evidence that genocide is taking place" (Nizich, 1992, p. 1). Genocide, "the most unspeakable crime in the lexicon" (Nizich, 1993, p. 2), has been documented in this initial phase of methodical inquiry, as have other "extreme violations of international humanitarian laws" (Nizich, 1992, p. 1).

### Culture as Cause

Culture dictates what constitutes criminality. Simic (in Ramet, 1992) explained that personal and societal behavior is condoned or penalized according to the operative moral field within a culture. People typically behave toward each other on the basis of ethnically perceived criteria, that is, culture-adopted rules embodying exemplars and directives honored by society as being good and proper. Behavior that does not correlate with standards implicit in a culture's moral field is regarded as being amoral.

Ramet (1992) observed that in applying moral field theory, actions such as murder, torture, and rape, which would be considered morally reprehensible when directed toward a person sharing one's moral field, might be regarded as morally commendable when committed against a person not associated with the moral field of one's culture.

Supported by cultural groups, moral fields become all the more fixed as time passes. Entrenchment is even further assured in past-oriented cultures. East Europeans, including people living in the Balkan area, in contrast to people in the United States of America who "think about the future almost compulsively," are typically "inclined to seek solace in the past" (Janos, 1994, p. 8). Among the nations of the former Yugoslavia, "The past has never been laid to rest. . . . The wounds of the past have never healed. . . . The past haunts the present" (Ramet, 1992, p. 40). Here, the prevailing ethnically and tribally grounded moral fields are not characterized by mutability.

Questioning the givens of such contrasting life adaptations by persons outside the Southern Slavic cultures, thereby perhaps encouraging introspective assessment by the members of these cultures, would probably be futile. Ramet (1992) reported that even the citizens of these separate nations not only speak different languages, but they also talk "past each other" (p. 175). As a result, these diverse peoples have failed to comprehend each other's cultures. Any effort to effect melding of moral fields would probably not be promising (Ramet, 1992).

Additional life factors reinforce cultural/moral intransigence. Hobsbawn (1990) suggested that the official adoption of the Serbo-Croat language by both Serbia and Croatia does not represent language hybridization, as the hyphenated title indicates. Traditionally speaking the kajkavian dialect, whereas Serbian people relied on the related stokavian dialect, Croatian litterateurs, interested in promoting an inclusive identity among people of the Adriatic coastal area, elected to write in stokavian, thereby indirectly proclaiming Slavic unity. Since mid-19th century, therefore, the Serbs and Croats have shared a common idiom, at least in its literary version. Smith (1986) pointed out that "Serbo-Croat represents a unified language which affords no basis for two nationalisms" (p. 27). He cautioned, however, that insight into cultural forces requires looking "beneath the immediate and salient sign of communication which a shared language expresses, to the underlying life-styles and values of the community" (p. 27). In the final analysis, linguistic as well as other cultural cleavages persevere between the two peoples, as the Roman Catholic Croats elect to write in Latin script, and the Orthodox Christian Serbs prefer Cyrillic script (Hobsbawn, 1990).

The factor of religion supersedes in importance the culturally consolidating factors of a history shared to a degree, and a long-standing mutual association with a specific territory. "It is the identification of an ethnic community with a salvationist religion that appears to secure survival more effectively" than any of the other components comprising the vital ethnic core (Arnason, 1990, p. 217). Hobsbawn (1990) observed that "the links between religion and national consciousness can be very close" (p. 67). For centuries, it has been through religious practices that people have experienced close communion with one another, along with a deepening sense of fellowship.

In all the former Yugoslav nations, the strength of the three dominant faiths indicates the accompanying magnitude of divisions in ethnic consciousness. Since the spring of 1990, a religious revival has been in evidence in the area, confirming signs during the late 1980s that indicated "a resurgence of religious belief, especially among young people" (Curtis, 1992, p. 108). The Islamic faith is thriving. Since World War II, approximately 800 mosques have been constructed in Yugoslav territory. In this Islamic community, which is the largest in any European country west of Turkey, the Sarajevo Islamic school of theology is the only one for that faith in Europe. The stability of the Greek Orthodox Church in the territory of former Yugoslavia is indicated by the decision of the government to complete the long-delayed Cathedral of St. Sava in Belgrade, which will be the largest Eastern Orthodox church structure in the world. In comparison, the press of the Roman Catholic Church, consisting of dozens of newspapers and periodicals, has attained a circulation that exceeds the remainder of the country's religious press, thereby reflecting the area's "most highly organized religious community" (Curtis, 1992, p. 110). Morality and ethnicity are thus deeply anchored in religion, each of these related aspects of life reciprocally strengthening the others, at once consolidating and segregating.

Secular explanations for the problematic cultural challenges in Eastern Europe must be noted as well. There exists in this large area, including the former Yugoslavia, an activist movement that is "ready to change the cultural makeup of society by changing its sexual constitution, by rejecting traditional proprieties, and by cultivating the symbols of the victim and the weak" (Janos, 1994, p. 25). Janos held that the rationale for resisting this sentiment "provides plausible explanation for bizarre rituals of brutality, and provides meaning to seemingly senseless acts of violence in the Balkans" (p. 25). Rebelling against this reformation ideal for society, the perpetrators of such violent acts lash out at people. Even further, "the mass rape of women and the subsequent use of force to ensure that they carry children to term are not just the depraved acts of men who lost their moorings in society, but an intuitively choreographed response to the cultural liberal agenda of 'choice' and 'empowerment' " (Janos, 1994, p. 25). These acts "are part of the political ritual of a Nietzchean counterrevolution of the 'strong' against what they [the perpetrators] see as power masquerading as the morality of the victim and the weak" (Janos, 1994, p. 27). In effect, these machinations of terror mirror the ultimate in symbolic politics.

Concurrently, all the axes of "European symbolic geography intersect in Yugoslavia," that is, in the new individual nation-states (Bakic-Hayden & Hayden, 1992, p. 4). As explained by Bakic-Hayden and Hayden, in "distinguishing disvalued Others" (p. 5) in cultural politics, one might envision an Oriental system of conceptual nesting. Ideationally, in large sweep, heralded progressive, modern, rational Europe can thus be set apart from the allegedly stagnant, backward, traditional, mystical Orient. In sharper focus, perhaps most salient in the former Yugoslav lands, is the claiming of European status for some groups while demeaning others as Balkan or Byzantine, and hence as undesirable others:

> [These distinctions] privilege the predominantly Catholic, formerly Hapsburg territories of Slovenia and Croatia over the predominantly Orthodox or Muslim formerly Ottoman territories in the rest of the country. ... In the northwest the European character and apparent advantages of the Hapsburg empire are stressed, while the Ottoman oriental is blamed for the ills of the rest of the country. (Bakic-Hayden & Hayden, 1992, p. 5)

## The Ideal of Nationalism

In regard to the former Yugoslav states, one should assign due weight to the ideal of nationalism in order to comprehend the "new surge of ethnic consciousness" (Tehranian, 1993, p. 204). Tehranian estimated that of the 120 violent conflicts being waged around the world, 72% of them could be classified as ethnic wars. Ethnic group identities strengthen individuals and pervade history; identity with one's nation is commonly recognized as a natural and lasting affiliation. Ethnic identities are such intense affect phenomena that they become values in themselves rather than definers of wide ranges of general values. As controlling as religious faith is in exacting unfaltering allegiance, the sacrificing of fealty to one's religion in favor of nationalism is not uncommon today (Armstrong, 1982). When constitutionally sanctioned, nationalism, as it is rooted in European thought, may result in reasoning that makes "military or bureaucratic 'ethnic cleansing,' if not genocide itself, inevitable" (Hayden, 1992, p. 673).

Gellner (1983) concluded: "Nations are not inscribed into the nature of things" (p. 49). They are instead crystallized from "their raw material—the cultural, historical, and other inheritances from the pre-nationalist world" (Gellner, 1983, p. 49). Nationalism, Gellner claimed, "usually conquers in the name of a putative folk culture. Its symbolism is drawn from the healthy, pristine, vigorous life of the peasants, of the *Volk*" (p. 57). Wherever and whenever nationalism vigorously asserts itself, as it does in the *palanka* of the former Yugoslav territory, it is a powerful force and must be reckoned with.

## Cultural Divisiveness Compounded

The divisiveness of nationalism, which many scholars believe is the bane of more socially rewarding cultural systems, dominates as a societal force in the Balkan region. Driven by nationalistic zeal coming not from a common mold but from antagonistic backgrounds, the nations that declared their independence from the Yugoslav confederation are compulsively adhering to a fated course. Divisiveness, blatantly open and seriously rationalized, has proven to be endemic. In the absence of unifying energy, there is "complete and total breakdown of intercultural contact and exchange" (Ramet, 1992, p. 3). When the governmental institutions in the former Yugoslavia that had espoused, even mandated, multiethnic coexistence disintegrated, the entire social structure collapsed (Varady, 1992). With this sudden vanishing, the "only persuasion ready to fill the void was that of nationalism" (Varady, 1992, p. 262). This reinvigorated political creed restored vitality to one-party consciousness.

Under Tito, dissidents had been ostracized; it had been assumed that "those who are ideologically different must be enemies and traitors" (Varady, 1992, p. 262). Now, minorities essentially have become encumbrances—"an obstacle by their different culture, language, alphabet—or by their very existence" (Varady, 1992, p. 262).

Of the various national rivalries among the former Yugoslav states, the deepest and oldest is that between the Serbs and Croats. For many today, a venerable saying appears pertinent: "In a conflict with authority, the Serb reaches for the sword and the Croat for his [sic] pen" (Curtis, 1992, p. 73). Curtis offered elucidation:

> The Serbian stereotype refers to the tradition of the *hajduk*, the idealized mountain renegade who responded violently to the oppressive anarchy of the Ottoman Empire during its last two centuries; the Croatian stereotype reflects the cultural influence of responding through the legal system to the Hapsburgs' high bureaucratized infringements on national and individual freedoms in Croatia. (pp. 73–74)

Huntington (1993) posited another explanation for divisiveness: Croatia, situated west of "the historic dividing line in central Europe," harbors a civilization that "shared the common experiences of European history—feudalism, the Renaissance, the Reformation, the Enlightenment, the French Revolution, the Industrial Revolution" (p. 30). East of this figurative line are Bosnia-Hercegovina and Serbia; in ages past, the civilizations of these cultures developed within the Ottoman and Tsarist empires, which were "not affected significantly through the centuries by the shaping forces in western Europe" (Huntington, 1993, p. 30).

In 1991, in a letter widely circulated to Slovenian intellectuals throughout the world, Peter Tancig (quoted in Bakic-Hayden and Hayden, 1992), Minister of Science and Technology in Slovenia, even more pointedly applied the nesting analysis discussed earlier:

> The basic reason for all the past/present "mess" is the incompatibility of two main frames of reference/civilization, unnaturally and forcibly joined in Yugoslavia. On one side you have a typical violent and crooked oriental-bizantine [sic] heritage, best exemplified by Serbia and Montenegro. . . . On the other side (Slovenia, Croatia) there is a more humble and diligent western-catholic tradition. (p. 12)

Thus, the westernized peoples of Slovenia and Croatia were clearly distinguished from the supposedly evil elements of life in the nations directly to the east.

Of the multiple causal forces of divisiveness characterizing the countries that had formerly constituted Yugoslavia, the prominent factor of religion is among the most primal. The 1993 census of the major religious faiths (*World Factbook*, 1994) illustrates the remarkable divergence in the three countries in this region most torn by strife today (see Table 11.1). In Bosnia-Hercegovina, with no religious majority, there is marked lack of ecclesiastical convergence; in contrast, in Crotia and in Serbia, disparate religious faiths clearly dominate. This fact makes Huntington's (1993) statement all the more timely: "Religion reinforces the revival of ethnic identities" (p. 33). If this can be accepted as factual representation, its potential repercussions must be regarded as foreboding. As people bear witness to their common ethnic/religious identities, "they are likely to see an 'us' versus 'them' relation existing between themselves and people of different ethnicity or religion" (Huntington, 1993, p. 29). Figuring prominently in the life of each of these warring nations as a factor central to individual existence, religion compounds the divisive effects of ardent nationalism, the roots of which exist in various dimensions of life.

Cultures, religion engrossed, not states, are warring in Yugoslav lands, contended Kaplan (1994). Referring to the wanton destruction of medieval monuments in the Croatian port of Dubrovnik, he noted that treasured cultural and religious monuments are militarily regarded as justifiable targets of war and as mere objects to be damaged or destroyed to demoralize the enemy even more.

Ideologies such as obsessive nationalism and overzealous religious fundamentalism, "*particular* forms of life that demand their general adoption and, therefore, the exclusion and/or repression of every other particular form of life—remain the biggest single threat to the diversity of identities that comprise Europe" (Keane, 1992, pp. 57–58, emphasis in original). These ideologies, the very fabric of the embattled Balkan nations, pose the most calamitous threat to peace in Europe and, by the thinking of many perceptive commentators, to peace in the entire world.

## In Contrast: A Base for Bonding

In this Balkan cultural matrix, is there another, more promising persuasion than that of consuming nationalism, steeled by religious fire? In this

TABLE 11.1
Religious Divergence Among Three Countries Comprising the Region of Former Yugoslavia

| | *Muslim* | *Orthodox Christianity* | *Roman Catholic* |
|---|---|---|---|
| Bosnia-Hercegovina | 40% | 31% | 15% |
| Croatia | 1% | 11% | 77% |
| Federal Republic of Yugoslavia (i.e., Serbia and Montenegro) | 19% | 65% | 4% |

ideologically charged conflict among Bosnia-Hercegovina, Croatia, and Serbia, must there be, either metaphorically or in actuality, another fateful Battle of Kosovo, which would probably result in a colossal routing and annihilating of the military forces of a particular government as the victor seizes coveted areas? In order to promote productive, satisfying intercultural communication within a context of peaceful international living, is there an option that would make more viable the innate human drive to attain a more secure, more content world community, leagued in its marvelous multiformity?

In our era, and in all eras preceding this one, an abiding, reassuring sense of shared community is the sine qua non of a peaceful life. True of families, true of towns and cities, true of nations, it is also true of our entire planet, in all its reaches of human habitat. Whether in peace or in war, corporate life is charted, battered, and ennobled by the character of the premises advocated by any group of people as the norms for their culture. In this cultural context, communal problems originate and develop within a rather firmly faceted prism. In the limits of this prism, or in well-structured enlarged limits, these problems will be coped with and mitigated or solved through insightful processing. If not, they will be continuously and chafingly tolerated as difficulties mount and intensify in their wounding of life.

To invigorate groups and enhance the quality of life itself, the principle of broadening can be effected to harmonize with the inherent nature of community. At any level of group existence, broadening of the community at its base, by number and/or in concept, can make for both vitality and cohesiveness. On the other hand, diminution, especially when caused by the course of events rather than by design, debilitates. Positive broadening can hardly be imposed from outside the community. To be purposely kinetic, this refinement process must be given impetus by knowledgeable, sagacious proponents who are respected citizens within the community. Forsaking neither the richness of cultural diversity nor the promise of overarching cultural unity, these leaders of public opinion are the ones to articulate the essential character of a better life. In the dynamics of community, if significant broadening in the numerical and/or conceptual base is to manifest in emerging situations, there must be verve and vision, and there must be an appreciation for fluidity in idea and practice. Most crucially, there must be an activating, urgent sense of need to change materially the conditions producing the constraints of the status quo.

By struggling to ameliorate and hopefully to obliterate the horrors of the compounded tragedy currently tormenting them, the independent nations in the former Yugoslav area harbor a deep desire to program profound, progressive change. Consumed for years by their boundaried view of themselves as they maim and kill each other, destroying emblems of the spiritual psyches of neighbors they perceive as enemies, the sovereign nations of Bosnia-Hercegovina, Croatia, Macedonia, Montenegro, Serbia, and Slovenia, and the autonomous Serbian provinces of Kosovo and Vojvodina, can grasp the opportunity to elevate their thinking to a higher plateau affording the larger view.

That larger view embodies the continent of Europe. These nations and provinces can gauge the probability that although a continental view does involve some risk, the subsequent problems may be less severe than those they now confront. They must try to fathom how their cultural trait of devotion to the cause of personal and corporate freedom might be more encouragingly accommodated by this enlarged orientation than by the deadly imbroglio in which they are now ensnared. Continuing coalesced in their national individualities within the proximate sphere, they have the opportunity to explore the feasibility and desirability of being integral to the larger community within the more spacious sphere.

The idea of a European community can no longer be dismissed as a theoretical novelty. It is neither ahead of our times nor behind our times—the concept is very much *in* our times. The "considerable strides" of the European Council provide stunning testimony of this fact (Kirchner, 1992, p. 145). By implementing a belief in interdependence within its own borders in the past, rather than adhering to the more conventional concept of the self-sufficiency of its various constituencies, Yugoslavia was definitely ahead of its times. In 1918, at the time of its formation, and in 1943, at the beginning of Tito's long tenure, "the concept of 'Europe' as an entity did not exist" (Bakic-Hayden & Hayden, 1992, p. 15). Today, as the former Yugoslavia is wracked by strife throughout its now-sovereign individual parts, there is revelation, painful to acknowledge, of their interdependence on each other. The overlapping aspects of life in the region, notwithstanding the different cultural factors, provide the key for any redefinition of these rebirthed political entities. The peaking of the complex crisis for these nations dictates that their ongoing identity "can no longer be defined through the ideology of the post-war communist era" (Bakic-Hayden & Hayden, 1992, p. 15). Rather, the region needs to deliberate, even invent, opportunities "to propel European constructions of itself past the seeming naturalness of bounded 'nations' and toward recognition of the interdependency" of people vis-à-vis people (Bakic-Hayden & Hayden, 1992, p. 15). In today's Europe and today's world, individual communities, understandably proud of their different heritages, do not have the choice of existing hermetically sealed from each other.

Even though it was European thought that "imprinted on the world the forceful power machine of the nation-state and the ideology of nationalism," this same influence also made indelible on world conscience "the universal ideas of freedom, equality, and fraternity" (Heller, 1992, p. 22). In the world of the 1990s, especially for the nations of Europe, "the tradition of the Other has become attractive rather than repulsive" (Heller, 1992, p. 25). The proposed new European culture does not require a merger of cultures, but features an "umbrella culture in whose framework local, partial, and national cultures may thrive" (Heller, 1992, p. 25). On the basis of his survey of contemporary social cross-cultural movements in Europe, Papcke (1992) concluded that "*Europe* may be . . . a very evocative notion" for fashioning a dynamic continental community (italics added; p. 73).

In this community of broader vista, to expect people to transform themselves, chameleonlike, from one cultural identity to another in response to demands of localities hardly merits serious contemplation. "There is no real reason or justification for imposing the renouncement of one's identity as a condition for living in a community" (Varady, 1992, p. 275). The civilized solution is based on the value of assuring equality for all citizens with their willingness at the same time to experience differences among themselves (Varady, 1992). Cultural homogenization is not the goal of either globalization or regionalization theories. Within any framework for enrichening and accepting cultural differences, a dual challenge is present: "The nations have a more or less pronounced tendency to become worlds in their own right, and in this capacity, they also face the task of coming to terms with the other lines of differentiation which are built into the global [or regional] condition" (Arnason, 1990, p. 225). In national matters, the cherished standards of freedom and independence can be honored; in matters deservedly recognized as having regional or even wider import, the necessary interdependence of nations can become the guiding standard.

This evolving new social construct in Europe would constitute an entirely new entity. A multilayered federal system would ensure equilibrium among all its parts (Keane, 1992). Admittedly, this goal is at once fundamental, indispensable, and paradoxical. "To understand this new model, we have to make a sort of intellectual quantum jump" (Collins, 1992, p. 75). For the present, the formidable task for all nations interested in creating a consolidated Europe is to nurture a pan-European "public spirit" (Keane, 1992, p. 59).

Although economic and political pressures may provide the major incentive to develop this shared spirit, "ideology production—notably, the creation of a shared history—is also critical" (Eriksen, 1993, p. 75). The cultivation of the required, vibrant continental mind-set is a task requiring the imaginative involvement of the most ubiquitous of all instructional agencies—the public media. As in any task-oriented venture, there must be the beginning. The print media have already entered this public service project. Among the recent European history books attempting to change traditional emphases, a leading work is Jean-Baptiste Duroselle's *Europe: A History of its People*, published concurrently in 1990 in several European languages. Advancing toward its path-making conclusion, "It should be possible . . . to build a united Europe," the book "explicitly intends to play down the role of individual nations, instead emphasizing the shared European heritage as well as the local and regional communities" (Eriksen, 1993, p. 75). In his book, Duroselle (Eriksen, 1993) has unassumingly made a substantive, stellar contribution to the pedagogical task of laying the groundwork for effective ideational change on the scene of mortal distress.

The insights of other ideologues relying on the total gamut of media can be brought to bear in this deliberating of alternatives. In this communication effort, rhetoric will have a central role. Christopher Tugendhat (in Pryce, 1987), former vice president of the European Council Commission, depicted the goal of rhetoric as pushing back "the frontiers of the possible": "[Rhetoric] appeals to the emotions and instincts, raises men's and women's eyes from their immediate and parochial concerns to more distant horizons and generates the ground swell and ultimately the popular demand that are necessary for the attainment of all great objectives. In a multinational system, lacking the cohesion of a nation-state, its role is particularly important" (pp. 274–275). More succinctly, Pryce specified that it is the rhetoric of European union that "provides the rationale, justification, and incentive for political action" (p. 275).

In the politically dismantled region of the former Yugoslavia, the broadening of the concept of community is the most compelling option in the pursuit of peace. Though not abandoning the culturally important image of nationhood, but moving beyond the experiencing of immediate locale, the imaging of the European continent as the mainstay of continued personal and corporate life can lead to an enhanced appreciation for a greater, controlling gestalt. Perceptions of the wholeness and the individual components of Europe can thus become intertwined.

The sobering 1989 counsel of President François Mitterand of France (in A. Clark, 1992) should not go unheeded: "No country in Europe can act without taking into account the others" (p. 163). The interdependence of nations, a key concept in current world cultural consciousness, is an available and promising persuasion to counteract the persuasion of tenacious, divisive nationalism. Not incorporating cultural nullification or oppression, it offers a realistic rationale for a modern base to promote the bonding of peoples in our world community in which nations find themselves living more closely to each other symbolically and actually than they ever have.

Proceeding in its ascendancy, the theme of interdependence among nations, empowered by a dedicated public spirit, could prove to encase the most imperative agenda for peace among the independent, warring nations that formerly comprised the confederation of Yugoslavia.

## REFERENCES

*Abuses continue in the former Yugoslavia: Serbia, Montenegro, and Bosnia-Hercegovina.* (1993). New York: Helsinki Watch.

Armstrong, J. A. (1982). *Nations before nationalism.* Chapel Hill: University of North Carolina Press.

Arnason, J. P. (1990). Nationalism, globalization, and modernity. In M. Featherstone (Ed.), *Global culture: Nationalism, globalism, and modernity* (pp. 207–236). London: Sage.

Ayer, A. J. (1972). *Probability and evidence.* New York: Columbia University Press.

Bakic-Hayden, M., & Hayden, R. M. (1992). Orientalist variations on the theme "Balkans": Symbolic geography in recent Yugoslav culture politics. *Slavic Review, 51,* 1–15.

Banac, I. (1991). Political change and national diversity. In S. R. Graubard (Ed.), *Eastern Europe, Central Europe, Europe* (pp. 145–164). Boulder, CO: Westview Press.

Banac, I. (1992). Post-Communism as post-Yugoslavism: The Yugoslav nonrevolutions of 1989–1990. In I. Banac (Ed.), *Eastern Europe in revolution* (pp. 168–187). Ithaca, NY: Cornell University Press.

Banac, I. (1993–1994). Misreading the Balkans. *Foreign Policy, 93,* 173–182.

Brock, P. (1993–1994). Dateline Yugoslavia: The partisan press. *Foreign Policy, 93,* 152–172.

Brown, J. F. (1991). *Surge to freedom: The end of communist rule in Eastern Europe.* Durham, NC: Duke University Press.

Clark, A. (1992). François Mitterand and the idea of Europe. In B. Nelson, D. Roberts, & W. Veit (Eds.), *The idea of Europe: Problems of national and transnational identity* (pp. 152–170). New York: Berg.

Clark, R. S. (1990). Crimes against humanity at Nuremberg. In G. Ginsburgs (Ed.), *The Nuremberg Trial and international law* (pp. 177–199). Dordrecht, Netherlands: Martinus Nijhoff.

Collins, M. J. (1992). *Western European integration.* New York: Praeger.

Curtis, G. E. (Ed.). (1992). *Yugoslavia: A country study.* Washington, DC: Library of Congress.

Djilas, A. (1993). A profile of Slobodan Milosevic. *Foreign Affairs, 72,* 81–96.

Doder, D. (1993). Yugoslavia: New war, old hatreds. *Foreign Policy, 91,* 3–23.

Donnelly, J. (1989). *Universal human rights in theory and practice.* Ithaca, NY: Cornell University Press.

Eriksen, T. H. (1993). *Ethnicity and nationalism: Anthropological perspectives.* London: Pluto Press.

The future of the Balkans: An interview with David Owen. (1993). *Foreign Affairs, 72,* 1–9.

Gellner, E. (1983). *Nations and nationalism.* Ithaca, NY: Cornell University Press.

Hayden, R. M. (1992). Constitutional nationalism in the formerly Yugoslav republics. *Slavic Review, 51,* 654–673.

Heller, A. (1992). Europe: An epilogue? In B. Nelson, D. Roberts, & W. Veit (Eds.), *The idea of Europe: Problems of national and transnational identity* (pp. 12–25). New York: Berg.

Hobsbawn, E. J. (1990). *Nations and nationalism since 1780: Programme, myth, reality.* New York: Cambridge University Press.

*Human Rights Watch World Report 1993.* (1992). New York: Human Rights Watch.

Huntington, S. P. (1993). The clash of civilizations? *Foreign Affairs, 72,* 22–49.

Janos, A. (1994). Continuity and change in Eastern Europe: Strategies of post-Communist politics. *East European Politics and Societies, 8,* 1–31.

Job, C. (1993). Yugoslavia's ethnic furies. *Foreign Policy, 92*, 53–74.

Kaplan, R. D. (1994). The coming anarchy. *The Atlantic Monthly, 273*, 44–76.

Keane, J. (1992). Questions for Europe. In B. Nelson, D. Roberts, & W. Veit (Eds.), *The idea of Europe: Problems of national and transnational identity* (pp. 55–60). New York: Berg.

Kirchner, E. J. (1992). *Decision-making in the European community.* Manchester, England: Manchester University Press.

Knezevic, A. (1992). *An analysis of Serbian propaganda.* Zagreb, Croatia: Domovina TT.

Livezey, L. W. (1988). *Nongovernmental organizations and the ideas of human rights.* Princeton, NJ: Center of International Studies.

Magas, B. (1993). *The destruction of Yugoslavia: Tracking the break-up, 1980–1992.* London: Verso.

Meron, T. (1993). The case for war crimes trials in Yugoslavia. *Foreign Affairs, 72*, 122–135.

Mrdjen, S. (1993). Pluralist mobilization as a catalyst for the dismemberment of Yugoslavia. In J. O'Laughlin & H. van der Wusten (Eds.), *The new political geography of Eastern Europe* (pp. 115–131). London: Belhaven Press.

Nixon, R. (1993). Of Balkans and Bantustans. *Transition: An International Review, 60*, 4–26.

Nizich, I. (1992). *War crimes in Bosnia-Hercegovina: A Helsinki Watch report.* New York: Human Rights Watch.

Nizich, I. (1993). *War crimes in Bosnia-Hercegovina: Helsinki Watch, II.* New York: Human Rights Watch.

Papcke, S. (1992). Who needs European identity and what could it be? In B. Nelson, D. Roberts, & W. Veit (Eds.), *The idea of Europe: Problems of national and transnational identity* (pp. 61–74). New York: Berg.

Perelman, C., & Olbrechts-Tyteca, L. (1969). *The new rhetoric: A treatise on argumentation.* Notre Dame, IN: University of Notre Dame Press.

Podunavac, M. (1985). Culture-based value systems in Yugoslavia. In M. Damjanovic & D. Voich (Eds.), *The impact of culture-based value systems on management politics and practices* (pp. 39–63). New York: Praeger.

*Prosecute now! Helsinki Watch release eight cases for war crimes tribunal on former Yugoslavia.* (1993). New York: Helsinki Watch.

Pryce, R. (1987). Past experiences and lessons for the future. In R. Pryce (Ed.), *The dynamics of European union* (pp. 273–296). London: Croom Helm.

Ramcharan, B. G. (1982a). Evidence. In B. G. Ramcharan (Ed.), *International law and fact-finding in the field of human rights* (pp. 64–82). The Hague, Netherlands: Martinus Nijhoff.

Ramcharan, B. G. (1982b). Introduction. In B. G. Ramcharan (Ed.), *International law and fact-finding in the field of human rights* (pp. 1–25). The Hague, Netherlands: Martinus Nijhoff.

Ramet, S. P. (1991a). The new church-state configuration in Eastern Europe. *East European Politics and Society, 5*, 247–267.

Ramet, S. P. (1991b). Serbia's Slobodan Milosevic: A profile. *Orbis: A Journal of World Affairs, 35*, 93–105.

Ramet, S. P. (1992). *Balkan Babel: Politics, culture, and religion in Yugoslavia.* Boulder, CO: Westview Press.

Sandifer, D. V. (1975). *Evidence before international tribunals.* Charlottesville: University Press of Virginia.

Smith, A. D. (1986). *The ethnic origins of nations.* Oxford, England: Basil Blackwell.

Tehranian, M. (1993). Ethnic discourse and the new world dysorder: A communitarian perspective. In C. Roach (Ed.), *Communication and culture in war and peace* (pp. 192–215). Newbury Park, CA: Sage.

Varady, T. (1992). Collective minority rights and problems in their legal protection: The example of Yugoslavia. *East European Politics and Societies, 6*, 260–282.

Weissbrodt, D. (1977). The role of international nongovernment organizations in the implementation of human rights. *Texas International Law Journal, 12,* 293–330.

Weissbrodt, D., & McCarthy, J. (1981). Fact-finding by international nongovernmental human rights organizations. *Virginia Journal of International Law, 22,* 1–89.

Weissbrodt, D., & McCarthy, J. (1982). Fact-finding by nongovernmental organizations. In B. G. Ramcharan (Ed.), *International law and fact-finding in the field of human rights* (pp. 186–230). The Hague, Netherlands: Martinus Nijhoff.

Wiseberg, L. S. (1992). Human rights fact-finding in former Yugoslavia: Is this enough to halt the genocidal killings? *Human Rights Tribune, 1,* 7–9.

*The World Factbook: 1993.* (1994). Washington, DC: U.S. Government Printing Office.

# 12

# Some Summary Thoughts

Fred L. Casmir
*Pepperdine University*

We face serious intranational or intercultural conflicts at a time when we imagined that we had left that kind of savagery behind us. Dealing with these problems requires that we do not lose sight of the larger picture. A recent issue of *Foreign Policy* included a number of essays that make exactly that point, some of which I cite in these concluding pages.

Another important issue to raise here is the unwillingness of at least some of us to simply accept the most destructive aspects of human nature. If we make a choice to be destructive and savage, it is obvious that somewhere, somehow many of us also have a capacity to choose the opposite and to work out a more positive future for human beings than seems possible at the moment. For that effort, all of us who have contributed to this book hope to have provided some insights, some direction, and an indication that the task before us requires new ideas, new roads to travel, and a perhaps unusual amount of cooperative work.

***Moving Beyond the Past.*** To the extent that we—human beings all—will be able to learn from the past, we may be able to move beyond what so far seems to be a replay of history.

***The Burdens of the Past.*** As Brenner (1993) reminded us, in times of uncertainty human societies, or more accurately their members, fear three things: "the unknown, a remembered past, and, often some part of themselves" (p. 33). If anything has emerged in the preceding pages, it is an image of these factors as they contribute to the malaise of Eastern Europe. What lies ahead seems no longer as predictable as it once was thought to be. The "Wirtschaftswunder" of the years following World War II cannot simply be regurgitated or even copied in the last decade of the 20th century. There remain the memories of Nazi Germany, linked to the intolerance, both past and present, toward those who are different or simply declared to be culturally and economically threatening. These are dark specters, feared not only by those outside of Germany, but also by many who live within that country's new borders.

***The Loss of Sovereign Power.*** One of the great ironies of our times is the fact that traditional approaches and wisdom clearly are not working. The malaise of Eastern Europe and Germany is the malaise of our entire world.

Kielinger and Otte (1993) repeatedly pointed to the fundamental changes in international systems that have developed during recent years. Many of the policies and institutions (NATO is one example of the latter, nuclear deterrence an example of the former) that were developed following World War II included a kind of built-in obsolescence. The creation of "devils" or enemies in that setting has left us with the choice of either abandoning such concepts altogether, or finding new opponents once the old ones disintegrated or were conquered. The traditional response has, of course, been the continuation or rediscovery of even older enemies, approaches, and policies, rather than an attempt to produce fundamental change.

Contemporary problems touch citizens on very personal levels every day. The case of East Germany, which provided a certain kind of economic and physical security for both men and women that can no longer be found in the unified Federal Republic, is a stark example of that fact. But governments everywhere find it impossible to adequately deal with such problems as escalating crime. The average citizens cannot overlook the ready accessibility of drugs and the huge amounts of money their sales generate for highly successful criminal "entrepreneurs" of our days. States once thought of as giants can no longer afford to pay for wars whose costliness is the result of the very economic systems they created. Increasingly, they cannot even provide the health care for their own citizens that technology has made possible, but that is so costly that it threatens entire economies. What may seem like an invulnerable economic empire today turns out to be tomorrow's savings and loan scandal or Japanese failure to adequately understand global economic forces. Once seemingly dependable foundations of statehood are trembling everywhere.

***Changes in Authority.*** As Brenner (1993) made clear, "In principle sovereign leaders and institutions have exclusive authority over the most vital aspects of a society's collective existence, namely its physical security and constitutional integrity" (p. 27). The problem is that the traditional, politically and economically based state no longer seems to be able to translate its assumed authority (and capabilities) into meaningful action that is responsive to its citizens' needs.

States, in effect, are admitting their individual weaknesses by trusting in some vague global arena or international political and economic associations, or by hoping that technology will bring about a global village that makes possible human interactions on levels that were the strength of that romanticized small community of the past.

***Inadequate Responses to Real Needs.*** Thus are born the dreams of a European Community (EC) with its promises of freedom of access and travel, as well as shared economic prosperity. The "salesmen" (and saleswomen) of our political world, each of them losing money on individual deals at home, hope, somehow, to make up their losses by "volume," as they propose various unification schemes. In that process, however, they do not mind stepping outside the very rules they claim to be inviolable for the development of democratic states. "Without serious public debate about the aims of this historic exercise in constitution building on a semi-continental scale, or the basis for its legitimation, leaders of the 12 member states [of the EC] committed their peoples to a plan for relocating the sovereign authority that governs them" (Brenner, 1993, p. 27). Violations of principles on which the development and use of legitimate, democratic power through consensus building rests, make trust and cooperation by individual citizens virtually impossible.

***The Role of Human Individuals.*** In all of that, it is vital to understand, however, that we are not merely dealing with institutions, with organizations, with states, with cultures, but that our central concern must be with human beings. Ultimately it is some part of ourselves that we fear, such as our inability to adequately cope with the future or the present, as well as our moral, physical, and spiritual weaknesses. In other words, everything that lies hidden within us, the human potential both for good and for evil, must be considered.

In the past we have sought comfort in association with others. Somehow it seemed possible to overcome individual weaknesses and failures by forming powerful political entities in which, it was hoped, those would emerge who could grow beyond their humanness in some kind of ideological framework. That attempt continues, in spite of the Hitlers, Mussolinis, Francos, Stalins, Tojos, Pavelics, Quislings and a multitude of other such leaders who emerged in the 20th century. Although history teaches us that there may not be ultimate security in such ideological approaches, they certainly do provide at least momentary comfort from the fears just discussed. Today's "answer" often is sought in extreme forms of nationalism, but, as Brenner (1993) reminded us, "Nationalism, as an unquestioned political creed, bears similarities to the communist ideology it may supplant in some places. It, too, offers the fateful bargain of trading individual and personal rights for comforts of an all-embracing belief and paternalistic state" (p. 32).

***The Public Response.*** We are faced with publics constantly influenced by the media in their interpretations of world conditions and conditions in their own countries or neighborhoods. The media may present distorted images, but those images are often the only "reality" individuals know. It becomes significant, for instance, when the 1993 economic meeting of the G7 in Tokyo (its host a Japanese prime minister facing political oblivion within days after the meeting) is identified in the media as a conference of "dwarfs," with the President of the United States being the "biggest" among them.

What Brenner (1993) discussed as ultimate or final authority over public matters thus is increasingly being questioned by the media and by their consumers within all countries of the world, including Germany, Russia, and the Eastern European countries. Under such circumstances, the desire to return to the past, or to the "fleshpots of Egypt," to use an Old Testament example, often becomes overwhelming, even as the slavery and suffering associated with earlier experiences is all too readily forgotten.

***The Age of Public Diplomacy and World Trade.*** We have moved into an age where communication media from trains to planes, from television to cassettes have, in most cases long ago, made the borders of states mere graphics on a printed map. Today, loyalty to a political entity has to be earned by the state and its representatives. Citizens constantly question authority and involve themselves even in decision-making processes that used to be absolutely controlled by diplomatic elites. Relocation to a different country may still not be easy, but it is done by millions every year who have come to know via media and word of mouth of the advantages other countries offer. Working for an international or global corporation that expects ultimate loyalty to its own goals for success, regardless of its employees' domicile in a given state, further weakens the traditional authority and reward structures of the state.

***The Individual, Media, and Culture.*** The traditional models of authority, power, and thus the state were largely based on a Western world view dominated by reason and reasonableness (Brenner, 1993). The human ability to reason, however, does not appear to have enabled us to deal adequately with the unforeseen and rapid changes of our age. When the European Community found itself faced with the realities of disintegration in the former Yugoslavia, it was virtually paralyzed.

Our always-present mass media, however, reach us on a very different, much more emotional level every day. Unfortunately, we have frequently overlooked that role of the mass media as they respond to the need of individuals to strive, live, and act in a secure environment based on the best information available to them. When politicians or leaders in a given state are no longer trusted, someone (in this case the media, even if they are not fully trusted themselves) will be assigned the role of informant and security blanket by the public.

For example, Germany has been criticized for its timidity as a leading power in Europe, yet it stunned much of the world in December of 1991 with its sudden recognition of Slovenia and Croatia as sovereign states. What had happened? "The German media had brought the war and its atrocities into every living room, raising a public outcry and making diplomatic recognition a popular demand well before it became official policy" (Kielinger & Otte, 1993, p. 55). Today media may be the most influential transmitters (or teachers) of common cultural values as well as information in our world.

***What Next?*** Kielinger and Otte (1993) pointed to the "new fears of losing German national and cultural identity in a unified Europe" (p. 58). Hopefully, their point is clear to readers of this book. If we are to understand contemporary developments in *all* of Eastern Europe, we must know their history and the cultural value systems involved. Furthermore, we must learn from our insights as I indicated earlier. One of the most important, if not *the* most important lesson to be learned is that many traditional foundations that the state could provide in the past no longer exist or can no longer be trusted. Thus people, almost automatically, return to those factors that shaped their societies over the centuries, all of them culturally and historically significant, even if they have become "mere" mythology, and though they supposedly had little relevance to the building and maintenance of modern states.

An interesting question addressed by Kober (1993) is what happens when "revolutions go bad"? One thing that is evident to him and many others is the fact that the defeat of Communism has not necessarily resulted in the triumph of democracy, but rather, in many cases, in the crassest kind of nationalism. He cited Czech president Václav Havel's insightful statement related to this disturbing phenomenon: "The sudden outburst of freedom has not only untied the strait jacket made by Communism, it has also unveiled the centuries-old, often thorny history of nations. People are now remembering their past kings and emperors, the states they formed far back in their past and the borders of those states . . ." (Havel, quoted in Kober, 1993, p. 77). Reminiscent of concepts Brenner (1993) evoked, Havel also pointed to the deep feeling of uncertainty that makes people turn to demagogues, populists, and authoritarians.

***Building a New Consensus.*** It would appear that concern with the individual, with consensus building, with creating new goals and relevant value systems *together*, has to replace systems where power could be assumed to reside in the state and its institutions. Of course, our institutional identifications and standards have always been flawed. They are and were primarily used for the purpose of maintaining a base for those who were in power, but they also resulted in a feeling of unity. By providing a feeling of mystic transcendency for organizations and institutions, disassociating them from the ambitions of individual rulers or leaders, the state took on a moral dimension and image of power far beyond those of individuals representing it. Of course, references to long-standing institutions also make it more difficult to disagree with decisions than would be the case if citizens oppose individual leaders. What we must not forget, however, is that it has always been human beings who have negotiated and who have made decisions, not states. Those who spoke for the state have always been individual human beings who were influenced by their own perceptions, backgrounds, failings, and strengths, regardless of their positions of power.

It would seem necessary to overcome the lethargy of our day that is based on the hope that if we "hang in there" long enough, things will get back to normal. Such responses to the unknown and the future need to be overcome mainly because they are too much based on fear. We do need to learn to use what technology and new ideas offer us in building our future. However, that must be done in a spirit of cooperative respect, which assumes that new foundations and value systems have to be found by all of us together, rather than by merely announcing new incentives so citizens will go along with old ideas.

***The Role of the Individual.*** The future, undoubtedly, requires a reevaluation of the role of individuals, the dignity of human beings, and the fact that the atrocities of the final decade of our century can only be overcome if the thinking of individual human beings changes. The mere exercise of power by individual states, or even states in concert, is no longer a real solution to many existing problems.

Kielinger and Otte (1993) provided one example of some of the insights now appearing in the work of many experts from a variety of backgrounds. The contributions of such thought leaders increasingly bring us to the conclusion that we need to find new solutions to old problems.

Kielinger and Otte (1993) referred to the specific example of Germany when they wrote, "In fact, the *mental* division of Germany is creating even more serious political problems than its economic hardships. In August 1992, the newsmagazine Der Spiegel ran a cover story, The New Division: Germans against Germans, contending that 'deep depression in the East and aloofness in the West have replaced the joy about unity' " (emphasis added; p. 47). What is lacking in that insightful article is an awareness that we cannot really speak of people in east or west Germany as the same kind of Germans, or as one *Volk*. In other words, the fact is ignored that new *intranational*, consensus-building rules and structures need to be developed before the building of a true German, or any other Eastern European community can proceed. Over the last 40 years, culturally and historically, East and West Germans have grown apart, not together, and similar divisions continue in Eastern Europe. No wonder that T-shirts with the inscription "I want my wall back" became popular in west Germany—another example of unrealistic attempts, as I explained earlier, to move back to the fleshpots of Egypt.

***Carpetbaggers or Intercultural Promoters of Unity?*** It seems strange that so few of us in the United States have noticed the relationship to, and the lessons to be learned from, our country's experience following the Civil War. Take the example of carpetbaggers from our North who invaded the South. They differed little, when it comes to substance, from west German carpetbaggers who invaded east Germany following unification, or from Western Europeans seeking to influence the future of Eastern Europe. All were and are driven by traditional concepts of power, a statist model, and the dream of economic advantage. Both were and are a detriment to the future of democratic consensus building from which Germany and Eastern Europe will suffer for a long time to come, unless we decide that we need to learn from the past. Imposing cultural values and political structures, history teaches us, can lead to centuries of repeated conflicts.

***Some Possible Solutions.*** Dealing with the challenges the United States and Europe face in today's world, Brenner (1993) offered some specific solutions, which are of interest to the scholar and the practitioner in the interrelated areas of intercultural and mass media communication. He wrote, "In truth, the only arrangement liable to be both effectual and politically viable is a truly multilateral one. But the politics of an egalitarian alliance are not easy to work out. Nor do they fit readily into popular American conceptions of allied cooperation" (p. 42).

What Brenner (1993) spoke of as "multilateral," I have extended in my own work beyond the mere process, to an *orientation*. Participants in the process must bring that orientation to their work in order to produce consensus building and lasting results. *Building third cultures* is the umbrella term under which I have discussed both the process and that orientation (see Casmir, 1978, 1991, 1992). The model is based on an acceptance of the fact that there is valuable diversity and complexity in our world. Only if we reach agreements that are not enforced from the outside, but that result from the needs of those participating in their formulation, can we hope to overcome the tragedies that have resulted when we did not learn from the past. The creation of artificial and oppressive states that ignore the diversity of people under their control, as well as the contributions all of them could make to the future of a people, has proven utterly unacceptable to human beings.

Communication scholars and students of human communication may now be able to make a contribution to a new kind of process, in spite of the fact that in the past their insights have been ignored in such fields as economics, political science, and diplomacy. If we are to reach agreement we need to learn to talk to each other, to accept and deal effectively with diversity, and we must build and use new models of human cooperation in which communication is not merely a technique, but a central ethical concern.

## REFERENCES

Brenner, M. J. (1993). EC: Confidence lost. *Foreign Policy, 91*, 24–43.

Casmir, F. L. (Ed.). (1978). *Intercultural and international communication*. Washington, DC: University Press of America.

Casmir, F. L. (Ed). (1991). *Communication in development*. Norwood, NJ: Ablex.

Casmir, F. L. (1992). Third-culture building: A paradigm shift for international and intercultural communication. In S. Deetz (Ed.), *Communication yearbook* (Vol. 16, pp. 407–436). Beverly Hills, CA: Sage.

Kielinger, T., & Otte, M. (1993). Germany: The pressured power. *Foreign Policy, 91*, 44–62.

Kober, S. (1993). Revolutions gone bad. *Foreign Policy, 91*, 63–84.

# The Authors

**Charles Quist Adade** is a Ghanian journalist/sociologist who lived in the former Soviet Union during the last decade (1982–1992). While there, he studied for his MA and PhD in journalism and sociology respectively at the [Leningrad] St. Petersburg State University. He was the correspondent for the British-syndicated Gemini News Service. He is currently a Visiting Scholar at the University of Windsor, Canada, where he is writing a book to be titled *Africa, the Kremlin and the Press: Africa's Image in the Mirror Soviet/Russian Press*. He also teaches sociology at the University of Windsor.

**Maryellen Boyle** is the author of *Capturing the East German Mind: Press and Politics in East Germany, 1945–1991* (forthcoming). Dr. Boyle is an Annenberg Scholar working on the problems of East German integration into West German political, social, and economic life. She spent several years in eastern Germany as a Fulbright Research Fellow at the Department of Journalism, Karl Marx University, and as a Friedrich Ebert Foundation research scholar. In 1991–1992 she was a recipient of a University of California Institute for Global Conflict and Cooperation Fellowship; in 1992–1993 she was a member of the faculty at the Department of Culture and Communication, New York University.

**Fred L. Casmir** (PhD, The Ohio State University, 1961) is Distinguished Professor of Communication at Pepperdine University, and author of publications on five continents, including *Communication in Development*

(Ablex, 1991), and *Building Communication Theories: A Socio/Cultural Approach* (Lawrence Erlbaum Associates, 1993). Consulted, lectured, and taught in the areas of intercultural and mass communication in various countries in Europe, Asia, Africa, Australia, and North America. He has served at Pepperdine University as coordinator of the Communication Division's graduate program, and is coordinator of the International Studies major.

**Eric Gilder** (PhD, 1992, Communication, The Ohio State University) is interested in the function of communication ethics in changing "civil societies." His other publications include, "The Process of Political Praxis: Efforts of the Gay Community to Transform the Social Signification of AIDS," *Communication Quarterly*, *37*(1), 27–38; and, "Communication for Development and Habermas' 'Ideal Speech Situation'," *Media Development*, *35*(4), 34–37. He is currently a visiting professor with the Soros Foundation, Romania.

**Dina Iordanova** received her PhD in Philosophy from the University of Sofia in 1986. She has worked at the Institute for Cultural Studies in Sofia, Bulgaria; the University of Sofia; Memorial University, St. John's, Canada; and the University of Ottawa, Canada. Dr. Iordanova is currently teaching East European media and Cultural Studies at the University of Texas at Austin. Her research interests include film, media, migrations, and women. She has published a number of scholarly papers and essays in both Bulgarian and English.

**Mary McKinley** is a visiting lecturer at the Budapest University of Economics and a communications doctoral candidate from the Union Institute in Cincinnati, Ohio. She is conducting dissertation research on the effect of telecommunications on economic development in Hungary. In 1992, she was a visiting professor at The International Management Center in Budapest. She received the master's degree from the University of Southern California's Annenberg School in 1990.

**Scott R. Olson** is Associate Professor of Communication and former Assistant Dean of Arts and Sciences at Central Connecticut State University. His publications include several book chapters and journal articles on the role of media in culture formation and maintenance. With colleagues from The Technical University of Wroclaw and the University of Wroclaw, he is helping to establish the first School of Communication in Poland.

**Dr. Carsten R. C. Pellicaan** (1970) is connected with the Research Center for International Mass Communication, Budapest Department. He conducted several studies on which parts of this chapter are based.

**Dr. Carl C. Rohde** (1953) is a cultural sociologist connected with the Department of Mass Communication, at Utrecht University. He coordinated Pan-European value studies and analyses, indicating the consequences value changes have on culture in general and communication in particular.

**Dorothy J. Rosenberg** was trained in the field of German Studies. Beginning in 1980, she has been a regular visitor at the universities of East and West Berlin with the Fulbright, IREX, and DAAD programs and has also received research grants from the NEH and the ACLS. In addition to work on the Weimar Republic and Nazi Germany, she has written extensively on women, literature, and culture in the GDR. Her volume (with Nancy Lukens) *Daughters of Eve: Women's Writing from the German Democratic Republic* appeared in Fall 1993. *Disjuncture: Women and Social Policy in the United Germany* is now in progress.

**Tim Stephen** (PhD, 1980) is Associate Professor of Communication in Rensselaer Polytechnic Institute's Department of Language, Literature, and Communication. Professor Stephen is president of Communication Institute for Online Scholarship. His research focuses on the influences of social structure on communication in ongoing relationships.

**Donald E. Williams** (PhD, 1958, Northwestern University) teaches at the University of Florida, Gainesville. Since 1976 he has held teaching/lecturing appointments in 13 countries on six continents. In 1992, he presented a paper at an international conference in Zagreb, Croatia, where he also served as Guest Professor at the University of Zagreb, Croatia. His scholarly focus is on the interrelationship between theories of rhetorical criticism and intercultural communication.

# Author Index

R



S

## T



## U



## V



## W



## Y



## Z

# Subject Index

C

## D



## E

J



K



L



M